चण्डी पाठः

Chaṇḍī Pāṭhaḥ

She Who Tears Apart Thought

Also Known As

The Durgā Saptaśatī

The Seven Hundred Verses
In Praise of She Who Removes
All Difficulties

And

The Devī Māhātmyam

The Glory of the Goddess

Translated By

स्वामी सत्यानन्द सरस्वती

Swami Satyananda Saraswati

"I dance, and all that you perceive are its manifestations. If you like you can watch me dance, or if you like you can make me stop. He who can make me stop, I make him a seer, a being of wisdom, one of Intuitive Vision, my husband, Lord Śiva, the Consciousness of Infinite Goodness."

Swami Satyananda Saraswati

Chaṇḍī Pāṭh, Sixth edition

000721760
ISBN 1-877795-52-6
Library of Congress Catalog Card Number 91-075809

Chaṇḍī Pāṭh, Swami Satyananda Saraswati
1. Hindu Religion. 2. Goddess Worship. 3. Spirituality.
4. Philosophy. I. Saraswati, Swami Satyananda.

Published by
Devi Mandir Publications
5950 Highway 128
Napa, CA 94558 USA
707-966-2802
www.shreemaa.org

Introduction

Every form in the universe is subject to evolution and devolution and the two intermediate positions, birth and death, the wheel of life. The waves of the sea rise and fall, vegetation rises from the earth and returns to it, animals born to existence ultimately decompose and mingle with the dust of the earth; even the sun sets at the close of every day. Seing this, and knowing fully well that every human being dies, even still, our minds wander in the attachments of the ego as though we are immortal. What is this delusion of ego, this ignorance of attachment, that binds our every thought and action? What are these dreams and illusions to which we are so bound?

We adorn our bodies as though they are never subject to decay, and cling to relationships with people and things as though they are the substance of our very existence. We eat when we are not hungry, kill when we don't need food, and copulate out of season; we intoxicate ourselves to forgetfulness, take tobacco or drugs even when we know it is injurious to our health, drive our cars as though there are no statistics of traffic fatalities.

We see a new desire take birth with every perception and helplessly watch it grow until it becomes an obsession regulating our every action. As one possessed, we see morality and convention, even common sense, yield to the ethics of convenience, in which we can rationalize any behavior that brings success.

Look at the reality of our lives, at our goals and aspirations. There are many among us who have no vision of the future. We are caught in the paradox of working to survive and surviving to work. Somehow a sense of boredom, frustration, and futility has taken over our entire being. We find no lasting satisfaction, no sustaining pleasure, no all-inclusive delight. Again when we find ourselves avidly pursuing some goal, we are constantly in strife. Our minds are harnessed to the thought without our control. A continual anxiety prevails in which the vision of success or failure recurs to us day and night.

Look at these thoughts. How many of them bear significance in the cosmic reality? How many of them are such transient and petty desires that we ourselves can't remember them even after a few hours or a few days, let alone in the context of the history of civilizations, or the evolution of human kind or the origin of the universe.

What delusion has possessed us, and how do we go about purifying the ego so as to get rid of this bondage, so we can maintain our divine perception as Gods and Goddesses in the Garden of Bliss? In the Durgā Saptaśatī Mother shows us how to do just that: give them all to Her. The continual recitation of this book is designed to accomplish this.

Every character mentioned in this book is within us: the forces that impel us to realize our own divinity, filling our lives with Love and Joy and a sense of meaningful purpose, as well as the forces that incline to diminish that perception. In the case of the enemies of the Gods, Asuras, which has been rendered as "Thoughts," primarily the root meanings of the words have been employed. Asuras in Vaidika usage is an epithet of both the Gods and their enemies alike. It means variously: spiritual, incorporeal, divine, a good spirit; an evil spirit, an opponent of the Gods. In the Puranic literature it is almost exclusively in this latter sense that the term is used. Just as the Gods or Devas are the forces of clear perception, their opponents must be those that obscure clear perception - self-centered, egotistical thoughts.

In the case of the Devas, the Vaidika tradition has been applied almost exclusively, with the exception of the Creative, Maintaining, and Dissolving Capacities of Consciousness, which are the Puranic conceptions of Brahmā, Viṣṇu, and Śiva. The symbolism of the weapons of war has been defined from a consensus of oral traditions combined with the available scriptural references in the Tantras. It is the qualities and characteristics of spiritual discipline symbolized in these words that is relevant, more so than the question of with what physical weapon did She strike. Hence these words will take significance in the individual meditations of the seeker, and their definitions will change with growth, development, and progress along the path.

This principle is even more true of the Goddess, the Mother of the Universe. In one sense She resides in the image, the photo, or idol of worship. In another application She is manifested in the physical body of the worshipper. And again, "Her feet cover the earth, and Her crown extends to the farthest reaches of the atmosphere." On every level the scripture is a commentary on the evolution of consciousness.

The Durgā Saptaśatī, or Chaṇḍī Pāṭhaḥ, is Puranic, comprising thirteen chapters of Mārkaṇḍeya Purāṇa, numbers eighty-one to ninety-three. It dates between 900 and 500 B.C. However, because the first writing in India was not widely used until the Third Century B.C., it is precarious to proclaim any accuracy as to the actual date. It most probably assumed its present form during the Fourth Century A.D. under the patronage of the Gupta Kings, when scholars collected, edited, and recorded the oral traditions of prose and poetry prevalent among the many peoples of the empire.

Certainly its root is Vaidika. The entire Chaṇḍī Pāṭhaḥ purports to be a commentary on the two Ṛg Vaidika hymns included at its beginning and end: "The Rātri Sūkta, Praise of the Night of Duality," and "The Devī Sūkta, Praise of the Goddess Who is Unity." We must dispel the darkness of egotism in order to realize that "I" am a divine being of Infinite Perception.

Chaṇḍī Pāṭhaḥ is a fundamental authoritative text of the Tantras. It gives definition to method and practice of the oral tradition that can only be learned from a qualified Guru, the practice of which, when mastered, opens up the doors to the secret and makes available all the "magic" of the tantra, a new way of perceiving ourselves and the world around us.

This is an intellectual interpretation of the Chaṇḍī. But to realize the real Chaṇḍī, we must strive to make the Goddess the sum and substance of our entire life. This may be accomplished by sitting in an āsana and pronouncing the mantras of this work, and by striving to make the āsana and the recitation longer. Do not worry about not understanding. Do not worry about pronouncing the Sanskṛt perfectly when you first begin your practice. Do not worry about anything. If you study this and other translations or commentaries and devotedly recite, Chaṇḍī will become known to you. The one who understands it completely is Lord Śiva, and to the extent we are capable, we become Him.

Thus the Durgā Saptaśatī is a practical training manual. As human beings we have become habituated to being beset with thought. Through the study and practice of this work, according to the prescribed procedure, we seek to free ourselves from this habit, to take the "Ego I" out of thought, to find the remedy of that all too chronic disease, Attachment, and to expand our awareness beyond the relationships of this physical body so as to intuit by direct perception the Bliss of the Universe.

Saptaśatī is a Way. Daily reciting the verses, we offer to Mother all our troubles, afflictions, all manner of thoughts and perturbations - even the very Ego itself; and one by one She cuts them down, purifies them with the vibrations of Her mantras, until we, too, become the One of Intuitive Vision who only desires the Highest Wisdom that removes the attachments of the Ego.

In translating this work I hope to put forth an effort that will please my parents, my gurus, the ṛṣis, the Gods, and the Mother of the Universe, and upon its completion to become Lord Śiva.

Swami Satyananda Saraswati,
Rishikesh, 1981

Introduction to the Sixth Edition

It is more than twenty seven years since I worked on the original translation of the Chaṇḍī Pāṭhaḥ. So much has changed in the world since I roamed the forests of India asking all the holy people I met how they could explain these verses. Over these many years Hinduism has become a global culture, the word Yoga has been assimilated into every modern language, and people are reciting the Chaṇḍī Pāṭhaḥ all across Europe, throughout North and South America, in the Far East, the Middle East, Australia and New Zealand, Japan and Malaysia, certainly throughout India, and wherever students of Oriental Culture and Hindu Philosophy congregate.

There were a few areas which needed to be updated from the original translation. Many students complained that I often wrote in Indian English, which is no doubt a dialect significantly different from Americaneze. Having lived in India so long, it was impossible to remember what proper American English was supposed to sound like. Therefore, this new edition has tried to edit out many of those uncomfortable useages.

Also, the scripture has always been just as applicable to women as to men. However, the grammar followed the cultural traditions that suggest the men performed tapasya and the women provided support, nourishment, and enabled the discipline. Whether or not this may have been true in ancient times, it is no longer applicable to the present circumstances. Both males and females have an equal right and authority to pray to God. This has been rectified in the current translation, which now remains neutral in matters of gender, except for the obvious references to the Gods and Goddesses.

Punctuation has been applied in a much more liberal doseage, and it is a delight to discover people who get paid by the comma. We hope that the additional ink on the paper will make this edition much more readable and discernable, although it is still a translation of a work which precedes Christianity by at least a thousand years or more.

But most important is the Goddess, the Divine Mother who has remained with me all these years. Her presence in my life is increasingly more vibrant and more tangible. The famous proverb reminds us that Love is such a commodity: the more you give it away, the more it will grow. I always remember that Samadhi, Pure Intuitive Vision, as he is called in the story, asked for the boon of eternal devotion to the Divine Mother, along with the wisdom which removes the attachments of egotism and possession. After She granted him that boon, he constantly traveled the world and set up altars to the Divine Mother and taught people the joy of submerging ourselves into the worship of divinity.

These last so many years we have been doing something similar by circumambulating the globe and translating the methods of worship into many languages. It is our absolute delight that because of these efforts the Chaṇḍī Pāṭhaḥ is being recited by many people in many lands, and the pūjās are being performed with sincerity, regularity, and a degree of efficiency which will make every devotee proud. After all, that is the meaning of a sādhu.

I want to thank Nanda, whose knowledge of English is exemplary, and Vittalananda, whose knowledge of computers is exact, and Shree Maa and the entire Devi Mandir Family who have worked so hard to point me in the right direction and to offer support. I only pray that all of these efforts bring about a better world filled with devotees who respect each other because of their love for God.

Swami Satyananda Saraswati
Devi Mandir, Napa, CA 2001

Table of Contents

श्री मन्महागणाधिपतये नमः

śrī manmahāgaṇādhipataye namaḥ

We bow to the Respected Great Lord of Wisdom.

लक्ष्मीनारायणाभ्यां नमः

lakṣmīnārāyaṇābhyāṃ namaḥ

We bow to Lakṣmī and Nārāyaṇa, The Goal of all Existence and the Perceiver of all.

उमामहेश्वराभ्यां नमः

umāmaheśvarābhyāṃ namaḥ

We bow to Umā and Maheśvara, She who protects existence, and the Great Consciousness or Seer of all.

वाणीहिरण्यगर्भाभ्यां नमः

vāṇīhiraṇyagarbhābhyāṃ namaḥ

We bow to Vāṇī and Hiraṇyagarbha, Sarasvatī and Brahmā, who create the cosmic existence.

शचीपुरन्दराभ्यां नमः

śacīpurandarābhyāṃ namaḥ

We bow to Śacī and Purandara, Indra and his wife, who preside over all that is divine.

मातापितृभ्यां नमः

mātāpitṛbhyāṃ namaḥ

We bow to the Mothers and Fathers.

इष्टदेवताभ्यो नमः

iṣṭadevatābhyo namaḥ

We bow to the chosen deity of worship.

कुलदेवताभ्यो नमः
kuladevatābhyo namaḥ
We bow to the family deity of worship.

ग्रामदेवताभ्यो नमः
grāmadevatābhyo namaḥ
We bow to the village deity of worship.

वास्तुदेवताभ्यो नमः
vāstudevatābhyo namaḥ
We bow to the (particular) household deity of worship.

स्थानदेवताभ्यो नमः
sthānadevatābhyo namaḥ
We bow to the established deity of worship.

सर्वेभ्यो देवेभ्यो नमः
sarvebhyo devebhyo namaḥ
We bow to all the Gods.

सर्वेभ्यो ब्राह्मणेभ्यो नमः
sarvebhyo brāhmaṇebhyo namaḥ
We bow to all the Knowers of Divinity.

खड्गं चक्रगदेषुचापपरिघाञ्छूलं भुशुण्डीं शिरः
शङ्खं संदधतीं करैस्त्रिनयनां सर्वाङ्गभूषावृताम् ।
नीलाश्मद्युतिमास्यपाददशकां सेवे महाकालिकां
यामस्तौत्स्वपिते हरौ कमलजो हन्तुं मधुं कैटभम् ॥

khaḍgaṃ cakra gadeṣu cāpa
parighāñ chūlaṃ bhuśuṇḍīṃ śiraḥ
śaṅkhaṃ saṃdadhatīṃ karai
strinayanāṃ sarvāṅga bhūṣāvṛtām ।
nīlāśmadyutimāsya pāda-
daśakāṃ seve mahākālikāṃ
yāmastaut svapite harau kamalajo
hantuṃ madhuṃ kaiṭabham ॥

Bearing in Her ten hands the sword of worship, the discus of revolving time, the club of articulation, the bow of determination, the iron bar of restraint, the pike of attention, the sling, the head of egotism, and the conch of vibrations, She has three eyes and displays ornaments on all Her limbs. Shining like a blue gem, She has ten faces and feet. I worship that Great Remover of Darkness whom the lotus-born Creative Capacity praised in order to slay Too Much and Too Little, when the Supreme Consciousness was in sleep.

अक्षस्रक्परशुं गदेषुकुलिशं पद्मं धनुः कुण्डिकां
दण्डं शक्तिमसिं च चर्म जलजं घण्टां सुराभाजनम् ।
शूलं पाशसुदर्शने च दधतीं हस्तैः प्रसन्नाननां
सेवे सैरिभमर्दिनीमिह महालक्ष्मीं सरोजस्थिताम् ॥

akṣasrak paraśuṃ gadeṣu kuliśaṃ
padmaṃ dhanuḥ kuṇḍikāṃ
daṇḍaṃ śaktim asiṃ ca carma
jalajaṃ ghaṇṭāṃ surābhājanam ।
śūlaṃ pāśa sudarśane ca
dadhatīṃ hastaiḥ prasannānanāṃ
seve sairibha mardinīmiha
mahālakṣmīṃ sarojasthitām ॥

She with the beautiful face, the Destroyer of the Great Ego, is seated upon the lotus of peace. In Her hands She holds the rosary of alphabets, the battle axe of good actions, the club of articulation, the arrow of speech, the thunderbolt of illumination, the lotus of peace, the bow of determination, the water pot of purification, the staff of discipline, energy, the sword of worship, the shield of faith, the conch of vibrations, the bell of continuous tone, the wine cup of joy, the pike of concentration, the net of unity, and the discus of revolving time named Excellent Intuitive Vision. I worship that Great Goddess of True Wealth.

घण्टाशूलहलानि शङ्खमुसले चक्रं धनुः सायकं
हस्ताब्जैर्दधतीं घनान्तविलसच्छीतांशुतुल्यप्रभाम् ।
गौरीदेहसमुद्भवां त्रिजगतामाधारभूतां महा-
पूर्वामत्र सरस्वतीमनुभजे शुम्भादिदैत्यार्दिनीम् ॥

ghaṇṭā śūla halāni śaṅkha
musale cakraṃ dhanuḥ sāyakaṃ
hastābjair dadhatīṃ ghanānta
vilasacchītāṃ śutulya prabhām |
gaurīdeha samudbhavāṃ
trijagatām ādhārabhūtāṃ mahā-
pūrvāmatra sarasvatīm anubhaje
śumbhādi daityārdinīm ||

Bearing in Her lotus hands the bell of continuous tone, the pike of concentration, the plow sowing the seeds of the Way of Truth to Wisdom, the conch of vibrations, the pestle of refinement, the discus of revolving time, the bow of determination, and the arrow of speech, whose radiance is like the moon in autumn, whose appearance is most beautiful, who is manifested from the body of She Who is Rays of Light, and is the support of the three worlds, that Great Goddess of All-Pervading Knowledge, who destroyed Self-Conceit and other thoughts, I worship.

या चण्डी मधुकैटभादिदैत्यदलनी या माहिषोन्मूलिनी
या धूम्रेक्षणचण्डमुण्डमथनी या रक्तबीजाशनी ।
शक्तिः शुम्भनिशुम्भदैत्यदलनी या सिद्धिदात्री परा
सा देवी नवकोटिमूर्तिसहिता मां पातु विश्वेश्वरी ॥

yā caṇḍī madhukaiṭabhādidaityadalanī
yā māhiṣonmūlinī
yā dhūmrekṣaṇacaṇḍamuṇḍamathanī
yā raktabījāśanī |
śaktiḥ śumbhaniśumbhadaityadalanī
yā siddhidātrī parā
sā devī navakoṭimūrtisahitā māṃ pātu viśveśvarī ||

That Chaṇḍī, who slays the negativities of Too Much and Too Little and other Thoughts; Who is the Destroyer of the Great Ego, and the Vanquisher of Sinful Eyes, Passion and Anger, and the Seed of Desire; the Energy that tears asunder Self-Conceit and Self-Deprecation, the Grantor of the highest attainment of perfection: may that Goddess who is represented by ninety million divine images, Supreme Lord of the Universe, remain close and protect me.

ॐ अग्निर्ज्योतिर्ज्योतिरग्निः स्वाहा ।
सूर्यो ज्योतिर्ज्योतिः सूर्यः स्वाहा ।
अग्निर्वर्चो ज्योतिर्वर्चः स्वाहा ।
सूर्यो वर्चो ज्योतिर्वर्चः स्वाहा ।
ज्योतिः सूर्यः सूर्यो ज्योतिः स्वाहा ॥

oṃ agnir jyotir jyotir agniḥ svāhā |
sūryo jyotir jyotiḥ sūryaḥ svāhā |
agnir varco jyotir varcaḥ svāhā |
sūryo varco jyotir varcaḥ svāhā |
jyotiḥ sūryaḥ sūryo jyotiḥ svāhā ||

Oṃ The Divine Fire is the Light, and the Light is the Divine Fire; I am One with God! The Light of Wisdom is the Light, and the Light is the Light of Wisdom; I am One with God! The Divine Fire is the offering, and the Light is the Offering; I am One with God! The Light of Wisdom is the Offering, and the Light is the Light of Wisdom; I am One with God!

(Wave light)

ॐ अग्निर्ज्योती रविर्ज्योतिश्चन्द्रो ज्योतिस्तथैव च ।
ज्योतिषमुत्तमो देवि दीपोऽयं प्रतिगृह्यतम् ॥
एष दीपः ॐ ऐं ह्रीं क्लीं चामुण्डायै विच्चे ॥

oṃ agnirjyotī ravirjyotiścandro jyotistathaiva ca |
jyotiṣamuttamo devi dīpo-yaṃ pratigṛhyatam ||
eṣa dīpaḥ oṃ aiṃ hrīṃ klīṃ cāmuṇḍāyai vicce ||

Oṃ The Divine Fire is the Light, the Light of Wisdom is the Light, the Light of Devotion is the Light as well. The Light of the Highest Bliss, Oh Goddess, is in the Light that we offer, the Light that we request you to accept. With the offering of Light, oṃ aiṃ hrīṃ klīṃ cāmuṇḍāyai vicce.

(Wave incense)

ॐ वनस्पतिरसोत्पन्नो गन्धात्ययी गन्ध उत्तमः ।
आघ्रेयः सर्व देवानां धूपोऽयं प्रतिगृह्यताम् ॥
एष धूपः ॐ ऐं ह्रीं क्लीं चामुण्डायै विच्चे ॥

oṃ vanaspatirasotpanno
gandhātyayī gandha uttamaḥ |
āghreyaḥ sarva devānāṃ dhūpo-yaṃ pratigṛhyatām ||
eṣa dhūpaḥ oṃ aiṃ hrīṃ klīṃ cāmuṇḍāyai vicce ||

Oṃ Spirit of the Forest, from you is produced the most excellent of scents. The scent most pleasing to all the Gods, that scent we request you to accept. With the offering of fragrant scent, oṃ aiṃ hrīṃ klīṃ cāmuṇḍāyai vicce.

ॐ पयः पृथिव्यां पय ओषधीषु
पयो दिव्यन्तरिक्षे पयो धाः ।
पयःस्वतीः प्रदिशः सन्तु मह्यम् ॥

oṃ payaḥ pṛthivyāṃ paya oṣadhīṣu
payo divyantarikṣe payo dhāḥ |
payaḥsvatīḥ pradiśaḥ santu mahyam ||

Oṃ Earth is a reservoir of nectar, all vegetation is a reservoir of nectar, the divine atmosphere is a reservoir of nectar, and also above. May all perceptions shine forth with the sweet taste of nectar for us.

ॐ अग्निर्देवता वातो देवता सूर्यो देवता चन्द्रमा देवता
वसवो देवता रुद्रो देवता ऽदित्या देवता मरुतो देवता विश्वे
देवा देवता बृहस्पतिर्देवतेन्द्रो देवता वरुणो देवता ॥

oṃ agnirdevatā vāto devatā sūryo devatā candramā devatā vasavo devatā rudro devatā-dityā devatā maruto devatā viśve devā devatā bṛhaspatirdevatendro devatā varuṇo devatā ||

Oṃ The Divine Fire (Light of Purity) is the shining God, the Wind is the shining God, the Sun (Light of Wisdom) is the shining God, the Moon (Lord of Devotion) is the shining God, the Protectors of the Wealth are the shining Gods, the Relievers of Sufferings are the shining Gods, the Sons of the Light are the shining Gods; the Emmancipated seers (Maruts) are the shining Gods, the Universal Shining Gods are the shining Gods, the Guru of the Gods is the shining God, the Ruler of the Gods is the shining God, the Lord of Waters is the shining God.

ॐ भूर्भुवः स्वः ।
तत् सवितुर्वरेण्यम् भर्गो देवस्य धीमहि ।
धियो यो नः प्रचोदयात् ॥

oṃ bhūr bhuvaḥ svaḥ |
tat savitur vareṇyam bhargo devasya dhīmahi |
dhiyo yo naḥ pracodayāt ||

Oṃ the Infinite Beyond Conception, the gross body, the subtle body and the causal body; we meditate on that Light of Wisdom that is the Supreme Wealth of the Gods. May it grant to us increase in our meditations.

ॐ भूः

oṃ bhūḥ

Oṃ the gross body

ॐ भुवः

oṃ bhuvaḥ

Oṃ the subtle body

ॐ स्वः

oṃ svaḥ

Oṃ the causal body

ॐ महः

oṃ mahaḥ

Oṃ the great body of existence

ॐ जनः

oṃ janaḥ

Oṃ the body of knowledge

ॐ तपः

oṃ tapaḥ

Oṃ the body of light

ॐ सत्यं

oṃ satyaṃ

Oṃ the body of Truth

ॐ तत् सवितुर्वरेण्यम् भर्गो देवस्य धीमहि ।
धियो यो नः प्रचोदयात् ॥

oṃ tat savitur vareṇyam bhargo devasya dhīmahi |
dhiyo yo naḥ pracodayāt ||

Oṃ we meditate on that Light of Wisdom that is the Supreme Wealth of the Gods. May it grant to us increase in our meditations.

ॐ आपो ज्योतीरसोमृतं ब्रह्म भूर्भुवस्स्वरोम् ॥

oṃ āpo jyotīrasomṛtaṃ brahma bhūrbhuvassvarom ||

Oṃ may the divine waters, luminous with the nectar of immortality of Supreme Divinity, fill the earth, the atmosphere, and the heavens.

ॐ मां माले महामाये सर्वशक्तिस्वरूपिणि ।
चतुर्वर्गस्त्वयि न्यस्तस्तस्मान्मे सिद्धिदा भव ॥

oṃ māṃ māle mahāmāye sarva śakti svarūpiṇi |
catur vargas tvayi nyastas
tasmān me siddhidā bhava ||

Oṃ my Rosary, The Great Measurement of Consciousness, containing all energy within as your intrinsic nature, give to me the attainment of your Perfection, fulfilling the four objectives of life.

ॐ अविघ्नं कुरु माले त्वं गृह्णामि दक्षिणे करे ।
जपकाले च सिद्ध्यर्थं प्रसीद मम सिद्धये ॥

oṃ avighnaṃ kuru māle tvaṃ gṛhṇāmi dakṣiṇe kare |
japakāle ca siddhyarthaṃ prasīda mama siddhaye ||

Oṃ Rosary, please remove all obstacles. I hold you in my right hand. At the time of recitation be pleased with me. Allow me to attain the Highest Perfection.

ॐ अक्षमालाधिपतये सुसिद्धिं देहि देहि सर्वमन्त्रार्थसाधिनि
साधय साधय सर्वसिद्धिं परिकल्पय परिकल्पय मे स्वाहा ॥

oṃ akṣa mālā dhipataye susiddhiṃ dehi dehi sarva
mantrārtha sādhini sādhaya sādhaya sarva siddhiṃ
parikalpaya parikalpaya me svāhā ||

Oṃ Rosary of rudrākṣa seeds, my Lord, give to me excellent attainment. Give to me, give to me. Illuminate the meanings of all mantras. Illuminate! Illuminate! Fashion me with all excellent attainments! Fashion me! I am One with God!

एते गन्धपुष्पे ॐ गं गणपतये नमः

ete gandhapuṣpe oṃ gaṃ gaṇapataye namaḥ

With these scented flowers, oṃ we bow to the Lord of Wisdom, Lord of the Multitudes.

एते गन्धपुष्पे ॐ आदित्यादि नवग्रहेभ्यो नमः

ete gandhapuṣpe oṃ ādityādi navagrahebhyo namaḥ

With these scented flowers, oṃ we bow to the Sun, the Light of Wisdom, along with the nine planets.

एते गन्धपुष्पे ॐ शिवादिपञ्चदेवताभ्यो नमः

ete gandhapuṣpe oṃ śivādipañcadevatābhyo namaḥ

With these scented flowers, oṃ we bow to Śiva, the Consciousness of Infinite Goodness, along with the five primary deities (Śiva, Śakti, Viṣṇu, Gaṇeśa, Sūrya).

एते गन्धपुष्पे ॐ इन्द्रादिदशदिक्पालेभ्यो नमः

ete gandhapuṣpe oṃ indrādi daśadikpālebhyo namaḥ

With these scented flowers, oṃ we bow to Indra, the Ruler of the Pure, along with the Ten Protectors of the ten directions.

एते गन्धपुष्पे ॐ मत्स्यादिदशावतारेभ्यो नमः

ete gandhapuṣpe oṃ matsyādi daśāvatārebhyo namaḥ

With these scented flowers, oṃ we bow to Viṣṇu, the Fish, along with the Ten Incarnations that He assumed.

एते गन्धपुष्पे ॐ प्रजापतये नमः

ete gandhapuṣpe oṃ prajāpataye namaḥ

With these scented flowers, oṃ we bow to the Lord of All Created Beings.

एते गन्धपुष्पे ॐ नमो नारायणाय नमः

ete gandhapuṣpe oṃ namo nārāyaṇāya namaḥ

With these scented flowers, oṃ we bow to the Perfect Perception of Consciousness.

एते गन्धपुष्पे ॐ सर्वेभ्यो देवेभ्यो नमः

ete gandhapuṣpe oṃ sarvebhyo devebhyo namaḥ

With these scented flowers, oṃ we bow to All the Gods.

एते गन्धपुष्पे ॐ सर्वाभ्यो देवीभ्यो नमः

ete gandhapuṣpe oṃ sarvābhyo devībhyo namaḥ

With these scented flowers, oṃ we bow to All the Goddesses.

एते गन्धपुष्पे ॐ श्री गुरवे नमः

ete gandhapuṣpe oṃ śrī gurave namaḥ

With these scented flowers, oṃ we bow to the Guru.

एते गन्धपुष्पे ॐ ब्राह्मणेभ्यो नमः

ete gandhapuṣpe oṃ brāhmaṇebhyo namaḥ

With these scented flowers, oṃ we bow to All Knowers of Wisdom.

Tie a piece of string around right middle finger or wrist

ॐ कुशासने स्थितो ब्रह्मा कुशे चैव जनार्दनः ।
कुशे ह्याकाशवद् विष्णुः कुशासन नमोऽस्तु ते ॥

oṃ kuśāsane sthito brahmā kuśe caiva janārdanaḥ |
kuśe hyākāśavad viṣṇuḥ kuśāsana namo-stu te ||

Brahmā is in the shining light (or kuśa grass), in the shining light resides Janārdana, the Lord of Beings. The Supreme all-pervading Consciousness, Viṣṇu, resides in the shining light. Oh Repository of the shining light, we bow down to you, the seat of kuśa grass.

ācaman

ॐ केशवाय नमः स्वाहा

oṃ keśavāya namaḥ svāhā

Oṃ We bow to the one of beautiful hair.

ॐ माधवाय नमः स्वाहा

oṃ mādhavāya namaḥ svāhā

Oṃ We bow to the one who is always sweet.

ॐ गोविन्दाय नमः स्वाहा

oṃ govindāya namaḥ svāhā

Oṃ We bow to He who is one-pointed light.

ॐ विष्णुः ॐ विष्णुः ॐ विष्णुः

oṃ viṣṇuḥ oṃ viṣṇuḥ oṃ viṣṇuḥ

Oṃ Consciousness, oṃ Consciousness, oṃ Consciousness.

ॐ तत् विष्णोः परमं पदम् सदा पश्यन्ति सूरयः ।
दिवीव चक्षुराततम् ॥

oṃ tat viṣṇoḥ paramaṃ padam
sadā paśyanti sūrayaḥ |
divīva cakṣurā tatam ||

Oṃ That Consciousness of the highest station, who always sees the Light of Wisdom, give us Divine Eyes.

ॐ तद् विप्र स पिपानोव जुविग्रन्सो सोमिन्द्रते ।
विष्णुः तत् परमं पदम् ॥

oṃ tad vipra sa pipānova juvigranso somindraṭe |
viṣṇuḥ tat paramaṃ padam ||

Oṃ That twice-born teacher who is always thirsty for accepting the nectar of devotion, Oh Consciousness, you are in that highest station.

ॐ अपवित्रः पवित्रो वा सर्वावस्थां गतोऽपि वा ।
यः स्मरेत् पुण्डरीकाक्षं स बाह्याभ्यन्तरः शुचिः ॥

oṃ apavitraḥ pavitro vā sarvāvasthāṃ gato-pi vā |
yaḥ smaret puṇḍarīkākṣaṃ
sa bāhyābhyantaraḥ śuciḥ ||

Oṃ the Impure and the Pure reside within all objects. Who remembers the lotus-eyed Consciousness is conveyed to radiant beauty.

ॐ सर्वमङ्गलमाङ्गल्यम् वरेण्यम् वरदं शुभं ।
नारायणं नमस्कृत्य सर्वकर्माणि कारयेत् ॥

oṃ sarva maṅgala māṅgalyam
vareṇyam varadaṃ śubhaṃ |
nārāyaṇaṃ namaskṛtya sarva karmāṇi kārayet ||

Oṃ All the Welfare of all Welfare, the highest blessing of Purity and Illumination, with the offering of respect we bow down to the Supreme Consciousness who is the actual performer of all action.

ॐ सूर्य्यश्चमेति मन्त्रस्य ब्रह्मा ऋषिः प्रकृतिश्छन्दः आपो देवता आचमने विनियोगः ॥

oṃ sūryyaścameti mantrasya brahmā ṛṣiḥ
prakṛtiśchandaḥ āpo devatā ācamane viniyogaḥ ||

Oṃ these are the mantras of the Light of Wisdom, the Creative Capacity is the Seer, Nature is the meter, the divine flow of waters is the deity, being applied in washing the hands and rinsing the mouth.

Draw the following yantra with some drops of water and/or sandalpaste at the front of your seat.
Place a flower on the bindu in the middle.

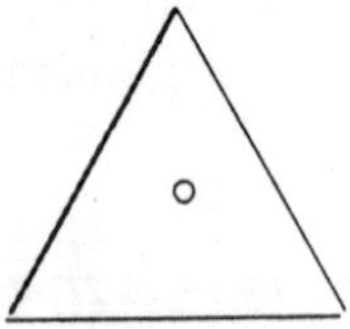

ॐ आसनस्य मन्त्रस्य मेरुपृष्ठ ऋषिः सुतलं छन्दः कूर्म्मो देवता आसनोपवेशने विनियोगः ॐ ॥

oṃ āsanasya mantrasya merupṛṣṭha ṛṣiḥ sutalaṃ chandaḥ kūrmmo devatā āsanopaveśane viniyogaḥ oṃ ||

Oṃ Introducing the mantras of the Purification of the seat. The Seer is He whose back is Straight, the meter is of very beautiful form, the tortoise who supports the earth is the deity. These mantras are applied to make the seat free from obstructions.

एते गन्धपुष्पे ॐ ह्रीं आधारशक्तये कमलासनाय नमः ॥

ete gandhapuṣpe oṃ hrīṃ ādhāra śaktaye kamalāsanāya namaḥ ||

With these scented flowers, Oṃ hrīṃ we bow to the Primal Energy situated in this lotus seat.

ॐ पृथ्वि त्वया धृता लोका देवि त्वं विष्णुना धृता ।
त्वञ्च धारय मां नित्यं पवित्रं कुरु चासनम् ॥

oṃ pṛthvi tvayā dhṛtā lokā devi tvaṃ viṣṇunā dhṛtā |
tvañca dhāraya māṃ nityaṃ
pavitraṃ kuru cāsanam ||

Oṃ Earth! You support the realms of the Goddess. You are supported by the Supreme Consciousness. Also bear me eternally and make pure this seat.

ॐ गुरुभ्यो नमः

oṃ gurubhyo namaḥ

Oṃ I bow to the Guru.

ॐ परमगुरुभ्यो नमः

oṃ paramagurubhyo namaḥ

Oṃ I bow to the Guru's Guru.

ॐ परापरगुरुभ्यो नमः

oṃ parāparagurubhyo namaḥ

Oṃ I bow to the Guru's Guru.

ॐ परमेष्ठिगुरुभ्यो नमः

oṃ parameṣṭhigurubhyo namaḥ

Oṃ I bow to the Supreme Guru's Guru.

ॐ गं गणेशाय नमः

oṃ gaṃ gaṇeśāya namaḥ

Oṃ I bow to the Lord of Wisdom.

ॐ अनन्ताय नमः

oṃ anantāya namaḥ

Oṃ I bow to the Infinite One.

ॐ ऐं ह्रीं क्लीं चामुण्डायै विच्चे
oṃ aiṃ hrīṃ klīṃ cāmuṇḍāyai vicce ||
Oṃ Wisdom, Māyā, Transformation.

ॐ नमः शिवाय
oṃ namaḥ śivāya
Oṃ I bow to the Consciousness of Infinite Goodness.

Clap hands three times and snap fingers in the ten directions (N, S, E, W, NE, SW, NW, SE, UP, DOWN) repeating:

ॐ ऐं ह्रीं क्लीं चामुण्डायै विच्चे
oṃ aiṃ hrīṃ klīṃ cāmuṇḍāyai vicce
Oṃ aiṃ hrīṃ klīṃ cāmuṇḍāyai vicce

saṅkalpa

विष्णुः ॐ तत् सत्। ॐ अद्य जम्बूद्वीपे (   ) देशे (   ) प्रदेशे (   ) नगरे (   ) मन्दिरे (   ) मासे (   ) पक्षे (   ) तिथौ (   ) गोत्र श्री (   ) कृतैतत् श्रीचण्डिकाकामः पूजाकर्माहं श्रीचण्डीपाठं करिष्ये ॥

viṣṇuḥ oṃ tat sat | oṃ adya jambūdvīpe (Country) deśe (State) pradeśe (City) nagare (Name of house or temple) mandire (month) māse (śukla or kṛṣṇa) pakṣe (name of day) tithau (name of) gotra śrī (your name) kṛtaitat śrī caṇḍikā kāmaḥ pūjā karmāhaṃ śrī caṇḍī pāṭhaṃ kariṣye ||

The Consciousness that Pervades All, Oṃ That is Truth. Presently, on the Planet Earth, in the Country of (Name), in the State of (Name), in the City of (Name), in the Temple of (Name), (Name of Month) Month, (Bright or Dark) fortnight, (Name of Day) Day, (Name of Sadhu Family), Śrī (Your Name) is performing the worship for the satisfaction of the Respected Chaṇḍī by reciting the Chaṇḍī Worship.

ॐ यज्जाग्रतो दूरमुदेति दैवं तदु सुप्तस्य तथैवैति ।
दूरङ्गमं ज्योतिषां ज्योतिरेकं तन्मे मनः शिवसङ्कल्पमस्तु ॥

oṃ yajjāgrato dūramudeti
daivaṃ tadu suptaśya tathaivaiti |
dūraṅgamamaṃ jyotiṣāṃ jyotirekaṃ
tanme manaḥ śiva saṅkalpamastu ||

Oṃ May our waking consciousness replace pain and suffering with divinity, as also our awareness when asleep. Far extending be our radiant aura of light, filling our minds with light. May that be the firm determination of the Consciousness of Infinite Goodness.

या गुङ्गूर्या सिनीवाली या राका या सरस्वती ।
ईन्द्राणीमह्व ऊतये वरुणानीं स्वस्तये ॥

yā guṅgūryā sinīvālī yā rākā yā sarasvatī |
īndrāṇīmahva ūtaye varuṇānīṃ svastaye ||

May that Goddess who wears the Moon of Devotion protect the children of Devotion. May that Goddess of All-Pervading Knowledge protect us. May the Energy of the Rule of the Pure rise up. Oh Energy of Equilibrium grant us the highest prosperity.

ॐ स्वस्ति न इन्द्रो वृद्धश्रवाः स्वस्ति नः पूषा विश्ववेदाः ।
स्वस्ति नस्तार्क्ष्यो अरिष्टनेमिः स्वस्ति नो बृहस्पतिर्दधातु ॥

oṃ svasti na indro vṛddhaśravāḥ
svasti naḥ pūṣā viśvavedāḥ |
svasti nastārkṣyo ariṣṭanemiḥ
svasti no bṛhaspatirdadhātu ||

Oṃ The Ultimate Prosperity to us, Oh Rule of the Pure, who perceives all that changes; the Ultimate Prosperity to us, Searchers for Truth, Knowers of the Universe; the Ultimate Prosperity to us, Oh Divine Being of Light, keep us safe; the Ultimate Prosperity to us, Oh Spirit of All-Pervading Delight, grant that to us.

ॐ गणानां त्वा गणपतिꣳ हवामहे
प्रियाणां त्वा प्रियपतिꣳ हवामहे
निधीनां त्वा निधिपतिꣳ हवामहे वसो मम ।
आहमजानि गर्ब्भधमा त्वमजासि गर्ब्भधम् ॥

oṃ gaṇānāṃ tvā gaṇapati guṃ havāmahe
priyāṇāṃ tvā priyapati guṃ havāmahe
nidhīnāṃ tvā nidhipati guṃ havāmahe vaso mama
āhamajāni garbbhadhamā tvamajāsi garbbhadham

Oṃ We invoke you with offerings, Oh Lord of the Multitudes; we invoke you with offerings, Oh Lord of Love; we invoke you with offerings, Oh Guardian of the Treasure. Sit within me, giving birth to the realm of the Gods within me; yes, giving birth to the realm of the Gods within me.

ॐ गणानां त्वा गणपतिꣳ हवामहे
कविं कवीनामुपमश्रवस्तमम् ।
ज्येष्ठराजं ब्रह्मणां ब्रह्मणस्पत
आ नः शृण्वन्नूतिभिः सीद सादनम् ॥

oṃ gaṇānāṃ tvā gaṇapati guṃ havāmahe
kaviṃ kavīnāmupamaśravastamam
jyeṣṭharājaṃ brahmaṇāṃ brahmaṇaspata
ā naḥ śṛṇvannūtibhiḥ sīda sādanam

Oṃ We invoke you with offerings, Oh Lord of the Multitudes, Seer among Seers, of unspeakable grandeur. Oh Glorious King, Lord of the Knowers of Wisdom, come speedily hearing our supplications and graciously take your seat amidst our assembly.

ॐ अदितिर्द्यौरदितिरन्तरिक्षमदितिर्माता स पिता स
पुत्रः । विश्वे देवा अदितिः पञ्च जना
अदितिर्जातमदितिर्जनित्वम् ॥

oṃ aditir dyauraditirantarikṣamaditirmātā
sa pitā sa putraḥ |
viśve devā aditiḥ pañca janā
aditirjātamaditirjanitvam ||

Oṃ The Mother of Enlightenment pervades the heavens; the Mother of Enlightenment pervades the atmosphere; the Mother of Enlightenment pervades Mother and Father and child. All Gods of the Universe are pervaded by the Mother, the five forms of living beings, all Life. The Mother of Enlightenment, She is to be known.

ॐ त्वं स्त्रीस्त्वं पुमानसि त्वं कुमार अत वा कुमारी ।
त्वं जिर्नो दण्डेन वञ्चसि त्वं जातो भवसि विश्वतोमुखः ॥

oṃ tvaṃ strīstvaṃ pumānasi
tvaṃ kumāra ata vā kumārī |
tvaṃ jirno daṇḍena vañcasi
tvaṃ jāto bhavasi viśvatomukhaḥ ||

Oṃ You are Female, you are Male; you are a young boy, you are a young girl. You are the word of praise by which we are singing; you are all creation existing as the mouth of the universe.

ॐ अम्बेऽम्बिकेऽम्बालिके न मा नयति कश्चन ।
ससस्त्यश्वकः सुभद्रिकां काम्पीलवासिनीम् ॥

oṃ ambe-mbike-mbālike na mā nayati kaścana |
sasastyaśvakaḥ subhadrikāṃ kāmpīlavāsinīm ||

Oṃ Mother of the Perceivable Universe, Mother of the Conceivable Universe, Mother of the Universe of Intuitive Vision, lead me to that True Existence. As excellent crops (or grains) are harvested, so may I be taken to reside with the Infinite Consciousness.

ॐ शान्ता द्यौः शान्तापृथिवी शान्तमिदमुर्वन्तरिक्षम् ।
शान्ता उदन्वतिरापः शान्ताः नः शान्त्वोषधीः ॥

oṃ śāntā dyauḥ śāntā pṛthivī
śāntam idamurvantarikṣam |
śāntā udanvatirāpaḥ śāntāḥ naḥ śāntvoṣadhī ||

Oṃ Peace in the heavens, Peace on the earth, Peace upwards and permeating the atmosphere; Peace upwards, over, on all sides and further; Peace to us, Peace to all vegetation;

ॐ शान्तानि पूर्वरूपाणि शान्तं नोऽस्तु कृताकृतम् ।
शान्तं भूतं च भव्यं च सर्वमेव शमस्तु नः ॥

oṃ śāntāni pūrva rūpāṇi śāntaṃ no-stu kṛtākṛtam |
śāntaṃ bhūtaṃ ca bhavyaṃ ca sarvameva śamastu naḥ ||

Oṃ Peace to all that has form, Peace to all causes and effects; Peace to all existence, and to all intensities of reality, including all and everything; Peace be to us.

ॐ पृथिवी शान्तिरन्तरिक्षं शान्तिर्द्यौः
शान्तिरापः शान्तिरोषधयः शान्तिः वनस्पतयः शान्तिर्विश्वे मे देवाः शान्तिः सर्वे मे देवाः शान्तिर्ब्रह्म शान्तिरापः शान्ति सर्व शान्तिरेधि शान्तिः शान्तिः सर्व शान्तिः सा मा शान्तिः शान्तिभिः ॥

oṃ pṛthivī śāntir antarikṣaṃ śāntir dyauḥ
śāntir āpaḥ śāntir oṣadhayaḥ śāntiḥ vanaspatayaḥ
śāntir viśve me devāḥ śāntiḥ sarve me devāḥ śāntir brahma śāntirāpaḥ śānti sarva śāntiredhi śāntiḥ śāntiḥ sarva śāntiḥ sā mā śāntiḥ śāntibhiḥ ||

Oṃ Let the earth be at Peace, the atmosphere be at Peace, the heavens be filled with Peace. Even further may Peace extend, Peace be to waters, Peace to all vegetation, Peace to All Gods of the Universe, Peace to All Gods within us, Peace to Creative Consciousness, Peace to Brilliant Light, Peace to All, Peace to Everything, Peace, Peace, altogether Peace, equally Peace, by means of Peace.

ताभिः शान्तिभिः सर्वशान्तिभिः समया मोहं यदिह घोरं
यदिह क्रूरं यधिह पापं तच्छान्तं तच्छिवं सर्वमेव
समस्तु नः ॥

**tābhiḥ śāntibhiḥ sarva śāntibhiḥ samayā mohaṃ
yadiha ghoraṃ yadiha krūraṃ yadiha pāpaṃ
tacchāntaṃ tacchivaṃ sarvameva samastu naḥ ॥**

Thus by means of Peace, altogether one with the means of
Peace, Ignorance is eliminated, Violence is eradicated,
Improper Conduct is eradicated, Confusion (sin) is eradicated,
all that is, is at Peace, all that is perceived, each and everything, altogether for us,

ॐ शान्तिः शान्तिः शान्तिः ॥

oṃ śāntiḥ śāntiḥ śāntiḥ ॥

Oṃ Peace, Peace, Peace

अथ सप्तश्लोकी दुर्गा

atha sapta ślokī durgā

Seven Verses That Express the Essence of
She Who Relieves all Difficulties

शिव उवाच

śiva uvāca

The Consciousness of Infinite Goodness said:

देवि त्वं भक्तसुलभे सर्वकार्यविधायिनी ।
कलौ हि कार्यसिद्ध्यर्थमुपायं ब्रूहि यत्नतः ॥

devi tvaṃ bhaktasulabhe sarvakāryavidhāyinī |
kalau hi kāryasiddhyarthamupāyaṃ brūhi yatnataḥ ||

Oh Goddess, You are accessible to your devotees as you give the effects of all actions. Please tell me the means of success in perfecting all desires in this Age of Darkness.

देव्युवाच

devyuvāca

The Goddess said:

शृणु देव प्रवक्ष्यामि कलौ सर्वेष्टसाधनम् ।
मया तवैव स्नेहेनाप्यम्बास्तुतिः प्रकाश्यते ॥

śṛṇu deva pravakṣyāmi kalau sarveṣṭasādhanam |
mayā tavaiva snehenāpyambāstutiḥ prakāśyate ||

Listen, Oh Divine Being, as I elucidate the highest path of Spiritual Discipline. Because of your unswerving love for me, I reveal this song of Praise of the Goddess.

ॐ अस्य श्रीदुर्गासप्तश्लोकीस्तोत्रमन्त्रस्य नारायण ऋषिः
अनुष्टुप् छन्दः श्रीमहाकालीमहालक्ष्मीमहासरस्वत्यो देवताः
श्रीदुर्गाप्रीत्यर्थं सप्तश्लोकीदुर्गापाठे विनियोगः ॥

oṃ asya śrīdurgā sapta ślokī stotra mantrasya nārāyaṇa ṛṣiḥ anuṣṭup chandaḥ śrīmahākālī mahālakṣmī mahāsarasvatyo devatāḥ śrīdurgā prītyarthaṃ sapta ślokī durgā pāṭhe viniyogaḥ ||

Oṃ Presenting the mantras of the Song of Seven Verses explaining the Respected Reliever of Difficulties, the All-Pervading Consciousness is the Seer; Anuṣṭup is the Meter (32 syllables to the verse); The Respected Remover of Darkness, The Great Goddess of True Wealth, and The Great Goddess of All Pervading Knowledge are the deities; for the satisfaction of the Reliever of Difficulties, these seven verses of Durgā are applied in recitation.

(Note: All Mantras have a Seer, who originally realized this knowledge and passed it along to us; a meter, a certain number of syllables with which it is expressed; a deity, whose attributes or actions are being extolled; a seed, or essential nature; a specific energy; and one or more specific principles that are incorporated into the purpose of recitation. Such a statement is called the Viniyogaḥ, Application, and is prefatory to the Mantras indicated.)

\- 1 -

ज्ञानिनामपि चेतांसि देवी भगवती हि सा ।
बलादाकृष्य मोहाय महामाया प्रयच्छति ॥

jñāninām api cetāṃsi devī bhagavatī hi sā |
balādākṛṣya mohāya mahāmāyā prayacchati ||

She, this Supreme Goddess, the Great Measurement of Consciousness, attracts the perceiving capacity of all sensible beings with such force as to thrust them into the ignorance of egotistic attachment.

\- 2 -

दुर्गे स्मृता हरसि भीतिमशेषजन्तोः
स्वस्थैः स्मृता मतिमतीव शुभां ददासि ।
दारिद्र्यदुःखभयहारिणि का त्वदन्या
सर्वोपकारकरणाय सदाऽऽर्द्रचित्ता ॥

durge smṛtā harasi bhītima śeṣajantoḥ
svasthaiḥ smṛtā matimatīva śubhāṃ dadāsi |
dāridrya duḥkha bhayahāriṇi kā tvadanyā
sarvopakāra karaṇāya sadā--rdracittā ||

Oh Reliever of Difficulties, remembering you the fear of all living beings is dispelled. When remembered by those individuals in the harmony of spiritual growth, you increase their welfare and intelligence. Who is like you, Oh Dispeller of Poverty, Pain, and Fear, whose sympathetic demeanor always extends compassionate assistance to everyone? Exposer of Consciousness, we bow to you.

- 3 -

सर्वमङ्गलमङ्गल्ये शिवे सर्वार्थसाधिके ।
शरण्ये त्र्यम्बके गौरि नारायणि नमोऽस्तु ते ॥

sarva maṅgala maṅgalye śive sarvārtha sādhike |
śaraṇye tryambake gauri nārāyaṇi namo-stu te ||

To the Auspicious of all Auspiciousness, to the Good, to the Accomplisher of all Objectives, to the Source of Refuge, to the Mother of the three worlds, to the Goddess Who is Rays of Light, Exposer of Consciousness, we bow to you.

- 4 -

शरणागतदीनार्तपरित्राणपरायणे ।
सर्वस्यार्तिहरे देवि नारायणि नमोऽस्तु ते ॥

śaraṇāgata dīnārta paritrāṇa parāyaṇe |
sarvasyārti hare devi nārāyaṇi namo-stu te ||

Those who are devoted to you and take refuge in you, even though lowly and humble, you save them from all discomfort and unhappiness. All worry you take away, Oh Goddess, Exposer of Consciousness, we bow to you.

- 5 -

सर्वस्वरूपे सर्वेशे सर्वशक्तिसमन्विते ।
भयेभ्यस्त्राहि नो देवि दुर्गे देवि नमोऽस्तु ते ॥

sarvasvarūpe sarveśe sarvaśakti samanvite |
bhayebhyastrāhi no devi durge devi namo-stu te ||

The Intrinsic Nature of All, the Supreme of All, and the Energy of All as well; you remove all fear from us, Oh Goddess; Reliever of Afflictions, Oh Goddess, we bow to you.

- 6 -

रोगानशेषानपहंसि तुष्टा
रुष्टा तु कामान् सकलानभीष्टान् ।
त्वामाश्रितानां न विपन्नराणां
त्वामाश्रिता ह्याश्रयतां प्रयान्ति ॥

rogānaśeṣānapahaṃsi tuṣṭā
ruṣṭā tu kāmān sakalānabhīṣṭān |
tvāmāśritānāṃ na vipannarāṇāṃ
tvāmāśritā hyāśrayatāṃ prayānti ||

When you are pleased you destroy all infirmities, and when you are displeased you frustrate all desires. No calamity or disease befalls those who take refuge in you, and those who take refuge in you invariably become a refuge to others.

- 7 -

सर्वाबाधाप्रशमनं त्रैलोक्यस्याखिलेश्वरि ।
एवमेव त्वया कार्यमस्मद्वैरिविनाशनम् ॥

sarvābādhā praśamanaṃ trailokyasyākhileśvari |
evameva tvayā kāryamasmadvairivināśanam ||

Oh Spirit of the Supreme Sovereign, terminate all disturbance in the three worlds and, in like manner, remove from us all hostility.

ॐ

oṃ

ॐ श्री दुर्गायै नमः

oṃ śrī durgāyai namaḥ

Oṃ We bow to the Respected Reliever of Difficulties

श्रीदुर्गाष्टोत्तरशतनामस्तोत्रम्

śrī durgāṣṭottara śatanāma stotram

The Song Containing One Hundred Eight Names of the Respected Reliever of Difficulties

ईश्वर उवाच

īśvara uvāca

The Supreme Lord said:

\- 1 -

शतनाम प्रवक्ष्यामि शृणुष्व कमलानने ।
यस्य प्रसादमात्रेण दुर्गा प्रीता भवेत् सती ॥

śatanāma pravakṣyāmi śṛṇuṣva kamalānane |
yasya prasādamātreṇa durgā prītā bhavet satī ||

Oh Lotus Eyed, I elucidate One Hundred Eight Names by means of which the Reliever of Difficulties truly becomes extremely pleased:

\- 2 -

ॐ सती साध्वी भवप्रीता भवानी भवमोचनी ।
आर्या दुर्गा जया चाद्या त्रिनेत्रा शूलधारिणी ॥

oṃ satī sādhvī bhavaprītā bhavānī bhavamocanī |
āryā durgā jayā cādyā trinetrā śūladhāriṇī ||

1. Embodiment of Truth
2. Embodiment of Virtue
3. Lover of the Universe
4. Embodiment of the Universe
5. Who Releases the Bonds of the Universe
6. Purified by Knowledge
7. Reliever of Difficulties
8. Victory
9. Foremost

10. Having Three Eyes
11. Bearer of the Spear

- 3 -

पिनाकधारिणी चित्रा चण्डघण्टा महातपाः ।

मनो बुद्धिरहंकारा चित्तरूपा चिता चितिः ॥

pinākadhāriṇī citrā caṇḍaghaṇṭā mahātapāḥ |
mano buddhir ahaṃkārā cittarūpā citā citiḥ ||

12. Bearer of the Trident
13. Characterized by Diversity
14. Who Makes Beautiful Subtle Sounds
15. Who Performs the Great Discipline of Austerities
16. Mind
17. Intellect
18. Ego
19. The Form of Recollection
20. All Recollection
21. Consciousness

- 4 -

सर्वमन्त्रमयी सत्ता सत्यानन्दस्वरूपिणी ।

अनन्ता भाविनी भाव्या भव्याभव्या सदागतिः ॥

sarva mantra mayī sattā satyānanda svarūpiṇī |
anantā bhāvinī bhāvyā bhavyā bhavyā sadāgatiḥ ||

22. The Essence of all Mantras
23. The Intrinsic Nature of Being
24. The Intrinsic Nature of the Bliss of Truth
25. Infinite
26. Who Brings Forth Creation
27. The Intensity of Reality
28. The Form of Welfare
29. Who is Always the Same
30. Who is Always in Motion

- 5 -

शाम्भवी देवमाता च चिन्ता रत्नप्रिया सदा ।

सर्वविद्या दक्षकन्या दक्षयज्ञविनाशिनी ॥

śāmbhavī devamātā ca cintā ratnapriyā sadā |
sarvavidyā dakṣakanyā dakṣayajña vināśinī ||

31. Beloved by Consciousness
32. Mother of the Gods
33. Contemplation
34. Beloved Jewel
35. All Knowledge
36. Daughter of Ability
37. Destroyer of Daksha's Sacrifice

- 6 -

अपर्णानेकवर्णा च पाटला पाटलावती ।
पट्टाम्बरपरीधाना कलमञ्जीररञ्जिनी ॥
aparṇānekavarṇā ca pāṭalā pāṭalāvatī |
paṭṭāmbara parīdhānā kalamañjīra rañjinī ||

38. Without Limbs
39. Of Various Colors, Castes, Tribes
40. Of Red Hue
41. Adorned by Red Flowers
42. Adorned by Silk Garments
43. Whose Anklets Make a Beautiful Sound

- 7 -

अमेयविक्रमा क्रूरा सुन्दरी सुरसुन्दरी ।
वनदुर्गा च मातङ्गी मतङ्गमुनिपूजिता ॥
ameya vikramā krūrā sundarī surasundarī |
vanadurgā ca mātaṅgī mataṅga muni pūjitā ||

44. Wielder of Infinite Strength
45. Who is Extremely Severe to Egos
46. Beautiful One
47. Beautiful One of the Gods
48. Reliever of Difficulties from the Forest
49. Embodiment of Thought
50. Worshipped by the Greatest of Munis

- 8 -

ब्राह्मी माहेश्वरी चैन्द्री कौमारी वैष्णवी तथा ।
चामुण्डा चैव वाराही लक्ष्मीश्च पुरुषाकृतिः ॥
brāhmī māheśvarī caindrī kaumārī vaiṣṇavī tathā |
cāmuṇḍā caiva vārāhī lakṣmīśca puruṣākṛtiḥ ||

51. Creative Energy
52. Energy of the Great Seer of All
53. Energy of the Rule of the Pure
54. Ever Pure One
55. Energy that Pervades All
56. Slayer of Passion and Anger
57. Most Excellent Desire of Union
58. Goddess of Wealth
59. Maker of Men

- 9 -

विमलोत्कर्षिणी ज्ञाना क्रिया नित्या च बुद्धिदा ।
बहुला बहुलप्रेमा सर्ववाहनवाहना ॥

vimalot karṣiṇī jñānā kriyā nityā ca buddhidā |
bahulā bahulapremā sarvavāhana vāhanā ||

60. Spotlessly Pure
61. Eminent One
62. Embodiment of Wisdom
63. Embodiment of Action
64. Eternal
65. Bestower of Wisdom
66. Extensive
67. Extensive Love
68. Carrier of all Carriers

- 10 -

निशुम्भशुम्भहननी महिषासुरमर्दिनी ।
मधुकैटभहन्त्री च चण्डमुण्डविनाशिनी ॥

niśumbha śumbha hananī mahiṣāsura mardinī |
madhu kaiṭabha hantrī ca caṇḍa muṇḍa vināśinī ||

69. Slayer of Self-Deprecation and Self-Conceit
70. Slayer of the Great Ego
71. Annihilator of Too Much and Too Little
72. Destroyer of Passion and Anger

- 11 -

सर्वासुरविनाशा च सर्वदानवघातिनी ।
सर्वशास्त्रमयी सत्या सर्वास्त्रधारिणी तथा ॥

sarvāsuravināśā ca sarvadānava ghātinī |
sarva śāstramayī satyā sarvāstra dhāriṇī tathā ||

73. Destroyer of All Egotistical Thought
74. Slayer of All Duality
75. Essence of All Scriptures
76. Truth
77. Bearer of All Weapons

\- 12 -

अनेकशस्त्रहस्ता च अनेकास्त्रस्य धारिणी ।
कुमारी चैककन्या च कैशोरी युवती यतिः ॥

aṇeka śastra hastā ca anekāstrasya dhāriṇī |
kumārī caika kanyā ca kaiśorī yuvatī yatiḥ ||

78. With Numerous Weapons in Her Hands
79. Bearer of Numerous Weapons
80. Ever Pure One
81. Sole Daughter
82. Incomparable Beauty
83. Eternal Youth
84. Ascetic

\- 13 -

अप्रौढा चैव प्रौढा च वृद्धमाता बलप्रदा ।
महोदरी मुक्तकेशी घोररूपा महाबला ॥

aprauḍhā caiva prauḍhā ca vṛddhamātā balapradā |
mahodarī muktakeśī ghorarūpā mahābalā ||

85. Never Aging
86. Advanced in Age
87. Mother of Old Age
88. Giver of Strength
89. Great Eminence
90. With Loose Hair
91. Of Formidable Appearance
92. One of Great Strength

\- 14 -

अग्निज्वाला रौद्रमुखी कालरात्रिस्तपस्विनी ।
नारायणी भद्रकाली विष्णुमाया जलोदरी ॥

agnijvālā raudramukhī kālarātristapasvinī |
nārāyaṇī bhadrakālī viṣṇu māyā jalodarī ||

93. Shining like Fire
94. Of Fearful Face
95. The Dark Night of Overcoming Egotism
96. Performer of Severe Spiritual Discipline
97. Exposer of Consciousness
98. Excellent One Beyond Time
99. Measurement of the All-Pervading Consciousness
100. Who Came from the Waters

- 15 -

शिवदूती कराली च अनन्ता परमेश्वरी ।
कात्यायनी च सावित्री प्रत्यक्षा ब्रह्मवादिनी ॥

śivadūtī karālī ca anantā parameśvarī |
kātyāyanī ca sāvitrī pratyakṣā brahma vādinī ||

101. Ambassador of Consciousness
102. Formidable One
103. Infinite
104. Supreme Sovereign
105. Ever Pure One
106. Bearer of Light
107. Perception of the Gross World
108. Who Speaks of Infinite Consciousness

- 16 -

य इदं प्रपठेन्नित्यं दुर्गानामशताष्टकम् ।
नासाध्यं विद्यते देवि त्रिषु लोकेषु पार्वति ॥

ya idaṃ prapaṭhen nityaṃ durgā nāmaśatāṣṭakam |
nāsādhyaṃ vidyate devi triṣu lokeṣu pārvati ||

Oh Goddess, Pārvati, He who recites these one hundred eight names of the Reliever of Difficulties every day will find no difficulties in the three worlds.

- 17 -

धनं धान्यं सुतं जायां हयं हस्तिनमेव च ।
चतुर्वर्गं तथा चान्ते लभेन्मुक्तिं च शाश्वतीम् ॥

dhanaṃ dhānyaṃ sutaṃ jāyāṃ
hayaṃ hastinameva ca |
caturvargaṃ tathā cānte labhenmuktiṃ ca śāśvatīm ||
He will find wealth, food, sons, a loving wife, horses, elephants,
and the four objectives of human life. At the end of his earthly
existence he will attain eternal liberation.

- 18 -

कुमारीं पूजयित्वा तु ध्यात्वा देवीं सुरेश्वरीम् ।
पूजयेत् परया भक्त्या पठेन्नामशताष्टकम् ॥

kumārīṃ pūjayitvā tu dhyātvā devīṃ sureśvarīm |
pūjayet parayā bhaktyā paṭhen nāmaśatāṣṭakam ||
One should worship the Ever Pure One and meditate upon the
female Ruler of Gods with the highest selfless devotion. Then
the recitation of these one hundred eight names should be com-
menced.

- 19 -

तस्य सिद्धिर्भवेद् देवि सर्वैः सुरवरैरपि ।
राजानो दासतां यान्ति राज्यश्रियमवाप्नुयात् ॥

tasya siddhir bhaved devi sarvaiḥ suravarairapi |
rājāno dāsatāṃ yānti rājya śriyamavāpnuyāt ||
Oh Goddess, who performs in this way attains the highest perfection of the Gods. Kings become his servants and he commands the wealth of kingdoms.

- 20 -

गोरोचनालक्तककुङ्कुमेन सिन्दूरकर्पूरमधुत्रयेण ।
विलिख्य यन्त्रं विधिना विधिज्ञो
भवेत् सदा धारयते पुरारिः ॥

gorocanā laktaka kuṅkumena
sindhura karpūra madhutrayeṇa |
vilikhya yantraṃ vidhinā vidhijño
bhavet sadā dhārayate purāriḥ ||

With fragrant gum, lac, red powders, camphor, ghee, sugar, and honey, one should draw the graphic representation of this truth according to the rules laid down in the scriptures. The knowledgeable one who wears such an inscription becomes one with the Consciousness of Infinite Goodness.

- 21 -

भौमावास्यानिशामग्रे चन्द्रे शतभिषां गते ।
विलिख्य प्रपठेत् स्तोत्रं स भवेत् संपदां पदम् ॥

bhaumāvāsyāniśāmagre candre śata bhiṣāṃ gate |
vilikhya prapaṭhet stotraṃ sa bhavet saṃpadāṃ padam ||

On the evening before the New Moon Day, known as Bhaumavatī, when the celestial configuration is in the asterism known as Śatabhiṣā, one who recites these mantras by putting them in writing becomes the Lord of Wealth.

ॐ

oṃ

ॐ ऐं आत्मतत्त्वं शोधयामि नमः स्वाहा

oṃ aiṃ ātmatattvaṃ śodhayāmi namaḥ svāhā

Oṃ Wisdom I purify the principle of the soul, I bow. I am One with God!

ॐ ह्रीं विद्यातत्त्वं शोधयामि नमः स्वाहा

oṃ hrīṃ vidyātattvaṃ śodhayāmi namaḥ svāhā

Oṃ Māyā I purify the principle of knowledge, I bow. I am One with God!

ॐ क्लीं शिवतत्त्वं शोधयामि नमः स्वाहा

oṃ klīṃ śivatattvaṃ śodhayāmi namaḥ svāhā

Oṃ Transformation I purify the principle of Infinite Goodness, I bow. I am One with God!

ॐ ऐं ह्रीं क्लीं सर्वतत्त्वं शोधयामि नमः स्वाहा

oṃ aiṃ hrīṃ klīṃ sarvatattvaṃ śodhayāmi namaḥ svāhā

Oṃ Wisdom, Māyā, Transformation I purify all principles, I bow. I am One with God!

ॐ नमो देव्यै महादेव्यै शिवायै सततं नमः ।
नमः प्रकृत्यै भद्रायै नियताः प्रणताः स्म ताम् ॥

oṃ namo devyai mahādevyai
śivāyai satataṃ namaḥ |
namaḥ prakṛtyai bhadrāyai
niyatāḥ praṇatāḥ sma tām ||

We bow to the Goddess, to the Great Goddess, to the Energy of Infinite Goodness at all times we bow. We bow to Nature, to the Excellent One. With discipline we have bowed down.

ध्यात्वा देवीं पञ्चपूजां कृत्वा योन्या प्रणम्य च ।
आधारं स्थाप्य मूलेन स्थापयेत्तत्र पुस्तकम् ॥
एते गन्धपुष्पे ॐ ह्रीं पुस्तकाय नमः

dhyātvā devīṃ pañcapūjāṃ
kṛtvā yonyā praṇamya ca |
ādhāraṃ sthāpya mūlena sthāpayettatra pustakam ||
ete gandhapuṣpe oṃ hrīṃ pustakāya namaḥ

Meditate upon the Goddess and offer Her five articles of worship, and then bow down to Her. Establish the primal energy with the bīja mantra, and then establish the book. With these scented flowers Oṃ we bow to the book.

शापोद्धार मन्त्रः

Dev: 03

śāpoddhāra mantraḥ

The mantra that removes the curses

ॐ ह्रीं क्लीं श्रीं क्रां क्रीं चण्डिकादेव्यै

शापनाशानुग्रहं कुरु कुरु स्वाहा ॥

oṃ hrīṃ klīṃ śrīṃ krāṃ krīṃ caṇḍikā devyai
śāpanāśānugrahaṃ kuru kuru svāhā ||

Repeat eleven times

Oṃ All existence, transformation, Increase, the Cause of Dissolution in the Gross Body, the Cause of Dissolution in the Causal Body, to the Goddess, She Who Tears Apart Thoughts, take away the curse, take away the curse, I am One with God!

उत्कीलन मन्त्रः

Dev: 04

utkīlana mantraḥ

The mantra that opens the pin

ॐ श्रीं क्लीं ह्रीं सप्तशति चण्डिके

उत्कीलनं कुरु कुरु स्वाहा ॥

oṃ śrīṃ klīṃ hrīṃ saptaśati caṇḍike
utkīlanaṃ kuru kuru svāhā ||

Repeat twenty-one times

Oṃ Increase, transformation, all existence, the seven hundred verses of the Chaṇḍī, remove the pin, remove the pin, I am One with God!

मृतसंजीवनी मन्त्रः

mṛtasaṃjīvanī mantraḥ

The mantra that bestows life from death

ॐ ह्रीं ह्रीं वं वं ऐं ऐं मृतसंजीवनि विद्ये
मृतमुत्थापयोत्थापय क्रीं ह्रीं ह्रीं वं स्वाहा ॥

**oṃ hrīṃ hrīṃ vaṃ vaṃ aiṃ aiṃ
mṛtasaṃjīvani vidye mṛtamutthāpayot
thāpaya krīṃ hrīṃ hrīṃ vaṃ svāhā ||**

Repeat eleven times

Oṃ all existence, all existence, vibrations, vibrations, wisdom, wisdom, Oh knowledge that bestows life from death, raise from death, transformation, all existence, all existence, vibrations, I am One with God!

शापविमोचनमन्त्रः

śāpavimocana mantraḥ

The mantra that removes the curses

ॐ श्रीं श्रीं क्लीं हूं ॐ ऐं क्षोभय मोहय
उत्कीलय उत्कीलय उत्कीलय ठं ठं ॥

**oṃ śrīṃ śrīṃ klīṃ hūṃ oṃ aiṃ kṣobhaya
mohaya utkīlaya utkīlaya utkīlaya ṭhaṃ ṭhaṃ ||**

Repeat eleven times

Oṃ Increase, increase, transformation, cut the ego! Erase the fears of ignorance, remove the pin, remove, remove, devotion, devotion.

अथ ब्रह्मादिशापविमोचनम्

atha brahmādi śāpa vimocanam

And now, The Removal of the Curses by Brahmā and others

ॐ अस्य श्रीचण्डिकायाब्रह्मवशिष्ठविश्वामित्रशाप-
विमोचनमन्त्रस्य वशिष्ठनारदसंवाद सामवेदाधिपति- ब्रह्माण
ऋषयः सर्वैश्वर्यकारिणी श्रीदुर्गा देवता चरित्रत्रयं बीजं ह्रीं
शक्तिः त्रिगुणात्मस्वरूपचण्डिकाशापविमुक्तौ मम
संकल्पितकार्यसिद्ध्यर्थे जपे विनियोगः ॥

oṃ asya śrī caṇḍikāyā brahma vaśiṣṭha viśvāmitra śāpa vimocana mantrasya vaśiṣṭha nārada saṃvāda sāma vedādhipati brahmāṇa ṛṣayaḥ sarvaiśvarya kāriṇī śrī durgā devatā caritratrayaṃ bījaṃ hrīṃ śaktiḥ triguṇātma svarūpa caṇḍikāśāpa vimuktau mama saṃkalpita kārya siddhyarthe jape viniyogaḥ ||

Oṃ Presenting the mantras that remove the curses of Brahmā, Vaśiṣṭha, and Viśvāmitra from the respected Chaṇḍī Pāṭhaḥ, as explained by Vaśiṣṭha to Nārada: The Lord of the Sāma Veda, Brahmā, is the Seer. Its purpose is the attainment of all imperishable qualities, the respected Reliever of Difficulties is the deity, the three episodes are the seed, the energy is hrīṃ, all existence. It is the intrinsic essence of the three qualities applied to remove the curses of the Chaṇḍī, and for the attainment of perfection in the object of my spiritual vow this recitation is applied.

- 1 -

ॐ ह्रीं रीं रेतःस्वरूपिण्यै मधुकैटभमर्दिन्यै
ब्रह्मवशिष्ठविश्वामित्रशापाद् विमुक्ता भव ॥

oṃ hrīṃ rīṃ retaḥ svarūpiṇyai madhu kaiṭabha mardinyai brahma vaśiṣṭha viśvāmitra śāpād vimuktā bhava ||

Oṃ Māyā, the subtle body merging into perfection, the intrinsic nature of the seed of existence, the balance between Too Much and Too Little, may the curses of Brahmā, Vaśiṣṭha, and Viśvāmitra be removed.

- 2 -

ॐ श्रीं बुद्धिस्वरूपिण्यै महिषासुरसैन्यनाशिन्यै

ब्रह्मवशिष्ठविश्वामित्रशापाद् विमुक्ता भव ॥

oṃ śrīṃ buddhi svarūpiṇyai mahiṣāsura sainya nāśinyai brahma vaśiṣṭha viśvāmitra śāpād vimuktā bhava ||

Oṃ Increase, the intrinsic nature of Intellect, the destroyer of the armies of the Great Ego, may the curses of Brahmā, Vaśiṣṭha, and Viśvāmitra be removed.

- 3 -

ॐ रं रक्तस्वरूपिण्यै महिषासुरमर्दिन्यै

ब्रह्मवशिष्ठविश्वामित्रशापाद् विमुक्ता भव ॥

oṃ raṃ rakta svarūpiṇyai mahiṣāsura mardinyai brahma vaśiṣṭha viśvāmitra śāpād vimuktā bhava ||

Oṃ Perfection of the subtle body, the intrinsic nature of desire, the destroyer of the Great Ego, may the curses of Brahmā, Vaśiṣṭha, and Viśvāmitra be removed.

- 4 -

ॐ क्षुं क्षुधास्वरूपिण्यै देववन्दितायै

ब्रह्मवशिष्ठविश्वामित्रशापाद् विमुक्ता भव ॥

oṃ kṣuṃ kṣudhā svarūpiṇyai devavanditāyai brahma vaśiṣṭha viśvāmitra śāpād vimuktā bhava ||

Oṃ Hunger, the intrinsic nature of Hunger, praised by the Gods in song, may the curses of Brahmā, Vaśiṣṭha, and Viśvāmitra be removed.

- 5 -

ॐ छां छायास्वरूपिण्यै दूतसंवादिन्यै

ब्रह्मवशिष्ठविश्वामित्रशापाद् विमुक्ता भव ॥

oṃ chāṃ chāyā svarūpiṇyai dūtasaṃvādinyai brahma vaśiṣṭha viśvāmitra śāpād vimuktā bhava ||

Oṃ Reflection, the intrinsic nature of appearance, receiving communication from the Ambassador of Self-Conceit, may the curses of Brahmā, Vaśiṣṭha, and Viśvāmitra be removed.

- 6 -

ॐ शं शक्तिस्वरूपिण्यै धूम्रलोचनघातिन्यै

ब्रह्मवशिष्ठविश्वामित्रशापाद् विमुक्ता भव ॥

oṃ śaṃ śakti svarūpiṇyai dhūmralocana ghātinyai
brahma vaśiṣṭha viśvāmitra śāpād vimuktā bhava ||

Oṃ Energy, the intrinsic nature of Energy, the destroyer of Sinful Eyes, may the curses of Brahmā, Vaśiṣṭha, and Viśvāmitra be removed.

- 7 -

ॐ तृं तृषास्वरूपिण्यै चण्डमुण्डवधकारिण्यै

ब्रह्मवशिष्ठविश्वामित्रशापाद् विमुक्ता भव ॥

oṃ tṛṃ tṛṣā svarūpiṇyai caṇḍa muṇḍa vadha kāriṇyai
brahma vaśiṣṭha viśvāmitra śāpād vimuktā bhava ||

Oṃ Thirst, the intrinsic nature of desire, the cause of destroying Passion and Anger, may the curses of Brahmā, Vaśiṣṭha, and Viśvāmitra be removed.

- 8 -

ॐ क्षां क्षान्तिस्वरूपिण्यै रक्तबीजवधकारिण्यै

ब्रह्मवशिष्ठविश्वामित्रशापाद् विमुक्ता भव ॥

oṃ kṣāṃ kṣānti svarūpiṇyai raktabīja vadha kāriṇyai
brahma vaśiṣṭha viśvāmitra śāpād vimuktā bhava ||

Oṃ Patient Forgiveness, the intrinsic nature of Patient Forgiveness, the cause of destroying the Seed of Desire, may the curses of Brahmā, Vaśiṣṭha, and Viśvāmitra be removed.

- 9 -

ॐ जां जातिस्वरूपिण्यै निशुम्भवधकारिण्यै

ब्रह्मवशिष्ठविश्वामित्रशापाद् विमुक्ता भव ॥

oṃ jāṃ jāti svarūpiṇyai niśumbha vadha kāriṇyai
brahma vaśiṣṭha viśvāmitra śāpād vimuktā bhava ||

Oṃ Birth, the intrinsic nature of All Beings Born, the cause of destroying Self-Deprecation, may the curses of Brahmā, Vaśiṣṭha, and Viśvāmitra be removed.

- 10 -

ॐ लं लज्जास्वरूपिण्यै शुम्भवधकारिण्यै

ब्रह्मवशिष्ठविश्वामित्रशापाद् विमुक्ता भव ॥

oṃ laṃ lajjā svarūpiṇyai śumbha vadha kāriṇyai brahma vaśiṣṭha viśvāmitra śāpād vimuktā bhava ||

Oṃ Humility, the intrinsic nature of Humility, the cause of destroying Self-Conceit, may the curses of Brahmā, Vaśiṣṭha, and Viśvāmitra be removed.

- 11 -

ॐ शां शान्तिस्वरूपिण्यै देवस्तुत्यै

ब्रह्मवशिष्ठविश्वामित्रशापाद् विमुक्ता भव ॥

oṃ śāṃ śānti svarūpiṇyai devastutyai brahma vaśiṣṭha viśvāmitra śāpād vimuktā bhava ||

Oṃ Peace, the intrinsic nature of Peace, the Gods sing a song of praise, may the curses of Brahmā, Vaśiṣṭha, and Viśvāmitra be removed.

- 12 -

ॐ श्रं श्रद्धास्वरूपिण्यै सकलफलदात्र्यै

ब्रह्मवशिष्ठविश्वामित्रशापाद् विमुक्ता भव ॥

oṃ śraṃ śraddhā svarūpiṇyai sakalaphala dātryai brahma vaśiṣṭha viśvāmitra śāpād vimuktā bhava ||

Oṃ Faith, the intrinsic nature of Faith, the Grantor of every fruit, may the curses of Brahmā, Vaśiṣṭha, and Viśvāmitra be removed.

- 13 -

ॐ कां कान्तिस्वरूपिण्यै राजवरप्रदायै

ब्रह्मवशिष्ठविश्वामित्रशापाद् विमुक्ता भव ॥

oṃ kāṃ kānti svarūpiṇyai rājavara pradāyai brahma vaśiṣṭha viśvāmitra śāpād vimuktā bhava ||

Oṃ Beauty Enhanced by Love, the intrinsic nature of Beauty Enhanced by Love, the Grantor of Boons to the King, may the curses of Brahmā, Vaśiṣṭha, and Viśvāmitra be removed.

- 14 -

ॐ मां मातृस्वरूपिण्यै अनर्गलमहिमसहितायै

ब्रह्मवशिष्ठविश्वामित्रशापाद् विमुक्ता भव ॥

oṃ māṃ mātṛ svarūpiṇyai anargalamahima sahitāyai brahma vaśiṣṭha viśvāmitra śāpād vimuktā bhava ||

Oṃ Mother, the intrinsic nature of Mother, together with unrestricted greatness, may the curses of Brahmā, Vaśiṣṭha, and Viśvāmitra be removed.

- 15 -

ॐ ह्रीं श्रीं दुं दुर्गायै सं सर्वैश्वर्यकारिण्यै

ब्रह्मवशिष्ठविश्वामित्रशापाद् विमुक्ता भव ॥

oṃ hrīṃ śrīṃ duṃ durgāyai saṃ sarvaiśvarya kāriṇyai brahma vaśiṣṭha viśvāmitra śāpād vimuktā bhava ||

Oṃ Māyā, Increase, Durgā, the Reliever of Difficulties, all together, the cause of all imperishable qualities, may the curses of Brahmā, Vaśiṣṭha, and Viśvāmitra be removed.

- 16 -

ॐ ऐं ह्रीं क्लीं नमः शिवायै अभेद्यकवचस्वरूपिण्यै

ब्रह्मवशिष्ठविश्वामित्रशापाद् विमुक्ता भव ॥

oṃ aiṃ hrīṃ klīṃ namaḥ śivāyai abhedya kavaca svarūpiṇyai brahma vaśiṣṭha viśvāmitra śāpād vimuktā bhava ||

Oṃ Wisdom, Māyā, Transformation, I bow to the Energy of Infinite Goodness, with the intrinsic nature of impermeable armor, may the curses of Brahmā, Vaśiṣṭha, and Viśvāmitra be removed.

- 17 -

ॐ क्रीं काल्यै कालि ह्रीं फट् स्वाहायै ऋग्वेदस्वरूपिण्यै

ब्रह्मवशिष्ठविश्वामित्रशापाद् विमुक्ता भव ॥

oṃ krīṃ kālyai kāli hrīṃ phaṭ svāhāyai ṛgveda svarūpiṇyai brahma vaśiṣṭha viśvāmitra śāpād vimuktā bhava ||

Oṃ Transformation, She who Takes Away Darkness, She who Takes Away Darkness, Māyā, cut the ego! I am One with God! The intrinsic nature of the Ṛg Veda, may the curses of Brahmā, Vaśiṣṭha, and Viśvāmitra be removed.

- 18 -

ॐ ऐं ह्रीं क्लीं महाकालीमहालक्ष्मीमहासरस्वतीस्वरूपिण्यै त्रिगुणात्मिकायै दुर्गादेव्यै नमः ॥

oṃ aiṃ hrīṃ klīṃ mahākālī mahālakṣmī mahā sarasvatī svarūpiṇyai triguṇātmikāyai durgā devyai namaḥ ||

Oṃ Wisdom, Māyā, Transformation, the intrinsic nature of She who Takes Away Darkness, the Great Goddess of True Wealth, the Great Goddess of All-Pervading Knowledge, the capacity of expression of the three qualities of Nature, I bow to the Goddess Durgā, the Reliever of Difficulties.

- 19 -

इत्येवं हि महामन्त्रान् पठित्वा परमेश्वर ।
चण्डीपाठं दिवा रात्रौ कुर्यादेव न संशयः ॥

ityevaṃ hi mahāmantrān paṭhitvā parameśvara |
caṇḍīpāṭhaṃ divā rātrau kuryā deva na saṃśayaḥ ||

These are the great mantras that were recited by the Supreme Lord of Existence. Whoever will recite this Chaṇḍī Pāṭhaḥ in the day and in the night will become a God without a doubt.

- 20 -

एवं मन्त्रं न जानाति चण्डीपाठं करोति यः ।

आत्मानं चैव दातारं क्षीणं कुर्यान्न संशयः ॥

evaṃ mantraṃ na jānāti caṇḍī pāṭhaṃ karoti yaḥ |
ātmānaṃ caiva dātāraṃ
kṣīṇaṃ kuryānna saṃśayaḥ ||

And whoever recites the Chaṇḍī Pāṭhaḥ without knowledge or proper understanding, his soul will go to the darkness of hell. Of this there is no doubt.

ॐ

oṃ

Devi 05

अथ देव्याः कवचम्

atha devyāḥ kavacam

The Armor of the Goddess

ॐ अस्य श्रीचण्डीकवचस्य ब्रह्मा ऋषिः अनुष्टुप् छन्दः
चामुण्डा देवता अङ्गन्यासोक्तमातरो बीजम्
दिग्बन्धदेवतास्तत्त्वम् श्रीजगदम्बाप्रीत्यर्थे सप्तशती
पाठाङ्गत्वेन जपे विनियोगः ।

oṃ asya śrī caṇḍīkavacasya brahmā ṛṣiḥ anuṣṭup chandaḥ cāmuṇḍā devatā aṅganyāsokta mātaro bījam digbandha devatās tattvam śrī jagad ambā prītyarthe saptaśatī pāṭhāṅga tvena jape viniyogaḥ |

Oṃ Presenting the Armor of the Respected She Who Tears Apart Thought, the Creative Capacity is the Seer, Anuṣṭup (32 syllables to the verse) is the meter, the Slayer of Passion and Anger is the deity, the establishment of the Mother of Unity in the body is the seed, that which binds the Gods of all the directions is the principle, for the satisfaction of the Respected Mother of the Universe this appendage of the Seven Hundred Verses is applied in recitation.

ॐ नमश्चण्डिकायै

oṃ namaścaṇḍikāyai

Oṃ We bow to the Goddess Who Tears Apart Thought.

मार्कण्डेय उवाच

mārkaṇḍeya uvāca

Mārkaṇḍeya said:

- 1 -

ॐ यद्गुह्यं परमं लोके सर्वरक्षाकरं नृणाम् ।
यन्न कस्यचिदाख्यातं तन्मे ब्रूहि पितामह ॥

oṃ yadguhyaṃ paramaṃ loke
sarva rakṣā karaṃ nṛṇām |
yanna kasya cidākhyātaṃ tanme brūhi pitāmaha ||
Oṃ. Grandfather, tell me the Supreme Mystical Secret, the one that is not well known, which affords all protection to all men.

ब्रह्मोवाच
brahmovāca
The Creative Capacity said:

- 2 -

अस्ति गुह्यतमं विप्र सर्वभूतोपकारकम् ।
देव्यास्तु कवचं पुण्यं तच्छृणुष्व महामुने ॥
asti guhyatamaṃ vipra sarva bhūtopakārakam |
devyāstu kavacaṃ puṇyaṃ tacchṛṇuṣva mahāmune ||
There is a mystical secret, Oh Learned One, that is beneficial to all existence, the meritorious Armor of the Goddess. Listen to that, Oh Man of Great Wisdom.

- 3 -

प्रथमं शैलपुत्री च द्वितीयं ब्रह्मचारिणी ।
तृतीयं चन्द्रघण्टेति कूष्माण्डेति चतुर्थकम् ॥
prathamaṃ śailaputrī ca dvitīyaṃ brahmacāriṇī |
tṛtīyaṃ candra ghaṇṭeti kūṣmāṇḍeti caturthakam ||
First is the Goddess of Inspiration, and second the Goddess of Sacred Study; third is the Goddess of the Delight of Practice, the Goddess of Purifying Austerity is fourth.

- 4 -

पञ्चमं स्कन्दमातेति षष्ठं कात्यायनीति च ।
सप्तमं कालरात्रीति महागौरीति चाष्टमम् ॥
pañcamaṃ skandamāteti ṣaṣṭhaṃ kātyāyanīti ca |
saptamaṃ kālarātrīti mahāgaurīti cāṣṭamam ||
Fifth is the Goddess who Nurtures Divinity, sixth is the One Who is Ever Pure; seventh is the Goddess of the Dark Night of Overcoming Egotism, the Goddess of the Great Radiant Light is eighth.

- 5 -

नवमं सिद्धिदात्री च नवदुर्गाः प्रकीर्तिताः ।
उक्तान्येतानि नामानि ब्रह्मणैव महात्मना ॥

navamaṃ siddhidātrī ca navadurgāḥ prakīrtitāḥ |
uktānyetāni nāmāni brahmaṇaiva mahātmanā ||

Ninth is the Goddess who Grants Perfection, the nine Durgās, Relievers of Difficulties, have been enumerated, and these names have been revealed by the great soul of the Supreme himself.

- 6 -

अग्निना दह्यमानस्तु शत्रुमध्ये गतो रणे ।
विषमे दुर्गमे चैव भयार्त्ताः शरणं गताः ॥

agninā dahyamānastu śatrumadhye gato raṇe |
viṣame durgame caiva bhayārttāḥ śaraṇaṃ gatāḥ ||

If one is being burned by fire, or in the midst of enemies on the field of battle, whenever thoughts are occupied with difficulties or any kind of fear, by taking refuge in the Mother,

- 7 -

न तेषां जायते किंचिदशुभं रणसंकटे ।
नापदं तस्य पश्यामि शोकदुःखभयं न हि ॥

na teṣāṃ jāyate kiṃcidaśubhaṃ raṇasaṃkaṭe |
nāpadaṃ tasya paśyāmi śoka duḥkha bhayaṃ na hi ||

no energetic opposition will conquer that individual, nor injury in the dangers of battle. I cannot foresee any sorrow, pain or fear to envelope such a person.

- 8 -

यैस्तु भक्त्या स्मृता नूनं तेषां वृद्धिः प्रजायते ।
ये त्वां स्मरन्ति देवेशि रक्षसे तान्न संशयः ॥

yaistu bhaktyā smṛtā nūnaṃ
teṣāṃ vṛddhiḥ prajāyate |
ye tvāṃ smaranti deveśi rakṣase tānna saṃśayaḥ ||

When She is remembered with devotion, all opposition ends

and immediately prosperity begins. For those who remember Her, the Supreme Goddess protects them without a doubt.

- 9 -

प्रेतसंस्था तु चामुण्डा वाराही महिषासना ।

ऐन्द्री गजसमारूढा वैष्णवी गरुडासना ॥

pretasaṃsthā tu cāmuṇḍā vārāhī mahiṣāsanā |
aindrī gaja samārūḍhā vaiṣṇavī garuḍāsanā ||

Standing upon the corpse of Inert Consciousness is the Slayer of Passion and Anger; She who is the Most Excellent Desire of Union sits upon the buffalo of perseverance. The Energy of the Rule of the Pure rides upon the elephant of Universal Love, while the Energy that Pervades All sits upon the bird of brilliant luster.

- 10 -

माहेश्वरी वृषारूढा कौमारी शिखिवाहना ।

लक्ष्मीः पद्मासना देवी पद्महस्ता हरिप्रिया ॥

māheśvarī vṛṣārūḍhā kaumārī śikhivāhanā |
lakṣmīḥ padmāsanā devī padmahastā haripriyā ||

The Energy of the Great Seer of All rides upon the bull of discipline; the Ever Pure One is carried by the peacock of beauty. The Goddess of Wealth sits upon the lotus of peace; the Goddess beloved of Consciousness has a lotus in Her hand.

- 11 -

श्वेतरूपधरा देवी ईश्वरी वृषवाहना ।

ब्राह्मी हंससमारूढा सर्वाभरणभूषिता ॥

śvetarūpa dharā devī īśvarī vṛṣa vāhanā |
brāhmī haṃsa samārūḍhā sarvābharaṇa bhūṣitā ||

Pure white is the form of the Goddess, Supreme Energy, carried by the bull of discipline. The Creative Energy rides upon the swans of controlled breath displaying all ornaments.

- 12 -

इत्येता मातरः सर्वाः सर्वयोगसमन्विताः ।

नानाभरणशोभाढ्या नानारत्नोपशोभिताः ॥

ityetā mātaraḥ sarvāḥ sarvayoga samanvitāḥ |
nānābharaṇaśobhāḍhyā nānāratno paśobhitāḥ ||

These are all the Mothers, all connected in succession in the path of union, displaying various ornaments and various jewels.

- 13 -

दृश्यन्ते रथमारूढा देव्यः क्रोधसमाकुलाः ।
शङ्खं चक्रं गदां शक्तिं हलं च मुसलायुधम् ॥

dṛśyante rathamārūḍhā devyaḥ krodhasamākulāḥ |
śaṅkhaṃ cakraṃ gadāṃ śaktiṃ
halaṃ ca musalāyudham ||

The Goddesses are seen angry and agitated, mounted upon chariots. The conch of vibrations, the discus of revolving time, the club of articulation, various forms of energy, the plow sowing the seeds of the Way of Truth to Wisdom, the pestle of refinement,

- 14 -

खेटकं तोमरं चैव परशुं पाशमेव च ।
कुन्तायुधं त्रिशूलं च शार्ङ्गमायुधमुत्तमम् ॥

kheṭakaṃ tomaraṃ caiva paraśuṃ pāśameva ca |
kuntāyudhaṃ triśūlaṃ ca
śārṅgamāyudham uttamam ||

the shield of method, the javelin of effort, the battle axe of good actions, the net of unity, the spear of concentration, the trident of harmony, and the excellent bow of determination;

- 15 -

दैत्यानां देहनाशाय भक्तानामभयाय च ।
धारयन्त्यायुधानीत्थं देवानां च हिताय वै ॥

daityānāṃ dehanāśāya bhaktānāmabhayāya ca |
dhārayantyāyu dhānītthaṃ devānāṃ ca hitāya vai ||

they display these weapons for the purpose of destroying the bodies of thoughts, to instill fearlessness in devotees, and for the welfare of the Gods.

- 16 -

नमस्तेऽस्तु महारौद्रे महाघोरपराक्रमे ।

महाबले महोत्साहे महाभयविनाशिनि ॥

namaste-stu mahāraudre mahāghoraparākrame |
mahābale mahotsāhe mahābhaya vināśini ||

We bow to you, Oh Great Fierce One, Oh Great One of dreadful prowess, Oh you of Great Strength, of Great Joy, the Great Destroyer of Fear.

- 17 -

त्राहि मां देवि दुष्प्रेक्ष्ये शत्रूणां भयवर्द्धिनि ।

प्राच्यां रक्षतु मामैन्द्री आग्नेय्यामग्निदेवता ॥

trāhi māṃ devi duṣprekṣye
śatrūṇāṃ bhayavarddhini |
prācyāṃ rakṣatu māmaindrī āgneyyām agni devatā ||

Protect me, Oh Goddess, difficult to perceive, you who increase the fear in our enemies. May the Energy of the Rule of the Pure protect me in the East; in the Southeast, the God who is the Light of Meditation.

- 18 -

दक्षिणेऽवतु वाराही नैर्ऋत्यां खड्गधारिणी ।

प्रतीच्यां वारुणी रक्षेद् वायव्यां मृगवाहिनी ॥

dakṣiṇe-vatu vārāhī nairṛtyāṃ khaḍgadhāriṇī |
pratīcyāṃ vāruṇī rakṣed vāyavyāṃ mṛgavāhinī ||

In the South, the Most Excellent Desire of Union. In the Southwest, She who wields the sword of worship. In the West, may the Energy of the Lord of Equilibrium give protection. In the Northwest, She who is carried by the deer of enthusiasm.

- 19 -

उदीच्यां पातु कौमारी ऐशान्यां शूलधारिणी ।

ऊर्ध्वं ब्रह्माणि मे रक्षेदधस्ताद् वैष्णवी तथा ॥

udīcyāṃ pātu kaumārī aiśānyāṃ śūladhāriṇī |
ūrdhvaṃ brahmāṇi me rakṣed
adhastād vaiṣṇavī tathā ||

In the North may the Ever Pure One protect. In the Northeast, the Wielder of the pike of concentration. Above may the Creative Energy protect me. And then below, the Energy that Pervades All.

- 20 -

एवं दश दिशो रक्षेच्चामुण्डा शववाहना ।
जया मे चाग्रतः पातु विजया पातु पृष्ठतः ॥

evaṃ daśa diśo rakṣeccāmuṇḍā śavavāhanā |
jayā me cāgrataḥ pātu vijayā pātu pṛṣṭhataḥ ||

And all ten directions may be protected by the Slayer of Passion and Anger, mounted upon the corpse of inert consciousness. In the front may Victory protect me, and may Conquest protect me in the rear.

- 21 -

अजिता वामपार्श्वे तु दक्षिणे चापराजिता ।
शिखामुद्योतिनी रक्षेदुमा मूर्ध्नि व्यवस्थिता ॥

ajitā vāmapārśve tu dakṣiṇe cāparājitā |
śikhāmudyotinī rakṣed umā mūrdhni vyavasthitā ||

On the left side may stand the Undefeated One, and on the right the Unconquerable. May the Luminous One guard the crown of the head, and may the Mother of Protective Energy safeguard residing on the head.

- 22 -

मालाधरी ललाटे च भ्रुवौ रक्षेद् यशस्विनी ।
त्रिनेत्रा च भ्रुवोर्मध्ये यमघण्टा च नासिके ॥

mālādharī lalāṭe ca bhruvau rakṣed yaśasvinī |
trinetrā ca bhruvor madhye yamaghaṇṭā ca nāsike ||

May the One who wears the garland protect in the forehead, and in the eyebrows the Bearer of Welfare; the Three-eyed One between the eyebrows, and Restrained Sound in the nose.

- 23 -

शङ्खिनी चक्षुषोर्मध्ये श्रोत्रयोर्द्वारवासिनी ।
कपोलौ कालिका रक्षेत्कर्णमूले तु शाङ्करी ॥

śaṅkhinī cakṣuṣor madhye śrotrayordvāravāsinī |
kapolau kālikā rakṣet karṇamūle tu śaṅkarī ||

The Bearer of the Constant Vibration between the eyes, in the
ears the Dweller at the Doors; in the cheeks may the Goddess
of Time protect, and behind the ears, the Energy that Causes
Peace.

- 24 -

नासिकायां सुगन्धा च उत्तरोष्ठे च चर्चिका ।
अधरे चामृतकला जिह्वायां च सरस्वती ॥

nāsikāyāṃ sugandhā ca uttaroṣṭhe ca carcikā |
adhare cāmṛtakalā jihvāyāṃ ca sarasvatī ||

In the nostrils, Excellent Scent, and on the upper lip, the Sweet
Taste; on the lower lip, a Drop of Nectar, and in the tongue, the
Spirit of All Knowledge.

- 25 -

दन्तान् रक्षतु कौमारी कण्ठदेशे तु चण्डिका ।
घण्टिकां चित्रघण्टा च महामाया च तालुके ॥

dantān rakṣatu kaumārī kaṇṭhadeśe tu caṇḍikā |
ghaṇṭikāṃ citraghaṇṭā ca mahāmāyā ca tāluke ||

May the Ever Pure One protect the teeth, and in the throat, She
Who Tears Apart Thought; in the uvula the One of Varied
Sound, and the Great Measurement of Consciousness in the
palate.

- 26 -

कामाक्षी चिबुकं रक्षेद् वाच मे सर्वमङ्गला ।
ग्रीवायां भद्रकाली च पृष्ठवंशे धनुर्धरी ॥

kāmākṣī cibukaṃ rakṣed vāca me sarvamaṅgalā |
grīvāyāṃ bhadrakālī ca pṛṣṭhavaṃśe dhanurdharī ||

May the Goddess who Causes Love protect the chin; All
Welfare protect my speech; the Excellent Remover of
Darkness, the neck; the wielder of the bow of determination,
the backbone.

- 27 -

नीलग्रीवा बहिःकण्ठे नलिकां नलकूबरी ।
स्कन्धयोः खड्गिनी रक्षेद् बाहू मे वज्रधारिणी ॥

nīlagrīvā bahiḥkaṇṭhe nalikāṃ nalakūbarī |
skandayoḥ khaḍginī rakṣed bāhū me vajradhāriṇī ||

In the outer neck, the Blue Necked One, in the throat-pipe, the Goddess of Inspired Songs; in the shoulders, may the Wielder of the Sword of Worship protect; in my arms, She who Bears the Thunderbolt of Illumination.

- 28 -

हस्तयोर्दण्डिनी रक्षेदम्बिका चाङ्गुलीषु च ।
नखाञ्छूलेश्वरी रक्षेत्कुक्षौ रक्षेत्कुलेश्वरी ॥

hastayor daṇḍinī rakṣed ambikā cāṅgulīṣu ca |
nakhāñchūleśvarī rakṣet kukṣau rakṣet kuleśvarī ||

May the Energy that Bears the Staff of Discipline protect my hands, and the Mother of the Universe the fingers; may the Ruler of the Trident of Harmony protect the nails; and in the abdomen, the Ruler of the Family.

- 29 -

स्तनौ रक्षेन्महादेवी मनःशोकविनाशिनी ।
हृदये ललिता देवी उदरे शूलधारिणी ॥

stanau rakṣen mahādevī manaḥ śokavināśinī |
hṛdaye lalitā devī udare śūladhāriṇī ||

May the Great Goddess protect my breasts, She Who Destroys All Sorrow in the Mind; in the heart, the Desired Goddess; and in the stomach, the Bearer of the Pike of Concentration.

- 30 -

नाभौ च कामिनी रक्षेद् गुह्यं गुह्येश्वरी तथा ।
पूतना कामिका मेढ्रं गुदे महिषवाहिनी ॥

nābhau ca kāminī rakṣed guhyaṃ guhyeśvarī tathā |
pūtanā kāmikā meḍhraṃ gude mahiṣavāhinī ||

May the Goddess of Love protect the navel; the private part, the Ruler of Mystical Secrets; may Purity of Desire protect the genital; and She who rides the Buffalo of Perseverance, the anus.

- 31 -

कट्यां भगवती रक्षेज्जानुनी विन्ध्यवासिनी ।

जङ्घे महाबला रक्षेत्सर्वकामप्रदायिनी ॥

kaṭyāṃ bhagavatī rakṣej jānunī vindhyavāsinī |
janghe mahābalā rakṣet sarvakāmapradāyinī ||

May the Supreme Goddess protect the hips; in the knees, She Who Resides in Knowledge; in the shanks may the Great Strength protect, the Grantor of All Desires.

- 32 -

गुल्फयोर्नारसिंही च पादपृष्ठे तु तैजसी ।

पादाङ्गुलीषु श्री रक्षेत्पादाधस्तलवासिनी ॥

gulphayor nārasiṃhī ca pādapṛṣṭhe tu taijasī |
pādāṅgulīṣu śrī rakṣet pādādhastalavāsinī ||

In the ankles, the Goddess of Courageous Fortitude; on the top of the feet, She who is Heat and Light; in the toes, may Prosperity protect; and in the soles, She who Dwells in Support.

- 33 -

नखान् दंष्ट्राकराली च केशांश्चैवोर्ध्वकेशिनी ।

रोमकूपेषु कौबेरी त्वचं वागीश्वरी तथा ॥

nakhān daṃṣṭrākarālī ca keśāṃś-caivordhvakeśinī |
romakūpeṣu kauberī tvacaṃ vāgīśvarī tathā ||

On the nails, She with Great Tusks; and She with Great Hairs, the hair; in the pores of the skin, the Energy of Wealth, and the skin, the Energy that Rules Vibrations.

- 34 -

रक्तमज्जावसामांसान्यस्थिमेदांसि पार्वती ।

अन्त्राणि कालरात्रिश्च पित्तं च मुकुटेश्वरी ॥

raktamajjāvasāmāṃsān yasthi medāṃsi pārvatī |
antrāṇi kālarātriśca pittaṃ ca mukuṭeśvarī ||

May the Daughter of Spiritual Discipline protect my blood, marrow, fat, flesh, bones, and lymph; the entrails, the Dark Night of Overcoming Egotism; and the bile, the Crowned Sovereign.

\- 35 -

पद्मावती पद्मकोशे कफे चूडामणिस्तथा ।
ज्वालामुखी नखज्वालामभेद्या सर्वसन्धिषु ॥

padmāvatī padmakośe kaphe cūḍāmaṇis tathā |
jvālāmukhī nakha jvālām abhedyā sarva sandhiṣu ||

May the Goddess of the Lotus of Peace protect the lungs, and She with the Crest Jewel, the phlegm; She with the Radiant face, the luster of the nails, and the Unbreakable One, all the joints.

\- 36 -

शुक्रं ब्रह्माणि मे रक्षेच्छायां छत्रेश्वरी तथा ।
अहंकारं मनो बुद्धिं रक्षेन्मे धर्मधारिणी ॥

śukraṃ brahmāṇi me rakṣec
chāyāṃ chatreśvarī tathā |
ahaṃkāraṃ mano buddhiṃ
rakṣenme dharmadhāriṇī ||

May the Creative Energy protect my semen; and the Goddess with the Supreme Umbrella, my shadow; may my ego, mind, and intellect be protected by She who Supports the Way of Truth to Wisdom.

\- 37 -

प्राणापानौ तथा व्यानमुदानं च समानकम् ।
वज्रहस्ता च मे रक्षेत्प्राणं कल्याणशोभना ॥

prāṇā pānau tathā vyānam udānaṃ ca samānakam |
vajra hastā ca me rakṣet prāṇaṃ kalyāṇaśobhanā ||

May She who Holds the Thunderbolt of Illumination in Her hands protect my life, welfare, and five vital breaths: inhaling, exhaling, diffusing, rising, and equalizing.

\- 38 -

रसे रूपे च गन्धे च शब्दे स्पर्शे च योगिनी ।
सत्त्वं रजस्तमश्चैव रक्षेन्नारायणी सदा ॥

rase rūpe ca gandhe ca śabde sparśe ca yoginī |
sattvaṃ rajas tamaścaiva rakṣen nārāyaṇī sadā ||

Taste, form, smell, sound, and feeling may the Goddess of Union protect, and may knowledge, action, and desire always be protected by the Exposer of Consciousness.

- 39 -

आयू रक्षतु वाराही धर्मं रक्षतु वैष्णवी ।
यशः कीर्तिं च लक्ष्मीं च धनं विद्यां च चक्रिणी ॥

āyū rakṣatu vārāhī dharmaṃ rakṣatu vaiṣṇavī |
yaśaḥ kīrtiṃ ca lakṣmīṃ ca
dhanaṃ vidyāṃ ca cakriṇī ||

May the Most Excellent Desire of Union protect life, and the Energy of That which Pervades All protect the Way of Truth to Wisdom; may welfare, repute, prosperity, wealth, knowledge be protected by She who Holds the Discus of Revolving Time.

- 40 -

गोत्रमिन्द्राणि मे रक्षेत्पशून्मे रक्ष चण्डिके ।
पुत्रान् रक्षेन्महालक्ष्मीर्भार्यां रक्षतु भैरवी ॥

gotramindrāṇi me rakṣet paśūnme rakṣa caṇḍike |
putrān rakṣen mahālakṣmīr
bhāryāṃ rakṣatu bhairavī ||

May the Energy of the Rule of the Pure protect my lineage, and may She Who Tears Apart Thought protect my animals; may the Great Goddess of True Wealth protect my children, and the Formidable Goddess protect my mate.

- 41 -

पन्थानं सुपथा रक्षेन्मार्गं क्षेमकरी तथा ।
राजद्वारे महालक्ष्मीर्विजया सर्वतः स्थिता ॥

panthānaṃ supathā rakṣen mārgaṃ kṣemakarī tathā |
rājadvāre mahālakṣmīr vijayā sarvataḥ sthitā ||

May the Goddess of Excellent Paths protect my path, and the Giver of Salvation, my way; may the Great Goddess of True Wealth protect me at the gate to the royal palace where victory always dwells.

- 42 -

रक्षाहीनं तु यत्स्थानं वर्जितं कवचेन तु ।
तत्सर्वं रक्ष मे देवि जयन्ती पापनाशिनी ॥

rakṣāhīnaṃ tu yatsthānaṃ varjitaṃ kavacena tu |
tat sarvaṃ rakṣa me devi jayantī pāpanāśinī ||

Oh Goddess, protect all those places not mentioned in this my armor, Oh You Who Conquer and Destroy all Sin.

- 43 -

पदमेकं न गच्छेत्तु यदीच्छेच्छुभमात्मनः ।
कवचेनावृतो नित्यं यत्र यत्रैव गच्छति ॥

padamekaṃ na gacchettu
yadīcchecchubham ātmanaḥ |
kavacenā vṛto nityaṃ yatra yatraiva gacchati ||

For the welfare of his or her own soul, a person should not take one step without this armor. But if he or she always proceeds with the armor, wherever that person goes,

- 44 -

तत्र तत्रार्थलाभश्च विजयः सार्वकामिकः ।
यं यं चिन्तयते कामं तं तं प्राप्नोति निश्चितम् ।
परमैश्वर्यमतुलं प्राप्स्यते भूतले पुमान् ॥

tatra tatrārtha lābhaśca vijayaḥ sārva kāmikaḥ |
yaṃ yaṃ cintayate kāmaṃ
taṃ taṃ prāpnoti niścitam |
paramaiśvaryamatulaṃ prāpsyate bhūtale pumān ||

there the objectives are accomplished, conquering all desires. Whatever desires one contemplates, he or she attains them without a doubt. A human being becomes equivalent to the Supreme Sovereign of All.

- 45 -

निर्भयो जायते मर्त्यः संग्रामेष्वपराजितः ।
त्रैलोक्ये तु भवेत्पूज्यः कवचेनावृतः पुमान् ॥

nirbhayo jāyate martyaḥ saṅgrāmeṣvaparājitaḥ |
trailokye tu bhavet pūjyaḥ kavacenāvṛtaḥ pumān ||

Unafraid, a mortal conquers and is undefeated in any encounter. The human who proceeds with this armor becomes worthy of worship in the three worlds.

\- 46 -

इदं तु देव्याः कवचं देवानामपि दुर्लभम् ।
यः पठेत्प्रयतो नित्यं त्रिसन्ध्यं श्रद्धयान्वितः ॥

idaṃ tu devyāḥ kavacaṃ devānāmapi durlabham |
yaḥ paṭhet prayato nityaṃ
trisandhyaṃ śraddhayānvitaḥ ||

This is the armor of the Goddess, which is difficult for even the Gods. Whoever will constantly make its recitation at the three times of prayer with faith and self-control,

\- 47 -

दैवी कला भवेत्तस्य त्रैलोक्येष्वपराजितः ।
जीवेद् वर्षशतं साग्रमपमृत्युविवर्जितः ॥

daivī kalā bhavettasya trailokyeṣvaparājitaḥ |
jīved varṣaśataṃ sāgram apamṛtyu vivarjitaḥ ||

will assume the brilliance of the Goddess and become unconquerable in the three worlds. His or her life will last a hundred years, and death will be from natural causes.

\- 48 -

नश्यन्ति व्याधयः सर्वे लूताविस्फोटकादयः ।
स्थावरं जङ्गमं चैव कृत्रिमं चापि यद्विषम् ॥

naśyanti vyādhayaḥ sarve lūtāvisphoṭakādayaḥ |
sthāvaraṃ jaṅgamaṃ caiva
kṛtrimaṃ cāpi yadviṣam ||

All maladies will be destroyed, even those arising from infectious cuts and eruptions; all types of poisons will be rendered ineffective.

\- 49 -

अभिचाराणि सर्वाणि मन्त्रयन्त्राणि भूतले ।
भूचराः खेचराश्चैव जलजाश्चोपदेशिकाः ॥

abhicārāṇi sarvāṇi mantra yantrāṇi bhūtale |
bhūcarāḥ khecarāś caiva jalajāśco padeśikāḥ ||

All spells, mantras, amulets in existence, or those who move on the earth, or those who move in the air, or those born in water, or those counselled by others,

- 50 -

सहजा कुलजा माला डाकिनी शाकिनी तथा ।
अन्तरिक्षचरा घोरा डाकिन्यश्च महाबलाः ॥

sahajā kulajā mālā ḍākinī śākinī tathā |
antarikṣa carā ghorā ḍākinyaśca mahābalāḥ ||

or those born by themselves, or born in a family, those wearing a garland, those who feed on flesh, those who feed on vegetables, or those terrible beings of great strength who move in the atmosphere,

- 51 -

ग्रहभूतपिशाचाश्च यक्षगन्धर्वराक्षसाः ।
ब्रह्मराक्षसवेतालाः कूष्माण्डा भैरवादयः ॥

graha bhūta piśācāśca yakṣa gandharva rākṣasāḥ |
brahma rākṣasa vetālāḥ kūṣmāṇḍā bhairavādayaḥ ||

or spirits of the planets, heavenly nymphs, celestial minstrels, demons, those proud of learning, goblins, demons causing disease, terrifying ones,

- 52 -

नश्यन्ति दर्शनात्तस्य कवचे हृदि संस्थिते ।
मानोन्नतिर्भवेद् राज्ञस्तेजोवृद्धिकरं परम् ॥

naśyanti darśanāttasya kavace hṛdi saṃsthite |
mānonnatir bhaved rājñas tejo vṛddhi karaṃ param ||

all perish at the sight of one in whose heart resides this armor. His or her respect with superiors will rise, and the aura of light will have excellent increase.

- 53 -

यशसा वर्द्धते सोऽपि कीर्तिमण्डितभूतले ।
जपेत्सप्तशतीं चण्डीं कृत्वा तु कवचं पुरा ॥

yaśasā varddhate so-pi kīrti maṇḍita bhūtale |
japet saptaśatīṃ caṇḍīṃ kṛtvā tu kavacaṃ purā ||

Welfare will grow, and the fame of that person will spread throughout the world. First one should perform this armor, and then recite the seven hundred verses of the Chaṇḍī Pāṭhaḥ.

- 54 -

यावद्भूमण्डलं धत्ते सशैलवनकाननम् ।
तावत्तिष्ठति मेदिन्यां सन्ततिः पुत्रपौत्रिकी ॥

yāvad bhūmaṇḍalaṃ dhatte saśaila vana kānanam |
tāvat tiṣṭhati medinyāṃ santatiḥ putra pautrikī ||

So long as the hills and forests of trees last upon this earth, the descendants of sons and grandsons of that individual will remain.

- 55 -

देहान्ते परमं स्थानं यत्सुरैरपि दुर्लभम् ।
प्राप्नोति पुरुषो नित्यं महामायाप्रसादतः ॥

dehānte paramaṃ sthānaṃ yat surairapi durlabham |
prāpnoti puruṣo nityaṃ mahāmāyā prasādataḥ ||

At the end of the earthly body, with the blessing of the Great Measurement, that individual will attain the supreme station which is difficult even for Gods to attain.

- 56 -

लभते परमं रूपं शिवेन सह मोदते ॥

labhate paramaṃ rūpaṃ śivena saha modate ||

That person will attain the Ultimate form of Goodness and enjoy perfect bliss.

ॐ

oṃ

Dev.06

अथार्गलास्तोत्रम्
athārgalā stotram
The Praise That Unfastens the Bolt

ॐ अस्य श्रीअर्गलास्तोत्रमन्त्रस्य विष्णुर्ऋषिः अनुष्टुप् छन्दः श्रीमहालक्ष्मीर्देवता श्रीजगदम्बाप्रीत्यर्थे सप्तशतीपाठाङ्गत्वेन जपे विनियोगः ।

oṃ asya śrī argalā stotra mantrasya viṣṇur ṛṣiḥ anuṣṭup chandaḥ śrī mahālakṣmīr devatā śrī jagadambā prītyarthe saptaśatīpāṭhāṅga tvena jape viniyogaḥ |

Oṃ Presenting the respected mantras of The Praise that Unfastens the Bolt, the Consciousness that Pervades All is the seer, Anuṣṭup (32 syllables to the verse) is the meter, the respected Great Goddess of True Wealth is the deity, for the satisfaction of the respected Mother of the Universe this appendage of the Seven Hundred Verses is applied in recitation.

ॐ नमश्चण्डिकायै

oṃ namaścaṇḍikāyai

Oṃ We bow to the Goddess Who Tears Apart Thought.

मार्कण्डेय उवाच
mārkaṇḍeya uvāca
Mārkaṇḍeya said:

\- 1 -

ॐ जयन्ती मङ्गला काली भद्रकाली कपालिनी ।
दुर्गा क्षमा शिवा धात्री स्वाहा स्वधा नमोऽस्तु ते ॥

oṃ jayantī maṅgalā kālī bhadra-kālī kapālinī |
durgā kṣamā śivā dhātrī svāhā svadhā namo-stu te ||

Oṃ She Who Conquers Over All, All-Auspicious, the Remover of Darkness, the Excellent One Beyond Time, the Bearer of the

Skulls of Impure Thought, the Reliever of Difficulties, Loving Forgiveness, Supporter of the Universe, Oblations of I am One with God, Oblations of Ancestral Praise, to You, we bow.

- 2 -

जय त्वं देवि चामुण्डे जय भूतार्तिहारिणि ।
जय सर्वगते देवि कालरात्रि नमोऽस्तु ते ॥

jaya tvaṃ devi cāmuṇḍe jaya bhūtārtihāriṇi |
jaya sarvagate devi kālarātri namo-stu te ||

Conquer, Oh Goddess, Slayer of Passion and Anger! Conquer, Reliever of the Troubles of all Existence! Conquer, Oh Goddess Who Pervades this All! The Dark Night of Egotism, we bow to you.

- 3 -

मधुकैटभविद्राविं विधातृवरदे नमः ।
रूपं देहि जयं देहि यशो देहि द्विषो जहि ॥

madhu kaiṭabha vidrāvi vidhātṛ varade namaḥ |
rūpaṃ dehi jayaṃ dehi yaśo dehi dviṣo jahi ||

To you who defeated Too Much and Too Little, Giver of the blessing to the Creative Capacity, we bow. Give us your form, give us victory, give us welfare, remove all hostility.

- 4 -

महिषासुरनिर्णाशि भक्तानां सुखदे नमः ।
रूपं देहि जयं देहि यशो देहि द्विषो जहि ॥

mahiṣāsura nirṇāśi bhaktānāṃ sukhade namaḥ |
rūpaṃ dehi jayaṃ dehi yaśo dehi dviṣo jahi ||

To you who caused the destruction of the Great Ego, Giver of Happiness to devotees, we bow. Give us your form, give us victory, give us welfare, remove all hostility.

- 5 -

रक्तबीजवधे देवि चण्डमुण्डविनाशिनि ।
रूपं देहि जयं देहि यशो देहि द्विषो जहि ॥

raktabījavadhe devi caṇḍamuṇḍa vināśini |
rūpaṃ dehi jayaṃ dehi yaśo dehi dviṣo jahi ||

To you who slew the Seed of Desire, Oh Goddess, Destroyer of Passion and Anger. Give us your form, give us victory, give us welfare, remove all hostility.

- 6 -

शुम्भस्यैव निशुम्भस्य धूम्राक्षस्य च मर्दिनि ।
रूपं देहि जयं देहि यशो देहि द्विषो जहि ॥

śumbhasyaiva niśumbhasya
dhūmrākṣasya ca mardini |
rūpaṃ dehi jayaṃ dehi yaśo dehi dviṣo jahi ||

Slayer of Self-Conceit, Self-Deprecation, and Sinful Eyes, give us your form, give us victory, give us welfare, remove all hostility.

- 7 -

वन्दिताङ्घ्रियुगे देवि सर्वसौभाग्यदायिनि ।
रूपं देहि जयं देहि यशो देहि द्विषो जहि ॥

vanditāṅghiyuge devi sarva saubhāgya dāyini |
rūpaṃ dehi jayaṃ dehi yaśo dehi dviṣo jahi ||

All revere your lotus feet, Oh Goddess, Giver of all that is beautiful. Give us your form, give us victory, give us welfare, remove all hostility.

- 8 -

अचिन्त्यरूपचरिते सर्वशत्रुविनाशिनि ।
रूपं देहि जयं देहि यशो देहि द्विषो जहि ॥

acintya rūpa carite sarva śatru vināśini |
rūpaṃ dehi jayaṃ dehi yaśo dehi dviṣo jahi ||

You of unthinkable form and activity, Destroyer of all Opposition, give us your form, give us victory, give us welfare, remove all hostility.

- 9 -

नतेभ्यः सर्वदा भक्त्या चण्डिके दुरितापहे ।
रूपं देहि जयं देहि यशो देहि द्विषो जहि ॥

natebhyaḥ sarvadā bhaktyā caṇḍike duritāpahe |
rūpaṃ dehi jayaṃ dehi yaśo dehi dviṣo jahi ||

For those who bow to you with devotion, you remove all distress. Give us your form, give us victory, give us welfare, remove all hostility.

- 10 -

स्तुवद्भ्यो भक्तिपूर्वं त्वां चण्डिके व्याधिनाशिनि ।

रूपं देहि जयं देहि यशो देहि द्विषो जहि ॥

stuvadbhyo bhaktipūrvaṃ tvāṃ
caṇḍike vyādhināśini |
rūpaṃ dehi jayaṃ dehi yaśo dehi dviṣo jahi ||

For those who praise you with full devotion, Oh you who Tear Apart Thought, you destroy all maladies, give us your form, give us victory, give us welfare, remove all hostility.

- 11 -

चण्डिके सततं ये त्वामर्चयन्तीह भक्तितः ।

रूपं देहि जयं देहि यशो देहि द्विषो जहि ॥

caṇḍike satataṃ ye tvāmarcayantīha bhaktitaḥ |
rūpaṃ dehi jayaṃ dehi yaśo dehi dviṣo jahi ||

Oh Goddess who Tears Apart Thought, for those who constantly worship you with devotion, give us your form, give us victory, give us welfare, remove all hostility.

- 12 -

देहि सौभाग्यमारोग्यं देहि मे परमं सुखम् ।

रूपं देहि जयं देहि यशो देहि द्विषो जहि ॥

dehi saubhāgyamārogyaṃ
dehi me paramaṃ sukham |
rūpaṃ dehi jayaṃ dehi yaśo dehi dviṣo jahi ||

Give beauty, freedom from disease; give me supreme happiness. Give us your form, give us victory, give us welfare, remove all hostility.

- 13 -

विधेहि द्विषतां नाशं विधेहि बलमुच्चकैः ।

रूपं देहि जयं देहि यशो देहि द्विषो जहि ॥

vidhehi dviṣatāṃ nāśaṃ vidhehi balamuccakaiḥ |
rūpaṃ dehi jayaṃ dehi yaśo dehi dviṣo jahi ||

Grant the destruction of all that is disruptive; grant increase in strength. Give us your form, give us victory, give us welfare, remove all hostility.

- 14 -

विधेहि देवि कल्याणं विधेहि परमां श्रियम् ।
रूपं देहि जयं देहि यशो देहि द्विषो जहि ॥

vidhehi devi kalyāṇaṃ vidhehi paramāṃ śriyam |
rūpaṃ dehi jayaṃ dehi yaśo dehi dviṣo jahi ||

Oh Goddess, grant welfare, grant supreme prosperity. Give us your form, give us victory, give us welfare, remove all hostility.

- 15 -

सुरासुरशिरोरत्ननिघृष्टचरणेऽम्बिके ।
रूपं देहि जयं देहि यशो देहि द्विषो जहि ॥

surāsura śiroratna nighṛṣṭa caraṇe-mbike |
rūpaṃ dehi jayaṃ dehi yaśo dehi dviṣo jahi ||

Oh Mother of the Universe, whose feet are rubbed by the crest jewels of Gods and enemies alike, give us your form, give us victory, give us welfare, remove all hostility.

- 16 -

विद्यावन्तं यशस्वन्तं लक्ष्मीवन्तं जनं कुरु ।
रूपं देहि जयं देहि यशो देहि द्विषो जहि ॥

vidyāvantaṃ yaśasvantaṃ
lakṣmīvantaṃ janaṃ kuru |
rūpaṃ dehi jayaṃ dehi yaśo dehi dviṣo jahi ||

Make this person endowed with knowledge, endowed with welfare, endowed with True Wealth. Give us your form, give us victory, give us welfare, remove all hostility.

- 17 -

प्रचण्डदैत्यदर्पघ्ने चण्डिके प्रणताय मे ।
रूपं देहि जयं देहि यशो देहि द्विषो जहि ॥

pracaṇḍadaitya darpaghne caṇḍike praṇatāya me I
rūpaṃ dehi jayaṃ dehi yaśo dehi dviṣo jahi II

You who destroy the great egotism of thought, you who Tear Apart Thought, to us who bow to you, give us your form, give us victory, give us welfare, remove all hostility.

- 18 -

चतुर्भुजे चतुर्वक्त्रसंस्तुते परमेश्वरि ।
रूपं देहि जयं देहि यशो देहि द्विषो जहि ॥

caturbhuje caturvaktra saṃstute parameśvari I
rūpaṃ dehi jayaṃ dehi yaśo dehi dviṣo jahi II

The four-faced Creative Capacity, Brahmā, sings the praise of the four-armed Energy of the Supreme Sovereign. Give us your form, give us victory, give us welfare, remove all hostility.

- 19 -

कृष्णेन संस्तुते देवि शश्वद्भक्त्या सदम्बिके ।
रूपं देहि जयं देहि यशो देहि द्विषो जहि ॥

kṛṣṇena saṃstute devi śaśvadbhaktyā sadambike I
rūpaṃ dehi jayaṃ dehi yaśo dehi dviṣo jahi II

Oh Goddess, Oh Mother of the Universe, your praise is always sung by the Doer of All. Give us your form, give us victory, give us welfare, remove all hostility.

- 20 -

हिमाचलसुतानाथसंस्तुते परमेश्वरि ।
रूपं देहि जयं देहि यशो देहि द्विषो जहि ॥

himācala sutānātha saṃstute parameśvari I
rūpaṃ dehi jayaṃ dehi yaśo dehi dviṣo jahi II

The Lord of the Daughter of the Himalayas (Śiva) sings the praise of the Energy of the Supreme Sovereign. Give us your form, give us victory, give us welfare, remove all hostility.

- 21 -

इन्द्राणीपतिसद्भावपूजिते परमेश्वरि ।
रूपं देहि जयं देहि यशो देहि द्विषो जहि ॥

indrāṇīpati sadbhāva pūjite parameśvari |
rūpaṃ dehi jayaṃ dehi yaśo dehi dviṣo jahi ||
The husband of the Energy of the Rule of the Pure (Indra) worships the Energy of the Supreme Sovereign with pure feeling. Give us your form, give us victory, give us welfare, remove all hostility.

- 22 -

देवि प्रचण्डदोर्दण्डदैत्यदर्पविनाशिनि ।
रूपं देहि जयं देहि यशो देहि द्विषो जहि ॥

devi pracaṇḍa dordaṇḍa daitya darpa vināśini |
rūpaṃ dehi jayaṃ dehi yaśo dehi dviṣo jahi ||
Oh Goddess, with your great Staff of Discipline you destroy the egotism of thought. Give us your form, give us victory, give us welfare, remove all hostility.

- 23 -

देवि भक्तजनोद्दामदत्तानन्दोदयेऽम्बिके ।
रूपं देहि जयं देहि यशो देहि द्विषो जहि ॥

devi bhakta janoddāmadattānandodaye-mbike |
rūpaṃ dehi jayaṃ dehi yaśo dehi dviṣo jahi ||
Oh Goddess, Mother of the Universe, to the people who are devoted to you, you give inexpressible Peace and Delight. Give us your form, give us victory, give us welfare, remove all hostility.

- 24 -

पत्नीं मनोरमां देहि मनोवृत्तानुसारिणीम् ।
तारिणीं दुर्गसंसार सागरस्य कुलोद्भवाम् ॥

patnīṃ manoramāṃ dehi manovṛttānusāriṇīm |
tāriṇīṃ durga saṃsāra sāgarasya kulodbhavām ||
Give me a wife in harmony with my mind, who follows the changes of mind, and who can lead a family of noble birth across the difficulties of the ocean of objects and their relationships.

- 25 -

इदं स्तोत्रं पठित्वा तु महास्तोत्रं पठेन्नरः ।
स तु सप्तशतीसंख्यावरमाप्नोति सम्पदाम् ॥

idaṃ stotraṃ paṭhitvā tu mahāstotraṃ paṭhen naraḥ |
sa tu saptaśatīsaṃkhyā varamāpnoti sampadām ||

After reciting this hymn of praise one should recite the great hymn of praise the number of which is seven hundred verses, and he or she will attain to supreme perfection.

ॐ

oṃ

Devi: 07

अथ कीलकम्
atha kīlakam
The Praise That Removes the Pin

ॐ अस्य श्रीकीलकमन्त्रस्य शिव ऋषिः अनुष्टुप् छन्दः
श्रीमहासरस्वती देवता श्रीजगदम्बाप्रीत्यर्थं
सप्तशतीपाठाङ्गत्वेन जपे विनियोगः ।

oṃ asya śrī kīlaka mantrasya śiva ṛṣiḥ anuṣṭup chandaḥ śrī mahāsarasvatī devatā śrī jagadambā prītyarthaṃ saptaśatī pāṭhāṅga tvena jape viniyogaḥ |

Oṃ Presenting the respected mantras of the Praise That Removes the Pin, The Consciousness of Infinite Goodness is the Seer, Anuṣṭup (32 syllables to the verse) is the meter, the Respected Great Goddess of All-Pervading Knowledge is the deity, for the satisfaction of the Respected Mother of the Universe this appendage of the Seven Hundred Verses is applied in recitation.

ॐ नमश्चण्डिकायै

oṃ namaścaṇḍikāyai

Oṃ We bow to the Goddess Who Tears Apart Thought.

मार्कण्डेय उवाच
mārkaṇḍeya uvāca
Mārkaṇḍeya said:

- 1 -

ॐ विशुद्धज्ञानदेहाय त्रिवेदीदिव्यचक्षुषे ।
श्रेयःप्राप्तिनिमित्ताय नमः सोमार्द्धधारिणे ॥

oṃ viśuddha jñāna dehāya trivedī divya cakṣuṣe |
śreyaḥprāpti nimittāya namaḥ somārddha dhāriṇe ||

Oṃ Pure Knowledge is His body, and the three V :das are the vision in His divine eyes. He is the cause of a·taining the ultimate. We bow to Him who wears the half-moon of the Bliss of Devotion.

- 2 -

सर्वमेतद्विजानीयान्मन्त्राणामभिकीलकम् ।
सोऽपि क्षेममवाप्नोति सततं जाप्यतत्परः ॥

sarva metad vijānīyān mantrāṇām abhi kīlakam |
so-pi kṣemamavāpnoti satatam jāpyatatparaḥ ||

One should understand the mantras that remove the pin. Whoever constantly recites all of these mantras attains peace and security.

- 3 -

सिद्ध्यन्त्युच्चाटनादीनि वस्तूनि सकलान्यपि ।
एतेन स्तुवतां देवी स्तोत्रमात्रेण सिद्ध्यति ॥

siddhyant yuccāṭanādīni vastūni sakalānyapi |
etena stuvatāṃ devī stotra mātreṇa siddhyati ||

Those who praise by means of this, Oh Goddess, by means of the mantras of this hymn, they attain the perfection of indifference to each and every object of existence.

- 4 -

न मन्त्रो नौषधं तत्र न किञ्चिदपि विद्यते ।
विना जाप्येन सिद्ध्येत सर्वमुच्चाटनादिकम् ॥

na mantro nauṣadhaṃ tatra na kiñcidapi vidyate |
vinā jāpyena siddhyeta sarvam uccāṭanādikam ||

There is no mantra, no medicine, nor anything else known, by which indifference to all can be attained without repeated application.

- 5 -

समग्राण्यपि सिद्ध्यन्ति लोकशङ्कामिमां हरः ।
कृत्वा निमन्त्रयामास सर्वमेवमिदं शुभम् ॥

samagrāṇyapi siddhyanti loka śaṅkāmimāṃ haraḥ |
kṛtvā nimantra yāmāsa sarvamevamidaṃ śubham ||

The Great Reliever perfects every doubt in the world and fills all this with bliss for those who perform these mantras.

- 6 -

स्तोत्रं वै चण्डिकायास्तु तच्च गुप्तं चकार सः ।
समाप्तिर्न च पुण्यस्य तां यथावन्नियन्त्रणाम् ॥

stotram vai caṇḍikāyāstu tacca guptaṃ cakāra saḥ ।
samāptirna ca puṇyasya tāṃ yathā vanni yantraṇām ॥

He made the praise of She Who Tears Apart Thought, and He made it secret. There is no end of its merit; thus He attached a restraint.

- 7 -

सोऽपि क्षेममवाप्नोति सर्वमेवं न संशयः ।
कृष्णायां वा चतुर्दश्यामष्टम्यां वा समाहितः ॥

so-pi kṣema mavāpnoti sarvamevaṃ na saṃśayaḥ ।
kṛṣṇāyāṃ vā caturdaśyām aṣṭamyāṃ vā samāhitaḥ ॥

Whoever with full concentration of mind will meditate upon all these on the fourteenth and eighth days of the dark lunar fortnight will undoubtedly attain bliss.

- 8 -

ददाति प्रतिगृह्णाति नान्यथैषा प्रसीदति ।
इत्थंरूपेण कीलेन महादेवेन कीलितम् ॥

dadāti prati gṛhṇāti nānyathaiṣā prasīdati ।
itthaṃ rūpeṇa kīlena mahādevena kīlitam ॥

As one gives, so in return does one receive, and by no other means is She pleased. And this is the form of the pin by which it has been bound by the Great God.

- 9 -

यो निष्कीलां विधायैनां नित्यं जपति संस्फुटम् ।
स सिद्धः स गणः सोऽपि गन्धर्वो जायते नरः ॥

yo niṣkīlāṃ vidhāyaināṃ nityaṃ japati saṃsphuṭam ।
sa siddhaḥ sa gaṇaḥ so-pi gandharvo jāyate naraḥ ॥

The person who constantly recites, clearly removes the pin and becomes an attained one. That person joins the retinue of the Goddess and becomes a celestial singer.

- 10 -

न चैवाप्यटतस्तस्य भयं क्वापीह जायते ।
नापमृत्युवशं याति मृतो मोक्षमवाप्नुयात् ॥

na caivāp yaṭatastasya bhayaṃ kvāpīha jāyate |
nāpa mṛtyu vaśaṃ yāti mṛto mokṣama vāpnuyāt ||

Wherever such a person may move, they are free from fear. Neither would that person be subjected to untimely death, and upon leaving his or her body, that individual attains liberation.

- 11 -

ज्ञात्वा प्रारभ्य कुर्वीत न कुर्वाणो विनश्यति ।
ततो ज्ञात्वैव सम्पन्नमिदं प्रारभ्यते बुधैः ॥

jñātvā prārabhya kurvīta na kurvāṇo vinaśyati |
tato jñātvaiva sampannam
idaṃ prārabhyate budhaiḥ ||

Having understood, one should commence and practice it; by not performing, it will perish. Again by having understood comes fulfillment. This is undertaken by those who know.

- 12 -

सौभाग्यादि च यत्किञ्चिद् दृश्यते ललनाजने ।
तत्सर्वं तत्प्रसादेन तेन जाप्यमिदं शुभम् ॥

saubhāgyādi ca yat kiñcid dṛśyate lalanājane |
tat sarvaṃ tat prasādena tena jāpyamidaṃ śubham ||

All that is beautiful or any other auspicious quality seen in women is all the blessing of the Divine, and therefore this goodness should be recited.

- 13 -

शनैस्तु जप्यमानेऽस्मिन् स्तोत्रे सम्पत्तिरुच्चकैः ।
भवत्येव समग्रापि ततः प्रारभ्यमेव तत् ॥

śanaistu japyamāne-smin stotre sampatti ruccakaiḥ |
bhavat yeva samagrāpi tataḥ prārabhyam eva tat ||

Great wealth is attained for those who recite in moderate tone, and for those of higher tone, it is completely fulfilled. Therefore it must be undertaken.

- 14 -

ऐश्वर्यं यत्प्रसादेन सौभाग्यारोग्यसम्पदः ।

शत्रुहानिः परो मोक्षः स्तूयते सा न किं जनैः ॥

aiśvaryaṃ yat prasādena

saubhāgyārogya sampadaḥ |

śatruhāniḥ paro mokṣaḥ stūyate sā na kiṃ janaiḥ ||

When the blessing of the Supreme Sovereign is welfare, health, fulfillment, the destruction of all enmity, and the ultimate liberation, why will people not sing Her praise?

ॐ

oṃ

There is a significant mystical tradition associated with the Kīlaka Stotram that Mother will reveal at a certain stage in the development of an aspirant. It includes the removal of the pin by which all these mantras of the Saptaśatī have been bound, and the lifting of the curses that open the door to the secret. These are part of that body of doctrine of the Tantra that is generally held to be "magic," and indeed it most certainly is, but perhaps not in the ordinary sense as the public construes.

As a consequence, the grammatical construction of these verses is obscure, and they have been variously translated in a number of sources consulted. This rendering attempts to come as close as possible to the spirit and theme, but the meaning will become more clear after initiation in the Utkīlana and Śāpoddhāra mantras.

This we must determine for ourselves after having the experience, and it is recommended that our most respected Gurus show the way to its attainment. Unfortunately no other intellectual explanation will be of any further value.

Devi: 08

अथ वेदोक्तं रात्रिसूक्तम्

atha vedoktaṃ rātri sūktam

The Praise to the Night of Duality

ॐ रात्रीति सूक्तस्य कुशिक ऋषिः रात्रिर्देवता गायत्री छन्दः देवीमाहात्म्यपाठादौ जपे विनियोगः ।

oṃ rātrīti sūktasya kuśika ṛṣiḥ rātrirdevatā gāyatrī chandaḥ devīmāhātmya pāṭhādau jape viniyogaḥ I

Oṃ Presenting the meditation of the Gods for the Goddess of Night, Kuśikaḥ is the Seer, Gāyatrī (24 syllables to the verse) is the meter, The Goddess of Night is the deity, this appendage to the presentation of the Glory of the Goddess is applied in recitation.

- 1 -

ॐ रात्री व्यख्यदायती पुरुत्रा देव्यक्षभिः ।
विश्वा अधि श्रियोऽधित ॥

oṃ rātrī vyakhya dāyatī purutrā devyakṣabhiḥ I
viśvā adhi śriyo-dhita II

Oṃ The Night of Duality gives individuality in many forms and times perceivable by the divine power of sense.

- 2 -

ओर्वप्रा अमर्त्या निवतो देव्युद्वतः ।
ज्योतिषा बाधते तमः ॥

orvaprā amartyā nivato devyudvataḥ I
jyotiṣā bādhate tamaḥ II

Omnipresent, immortal, the Goddess of places high and low; Darkness is repelled by the Light.

- 3 -

निरु स्वसारमस्कृतोषसं देव्यायती ।
अपेदु हासते तमः ॥

niru svasāramaskṛtoṣasaṃ devyā yatī I
apedu hāsate tamaḥ II

She gave definition to Her sister, the Dawning Light, the Goddess who comes. And the Darkness departs.

\- 4 -

सा नो अद्य यस्या वयं नि ते यामन्नविक्ष्महि ।
वृक्षे न वसतिं वयः ॥

sā no adya yasyā vayaṃ ni te yāmannavikṣmahi I
vṛkṣe na vasatiṃ vayaḥ II

She is ours now. May we see Her effortless, unimpaired movements upon the earth as a bird sees from its dwelling in a tree, (remaining only the witness).

\- 5 -

नि ग्रामासो अविक्षत नि पद्वन्तो नि पक्षिणः ।
नि श्येनासश्चिदर्थिनः ॥

ni grāmāso avikṣata ni padvanto ni pakṣiṇaḥ I
ni śyenāsaścidarthinaḥ II

For the entire host of humanity, for animals who traverse by foot, or birds who fly in the air, She is the object of desperate search.

\- 6 -

यावया वृक्यं वृकं यवय स्तेनमूर्म्ये ।
अथा नः सुतरा भव ॥

yāvayā vṛkyaṃ vṛkaṃ yavaya stena mūrmye I
athā naḥ sutarā bhava II

Drive away the wolves of confusion, dispel the wolves of egotism, the thieves: hunger, thirst, greed, illusion, grief, and death Then be to us the excellent crossing to Wisdom.

\- 7 -

उप मा पेपिशत्तमः कृष्णं व्यक्तमस्थित ।
उष ऋणेव यातय ॥

upa mā pepiśattamaḥ kṛṣṇaṃ vyaktamasthita I
uṣa ṛṇeva yātaya II

The all-pervasive Darkness is near me, existing as individual forms in the blackness. Oh Dawning Light, dismiss this ignorance.

- 8 -

उप ते गा इवाकरं वृणीष्व दुहितर्दिवः ।
रात्रि स्तोमं न जिग्युषे ॥

upa te gā ivākaraṃ vṛnīṣva duhitardivaḥ |
rātri stomaṃ na jigyuṣe ||

Oh Daughter of the Heavens, you have been gratified as by a privileged cow. Oh Night of Duality, may this hymn be victorious.

ॐ

oṃ

अथ तन्त्रोक्तं रात्रिसूक्तम्

atha tantroktaṃ rātri sūktam

The Tantric Praise to the Night of Duality

- 1 -

ॐ विश्वेश्वरीं जगद्धात्रीं स्थितिसंहारकारिणीम् ।
निद्रां भगवतीं विष्णोरतुलां तेजसः प्रभुः ॥

oṃ viśveśvarīṃ jagaddhātrīṃ sthiti saṃhārakāriṇīm |
nidrāṃ bhagavatīṃ viṣṇoratulāṃ tejasaḥ prabhuḥ ||

The Revered One of Brilliant Light extolled the Ruler of the Universe, Creator of the Perceivable World, Cause of evolution and devolution, Goddess of Sleep, the unequaled Energy of Consciousness.

ब्रह्मोवाच

brahmovāca

The Creative Capacity said:

- 2 -

त्वं स्वाहा त्वं स्वधा त्वं हि वषट्कारः स्वरात्मिका ।
सुधा त्वमक्षरे नित्ये त्रिधा मात्रात्मिका स्थिता ॥

tvaṃ svāhā tvaṃ svadhā tvaṃ hi
vaṣaṭkāraḥsvarātmikā |
sudhā tvamakṣare nitye tridhā mātrātmikā sthitā ||

You are oblations of I am One with God, you are oblations of Union with Ancestors. You are oblations of Purity, and the Consciousness of all sound. You are the eternal essence of all the letters, and the consciousness of the three vowels (A, U, M; aiṃ, hrīṃ, klīṃ).

- 3 -

अर्धमात्रास्थिता नित्या यानुच्चार्या विशेषतः ।
त्वमेव सन्ध्या सावित्री त्वं देवि जननी परा ॥

ardhamātrā sthitā nityā yānuccāryā viśeṣataḥ |
tvameva sandhyā sāvitrī tvaṃ devi jananī parā ||

You are the eternal half-vowel and its special mode of pronunciation. You are the Time of Prayer, you are the Bearer of the Light, you are the Goddess above all beings born.

- 4 -

त्वयैतद्धार्यते विश्वं त्वयैतत्सृज्यते जगत् ।
त्वयैतत्पाल्यते देवि त्वमत्स्यन्ते च सर्वदा ॥

tvayai taddhāryate viśvaṃ tvayai tat sṛjyate jagat |
tvayaitat pālyate devi tvamatsyante ca sarvadā ||

The universe is sustained by you, and the perceivable world is created by you. You protect what you create, Oh Divine Goddess, and you are the end for all.

- 5 -

विसृष्टौ सृष्टिरूपा त्वं स्थितिरूपा च पालने ।
तथा संहृतिरूपान्ते जगतोऽस्य जगन्मये ॥

visṛṣṭau sṛṣṭi rūpā tvaṃ sthiti rūpā ca pālane |
tathā saṃhṛti rūpānte jagato-sya jaganmaye ||

As the Creator, you are the form of the creation, and as the form of circumstance, you are its maintenance. Then at the conclusion as the form of dissolution of perceivable existence, you are the All-Mighty Measurement of Being.

- 6 -

महाविद्या महामाया महामेधा महास्मृतिः ।
महामोहा च भवती महादेवी महासुरी ॥

mahāvidyā mahāmāyā mahāmedhā mahāsmṛtiḥ |
mahāmohā ca bhavatī mahādevī mahāsurī ||

The Great Knowledge, The Great Measurement, The Great Intellect, The Great Recollection; The Great Ignorance too, and your Ladyship, the Great Goddess and Great Source of Strength.

- 7 -

प्रकृतिस्त्वं च सर्वस्य गुणत्रयविभाविनी ।
कालरात्रिर्महारात्रिर्मोहरात्रिश्च दारुणा ॥

prakṛtistvaṃ ca sarvasya guṇa traya vibhāvinī |
kālarātrir mahārātrir moharātriśca dāruṇā ||

You are Nature, and the three qualities that you manifest in all: the Night of Time, the Great Night, and the Night of Ignorance.

- 8 -

त्वं श्रीस्त्वमीश्वरी त्वं ह्रीस्त्वं बुद्धिर्बोधलक्षणा ।

लज्जा पुष्टिस्तथा तुष्टिस्त्वं शान्तिः क्षान्तिरेव च ॥

tvaṃ śrīs tvam īśvarī tvaṃ hrīs
tvaṃ buddhir bodhalakṣaṇā |
lajjā puṣṭis tathā tuṣṭis tvaṃ śāntiḥ kṣāntireva ca ||

You are Prosperity, you are the Consciousness of All. You are Humility, you are the Intellect, and the goal of all knowledge: modesty, increase, then complete satisfaction. You are Peace and Patient Forgiveness.

- 9 -

खड्गिनी शूलिनी घोरा गदिनी चक्रिणी तथा ।

शङ्खिनी चापिनी बाणभुशुण्डी परिघायुधा ॥

khaḍginī śūlinī ghorā gadinī cakriṇī tathā |
śaṅkhinī cāpinī bāṇabhuśuṇḍī parighāyudhā ||

You bear the sword of Wisdom and the pike of concentration, the club of articulation and the discus of revolving time as you present a frightful form. You bear the conch of vibrations and the bow of determination and other weapons as well.

- 10 -

सौम्या सौम्यतराशेषसौम्येभ्यस्त्वतिसुन्दरी ।

परापराणां परमा त्वमेव परमेश्वरी ॥

saumyā saumya tarā śeṣa saumyebhyastvati sundarī |
parā parāṇāṃ paramā tvameva parameśvarī ||

You are mild and gentle and the ultimate of attractiveness and incomparable beauty. Above and beyond that, and even again superior, you are the Supreme Consciousness.

- 11 -

यच्च किञ्चित् क्वचिद्वस्तु सदसद्वाखिलात्मिके ।

तस्य सर्वस्य या शक्तिः सा त्वं किं स्तूयसे तदा ॥

yacca kiñcit kvacidvastu sadasadvākhilātmike |
taśya sarvasya yā śaktiḥ sā tvaṃ kiṃ stūyase tadā ||

Whatsoever exists in thought or perception, whether true or untrue, the energy of everything in all is you. Then what can be sung in your praise?

- 12 -

यया त्वया जगत्स्रष्टा जगत्पात्यत्ति यो जगत् ।

सोऽपि निद्रावशं नीतः कस्त्वां स्तोतुमिहेश्वरः ॥

yayā tvayā jagat sraṣṭā jagat pātyatti yo jagat |
so-pi nidrā vaśaṃ nītaḥ kastvāṃ stotumiheśvaraḥ ||

If He who is the evolution, circumstance, and devolution of the perceivable world is subject to the sleep that you have caused, then what can be sung in your praise?

- 13 -

विष्णुः शरीरग्रहणमहमीशान एव च ।

कारितास्ते यतोऽतस्त्वां कः स्तोतुं शक्तिमान् भवेत् ॥

viṣṇuḥ śarīra grahaṇa mahamīśāna eva ca |
kāritāste yato-tastvāṃ kaḥ stotuṃ śaktimān bhavet ||

You cause the Maintaining Capacity and the Dissolving Capacity and myself as well to wear bodies. Hence for this reason and for this cause, who has sufficient ability to sing your praise?

- 14 -

सा त्वमित्थं प्रभावैः स्वैरुदारैर्देवि संस्तुता ।

मोहयैतौ दुराधर्षावसुरौ मधुकैटभौ ॥

sā tvamitthaṃ prabhāvaiḥ svairudārairdevi saṃstutā |
mohayaitau durādharṣā vasurau madhu kaiṭabhau ||

Oh Divine Goddess, you and your heavenly and bounteous manifestations have been extolled. Cause the ignorance of egotism to fall upon those two thoughts so difficult to understand, Too Much and Too Little.

- 15 -

प्रबोधं च जगत्स्वामी नीयतामच्युतो लघु ।

बोधश्च क्रियतामस्य हन्तुमेतौ महासुरौ ॥

prabodhaṃ ca jagat svāmī nīyatā macyuto laghu |
bodhaśca kriya tāmasya hantu metau mahāsurau ||
Awaken the Consciousness of the Master of the World and rouse Him from sleep. Let Him conquer these two great thoughts for me and beget Wisdom.

ॐ

oṃ

अथ श्रीदेव्यथर्वशीर्षम्

atha śrī devyatharvaśīrṣam

The Highest Meaning of the Goddess

\- 1 -

ॐ सर्वे वै देवा देवीमुपतस्थुः कासि त्वं महादेवीति ॥

oṃ sarve vai devā devīmupatasthuḥ kāsi tvaṃ mahādevīti ||

All of the Gods collected near the Goddess and with great respect asked of the Great Goddess, "Who are you?"

\- 2 -

साब्रवीत् -- अहं ब्रह्मस्वरूपिणी ।

मत्तः प्रकृतिपुरुषात्मकं जगत् । शून्यं चाशून्यं च ॥

sābravīt -- ahaṃ brahmasvarūpiṇī | mattaḥ prakṛti puruṣātmakaṃ jagat | śūnyaṃ caśūnyaṃ ca ||

She replied, I am the intrinsic nature of Consciousness. From me both Nature and Consciousness have taken birth, this world of true existence and untrue appearance.

\- 3 -

अहमानन्दानानन्दौ । अहं विज्ञानाविज्ञाने ।

अहं ब्रह्माब्रह्मणी वेदितव्ये । अहं पञ्चभूतान्यपञ्चभूतानि ।

अहमखिलं जगत् ॥

ahamānandānānandau | ahaṃ vijñānāvijñāne |
ahaṃ brahmābrahmaṇī veditavye |
ahaṃ pañcabhūtānya pañcabhūtāni |
aham akhilaṃ jagat ||

I am the form of bliss and blisslessness. I am the form of the Wisdom of Unity and lack of wisdom as well. I am the capacity of understanding what is Brahmā, the Supreme Consciousness, and what is not Brahmā. I am the great elements of existence as they unite in forms and in their ununited individual aspects as well. I am this entire perceivable universe.

- 4 -

वेदोऽहमवेदोऽहम् । विद्याहमविद्याहम् ।

अजाहमनजाहम् । अधश्चोर्ध्वं च तिर्यक्चाहम् ॥

vedo-hamavedo-ham | vidyāham avidyāham
ajāhamanajāham | adhaścordhvaṃ ca tiryakcāham ||

I am the Wisdom of Eternal Harmony, and I am lack of Wisdom; I am Knowledge and I am Ignorance; I am unborn and again I take birth; I am above and below, and even beyond.

- 5 -

ॐ अहं रुद्रेभिर्वसुभिश्चरामि । अहमादित्यैरुत विश्वदेवैः ।

अहं मित्रावरुणावुभौ बिभर्मि । अहमिन्द्राग्नी

अहमश्विनावुभौ ॥

oṃ ahaṃ rudrebhir vasubhiṣ carāmi | ahamādityairu-
ta viśva devaiḥ | ahaṃ mitrā varuṇāvubhau
bibharmi | aham indrāgnī aham aśvināvubhau ||

I travel with the Relievers of Suffering, with the Finders of the Wealth, with the Sons of Enlightenment, as also with All Gods. I hold aloft Friendship and Equanimity, the Rule of the Pure, the Light of Meditation and the Divine Urge to Union.

- 6 -

अहं सोमं त्वष्टारं पूषणं भगं दधामि ।

अहं विष्णुमुरुक्रमं ब्रह्माणमुत प्रजापतिं दधामि ॥

ahaṃ somaṃ tvaṣṭāraṃ pūṣaṇaṃ bhagaṃ dadhāmi |
ahaṃ viṣṇumurukramaṃ brahmāṇamuta prajāpatiṃ
dadhāmi ||

I perform the functions of Great Devotion, Creative Intelligence, Searchers for Truth, and the Wealth of Realization. I perform the functions of the All-Pervading Consciousness, the Creative Capacity, and the Lord of Beings.

- 7 -

अहं दधामि द्रविणं हविष्मते सुप्राव्ये यजमानाय सुन्वते । अहं राष्ट्री सङ्गमनी वसूनां चिकितुषी प्रथमा यज्ञियानाम् । अहं सुवे पितरमस्य मूर्धन्मम योनिरप्स्वन्तः समुद्रे । य एवं वेद । स दैवीं सम्पदमाप्नोति ॥

ahaṃ dadhāmi draviṇaṃ haviṣmate suprāvye yajamānāya sunvate | ahaṃ rāṣṭrī saṅgamanī vasūnāṃ cikituṣī prathamā yajñiyānām | ahaṃ suve pitaramasya mūrdhanmama yonirapsvantaḥ samudre | ya evaṃ veda | sa daivīṃ sampadamāpnoti ||

I give wealth to the sacrificer who presses out the offering of devotion with attention. I am the Queen, the united mind of the Guardians of the Treasure, the Supreme Consciousness of those who are offered sacrifice. I give birth to the Supreme Father of this All; my creative energy is in the waters of the inner ocean. For such a one who knows this, the wealth of the Goddess increases.

- 8 -

ते देवा अब्रुवन्--नमो देव्यै महादेव्यै शिवायै सततं नमः । नमः प्रकृत्यै भद्रायै नियताः प्रणताः स्म ताम् ॥

te devā abruvan--namo devyai mahādevyai śivāyai satataṃ namaḥ | namaḥ prakṛtyai bhadrāyai niyatāḥ praṇatāḥ sma tām ||

Then the Gods replied, We bow to the Goddess, to the Great Goddess, to the Energy of Infinite Goodness at all times we bow. We bow to Nature, to the Excellent One, with discipline we have bowed down.

- 9 -

तामग्निवर्णां तपसा ज्वलन्तीं वैरोचनीं कर्मफलेषु जुष्टाम् । दुर्गां देवीं शरणं प्रपद्यामहेऽसुरान्नाशयित्र्यै ते नमः ॥

tāmagnivarṇāṃ tapasā jvalantīṃ
vairocanīṃ karmaphaleṣu juṣṭām |
durgāṃ devīṃ śaraṇaṃ prapadyā
mahe-surānnāśayitryai te namaḥ ||

We take the refuge of She who is of the nature of Fire, who illuminates the Light of Wisdom in Meditation, the bestower of the fruits of all actions, the Goddess Durgā, the Reliever of all Difficulties. To the Destroyer of All Thoughts, we bow down to you.

- 10 -

देवीं वाचमजनयन्त देवास्तां विश्वरूपाः पशवो वदन्ति ।
सा नो मन्द्रेषमूर्जं दुहाना धेनुर्वागस्मानुप सुष्टुतैतु ॥

devīṃ vācamajanayanta devās
tāṃ viśvarūpāḥ paśavo vadanti |
sā no mandreṣamūrjaṃ duhānā
dhenurvāgasmānupa śuṣṭutaitu ||

The Gods have offered forth many loving vibrations to the Goddess. All living beings call Her the form of the universe. May She who is like the cow granting all desires, Giver of Bliss and Strength, the form of all sound, may that Ultimate Goddess, being pleased with our hymns, present Herself before us.

- 11 -

कालरात्रीं ब्रह्मस्तुतां वैष्णवीं स्कन्दमातरम् ।
सरस्वतीमदितिं दक्षदुहितरं नमामः पावनां शिवाम् ॥

kālarātrīṃ brahmastutāṃ
vaiṣṇavīṃ skandamātaram |
sarasvatīm aditiṃ dakṣaduhitaraṃ
namāmaḥ pāvanāṃ śivām ||

We bow to the Time of Darkness, to She who is praised by the Creative Capacity, to the Energy of Universal Consciousness, to the Mother of Divinity, to the Spirit of All-Pervading Knowledge, to the Mother of Enlightenment, to the Daughter of Ability, to the Energy of Goodness.

- 12 -

महाल्क्ष्म्यै च विद्महे सर्वशक्त्यै च धीमहि ।

तन्नो देवी प्रचोदयात् ॥

mahālakṣmyai ca vidmahe sarva śaktyai ca dhīmahi |
tanno devī pracodayāt ||

We know the Goddess Mahālakṣmi, and we meditate upon She who embodies all energy. May that Goddess grant us increase in wisdom.

- 13 -

अदितिर्ह्यजनिष्ट दक्ष या दुहिता तव ।

तां देवा अन्वजायन्त भद्रा अमृतबन्धवः ॥

aditirhyajaniṣṭa dakṣa yā duhitā tava |
tāṃ devā anvajāyanta bhadrā amṛtabandhavaḥ ||

Now Ability, your daughter, the Mother of Enlightenment, has taken birth, and also the excellent Gods of Eternal Bliss.

- 14 -

कामो योनिः कमला वज्रपाणि

र्गुहा हसा मातरिश्वाभ्रमिन्द्रः ।

पुनर्गुहा सकला मायया च

पुरूच्यैषा विश्वमातादिविद्योम् ॥

kāmo yoniḥ kamalā vajrapāṇir
guhā hasā mātariśvābhramindraḥ |
punarguhā sakalā māyayā ca
purūcyaiṣā viśvamātādi vidyom ||

Desire (ka), the womb of creation (e), the lotus Lakṣmi (ī), She with the thunderbolt in hand (la), the cave (hrīṃ), the letters (ha) (sa), the emancipated Lord of Wind (ka), the atmosphere (ha), the Rule of the Pure (la), again the cave (hrīṃ), the letters (sa) (ka) (la), Māyā (hrīṃ), this is the root of the knowledge of the Divine Mother.

Note:

Causal Body

ka	Wisdom, Ultimate Objective, Dissolution, Tamo Guṇa
e	Desire, Creation, Rajo Guṇa
ī	Action, Preservation, Sattva Guṇa
la	Manifestation
hrīṃ	Māyā, the One looking to the One

Subtle Body

ha	The Divine I, Īśvara, Puruṣa
sa	That, Prakṛti
ka	Heaven, Svaḥ
ha	Atmosphere, Bhuvaḥ
la	Earth, Bhūr
hrīṃ	Māyā, the One looking to the many, the many looking to the One

Gross Body

sa	All
ka	Desires, Objectives
la	Individual Manifestations
hrīṃ	Māyā, the many looking to the many

This is how the code works. Each word is reduced to its abbreviated form as a Bīja Mantra, a Seed Mantra, and the unity of all the bījas, the seeds, spells out the Śrī Vidyā, the Knowledge of the Ultimate Prosperity: how God sees Himself; how God sees the world and the world sees God; and how the world sees the world; the three forms of Māyā: Māyā as illusion, Māyā as the universal body of Nature, Māyā as the One Consciousness in harmony with its own self.

In the Nityāśodaśikārṇava another interpretation is offered: Śiva-Śakti of undifferentiated form; the potentiality of Brahmā, Viṣṇu, and Śiva (Creative, Maintaining, and Dissolving Capacities of Consciousness); the form of Sarasvatī, Lakṣmī, and Gaurī (Rajo, Sattva, and Tamo Guṇas: knowledge, action, and desire); the capacity of impure, mixed, and pure spiritual discipline; unity of existence, of Śiva-Śakti; the intrinsic nature of Brahma (Supreme Consciousness); bestower of Supreme Wisdom beyond thought or form; manifesting all the principles; the great threefold beauty.

This is the Bhāvarthā or purport of the mantra, the meaning according to the intensity of intuition as per the development of an aspirant's discipline. This mantra is defined in six different ways: according to the intensity of intuition, spoken meaning, meaning according to the schools of philosophy, according to the monastic order, secret meaning, and the meaning according to the principles. The definition we have presented purports to be an accurate rendition of the secret meaning, and is also in conformity with the principles of Tantra Tattvas.

- 15 -

एषाऽऽत्मशक्तिः । एषा विश्वमोहिनी । पाशाङ्कुशधनुर्बाण-

धरा । एषा श्रीमहाविद्या । य एवं वेद स शोकं तरति ॥

eṣā--tmaśaktiḥ | eṣā viśva mohinī | pāśāṅkuśa dhanur bāṇadharā | eṣā śrī mahāvidyā | ya evaṃ veda sa śokaṃ tarati ||

This is the Energy of the Universal Soul; this is the delusion of the world; this is She who hoids in Her four arms the net, the curved sword, the bow and arrow; this is the Great Śrī Vidyā - the Great Knowledge of Ultimate Prosperity; one who understands this may never sorrow again.

- 16 -

नमस्ते अस्तु भगवति मातरस्मान् पाहि सर्वतः ॥

namaste astu bhagavati mātarasmān pāhi sarvataḥ ||

Oh Bhagavatī, Empress of the Universe, we bow to you! Oh Mother, protect us in every way.

- 17 -

सैषाष्टौ वसवः । सैषैकादश रुद्राः । सैषा द्वादशादित्याः ।

सैषा विश्वेदेवाः सोमपा असोमपाश्च । सैषा यातुधाना असुरा

रक्षांसि पिशाचा यक्षाः सिद्धाः ।

सैषा सत्त्वरजस्तमांसि । सैषा ब्रह्मविष्णुरुद्ररूपिणी ।

सैषा प्रजापतीन्द्रमनवः । सैषा ग्रहनक्षत्रज्योतींषि ।

कलाकाष्ठादिकालरूपिणी । तामहं प्रणौमि नित्यम् ॥

saiṣāṣṭau vasavaḥ | saiṣaikādaśa rudrāḥ | saiṣā dvā-daśādityāḥ | saiṣā viśvedevāḥ somapā asomapāśca | saiṣā yātudhānā asurā rakṣāṃsi piśācā yakṣāḥ siddhāḥ | saiṣā sattva rajas tamāṃsi | saiṣā brahma viṣṇu rudra rūpiṇī | saiṣā prajāpatīndra manavaḥ | saiṣā grahanakṣatra jyotīṃṣi | kalākāṣṭhādi kālarūpiṇī | tāmahaṃ praṇaumi nityam ||

पापापहारिणीं देवीं भुक्तिमुक्तिप्रदायिनीम् ।
अनन्तां विजयां शुद्धां शरण्यां शिवदां शिवाम् ॥

pāpāpahāriṇīṃ devīṃ bhukti mukti pradāyinīm |
anantāṃ vijayāṃ śuddhāṃ
śaraṇyāṃ śivadāṃ śivām ||

(The Seer of the mantra says:) She is the eight forms of wealth; She is the Eleven Relievers from Sufferings; She is the twelve Sons of Enlightenment; She is All Gods who drink the nectar of Devotion and She is those who do not; She is the lowest concerns of the mind, thoughts, confusions, conflicts, good spirits, and attainments of perfection. She is Truth and Light, Activity and Rest. She is the form of Brahmā, Viṣṇu, and Rudra. She is the Lord of Beings, the Rule of the Pure, the manifestation of Reason. She is the planets and the Light of the stars. She is the form of time and its divisions. We continually bow down to Her.

To She who Destroys Confusion, to the Grantor of Enjoyment and Liberation, who resides within, Giver of Victory, without flaw or imperfection, the True Competent Refuge, Bestower of Welfare, and the Energy of Infinite Goodness, to that Goddess we continually bow down.

- 18 -

वियदीकारसंयुक्तं वीतिहोत्रसमन्वितम् ।
अर्धेन्दुलसितं देव्या बीजं सर्वार्थसाधकम् ॥

viyadīkārasaṃyuktaṃ vītihotra samanvitam |
ardhendulasitaṃ devyā bījaṃ sarvārtha sādhakam ||

Atmosphere (ha) plus the letter (ī), the Divine Fire that is the Light of Meditation (ra), anusvāra (ṃ) the beautiful ornament of the Goddess, the seed mantra that accomplishes all objectives.

- 19 -

एवमेकाक्षरं ब्रह्म यतयः शुद्धचेतसः ।
ध्यायन्ति परमानन्दमया ज्ञानाम्बुराशयः ॥

evamekākṣaraṃ brahma yatayaḥ śuddha cetasaḥ |
dhyāyanti paramānandamayā jñānāmburāśayaḥ ||

Who meditates upon this one-syllabled deity, his consciousness becomes pure, he becomes filled with the ultimate bliss, and he becomes the ocean of Wisdom.

- 20 -

वाङ्माया ब्रह्मसुस्तस्मात् षष्ठं वक्त्रसमन्वितम् ।
सूर्योऽवामश्रोत्रबिन्दुसंयुक्तष्टात्तृतीयकः ।
नारायणेन संमिश्रो वायुश्चाधरयुक् ततः ।
विच्चे नवार्णकोऽर्णः स्यान्महदानन्ददायकः ॥

vāṅmāyā brahmasustasmāt ṣaṣṭhaṃ vaktra samanvitam | sūryo-vāmaśrotra bindu saṃyuktaṣṭāt tṛtīyakaḥ | nārāyaṇena saṃmiśro vāyuścādharayuk tataḥ | vicce navārṇako-rṇaḥ syān mahadānanda dāyakaḥ ||

Sound (aiṃ); Māyā (hrīṃ); Ultimate Objective (klīṃ); six letters forward from ka = ca + a = cā; the Sun (ma); the letter of the right ear (u) + anusvāra = muṇ; from ṭa three letters forward = ḍa + the seed mantra of Nārāyaṇa (ā) = ḍā; Vāyu's seed mantra (ya) + ai = yai and vicce - this is the Navārṇa Mantra, which gives meditators the highest bliss and unites them in the being of the Supreme Reality.

- 21 -

हृत्पुण्डरीकमध्यस्थां प्रातःसूर्यसमप्रभाम् ।
पाशाङ्कुशधरां सौम्यां वरदाभयहस्तकाम् ।
त्रिनेत्रां रक्तवसनां भक्तकामदुघां भजे ॥

hṛtpuṇḍarīkamadhyasthām
prātaḥ sūrya sama prabhām |
pāśāṅkuśa dharāṃ saumyāṃ varadābhaya hastakām |
trinetrāṃ raktavasanāṃ bhaktakāmadughāṃ bhaje ||

Who resides in the lotus of the heart, whose radiance is like the luster of the rising sun, who holds in Her hands the net and curved sword, of beautiful appearance, and who shows the mudras bestowing fearlessness and granting boons; displaying three eyes, wearing a red cloth, who fulfills the desires of devotees, that Goddess I worship.

\- 22 -

नमामि त्वां महादेवीं महाभयविनाशिनीम् ।
महादुर्गप्रशमनीं महाकारुण्यरूपिणीम् ॥

namāmi tvāṃ mahādevīṃ mahābhayavināśinīm |
mahādurga praśamanīṃ mahākāruṇya rūpiṇīm ||

I bow down to you, the Great Goddess, the Great Destroyer of all Fear, the Great Reliever of all Difficulties, the form of the Great Bestower of Compassion.

\- 23 -

यस्याः स्वरूपं ब्रह्मादयो न जानन्ति तस्मादुच्यते अज्ञेया । यस्या अन्तो न लभ्यते तस्मादुच्यते अनन्ता । यस्या लक्ष्यं नोपलक्ष्यते तस्मादुच्यते अलक्ष्या । यस्या जननं नोपलभ्यते तस्मादुच्यते अजा । एकैव सर्वत्र वर्तते तस्मादुच्यते एका । एकैव विश्वरूपिणी तस्मादुच्यते नैका । अत एवोच्यते अज्ञेयानन्तालक्ष्याजैका नैकेति ॥

yasyāḥ svarūpaṃ brahmādayo na jānanti tasmāducyate ajñeyā | yasyā anto na labhyate tasmāducyate anantā | yasyā lakṣyaṃ nopalakṣyate tasmāducyate alakṣyā | yasyā jananaṃ nopalabhyate tasmāducyate ajā | ekaiva sarvatra vartate tasmāducyate ekā | ekaiva viśvarūpiṇī tasmāducyate naikā | ata evocyate ajñeyānantālakṣyājaikā naiketi ||

Whose intrinsic nature Brahmā and other divinities cannot know, and therefore She is called Unknowable; whose end cannot be found, and therefore She is called Infinite; whose definition cannot be defined, and therefore She is called Undefinable; whose birth cannot be understood, and therefore She is called Unborn; whose presence is everywhere, and therefore She is called the ONE; who alone is the active principle in the form of the universe, and therefore She is called the many. Therefore She is called Unknowable, Infinite, Undefinable, Unborn, One, and Many.

- 24 -

मन्त्राणां मातृका देवी शब्दानां ज्ञानरूपिणी ।
ज्ञानानां चिन्मयातीता शून्यानां शून्यसाक्षिणी ।
यस्याः परतरं नास्ति सैषा दुर्गा प्रकीर्तिता ॥

mantrāṇāṃ mātṛkā devī śabdānāṃ jñānarūpiṇī |
jñānānāṃ cinmayātītā śūnyānāṃ śūnyasākṣiṇī |
yasyāḥ parataraṃ nāsti saiṣā durgā prakīrtitā ||

Oh Goddess, you reside in all mantras in the form of letters, in all words in the form of wisdom and meaning. In Wisdom you reside as the Bliss of Consciousness, and in silence you reside as the Ultimate Silence beyond which no greater exists. There you are known by the name of the Reliever of Difficulties.

- 25 -

तां दुर्गां दुर्गमां देवीं दुराचारविघातिनीम् ।
नमामि भवभीतोऽहं संसारार्णवतारिणीम् ॥

tāṃ durgāṃ durgamāṃ devīṃ durācāravighātinīm |
namāmi bhavabhīto-haṃ saṃsārārṇava tāriṇīm ||

I bow to the Reliever of Difficulties, to the Goddess who Destroys Confusion, who destroys all inappropriate conduct, who takes us across the sea of objects and relationships free from fear.

- 26 -

इदमथर्वशीर्षं योऽधीते स पञ्चाथर्वशीर्षजपफलमाप्नोति ।
इदमथर्वशीर्षमज्ञात्वा योऽर्चां स्थापयति --
शतलक्षं प्रजप्त्वापि सोऽर्चासिद्धिं न विन्दति ।
शतमष्टोत्तरं चास्य पुरश्चर्याविधिः स्मृतः ।
दशवारं पठेद् यस्तु सद्यः पापैः प्रमुच्यते ।
महादुर्गाणि तरति महादेव्याः प्रसादतः ॥

idamatharvaśīrṣaṃ yo-dhīte sa pañcātharvaśīrṣa japa phalamāpnoti | idamatharvaśīrṣamajñātvā yo-rcāṃ sthāpayati--śatalakṣaṃ prajaptvāpi so-rcāsiddhiṃ na vindati | śatamaṣṭottaraṃ cāsya puraścaryā vidhiḥ smṛtaḥ | daśavāraṃ paṭhed yastu sadyaḥ pāpaiḥ pra-mucyate | mahādurgāṇi tarati mahādevyāḥ prasdataḥ ||

Who studies this "Highest Meaning" receives the fruit of five complete recitations. Who does not understand the Highest Meaning, but installs a deity for worship, he may recite millions of mantras, but his worship will be without attainment. The system of fire worship with these mantras requires one hundred eight oblations. Who will recite these mantras ten times will be immediately freed from all sin, and with the grace of the Great Goddess all terrible difficulties will be alleviated.

सायमधीयानो दिवसकृतं पापं नाशयति । प्रातरधीयानो
रात्रिकृतं पापं नाशयति । सायं प्रातः प्रयुञ्जानो अपापो
भवति । निशीथे तुरीयसन्ध्यायां जप्त्वा वाक्सिद्धिर्भवति ।
नूतनायां प्रतिमायां जप्त्वा देवतासान्निध्यं भवति । प्राण-
प्रतिष्ठायां जप्त्वा प्राणानां प्रतिष्ठा भवति । भौमाश्विन्यां
महादेवीसन्निधौ जप्त्वा महामृत्युं तरति ।
स महामृत्युं तरति य एवं वेद । इत्युपनिषत् ॥

sāyamadhīyāno divasakṛtaṃ pāpaṃ nāśayati I
prātaradhīyāno rātrikṛtaṃ pāpaṃ nāśayati I
sāyaṃ prātaḥ prayuñjāno apāpo bhavati I
niśīthe turīyasandhyāyāṃ japtvā vāk siddhir bhavati I
nūtanāyāṃ pratimāyāṃ japtvā devatāsānnidhyaṃ bhavati I
prāṇa pratiṣṭhāyāṃ japtvā prāṇānāṃ pratiṣṭhā bhavati I
bhaumāśvinyāṃ mahādevī sannidhau japtvā mahāmṛtyuṃ tarati I
sa mahā mṛtyuṃ tarati ya evaṃ veda I
ityupaniṣat II

Who recites these mantras in the night will be freed from all sins committed during the day. Who recites these mantras in the morning will be freed from all sins committed during the night. Who recites in both the day and the night will be freed from all sin. Who recites at midnight (four times of worship are recommended for Śrī Vidyā meditators) will attain the perfection of auspicious vibrations. Who recites before a new image of the Goddess will attain Her proximity. If it is recited at the time of establishment of life within a deity, life will be established. If recited before the Goddess in the (astrological yoga) Union of Eternal Attainment (Amṛta Siddhi Yoga), then the Great Death is avoided.

Who understands this avoids the Great Death.
This is the Upanishad.

ॐ

oṃ

अथ नवार्णविधिः

atha navārṇa vidhiḥ

And now,
The System of Worship
with the Nine Lettered Mantra

श्रीगणपतिर्जयति

śrī gaṇapatir jayati

May the Lord of Wisdom be Victorious.

ॐ अस्य श्रीनवार्णमन्त्रस्य ब्रह्मविष्णुरुद्रा ऋषयः गायत्र्युष्णिगनुष्टुभश्छन्दांसि श्रीमहाकालीमहालक्ष्मीमहासरस्वत्यो देवताः ऐं बीजम् ह्रीं शक्तिः क्लीं कीलकम् श्रीमहाकालीमहालक्ष्मीमहासरस्वती प्रीत्यर्थे नवार्णसिद्ध्यर्थे जपे विनियोगः ।

oṃ asya śrī navārṇa mantrasya brahma viṣṇu rudrā ṛṣayaḥ gāyatryuṣṇig anuṣṭubhaś chandāṃsi śrī mahākālī mahālakṣmī mahāsarasvatyo devatāḥ aiṃ bījam hrīṃ śaktiḥ klīṃ kīlakam śrī mahākālī mahālakṣmī mahāsarasvatī prītyarthe navārṇa siddhyarthe jape viniyogaḥ |

Oṃ. Presenting the Highly Efficacious Mantra of Nine Letters. The Lords of Creation, Preservation, and Destruction are the Seers; Gāyatrī, Uṣṇig, and Anuṣṭup (24, 28, and 32 syllables to the verse) are the Meters; the Great Remover of Darkness, the Great Goddess of True Wealth, and the Great Goddess of All-Pervading Knowledge are the Deities; Aiṃ is the Seed; Hrīṃ is the Energy; Klīṃ is the Pin; for the Satisfaction of the Great Remover of Darkness, the Great Goddess of True Wealth, and the Great Goddess of All-Pervading Knowledge, this System is applied in recitation.

ऋष्यादिन्यासः

ṛṣyādi nyāsaḥ

Establishment of the Seers

ॐ ब्रह्मविष्णुरुद्रऋषिभ्यो नमः

oṃ brahma viṣṇu rudra ṛṣibhyo namaḥ *head*

I bow to the Seers, the Lords of Creation, Preservation, and Destruction

गायत्र्युष्णिगनुष्टुप् छन्दोभ्यो नमः

gāyatryuṣṇig anuṣṭup chandobhyo namaḥ *mouth*

I bow to the Meters Gāyatrī, Uṣṇig, and Anuṣṭup

महाकालीमहालक्ष्मीमहासरस्वतीदेवताभ्यो नमः

mahākālī mahālakṣmī mahāsarasvatī devatābhyo namaḥ *heart*

I bow to the Deities, the Remover of Darkness, the Great Goddess of True Wealth, and the Great Goddess of All-Pervading Knowledge

ऐं बीजाय नमः

aiṃ bījāya namaḥ *anus*

I bow to the Seed Aiṃ

ह्रीं शक्तये नमः

hrīṃ śaktaye namaḥ *feet*

I bow to the Energy Hrīṃ

क्लीं कीलकाय नमः

klīṃ kīlakāya namaḥ *navel*

I bow to the Pin Klīṃ

ॐ ऐं ह्रीं क्लीं चामुण्डायै विच्चे

oṃ aiṃ hrīṃ klīṃ cāmuṇḍāyai vicce

Oṃ Aiṃ Hrīṃ Klīṃ Cāmuṇḍāyai Vicce

करन्यासः

kara nyāsaḥ

Establishment in the Hands

ॐ ऐं अङ्गुष्ठाभ्यां नमः

oṃ aiṃ aṅguṣṭhābhyāṃ namaḥ *thumb-forefinger*

Oṃ I bow to Aiṃ in the thumb

ॐ ह्रीं तर्जनीभ्यां स्वाहा

oṃ hrīṃ tarjanībhyāṃ svāhā *thumb-forefinger*

Oṃ I bow to Hrīṃ in the forefinger, I Am One With God!

ॐ क्लीं मध्यमाभ्यां वषट्

oṃ klīṃ madhyamābhyāṃ vaṣaṭ *thumb-middle finger*

Oṃ I bow to Klīṃ in the middle finger, Purify!

ॐ चामुण्डायै अनामिकाभ्यां हुम्

oṃ cāmuṇḍāyai anāmikābhyāṃ huṃ *thumb-ring finger*

Oṃ I bow to Cāmuṇḍā in the ring finger, Cut The Ego!

ॐ विच्चे कनिष्ठिकाभ्यां वौषट्

oṃ vicce kaniṣṭhikābhyāṃ vauṣaṭ *thumb-little finger*

Oṃ I bow to Vicce in the little finger, Ultimate Purity!

ॐ ऐं ह्रीं क्लीं चामुण्डायै विच्चे
करतलकरपृष्ठाभ्यां अस्त्राय फट्

**oṃ aiṃ hrīṃ klīṃ cāmuṇḍāyai vicce
karatalakara pṛṣṭhābhyāṃ astrāya phaṭ**

(roll hand over hand front and back and clap)
Oṃ Aiṃ Hrīṃ Klīṃ Cāmuṇḍāyai Vicce
with the weapon of Virtue

ॐ ऐं ह्रीं क्लीं चामुण्डायै विच्चे

oṃ aiṃ hrīṃ klīṃ cāmuṇḍāyai vicce

Oṃ Aiṃ Hrīṃ Klīṃ Cāmuṇḍāyai Vicce

हृदयादिन्यासः

hṛdayādi nyāsaḥ

Establishment in the Heart

ॐ ऐं हृदयाय नमः

oṃ aiṃ hṛdayāya namaḥ *touch heart*
Oṃ I bow to Aiṃ in the heart

ॐ ह्रीं शिरसे स्वाहा

oṃ hrīṃ śirase svāhā *top of head*
Oṃ I bow to Hrīṃ on top of the head, I am One with God!

ॐ क्लीं शिखायै वषट्

oṃ klīṃ śikhāyai vaṣaṭ *back of head*
Oṃ I bow to Klīṃ on the back of the head, Purify!

ॐ चामुण्डायै कवचाय हुम्

oṃ cāmuṇḍāyai kavacāya huṃ *cross arms*
Oṃ I bow to Cāmuṇḍā crossing both arms, Cut the Ego!

ॐ विच्चे नेत्रत्रयाय वौषट्

oṃ vicce netratrayāya vauṣaṭ *touch three eyes*
Oṃ I bow to Vicce on the three eyes, Ultimate Purity!

ॐ ऐं ह्रीं क्ली चामुण्डायै विच्चे
करतलकरपृष्ठाभ्यां अस्त्राय फट्

oṃ aiṃ hrīṃ klīṃ cāmuṇḍāyai vicce
karatalakara pṛṣṭhābhyāṃ astrāya phaṭ
(roll hand over hand front and back and clap)
Oṃ Aiṃ Hrīṃ Klīṃ Cāmuṇḍāyai Vicce
with the weapon of Virtue.

ॐ ऐं ह्रीं क्लीं चामुण्डायै विच्चे

oṃ aiṃ hrīṃ klīṃ cāmuṇḍāyai vicce
Oṃ Aiṃ Hrīṃ Klīṃ Cāmuṇḍāyai Vicce

अक्षरन्यासः

akṣaranyāsaḥ
Establishment of the letters

ॐ ऐं नमः

oṃ aiṃ namaḥ *top of head*
Oṃ I bow to Aiṃ

ॐ ह्रीं नमः

oṃ hrīṃ namaḥ *right eye*
Oṃ I bow to Hrīṃ

ॐ क्लीं नमः

oṃ klīṃ namaḥ *left eye*
Oṃ I bow to Klīṃ

ॐ चां नमः

oṃ cāṃ namaḥ *right ear*
Oṃ I bow to Cāṃ

ॐ मुं नमः

oṃ muṃ namaḥ *left ear*

Oṃ I bow to muṇ

ॐ डां नमः

oṃ ḍāṃ namaḥ *right nostril*

Oṃ I bow to ḍāṃ

ॐ यैं नमः

oṃ yaiṃ namaḥ *left nostril*

Oṃ I bow to yaiṃ

ॐ विं नमः

oṃ viṃ namaḥ *mouth*

Oṃ I bow to viṃ

ॐ चें नमः

oṃ ceṃ namaḥ *anus*

Oṃ I bow to ceṃ

ॐ ऐं ह्रीं क्लीं चामुण्डायै विच्चे

oṃ aiṃ hrīṃ klīṃ cāmuṇḍāyai vicce

Oṃ Aiṃ Hrīṃ Klīṃ Cāmuṇḍāyai Vicce

दिङ्न्यासः

diṅ nyāsaḥ
Establishment in the Directions

ॐ ऐं उदीच्यै नमः
oṃ aiṃ udīcyai namaḥ *north*
Oṃ I bow to Aiṃ in the North

ॐ ह्रीं प्राच्यै नमः
oṃ hrīṃ prācyai namaḥ *east*
Oṃ I bow to Hrīṃ in the East

ॐ क्लीं दक्षिणायै नमः
oṃ klīṃ dakṣiṇāyai namaḥ *south*
Oṃ I bow to Klīṃ in the South

ॐ चामुण्डायै प्रतीच्यै नमः
oṃ cāmuṇḍāyai pratīcyai namaḥ *west*
Oṃ I bow to Cāmuṇḍā in the West

ॐ विच्चे वायव्यै नमः
oṃ vicce vāyavyai namaḥ *northwest*
Oṃ I bow to Vicce in the Northwest

ॐ ऐं ऐशान्यै नमः
oṃ aiṃ aiśānyai namaḥ *northeast*
Oṃ I bow to Aiṃ in the Northeast

ॐ ह्रीं आग्नेय्यै नमः
oṃ hrīṃ āgneyyai namaḥ *southeast*
Oṃ I bow to Hrīṃ in the Southeast

ॐ क्लीं नैर्ऋत्यै नमः
oṃ klīṃ nairṛtyai namaḥ *southwest*
Oṃ I bow to Klīṃ in the Southwest

ॐ चामुण्डायै ऊर्ध्वायै नमः

oṃ cāmuṇḍāyai ūrdhvāyai namaḥ *up*

Oṃ I bow to Cāmuṇḍā, looking up

ॐ विच्चे भूम्यै नमः

oṃ vicce bhūmyai namaḥ *down*

Oṃ I bow to Vicce, looking down

ॐ ऐं ह्रीं क्लीं चामुण्डायै विच्चे

oṃ aiṃ hrīṃ klīṃ cāmuṇḍāyai vicce *ten directions*

Oṃ Aiṃ Hrīṃ Klīṃ Cāmuṇḍāyai Vicce

ध्यानम्

dhyānam

Meditation

खड्गं चक्रगदेषुचापपरिघाञ्छूलं भुशुण्डीं शिरः
शङ्खं संदधतीं करैस्त्रिनयनां सर्वाङ्गभूषावृताम् ।
नीलाश्मद्युतिमास्यपाददशकां सेवे महाकालिकां
यामस्तौत्स्वपिते हरौ कमलजो हन्तुं मधुं कैटभम् ॥

khaḍgaṃ cakra gadeṣu cāpa
parighāñ chūlaṃ bhuśuṇḍīṃ śiraḥ
śaṅkhaṃ saṃdadhatīṃ karai
strinayanāṃ sarvāṅga bhūṣāvṛtām ।
nīlāśmadyutimāsya pāda
daśakāṃ seve mahākālikāṃ
yāmastaut svapite harau kamalajo
hantuṃ madhuṃ kaiṭabham ॥

Bearing in Her ten hands the sword of worship, the discus of revolving time, the club of articulation, the bow of determination, the iron bar of restraint, the pike of attention, the sling, the head of egotism, and the conch of vibrations, She has three eyes and displays ornaments on all Her limbs. Shining like a blue gem, She has ten faces. I worship that Great Remover of Darkness whom the lotus-born Creative Capacity praised in order to slay Too Much and Too Little when the Supreme Consciousness was in sleep.

अक्षस्रक्परशुं गदेषुकुलिशं पद्मं धनुः कुण्डिकां
दण्डं शक्तिमसिं च चर्म जलजं घण्टां सुराभाजनम् ।
शूलं पाशसुदर्शने च दधतीं हस्तैः प्रसन्नाननां
सेवे सैरिभमर्दिनीमिह महालक्ष्मीं सरोजस्थिताम् ॥

akṣasrak paraśuṃ gadeṣu kuliśaṃ
padmaṃ dhanuḥ kuṇḍikāṃ
daṇḍaṃ śaktim asiṃ ca carma
jalajaṃ ghaṇṭāṃ surābhājanam |
śūlaṃ pāśa sudarśane ca
dadhatīṃ hastaiḥ prasannānanāṃ
seve sairibha mardinīmiha
mahālakṣmīṃ sarojasthitām ||

She with the beautiful face, the Destroyer of the Great Ego, is seated upon the lotus of peace. In Her hands She holds the rosary of alphabets, the battle axe of good actions, the club of articulation, the arrow of speech, the thunderbolt of illumination, the lotus of peace, the bow of determination, the water pot of purification, the staff of discipline, energy, the sword of worship, the shield of faith, the conch of vibrations, the bell of continuous tone, the wine cup of joy, the pike of concentration, the net of unity, and the discus of revolving time, named Excellent Intuitive Vision. I worship that Great Goddess of True Wealth.

घण्टाशूलहलानि शङ्खमुसले चक्रं धनुः सायकं
हस्ताब्जैर्दधतीं घनान्तविलसच्छीतांशुतुल्यप्रभाम् ।
गौरीदेहसमुद्भवां त्रिजगतामाधारभूतां महा-
पूर्वामत्र सरस्वतीमनुभजे शुम्भादिदैत्यार्दिनीम् ॥

ghaṇṭā śūla halāni śaṅkha
musale cakraṃ dhanuḥ sāyakaṃ
hastābjair dadhatīṃ ghanānta
vilasacchītāṃśutulya prabhām |
gaurīdeha samudbhavāṃ
trijagatām ādhārabhūtāṃ mahā-
pūrvāmatra sarasvatīm anubhaje
śumbhādi daityārdinīm ||

Bearing in Her lotus hands the bell of continuous tone, the pike of concentration, the plow sowing the seeds of the Way of Truth to Wisdom, the conch of vibrations, the pestle of refinement, the discus of revolving time, the bow of determination, and the arrow of speech; whose radiance is like the moon in autumn; whose appearance is most beautiful; who is manifested from the body of She Who is Rays of Light; and is the support of the three worlds, that Great Goddess of All-Pervading Knowledge, who destroyed Self-Conceit and other thoughts, I worship.

ॐ ऐं ह्रीं अक्षमालिकायै नमः

oṃ aiṃ hrīṃ akṣa mālikāyai namaḥ
Oṃ Aiṃ Hrīṃ I bow to the Rosary of Letters

ॐ मां माले महामाये सर्वशक्तिस्वरूपिणि ।
चतुर्वर्गस्त्वयि न्यस्तस्तस्मान्मे सिद्धिदा भव ॥

oṃ māṃ māle mahāmāye sarva śakti svarūpiṇi |
catur vargas tvayi nyastas
tasmān me siddhidā bhava ||

Oṃ My Rosary, the Great Measurement of Consciousness, containing all energy within as your intrinsic nature, give to me the attainment of your Perfection, fulfilling the four objectives of life.

ॐ अविघ्नं कुरु माले त्वं गृह्णामि दक्षिणे करे ।
जपकाले च सिद्ध्यर्थं प्रसीद मम सिद्धये ॥

oṃ avighnaṃ kuru māle tvaṃ gṛhṇāmi dakṣiṇe kare |
japakāle ca siddhyarthaṃ prasīda mama siddhaye ||
Oṃ Rosary, You please remove all obstacles. I hold you in my right hand. At the time of recitation be pleased with me. Allow me to attain the Highest Perfection.

ॐ अक्षमालाधिपतये सुसिद्धिं देहि देहि सर्वमन्त्रार्थसाधिनि
साधय साधय सर्वसिद्धिं परिकल्पय परिकल्पय मे स्वाहा ॥
oṃ akṣa mālā dhipataye susiddhiṃ dehi dehi sarva mantrārtha sādhini sādhaya sādhaya sarva siddhiṃ parikalpaya parikalpaya me svāhā ||
Oṃ Rosary of rudrākṣa seeds, my Lord, give to me excellent attainment. Give to me, give to me. Illuminate the meanings of all mantras, illuminate, illuminate! Fashion me with all excellent attainments, fashion me! I am One with God!

ॐ ऐं ह्रीं क्लीं चामुण्डायै विच्चे
oṃ aiṃ hrīṃ klīṃ cāmuṇḍāyai vicce 108 times
Oṃ Aiṃ Hrīṃ Klīṃ Cāmuṇḍāyai Vicce

ॐ गुह्यातिगुह्यगोप्त्री त्वं गृहाणास्मत्कृतं जपम् ।
सिद्धिर्भवतु मे देवि त्वत्प्रसादान्महेश्वरि ॥
oṃ guhyātiguhyagoptrī tvaṃ
gṛhāṇās matkṛtaṃ japam |
siddhir bhavatu me devi tvat prasādān maheśvari ||
Oh Goddess, You are the Protector of the most secret of mystical secrets. Please accept the recitation that I have offered and grant to me the attainment of Perfection.

ध्यानम्

dhyānam
Meditation

ॐ विद्युद्दामसमप्रभां मृगपतिस्कन्धस्थितां भीषणां
कन्याभिः करवालखेटविलसद्धस्ताभिरासेविताम् ।
हस्तैश्चक्रगदासिखेटविशिखांश्चापं गुणं तर्जनीं
बिभ्राणामनलात्मिकां शशिधरां दुर्गां त्रिनेत्रां भजे ॥

oṃ vidyud dāmasamaprabhāṃ
mṛgapati skandhasthitāṃ bhīṣaṇāṃ
kanyābhiḥ karavālakheṭa
vilasaddhastābhirā sevitām ।
hastaiścakra gadāsi kheṭa
viśikhāṃścāpaṃ guṇaṃ tarjanīṃ
bibhrāṇāmanalātmikāṃ śaśidharāṃ
durgāṃ trinetrāṃ bhaje ॥

I meditate upon the three-eyed Goddess, Durgā, the Reliever of Difficulties; the luster of Her beautiful body is like lightning. She sits upon the shoulders of a lion and appears very fierce. Many maidens holding the double-edged sword and shield in their hands are standing at readiness to serve Her. She holds in Her hands the discus, club, double-edged sword, shield, arrow, bow, net, and the mudrā connecting the thumb and the pointer finger, with the other three fingers extended upwards, indicating the granting of wisdom. Her intrinsic nature is fire, and upon her head She wears the moon as a crown.

ॐ

oṃ

Devi 13

श्री दुर्गायै नमः
śrī durgāyai namaḥ
We bow to She who Removes All Difficulties

अथ श्रीदुर्गासप्तशती
atha śrī durgā saptaśatī
And Now,
The Seven Hundred Verses in Praise of
She Who Removes all Difficulties

प्रथमोऽध्यायः
prathamo-dhyāyaḥ
Chapter One

विनियोगः
viniyogaḥ
Application

ॐ प्रथमचरित्रस्य ब्रह्मा ऋषिः महाकाली देवता गायत्री छन्दः नन्दा शक्तिः रक्तदन्तिका बीजम् अग्निस्तत्त्वम् ऋग्वेदः स्वरूपम् श्रीमहाकालीप्रीत्यर्थे प्रथमचरित्रजपे विनियोगः ।

oṃ prathama caritrasya brahmā ṛṣiḥ mahākālī devatā gāyatrī chandaḥ nandā śaktiḥ raktadantikā bījam agnistattvam ṛgvedaḥ svarūpam śrī mahākālī prītyarthe prathama caritra jape viniyogaḥ |

Oṃ Presenting the first episode, the Creative Capacity is the Seer, the Great Remover of Darkness is the deity, Gāyatrī (24 syllables to the verse) is the meter, Nandā is the energy, Raktadantikā is the seed, Fire is the principle, Ṛg Veda is the intrinsic nature, and for the satisfaction of the Great Remover of Darkness this first episode is being applied in recitation.

ध्यानम्

dhyānam

Meditation

खड्गं चक्रगदेषुचापपरिघाञ्छूलं भुशुण्डीं शिरः
शङ्खं संदधतीं करैस्त्रिनयनां सर्वाङ्गभूषावृताम् ।
नीलाश्मद्युतिमास्यपाददशकां सेवे महाकालिकां
यामस्तौत्स्वपिते हरौ कमलजो हन्तुं मधुं कैटभम् ॥

khaḍgaṃ cakra gadeṣu cāpa
parighāñ chūlaṃ bhuśuṇḍīṃ śiraḥ
śaṅkhaṃ saṃdadhatīṃ karai
strinayanāṃ sarvāṅga bhūṣāvṛtām ।
nīlāśmadyutimāsya pāda
daśakāṃ seve mahākālikāṃ
yāmastaut svapite harau kamalajo
hantuṃ madhuṃ kaiṭabham ॥

Bearing in Her ten hands the sword of worship, the discus of revolving time, the club of articulation, the bow of determination, the iron bar of restraint, the pike of attention, the sling, the head of egotism, and the conch of vibrations, She has three eyes and displays ornaments on all Her limbs. Shining like a blue gem, She has ten faces. I worship that Great Remover of Darkness whom the lotus-born Creative Capacity praised in order to slay Too Much and Too Little, when the Supreme Consciousness was in sleep.

ॐ नमश्चण्डिकायै

oṃ namaścaṇḍikāyai

Oṃ We bow to She Who Tears Apart Thought.

- 1 -

ॐ ऐं मार्कण्डेय उवाच ॥

oṃ aiṃ mārkaṇḍeya uvāca ||

Oṃ Aiṃ Mārkaṇḍeya said:

- 2 -

सावर्णिः सूर्यतनयो यो मनुः कथ्यतेऽष्टमः ।

निशामय तदुत्पत्तिं विस्तराद् गदतो मम ॥

sāvarṇiḥ sūryatanayo yo manuḥ kathyate-ṣṭamaḥ |
niśāmaya tadutpattiṃ vistarād gadato mama ||

He who belongs to all colors, tribes, and castes, the son of the Light of Wisdom, is known as the eighth Manifestation of Wisdom. I describe his origins at length. Listen.

- 3 -

महामायानुभावेन यथा मन्वन्तराधिपः ।

स बभूव महाभागः सावर्णिस्तनयो रवेः ॥

mahāmāyā nubhāvena yathā manvantarādhipaḥ |
sa babhūva mahā bhāgaḥ sāvarṇistanayo raveḥ ||

With the grace of the Supreme Goddess, the Great Measurement of Consciousness, the son of the Light, He Who Belongs to All, became the highly eminent master of the fourteenth part of a day of the Infinite. On this subject I speak.

- 4 -

स्वारोचिषेऽन्तरे पूर्वं चैत्रवंशसमुद्भवः ।

सुरथो नाम राजाभूत्समस्ते क्षितिमण्डले ॥

svārociṣe-ntare pūrvaṃ caitravaṃśa samudbhavaḥ |
suratho nāma rājābhūt samaste kṣiti maṇḍale ||

In times of old, in the period ruled by He who makes Himself Radiant, there was a King named the Conveyor of Good Thoughts, born of the lineage of Those Who Dwell in Consciousness, and he had authority over all the regions of the earth.

- 5 -

तस्य पालयतः सम्यक् प्रजाः पुत्रानिवौरसान् ।
बभूवुः शत्रवो भूपाः कोलाविध्वंसिनस्तदा ॥

tasya pālayataḥ samyak prajāḥ putrā nivaurasān I
babhūvuḥ śatravo bhūpāḥ kolā vidhvaṃsi nastadā II

He protected his subjects in the Way of Truth as a father to his children. At that time the kings who were the Destroyers of Worship became his enemies.

- 6 -

तस्य तैरभवद् युद्धमतिप्रबलदण्डिनः ।
न्यूनैरपि स तैर्युद्धे कोलाविध्वंसिभिर्जितः ॥

tasya tairabhavad yuddham ati prabala daṇḍinaḥ I
nyūnairapi sa tairyuddhe kolāvidhvaṃsibhirjitaḥ II

Good Thoughts moved against the Destroyers of Worship to engage in battle, and even though they were fewer in numbers, nevertheless Good Thoughts was defeated.

- 7 -

ततः स्वपुरमायातो निजदेशाधिपोऽभवत् ।
आक्रान्तः स महाभागस्तैस्तदा प्रबलारिभिः ॥

tataḥ svapura māyāto nija deśā dhipo-bhavat I
ākrāntaḥ sa mahā bhāgas taistadā prabalāribhiḥ II

Then he returned to his own city, renouncing his authority over the earth, and continued to rule in his own land. But there, too, the powerful enemies pursued that illustrious one and again attacked.

- 8 -

अमात्यैर्बलिभिर्दुष्टैर्दुर्बलस्य दुरात्मभिः ।
कोशो बलं चापहृतं तत्रापि स्वपुरे ततः ॥

amātyair balibhir duṣṭair durbalasya durātmabhiḥ I
kośo balaṃ cāpahṛtaṃ tatrāpi svapure tataḥ II

The King's strength was severely depleted, his enemies were mighty, and his unscrupulous ministers took over the army and the treasury.

- 9 -

ततो मृगयाव्याजेन हृतस्वाम्यः स भूपतिः ।

एकाकी हयमारुह्य जगाम गहनं वनम् ॥

tato mṛgayāvyājena hṛtasvāmyaḥ sa bhūpatiḥ |

ekākī hayamāruhya jagāma gahanaṃ vanam ||

Good Thought's sovereignty was lost, and therefore riding alone upon his horse, he fled into the dense forest on the pretext of hunting.

- 10 -

स तत्राश्रममद्राक्षीद् द्विजवर्यस्य मेधसः ।

प्रशान्तश्वापदाकीर्णं मुनिशिष्योपशोभितम् ॥

sa tatrāśramamadrākṣīd dvija varyasya medhasaḥ |

praśāntaśvā padākīrṇaṃ muni śiṣyo paśobhitam ||

There he came upon the hermitage of a great wise master, the Intellect of Love, where he saw so many dangerous animals living together in the greatest of peace. Many disciples to the Great Wise One were enhancing the magnificence of the forest.

- 11 -

तस्थौ कंचित्स कालं च मुनिना तेन सत्कृतः ।

इतश्चेतश्च विचरंस्तस्मिन्मुनिवराश्रमे ॥

tasthau kaṃcitsa kālaṃ ca muninā tena satkṛtaḥ |

itaśce taśca vicaraṃs tasmin muni varāśrame ||

The Great Wise One made him welcome there with respect, and the King wandered about the hermitage for some time.

- 12 -

सोऽचिन्तयत्तदा तत्र ममत्वाकृष्टचेतनः ।

मत्पूर्वैः पालितं पूर्वं मया हीनं पुरं हि तत् ॥

so-cintayat tadā tatra mamatvā kṛṣṭa cetanaḥ |

matpūrvaiḥ pālitaṃ pūrvaṃ

mayā hīnaṃ puraṃ hi tat ||

Then his contemplations were overcome with egotism and attachment, and he thought, "The city that my ancestors protected in former times has now gone from me.

- 13 -

मद्भृत्यैस्तैरसद्वृत्तैर्धर्मतः पाल्यते न वा ।

न जाने स प्रधानो मे शूरहस्ती सदामदः ॥

madbhṛtyais tairasad vṛttair
dharmataḥ pālyate na vā ।
na jāne sa pradhāno me śūrahastī sadāmadaḥ ॥

Are my unprincipled employees protecting and righteously preserving the kingdom in my absence? And my foremost elephant, heroic and continually delighted,

- 14 -

मम वैरिवशं यातः कान् भोगानुपलप्स्यते ।

ये ममानुगता नित्यं प्रसादधनभोजनैः ॥

mama vairivaśaṃ yātaḥ kān bhogānupalapsyate ।
ye mamānugatā nityaṃ prasāda dhana bhojanaiḥ ॥

will not experience the pleasures he enjoyed during my time. Those who followed me with the eternal way of offering wealth and food,

- 15 -

अनुवृत्तिं ध्रुवं तेऽद्य कुर्वन्त्यन्यमहीभृताम् ।

असम्यग्व्ययशीलैस्तैः कुर्वद्भिः सततं व्ययम् ॥

anuvṛttiṃ dhruvaṃ te-dya
kurvantyan yamahībhṛtām ।
asamyagvyayaśīlaistaiḥ
kurvadbhiḥ satataṃ vyayam ॥

definitely may now be serving other kings, who are spending without restraint in continual extravagance."

- 16 -

संचितः सोऽतिदुःखेन क्षयं कोशो गमिष्यति ।

एतच्चान्यच्च सततं चिन्तयामास पार्थिवः ॥

saṃcitaḥ so-tiduḥkhena kṣayaṃ kośo gamiṣyati ।
etaccānyacca satataṃ cintayāmāsa pārthivaḥ ॥

And as the King went into deeper contemplation of the loss of his wealth and his present situation, his mind became absorbed in pain and his thoughts controlled by worldly attachments.

\- 17 -

तत्र विप्राश्रमाभ्याशे वैश्यमेकं ददर्श सः ।
स पृष्टस्तेन कस्त्वं भो हेतुश्चागमनेऽत्र कः ॥

tatra viprāśram ābhyāśe vaiśyamekaṃ dadarśa saḥ |
sa pṛṣṭastena kastvaṃ bho hetuścāgamane-tra kaḥ ||

There in the hermitage of the great teacher he saw a businessman, and after greeting him, asked, "Who are you, and what is the reason for your coming here?

\- 18 -

सशोक इव कस्मात्त्वं दुर्मना इव लक्ष्यसे ।
इत्याकर्ण्य वचस्तस्य भूपतेः प्रणयोदितम् ॥

saśoka iva kasmāttvaṃ durmanā iva lakṣyase |
ityākarṇya vacastasya bhūpateḥ praṇayoditam ||

Why do you appear to be in a great sorrow as though your mind were far from its goal?" asked the King in a pleasant voice and friendly spirit.

\- 19 -

प्रत्युवाच स तं वैश्यः प्रश्रयावनतो नृपम् ॥

pratyuvāca sa taṃ vaiśyaḥ praśrayāvanato nṛpam ||

And with words full of modesty and humble respect, the businessman replied to the King.

\- 20 -

वैश्य उवाच ॥

vaiśya uvāca ||

The Businessman said:

\- 21 -

समाधिर्नाम वैश्योऽहमुत्पन्नो धनिनां कुले ॥

samādhirnāma vaiśyo-hamutpanno dhaninām kule ||

Pure Intuitive Perception is my name, and I'm a businessman born in the lineage of those who worship Infinite Energy.

- 22 -

पुत्रदारैर्निरस्तश्च धनलोभादसाधुभिः ।
विहीनश्च धनैर्दारैः पुत्रैरादाय मे धनम् ॥

putradārair nirastaśca dhana lobhāda sādhubhiḥ |
vihīnaśca dhanairdāraiḥ putrairādāya me dhanam ||

My wife and children have cast me out because of their greed for wealth, and have caused me to become an ascetic Seeker of Truth. I have been deprived of wealth, and my wife and sons have seized my estate,

- 23 -

वनमभ्यागतो दुःखी निरस्तश्चाप्तबन्धुभिः ।
सोऽहं न वेद्मि पुत्राणां कुशलाकुशलात्मिकाम् ॥

vanamabhyāgato duḥkhī nirastaścāpta bandhubhiḥ |
so-haṃ na vedmi putrāṇāṃ kuśalākuśalāt mikām ||

and having been cast out by my trusted kinsmen and bound by sorrow, I have come into the forest. But now I don't know if happiness or unhappiness is with my children.

- 24 -

प्रवृत्तिं स्वजनानां च दाराणां चात्र संस्थितः ।
किं नु तेषां गृहे क्षेममक्षेमं किं नु साम्प्रतम् ॥

pravṛttiṃ svajanānāṃ ca dārāṇāṃ cātra saṃsthitaḥ |
kiṃ nu teṣāṃ gṛhe kṣema
makṣemaṃ kiṃ nu sāmpratam ||

Staying here I am unaware of the activities of my family. Do they experience tranquility at present or does discomfort reign?

- 25 -

कथं ते किं नु सद्वृत्ता दुर्वृत्ताः किं नु मे सुताः ॥

kathaṃ te kiṃ nu sad vṛttā
durvṛttāḥ kiṃ nu me sutāḥ ||

Are my sons observing good conduct, or are they behaving with evil and wickedness?

- 26 -

राजोवाच ॥

rājovāca ॥

The King said:

- 27 -

यैर्निरस्तो भवांल्लुब्धैः पुत्रदारादिभिर्धनैः ॥

yairnirasto bhavāmllubdhaiḥ
putradārādibhir dhanaiḥ ॥

You have been cast out by your wife and children because of their avarice and greed;

- 28 -

तेषु किं भवतः स्नेहमनुबध्नाति मानसम् ॥

teṣu kiṃ bhavataḥ sneham anubadhnāti mānasam ॥

Why are your thoughts so bound in love for them?

- 29 -

वैश्य उवाच ॥

vaiśya uvāca ॥

The Businessman said:

- 30 -

एवमेतद्यथा प्राह भवानस्मद्गतं वचः ॥

evametadyathā prāha bhavānasmadgataṃ vacaḥ ॥

Just as you were speaking to me I was having this same thought.

- 31 -

किं करोमि न बध्नाति मम निष्ठुरतां मनः ।
यैः संत्यज्य पितृस्नेहं धनलुब्धैर्निराकृतः ॥

kiṃ karomi na badhnāti mama niṣṭhuratāṃ manaḥ ।
yaiḥ saṃtyajya pitṛsnehaṃ dhana lubdhair nirākṛtaḥ ॥

- 32 -

पतिस्वजनहार्दं च हार्दि तेष्वेव मे मनः ।
किमेतन्नाभिजानामि जानन्नपि महामते ॥

patisvajanahārdaṃ ca hārdi teṣveva me manaḥ ।
ki me tannābhi jānāmi jānannapi mahā mate ॥

31-32. But what can I do? My mind does not entertain severity. They have sacrificed a father's love, and affection for a master and kinsman, in their greed for wealth, yet my mind joins them all in affection. Though knowing all this, Oh Great Learned One, I fail to understand how

- 33 -

यत्प्रेमप्रवणं चित्तं विगुणेष्वपि बन्धुषु ।
तेषां कृते मे निःश्वासो दौर्मनस्यं च जायते ॥

yat prema pravaṇaṃ cittaṃ viguṇeṣvapi bandhuṣu I
teṣāṃ kṛte me niḥśvāso daurmanasyaṃ ca jāyate II

my contemplations are disposed to love even characterless relations. Because of their actions, I heave a sigh and feel dejection and despair.

- 34 -

करोमि किं यन्न मनस्तेष्वप्रीतिषु निष्ठुरम् ॥

karomi kiṃ yanna manasteṣ vaprītiṣu niṣṭhuram II

But what can I do? My mind does not become hard, even for those who are devoid of love for me.

- 35 -

मार्कण्डेय उवाच ॥

mārkaṇḍeya uvāca II

Mārkaṇḍeya said:

- 36 -

ततस्तौ सहितौ विप्र तं मुनिं समुपस्थितौ ॥

tatastau sahitau vipra taṃ muniṃ samupasthitau II

- 37 -

समाधिर्नाम वैश्योऽसौ स च पार्थिवसत्तमः ।
कृत्वा तु तौ यथान्यायं यथार्हं तेन संविदम् ॥

samādhirnāma vaiśyo-sau sa ca pārthiva sattamaḥ I
kṛtvā tu tau yathānyāyaṃ
yathārhaṃ tena saṃvidam II

- 38 -

उपविष्टौ कथाः काश्चिच्चक्रतुर्वैश्यपार्थिवौ ॥

upaviṣṭau kathāḥ kāścic cakraturvaiśya pārthivau II

36-38. Then together the two, Pure Intuitive Perception, (the businessman), and the very noble monarch, (Good Thoughts, the king), arrived in the circular sacrificial area in the presence of the Great Wise Master. Observing the proper customs and congenialities for learning, they sat down and engaged in conversation.

- 39 -

राजोवाच ॥

rājovāca ||

The King said:

- 40 -

भगवंस्त्वामहं प्रष्टुमिच्छाम्येकं वदस्व तत् ॥

bhagavaṃstvāmahaṃ praṣṭum
icchām yekaṃ vadasva tat ||

You who have united with the Infinite Self, I wish to ask only one question of you, and please be pleased to speak on that.

- 41 -

दुःखाय यन्मे मनसः स्वचित्तायत्ततां विना ।
ममत्वं गतराज्यस्य राज्याङ्गेष्वखिलेष्वपि ॥

duḥkhāya yanme manasaḥ svacit tāyat tatāṃ vinā |
mamatvaṃ gatarājyasya rājyāṅgeṣva khileṣvapi ||

My reflections are without control and give much pain to my mind. I have great attachment to the kingdom and to every aspect of the status that has gone from me.

- 42 -

जानतोऽपि यथाज्ञस्य किमेतन्मुनिसत्तम ।
अयं च निकृतः पुत्रैर्दारैर्भृत्यैस्तथोज्झितः ॥

jānato-pi yathā jñasya kimetan muni sattama |
ayaṃ ca nikṛtaḥ putrair dārair bhṛtyaistathoj jhitaḥ ||

But even with this knowledge, in the manner of one who is ignorant, I still feel pain. Why is that, Oh Great Learned One? And here this humble man, cheated and deceived by his wife and children and employees, and cast out;

- 43 -

स्वजनेन च संत्यक्तस्तेषु हार्दी तथाप्यति ।

एवमेष तथाहं च द्वावप्यत्यन्तदुःखितौ ॥

svajanena ca saṃtyaktas teṣu hārdī tathāpyati |

evameṣa tathāhaṃ ca dvāvap yatyanta duḥkhitau ||

even deserted by his own relations, he still maintains the greatest affection for them. Thus both of us are feeling pain.

- 44 -

दृष्टदोषेऽपि विषये ममत्वाकृष्टमानसौ ।

तत्किमेतन्महाभाग यन्मोहो ज्ञानिनोरपि ॥

dṛṣṭa doṣe-pi viṣaye mamatvā kṛṣṭa mānasau |

tat kimetan mahā bhāga yanmoho jñāni norapi ||

Even though we see the defects in our contemplations, nevertheless our minds are drawn into attachment and egotism. What is it, Oh Exalted One, that causes this ignorance, even in the presence of our wisdom and understanding?

- 45 -

ममास्य च भवत्येषा विवेकान्धस्य मूढता ॥

mamāsya ca bhavat yeṣā vivekāndhasya mūḍhatā ||

He and I are as fools without the capacity of discrimination.

- 46 -

ऋषिरुवाच ॥

ṛṣi ruvāca ||

The Ṛṣi said:

- 47 -

ज्ञानमस्ति समस्तस्य जन्तोर्विषयगोचरे ॥

jñānamasti samastasya jantorviṣaya gocare ||

Oh Great Light of Luminous Splendor, all that lives has knowledge of objects perceived by the senses.

- 48 -

विषयश्च महाभाग याति चैवं पृथक् पृथक् ।

दिवान्धाः प्राणिनः केचिद्रात्रावन्धास्तथापरे ॥

viṣayaśca mahābhāga yāti caivaṃ pṛthak pṛthak |
divāndhāḥ prāṇinaḥ kecid rātrāvandhās tathāpare ||

But the objects of the senses are perceived differently by all beings. Some beings are unable to see in the day, while others are unable to see in the night.

\- 49 -

केचिद्दिवा तथा रात्रौ प्राणिनस्तुल्यदृष्टयः ।
ज्ञानिनो मनुजाः सत्यं किं तु ते न हि केवलम् ॥

keciddivā tathā rātrau prāṇinastulyadṛṣṭayaḥ |
jñānino manujāḥ satyaṃ kiṃ tu te na hi kevalam ||

Still others have the capacity to see equally well in the day and in the night. It is true that humans have a capacity of understanding, but not only humans.

\- 50 -

यतो हि ज्ञानिनः सर्वे पशुपक्षिमृगादयः ।
ज्ञानं च तन्मनुष्याणां यत्तेषां मृगपक्षिणाम् ॥

yato hi jñāninaḥ sarve paśu pakṣi mṛgādayaḥ |
jñānaṃ ca tanmanuṣyāṇāṃ
yatteṣāṃ mṛgapakṣiṇām ||

This knowledge is common to all animals, whether beasts of the forest or birds of the air; all living beings possess this understanding just as human beings.

\- 51 -

मनुष्याणां च यत्तेषां तुल्यमन्यत्तथोभयोः ।
ज्ञानेऽपि सति पश्यैतान् पतङ्गाञ्छावचञ्चुषु ॥

manuṣyāṇāṃ ca yatteṣāṃ tulyamanyat tathobhayoḥ |
jñāne-pi sati paśyaitān pataṅgāñchā vacañcuṣu ||

Then just as in humans, the capacity of understanding exists in all animals, and this is a general principle that the understanding of the two is alike. Look at those birds.

\- 52 -

कणमोक्षादृतान्मोहात्पीड्यमानानपि क्षुधा ।
मानुषा मनुजव्याघ्र साभिलाषाः सुतान् प्रति ॥

kaṇamokṣā dṛtānmohāt pīḍyamānānapi kṣudhā |
mānuṣā manu javyāghra sābhilāṣāḥ sutān prati ||
Though they have knowledge, because of attachment they are ignoring their own hunger and are busy putting food into the mouths of their children. But Supreme Among Men, humans are different because they are desirous of obtaining reciprocal assistance from their children in their need.

- 53 -

लोभात्प्रत्युपकाराय नन्वेतान् किं न पश्यसि ।

तथापि ममतावर्त्ते मोहगर्ते निपातिताः ॥

lobhāt pratyupakārāya nanvetān kiṃ na paśyasi |
tathāpi mamatāvartte mohagarte nipātitāḥ ||
Can't you see that desire in their greed? People are hurled into the whirlpool of attachment and the pit of delusion

- 54 -

महामायाप्रभावेण संसारस्थिति कारिणा ।

तन्नात्र विस्मयः कार्यो योगनिद्रा जगत्पतेः ॥

mahāmāyā prabhāveṇa saṃsāra sthiti kāriṇā |
tannātra vismayaḥ kāryo yoganidrā jagat pateḥ ||
by the Great Measurement of Consciousness, who is the cause of the circumstance of all objects in the creation and of their relationships. For this there is no need to wonder. The Consciousness of the Universe, the Supreme Lord, is put into the sleep of divine union

- 55 -

महामाया हरेश्चैषा तया संमोह्यते जगत् ।

ज्ञानिनामपि चेतांसि देवी भगवती हि सा ॥

mahāmāyā hareścaiṣā tayā saṃmohyate jagat |
jñāninâmapi cetāṃsi devī bhagavatī hi sā ||
by the Great Measurement, and therefore the world is deluded by Her. She, this Supreme Goddess, the Great Measurement of Consciousness, attracts the perceiving capacity of all sensible beings

- 56 -

बलादाकृष्य मोहाय महामाया प्रयच्छति ।

तया विसृजते विश्वं जगदेतच्चराचरम् ॥

balādākṛṣya mohāya mahāmāyā prayacchati |

tayā visṛjate viśvaṃjagadetac carācaram ||

with such force as to thrust them into the ignorance of egotistic attachment. The universe is born from Her, the perceivable world with all that moves and moves not,

- 57 -

सैषा प्रसन्ना वरदा नृणां भवति मुक्तये ।

सा विद्या परमा मुक्तेर्हेतुभूता सनातनी ॥

saiṣā prasannā varadā nṛṇāṃ bhavati muktaye |

sā vidyā paramā mukter hetu bhūtā sanātanī ||

and it is She who, after satisfaction, bestows upon humans the blessing of liberation. It is She who is the ultimate knowledge, the cause of the liberation of Consciousness, the Eternal Existence;

- 58 -

संसारबन्धहेतुश्च सैव सर्वेश्वरेश्वरी ॥

saṃsāra bandha hetuśca saiva sarveśvareśvarī ||

and She is the cause of the bondage of Consciousness to objects and their relationships, the full and complete Supreme over all sovereigns.

- 59 -

राजोवाच ॥

rājovāca ||

The King said:

- 60 -

भगवन् का हि सा देवी महामायेति यां भवान् ॥

bhagavan kā hi sā devī mahāmāyeti yāṃ bhavān ||

Revered One, who is that Goddess, the Great Measurement of Consciousness, of whom you speak?

- 61 -

ब्रवीति कथमुत्पन्ना सा कर्मास्याश्च किं द्विज ।
यत्प्रभावा च सा देवी यत्स्वरूपा यदुद्भवा ॥

bravīti kathamutpannā sā karmāsyāśca kiṃ dvija |
yat prabhāvā ca sā devī yat svarūpā yadudbhavā ||

Tell, Oh Wise One, of the actions by which She is known. What is the cause of this Goddess, what is Her intrinsic nature, what of Her birth?

- 62 -

तत्सर्वं श्रोतुमिच्छामि त्वत्तो ब्रह्मविदां वर ॥

tatsarvaṃ śrotumicchāmi tvatto brahma vidāṃ vara ||

All this I wish to hear from you, Oh Most Excellent among the Knowers of the One Self-Existent Being.

- 63 -

ऋषिरुवाच ॥

ṛṣi ruvāca ||

The Ṛṣi said:

- 64 -

नित्यैव सा जगन्मूर्तिस्तया सर्वमिदं ततम् ॥

nityaiva sā jaganmūrtis tayā sarvam idaṃ tatam ||

She is Eternal, and the gross world and all the individual phenomena in it are Her visible forms. In many ways She is manifest. Hear of them from me.

- 65 -

तथापि तत्समुत्पत्तिर्बहुधा श्रूयतां मम ।
देवानां कार्यसिद्ध्यर्थमाविर्भवति सा यदा ॥

tathāpi tat samutpattir bahudhā śrūyatāṃ mama |
devānāṃ kārya siddhyartham āvirbhavati sā yadā ||

- 66 -

उत्पन्नेति तदा लोके सा नित्याप्यभिधीयते ।
योगनिद्रां यदा विष्णुर्जगत्येकार्णवीकृते ॥

utpanneti tadā loke sā nityāpyabhi dhīyate |
yoganidrāṃ yadā viṣṇur jagat yekārṇa vīkṛte ||

- 67 -

आस्तीर्य शेषमभजत्कल्पान्ते भगवान् प्रभुः ।
तदा द्वावसुरौ घोरौ विख्यातौ मधुकैटभौ ॥

āstīrya śeṣamabhajat kalpānte bhagavān prabhuḥ |
tadā dvāvasurau ghorau vikhyātau madhu kaiṭabhau ||

- 68 -

विष्णुकर्णमलोद्भूतौ हन्तुं ब्रह्माणमुद्यतौ ।
स नाभिकमले विष्णोः स्थितो ब्रह्मा प्रजापतिः ॥

viṣṇukarṇamalod bhūtau
hantuṃ brahmāṇamudyatau |
sa nābhi kamale viṣṇoḥ sthito brahmā prajāpatiḥ ||

65-68. Notwithstanding that She is eternal and unborn, nevertheless when divine ones perform actions for the attainment of this cause, She becomes manifest in the world. At the end of the period for manifestation when the gross world was indistinguishable potentiality, the revered Divine Lord, the Universal Consciousness, rested at the end of infinity in the sleep of divine union. Then from the dirt of the ears of this Perceiving Capacity arose two terrible thoughts, known as Too Much and Too Little. They were ready to slay the divine Creative Capacity, who was seated in the lotus blossom in the navel of Consciousness. The Creative Capacity, the Ruler of Beings,

- 69 -

दृष्ट्वा तावसुरौ चोग्रौ प्रसुप्तं च जनार्दनम् ।
तुष्टाव योगनिद्रां तामेकाग्रहृदयस्थितः ॥

dṛṣṭvā tāvasurau cograu prasuptaṃ ca janārdanam |
tuṣṭāva yoganidrāṃ tāmekāgra hṛdayasthitaḥ ||

seeing the approach of the two thoughts and the Causer of Being indifferently asleep in Divine Union, then with one-pointed attention He began to praise Divine Union from His heart.

- 70 -

विबोधनार्थाय हरेर्हरिनेत्रकृतालयाम् ।
विश्वेश्वरीं जगद्धात्रीं स्थितिसंहारकारिणीम् ॥

vibodhanārthāya harer hari netra kṛtālayām |
viśveśvarīṃ jagaddhātrīṃ sthiti saṃhārakāriṇīm ||
For the purpose of awakening the eyes of Consciousness, the Revered One of Brilliant Light extolled the Ruler of the Universe, Creator of the Perceivable World, Cause of evolution and devolution,

\- 71 -

निद्रां भगवतीं विष्णोरतुलां तेजसः प्रभुः ॥
nidrāṃ bhagavatīṃ viṣṇoratulāṃ tejasaḥ prabhuḥ ||
Goddess of Sleep, the unequaled Energy of Consciousness.

\- 72 -

ब्रह्मोवाच ॥
brahmovāca ||
The Creative Capacity said:

\- 73 -

त्वं स्वाहा त्वं स्वधा त्वं हि वषट्कारः स्वरात्मिका ॥
tvaṃ svāhā tvaṃ svadhā tvaṃ hi
vaṣaṭkāraḥ svarātmikā ||
You are oblations of I am One with God, you are oblations of Union with Ancestors. You are oblations of Purity, and the Consciousness of all sound.

\- 74 -

सुधा त्वमक्षरे नित्ये त्रिधा मात्रात्मिका स्थिता ।
अर्धमात्रास्थिता नित्या यानुच्चार्या विशेषतः ॥
sudhā tvamakṣare nitye tridhā mātrātmikā sthitā |
ardhamātrā sthitā nityā yānuccāryā viśeṣataḥ ||
You are the eternal essence of all the letters, and the consciousness of the three vowels (A, U, M; aiṃ, hrīṃ, klīṃ). You are the eternal half-vowel and its special mode of pronunciation.

\- 75 -

त्वमेव सन्ध्या सावित्री त्वं देवि जननी परा ।
त्वयैतद्धार्यते विश्वं त्वयैतत्सृज्यते जगत् ॥

tvameva sandhyā sāvitrī tvaṃ devi jananī parā |
tvayai taddhāryate viśvaṃ tvayai tatsṛjyate jagat ||

You are the Time of Prayer, you are the Bearer of the Light, you are the Goddess above all beings born. The universe is sustained by you, and the perceivable world is created by you.

- 76 -

त्वयैतत्पाल्यते देवि त्वमत्स्यन्ते च सर्वदा ।
विसृष्टौ सृष्टिरूपा त्वं स्थितिरूपा च पाल्ने ॥

tvayaitat pālyate devi tvamatsyante ca sarvadā |
visṛṣṭau sṛṣṭi rūpā tvaṃ sthiti rūpā ca pālane ||

You protect what you create, Oh Divine Goddess, and you destroy it in the end. As the Creator, you are the form of the creation, and as the form of circumstance, you are its maintenance.

- 77 -

तथा संहृतिरूपान्ते जगतोऽस्य जगन्मये ।
महाविद्या महामाया महामेधा महास्मृतिः ॥

tathā saṃhṛti rūpānte jagato-sya jaganmaye |
mahāvidyā mahāmāyā mahāmedhā mahāsmṛtiḥ ||

Then at the conclusion as the form of dissolution of perceivable existence, you are the All-mighty Measurement of Being. The Great Knowledge, The Great Measurement, The Great Intellect, The Great Recollection;

- 78 -

महामोहा च भवती महादेवी महासुरी ।
प्रकृतिस्त्वं च सर्वस्य गुणत्रयविभाविनी ॥

mahāmohā ca bhavatī mahādevī mahāsurī |
prakṛtistvaṃ ca sarvasya guṇa traya vibhāvinī ||

The Great Ignorance too, and your Ladyship, the Great Goddess and Great Source of Strength. You are Nature, and the three qualities that you manifest in all:

- 79 -

कालरात्रिर्महारात्रिर्मोहरात्रिश्च दारुणा ।
त्वं श्रीस्त्वमीश्वरी त्वं ह्रीस्त्वं बुद्धिर्बोधलक्षणा ॥

kāla rātrir mahārātrir moharātriśca dāruṇā |
tvaṃ śrīs tvam īśvarī tvaṃ hrīs
tvaṃ buddhir bodhalakṣaṇā ||

the Night of Time, the Great Night, and the Night of Ignorance. You are Prosperity, you are the Consciousness of All. You are Humility, you are the Intellect, and the goal of all knowledge:

- 80 -

लज्जा पुष्टिस्तथा तुष्टिस्त्वं शान्तिः क्षान्तिरेव च ।
खड्गिनी शूलिनी घोरा गदिनी चक्रिणी तथा ॥

lajjā puṣṭis tathā tuṣṭis tvaṃ śāntiḥ kṣāntireva ca |
khaḍginī śūlinī ghorā gadinī cakriṇī tathā ||

modesty, increase, then complete satisfaction. You are Peace and Patient Forgiveness. You bear the sword of Wisdom and the pike of concentration, the club of articulation and the discus of revolving time as you present a frightful form.

- 81 -

शङ्खिनी चापिनी बाणभुशुण्डीपरिघायुधा ।
सौम्या सौम्यतराशेषसौम्येभ्यस्त्वतिसुन्दरी ॥

śaṅkhinī cāpinī bāṇabhuśuṇḍī parighāyudhā |
saumyā saumyatarāśeṣa saumyebhyastvati sundarī ||

You bear the conch of vibrations and the bow of determination, and other weapons as well. You are mild and gentle and the ultimate of attractiveness and incomparable beauty.

- 82 -

परापराणां परमा त्वमेव परमेश्वरी ।
यच्च किंचित्क्वचिद्वस्तु सदसद्वाखिलात्मिके ॥

parā parāṇāṃ paramā tvameva parameśvarī |
yacca kiṃcit kvacidvastu sadasadvākhilātmike ||

Above and beyond that, and even again superior, you are the Supreme Consciousness. Whatsoever exists in thought or perception, whether true or untrue,

- 83 -

तस्य सर्वस्य या शक्तिः सा त्वं किं स्तूयसे तदा ।
यया त्वया जगत्स्रष्टा जगत्पात्यत्ति यो जगत् ॥

tasya sarvasya yā śaktiḥ sā tvaṃ kiṃ stūyase tadā |
yayā tvayā jagat sraṣṭā jagat pātyatti yo jagat ||
the energy of everything in all is you. Then what can be sung in your praise? If He who is the evolution, circumstance, and devolution of the perceivable world

- 84 -

सोऽपि निद्रावशं नीतः कस्त्वां स्तोतुमिहेश्वरः ।
विष्णुः शरीरग्रहणमहमीशान एव च ॥

so-pi nidrā vaśaṃ nītaḥ kastvāṃ stotumiheśvaraḥ |
viṣṇuḥ śarīra grahaṇa mahamīśāna eva ca ||
is subject to the sleep that you have caused, then what can be sung in your praise? You cause the Maintaining Capacity and the Dissolving Capacity and myself as well to wear bodies.

- 85 -

कारितास्ते यतोऽतस्त्वां कः स्तोतुं शक्तिमान् भवेत् ।
सा त्वमित्थं प्रभावैः स्वैरुदारैर्देवि संस्तुता ॥

kāritāste yato-tastvāṃ kaḥ stotuṃ śaktimān bhavet |
sā tvamitthaṃ prabhāvaiḥ svair
udārairdevi saṃstutā ||
Hence for this reason and for this cause, who has sufficient ability to sing your praise? Oh Divine Goddess, you and your heavenly and bounteous manifestations have been extolled.

- 86 -

मोहयैतौ दुराधर्षावसुरौ मधुकैटभौ ।
प्रबोधं च जगत्स्वामी नीयतामच्युतो लघु ॥

mohayaitau durādharṣā vasurau madhu kaiṭabhau |
prabodhaṃ ca jagat svāmī nīyatāmacyuto laghu ||
Cause the ignorance of egotism to fall upon those two thoughts so difficult to understand, Too Much and Too Little. Awaken the Consciousness of the Master of the World and rouse Him from sleep.

- 87 -

बोधश्च क्रियतामस्य हन्तुमेतौ महासुरौ ॥

bodhaśca kriya tāmasya hantu metau mahāsurau ||

Let Him conquer these two great thoughts for me and beget Wisdom.

\- 88 -

ऋषिरुवाच ॥

ṛṣi ruvāca ||

The Ṛṣi said:

\- 89 -

एवं स्तुता तदा देवी तामसी तत्र वेधसा ॥

evaṃ stutā tadā devī tāmasī tatra vedhasā ||

Thus praised by the pious worshipper, the Goddess of Rest, in order to awaken

\- 90 -

विष्णोः प्रबोधनार्थाय निहन्तुं मधुकैटभौ ।

नेत्रास्यनासिकाबाहुहृदयेभ्यस्तथोरसः ॥

viṣṇoḥ prabodhanārthāya

nihantuṃ madhu kaiṭabhau |

netrāsya nāsikā bāhu hṛdayebhyas tathorasaḥ ||

the awareness of the Supreme Consciousness to kill Too Much and Too Little, emerged from Her dwelling in the eyes, mouth, nose, arms, chest, and heart.

\- 91 -

निर्गम्य दर्शने तस्थौ ब्रह्मणोऽव्यक्तजन्मनः ।

उत्तस्थौ च जगन्नाथस्तया मुक्तो जनार्दनः ॥

nirgamya darśane tasthau

brahmaṇo-vyakta janmanaḥ |

uttasthau ca jagannāthas tayā mukto janārdanaḥ ||

That immovable, Imperceptible Existence became visible to the Creative Capacity who is born of the Unmanifest. Freed by Her, the Lord of the World, the Causer of Being,

\- 92 -

एकार्णवेऽहिशयनात्ततः स ददृशे च तौ ।

मधुकैटभौ दुरात्मानावतिवीर्यपराक्रमौ ॥

ekārṇave-hiśayanāt tataḥ sa dadṛśe ca tau |

madhu kaiṭabhau durātmānā vativīryaparākramau ||

rose from His couch on the Infinite Ocean of Being. He saw those two wicked warriors of great strength, Too Much and Too Little, marching forward to attack.

- 93 -

क्रोधरक्तेक्षणावत्तुं ब्रह्माणं जनितोद्यमौ ।
समुत्थाय ततस्ताभ्यां युयुधे भगवान् हरिः ॥

krodharaktekṣaṇāvattuṃ brahmāṇaṃ janitodyamau |
samuthāya tatastābhyāṃ yuyudhe bhagavān hariḥ ||

Red eyed with anger and ready in an instant to strike, they continued in their endeavor to devour the Creative Capacity. Then the Lord who Removes Confusion rose and waged battle with the two.

- 94 -

पञ्चवर्षसहस्राणि बाहुप्रहरणो विभुः ।
तावप्यति बलोन्मत्तौ महामायाविमोहितौ ॥

pañca varṣa sahasrāṇi bāhu praharaṇo vibhuḥ |
tāvap yati balon mattau mahāmāyā vimohitau ||

For five thousand years the All-Pervading, Omnipresent, Eternal wrestled with them arm in arm, and they became frenzied by their own strength under the delusion of the Great Measurement of Consciousness.

- 95 -

उक्तवन्तौ वरोऽस्मत्तो व्रियतामिति केशवम् ॥

uktavantau varo-smatto vriyatāmiti keśavam ||

Then they told the One of Beautiful Hair to choose of them a wish.

- 96 -

श्रीभगवानुवाच ॥

śrī bhagavān uvāca ||

The Lord of the Universe said:

- 97 -

भवेतामद्य मे तुष्टौ मम वध्यावुभावपि ॥

bhavetāmadya me tuṣṭau mama vadhyā vubhāvapi ||

If you are so satisfied with me, then both of you be slain by me now.

- 98 -

किमन्येन वरेणात्र एतावद्धि वृतं मम ॥

kimanyena vareṇātra etāvaddhi vṛtaṃ mama ||

What other wish could be regarded? This much I ask.

- 99 -

ऋषिरुवाच ॥

ṛṣi ruvāca ||

The Ṛṣi said:

- 100 -

वञ्चिताभ्यामिति तदा सर्वमापोमयं जगत् ॥

vañcitābhyāmiti tadā sarvam āpo mayaṃ jagat ||

Thus deceived, they saw that the entire gross world was covered with the waters of strife.

- 101 -

विलोक्य ताभ्यां गदितो भगवान् कमलेक्षणः ।

आवां जहि न यत्रोर्वी सलिलेन परिप्लुता ॥

vilokya tābhyāṃ gadito bhagavān kamalekṣaṇaḥ |

āvāṃ jahi na yatrorvī salilena pariplutā ||

Seeing that, they said to the Lord with lotus eyes, "Conquer us in the place that is not inundated by the flood of desire."

- 102 -

ऋषिरुवाच ॥

ṛṣi ruvāca ||

The Ṛṣi said:

- 103 -

तथेत्युक्त्वा भगवता शङ्खचक्रगदाभृता ।

कृत्वा चक्रेण वै च्छिन्ने जघने शिरसी तयोः ॥

tathet yuktvā bhagavatā śaṅkha cakra gadā bhṛtā |

kṛtvā cakreṇa vaicchinne jaghane śirasī tayoḥ ||

Saying, "Let it be so," the Glorious One who bears the conch of vibrations, the discus of revolving time, and the club of articulation, raised the two upon His loins and with the revolutions of time severed their heads.

- 104 -

एवमेषा समुत्पन्ना ब्रह्मणा संस्तुता स्वयम् ।
प्रभावमस्या देव्यास्तु भूयः शृणु वदामि ते ॥

evameṣā samutpannā brahmaṇā saṃstutā svayam I
prabhāvamasyā devyāstu bhūyaḥ śṛṇu vadāmi te II

Thus praised by the Creative Capacity, She manifested Herself. Now I declare more of the Glory of the Goddess. Listen as I speak to you.

ऐं ॐ

aiṃ oṃ

द्वितीयोऽध्यायः
dvitīyo-dhyāyaḥ
Chapter Two

विनियोगः
viniyogaḥ
Application

ॐ मध्यमचरित्रस्य विष्णुर्ऋषिः महालक्ष्मीर्देवता उष्णिक् छन्दः शाकम्भरी शक्तिः दुर्गा बीजं वायुस्तत्त्वं यजुर्वेदः स्वरूपं श्रीमहालक्ष्मीप्रीत्यर्थं मध्यमचरित्रजपे विनियोगः ।

oṃ madhyama caritrasya viṣṇur ṛṣiḥ mahālakṣmīr devatā uṣṇik chandaḥ śākambharī śaktiḥ durgā bījaṃ vāyustattvaṃ yajur vedaḥ svarūpaṃ śrī mahālakṣmī prītyarthaṃ madhyama caritra jape viniyogaḥ |

Oṃ Presenting the middle episode, the Consciousness That Pervades All is the Seer, the Great Goddess of True Wealth is the deity, Uṣnig (28 syllables to the verse) is the meter, Śākambharī is the energy, Durgā is the seed, Air is the principle, Yājur Veda is the intrinsic nature. For the satisfaction of the Great Goddess of True Wealth this middle episode is being applied in recitation.

ध्यानम्
dhyānam
Meditation

अक्षस्रक्परशुं गदेषुकुलिशं पद्मं धनुः कुण्डिकां
दण्डं शक्तिमसिं च चर्म जलजं घण्टां सुराभाजनम् ।
शूलं पाशसुदर्शने च दधतीं हस्तैः प्रसन्नाननां
सेवे सैरिभमर्दिनीमिह महालक्ष्मीं सरोजस्थिताम् ॥

akṣasrak paraśuṃ gadeṣu kuliśaṃ
padmaṃ dhanuḥ kuṇḍikāṃ
daṇḍaṃ śaktim asiṃ ca carma
jalajaṃ ghaṇṭāṃ surābhājanam |
śūlaṃ pāśa sudarśane ca
dadhatīṃ hastaiḥ prasannānanāṃ
seve sairibha mardinīmiha
mahālakṣmīṃ sarojasthitām ||

She with the beautiful face, the Destroyer of the Great Ego, is seated upon the lotus of Peace. In Her hands She holds the rosary of alphabets, the battle axe of good actions, the club of articulation, the arrow of speech, the thunderbolt of illumination, the lotus of peace, the bow of determination, the water pot of purification, the staff of discipline, energy, the sword of worship, the shield of faith, the conch of vibrations, the bell of continuous tone, the wine cup of joy, the pike of concentration, the net of unity, and the discus of revolving time named Excellent Intuitive Vision. I worship that Great Goddess of True Wealth.

- 1 -

ॐ ह्रीं ऋषिरुवाच ॥

oṃ hrīṃ ṛṣi ruvāca ||
Oṃ Hrīṃ the Ṛṣi said:

- 2 -

देवासुरमभूद्युद्धं पूर्णमब्दशतं पुरा ।
महिषेऽसुराणामधिपे देवानां च पुरन्दरे ॥

devā suramabhūdyuddhaṃ pūrṇamabdaśataṃ purā |
mahiṣe-surāṇāmadhipe devānāṃ ca purandare ||

In former times the forces of Peace and Divinity had a dreadful encounter with the forces of thought, which continued for a full hundred years. The commander of the army of thought was the Great Ego, and the leader of the army of clear perception was the Rule of the Pure.

- 3 -

तत्रासुरैर्महावीर्यैर्देवसैन्यं पराजितम् ।
जित्वा च सकलान् देवानिन्द्रोऽभून्महिषासुरः ॥

tatrā surair mahāvīryair devasainyaṃ parājitam |
jitvā ca sakalān devān indro-bhūn mahiṣāsuraḥ ||

The army of the Gods was vanquished by the very powerful thoughts, and all the Gods being subdued, the Great Ego assumed the authority of the Rule of the Pure.

- 4 -

ततः पराजिता देवाः पद्मयोनिं प्रजापतिम् ।
पुरस्कृत्य गतास्तत्र यत्रेशगरुडध्वजौ ॥

tataḥ parājitā devāḥ padmayoniṃ prajāpatim |
puraskṛtya gatās tatra yatreśagaruḍadhvajau ||

Then the defeated Gods, led by the lotus-born Lord of Being, went to where the Supreme Consciousness and the Brilliance that Pervades All were staying.

- 5 -

यथावृत्तं तयोस्तद्वन्महिषासुरचेष्टितम् ।
त्रिदशाः कथयामासुर्देवाभिभवविस्तरम् ॥

yathā vṛttaṃ tayostadvan mahiṣāsura ceṣṭitam |
tridaśāḥ kathayām āsur devābhi bhavavistaram ||

The Gods gave the narration of the exploits of the Great Ego at length, and told of their defeat by the forces of thought.

\- 6 -

सूर्येन्द्राग्न्यनिलेन्दूनां यमस्य वरुणस्य च ।
अन्येषां चाधिकारान् स स्वयमेवाधितिष्ठति ॥

sūryendrāgnyanilendūnāṃ yamasya varuṇasya ca |
anyeṣāṃ cādhikārān sa svayamevā dhitiṣṭhati ||

The authority of the Light of Wisdom, the Rule of the Pure the Light of Meditation, Emancipation, Devotion, the Power That Controls, the Lord of Equilibrium, and other Gods has been usurped by the Great Ego, and now he governs over all.

\- 7 -

स्वर्गान्निराकृताः सर्वे तेन देवगणा भुवि ।
विचरन्ति यथा मर्त्या महिषेण दुरात्मना ॥

svargān nirā kṛtāḥ sarve tena devagaṇā bhuvi |
vicaranti yathā martyā mahiṣeṇa durātmanā ||

That wicked Ego has cast all of the Gods from heaven, and now in the manner of men they wander about the earth.

\- 8 -

एतद्वः कथितं सर्वममरारिविचेष्टितम् ।
शरणं वः प्रपन्नाः स्मो वधस्तस्य विचिन्त्यताम् ॥

etadvaḥ kathitaṃ sarvamamarārivіceṣṭitam |
śaraṇaṃ vaḥ prapannāḥ smo
vadhastasya vicintyatām ||

"All that the thoughts have done has been reported to you. We have come for your protection. Now please think of the manner of their destruction."

\- 9 -

इत्थं निशम्य देवानां वचांसि मधुसूदनः ।
चकार कोपं शम्भुश्च भ्रुकुटीकुटिलाननौ ॥

itthaṃ niśamya devānāṃ vacāṃsi madhusūdanaḥ |
cakāra kopaṃ śambhuśca bhrukuṭī kuṭilānanau ||

Then the Slayer of Too Much and the Bliss of Being became enraged over the conduct of the thoughts, and their faces frowned in anger.

- 10 -

ततोऽतिकोपपूर्णस्य चक्रिणो वदनात्ततः ।
निश्चक्राम महत्तेजो ब्रह्मणः शङ्करस्य च ॥

tato-tikopa pūrṇasya cakriṇo vadanāt tataḥ I
niścakrāma mahattejo brahmaṇaḥ śaṅkarasya ca II

And in excessive rage a great light emanated from the face of He Who Holds the Discus of Revolving Time, and from the Creative Capacity and the Consciousness of Infinite Goodness as well.

- 11 -

अन्येषां चैव देवाना शक्रादीनां शरीरतः ।
निर्गतं सुमहत्तेजस्तच्चैक्यं समगच्छत ॥

anyeṣāṃ caiva devānāṃ śakrādīnāṃ śarīrataḥ I
nirgataṃ sumahattejas taccaikyaṃ samagacchata II

The Rule of the Pure and all the other Gods, too, emitted great lights from their bodies, and all the lights united to form one light of radiant splendor.

- 12 -

अतीव तेजसः कूटं ज्वलन्तमिव पर्वतम् ।
ददृशुस्ते सुरास्तत्र ज्वालाव्याप्तदिगन्तरम् ॥

atīva tejasaḥ kūṭaṃ jvalantamiva parvatam I
dadṛśuste surāstatra jvālā vyāpta digantaram II

The Gods saw that great collection of light like a blazing mountain that pervaded all the directions with its flames.

- 13 -

अतुलं तत्र तत्तेजः सर्वदेवशरीरजम् ।
एकस्थं तदभून्नारी व्याप्तलोकत्रयं त्विषा ॥

atulaṃ tatra tattejaḥ sarva deva śarīrajam I
ekasthaṃ tadabhūnnārī vyāpta loka trayaṃ tviṣā II

There was nothing to compare with this light that emanated from the bodies of all the Gods, and after collecting into one, it assumed a feminine form whose illumination was apparent throughout the three worlds.

- 14 -

यदभूच्छाम्भवं तेजस्तेनाजायत तन्मुखम् ।

याम्येन चाभवन् केशा बाहवो विष्णुतेजसा ॥

yadabhūcchāmbhavaṃ tejas tenājāyata tanmukham |

yāmyena cābhavan keśā bāhavo viṣṇu tejasā ||

From the light that had come from the Source of Bliss to Existence, Her face became manifested; from the Power That Controls, the hair; and from the Consciousness That Pervades All, Her arms.

- 15 -

सौम्येन स्तनयोर्युग्मं मध्यं चैन्द्रेण चाभवत् ।

वारुणेन च जङ्घोरू नितम्बस्तेजसा भुवः ॥

saumyena stanayoryugmaṃ

madhyaṃ caindreṇa cābhavat |

vāruṇena ca jaṅghorū nitambas tejasā bhuvaḥ ||

From the light of Devotion came Her breasts, and from the light of the Rule of the Pure, Her midsection. From the light of the Lord of Equilibrium, came Her legs and thighs, and from the light of Earth, Her buttocks and hips.

- 16 -

ब्रह्मणस्तेजसा पादौ तदङ्गुल्योऽर्कतेजसा ।

वसूनां च कराङ्गुल्यः कौबेरेण च नासिका ॥

brahmaṇas tejasā pādau tadaṅgulyo-rka tejasā |

vasūnāṃ ca karāṅgulyaḥ kaubereṇa ca nāsikā ||

From the light of the Creative Capacity came Her feet, and from the light of Radiance, Her toes. From the Finders of the Wealth came Her fingers, and from the Guardian of the Treasure, Her nose.

- 17 -

तस्यास्तु दन्ताः सम्भूताः प्राजापत्येन तेजसा ।

नयनत्रितयं जज्ञे तथा पावकतेजसा ॥

tasyāstu dantāḥ sambhūtāḥ prājāpatyena tejasā |

nayanatritayaṃ jajñe tathā pāvaka tejasā ||

All of Her teeth came from the Lord of Being, and from the Clarity of Meditation, Her three eyes became apparent.

- 18 -

भ्रुवौ च सन्ध्ययोस्तेजः श्रवणावनिलस्य च ।
अन्येषां चैव देवानां सम्भवस्तेजसां शिवा ॥

bhruvau ca sandhyayostejaḥ śravaṇā vanilasya ca |
anyeṣāṃ caiva devānāṃ sambhavas tejasāṃ śivā ||

From the light of the Time of Worship Her eyebrows were manifested, and from Desiring Excellence, Her ears came into being. And all the other Gods too gave their lights to the formation of the Energy of Infinite Goodness.

- 19 -

ततः समस्तदेवानां तेजोराशिसमुद्भवाम् ।
तां विलोक्य मुदं प्रापुरमरा महिषार्दिताः ॥

tataḥ samasta devānāṃ tejo rāśi samudbhavām |
tāṃ vilokya mudaṃ prāpuramarā mahiṣārditāḥ ||

Then the Gods who were troubled by the Great Ego, seeing the grandeur of the Goddess manifested from their united lights, experienced extreme joy!

- 20 -

शूलं शूलाद्विनिष्कृष्य ददौ तस्यै पिनाकधृक् ।
चक्रं च दत्तवान् कृष्णः समुत्पाद्य स्वचक्रतः ॥

śūlaṃ śūlād viniṣkṛṣya dadau tasyai pinākadhṛk |
cakraṃ ca dattavān kṛṣṇaḥ samutpādya svacakrataḥ ||

The Bearer of the Trident of Unity took from His trident another trident and presented it to the Goddess. Then the Doer of All, taking from the discus of revolving time, manifested a second discus and bestowed it upon Her.

- 21 -

शङ्खं च वरुणः शक्तिं ददौ तस्यै हुताशनः ।
मारुतो दत्तवांश्चापं बाणपूर्णे तथेषुधी ॥

śaṅkhaṃ ca varuṇaḥ śaktiṃ dadau tasyai hutāśanaḥ |
māruto dattavāṃścāpaṃ bāṇa pūrṇe tatheṣudhī ||

Equilibrium donated the conch of vibrations, and the Light of

Meditation gave His energy. Emancipation gave His bow of determination and two quivers full of arrows.

- 22 -

वज्रमिन्द्रः समुत्पाद्य कुलिशादमराधिपः ।
ददौ तस्यै सहस्राक्षो घण्टामैरावताद् गजात् ॥

vajram indraḥ samutpādya kuliśādamarādhipaḥ |
dadau tasyai sahasrākṣo ghaṇṭā mairāvatād gajāt ||

The Rule of the Pure with a thousand eyes took from His thunderbolt of illumination a second thunderbolt and presented it to the Goddess, and from His elephant, Love for All, a bell of continuous tone was donated.

- 23 -

कालदण्डाद्यमो दण्डं पाशं चाम्बुपतिर्ददौ ।
प्रजापतिश्चाक्षमालां ददौ ब्रह्मा कमण्डलुम् ॥

kāla daṇḍā dyamo daṇḍaṃ
pāśaṃ cāmbupatir dadau |
prajāpatiścākṣamālāṃ dadau brahmā kamaṇḍalum ||

From the Power That Controls came the staff of discipline, and the Lord of Equilibrium presented the net of unity; the Lord of Being, a rosary of letters; the Creative Capacity, the bowl of renunciation.

- 24 -

समस्तरोमकूपेषु निजरश्मीन् दिवाकरः ।
कालश्च दत्तवान् खड्गं तस्याश्चर्म च निर्मलम् ॥

samasta roma kupeṣu nijaraśmīn divākaraḥ |
kālaśca dattavān khaḍgaṃ tasyāścarma ca nirmalam ||

The Divine Being of Light filled the pores of Her skin with rays of light, and Time gave the sword of worship and a brilliant shield.

- 25 -

क्षीरोदश्चामलं हारमजरे च तथाम्बरे ।
चूडामणिं तथा दिव्यं कुण्डले कटकानि च ॥

kṣīrodaścāmalaṃ hāramajare ca tathāmbare |
cūḍāmaṇiṃ tathā divyaṃ kuṇḍale kaṭakāni ca ||

- 26 -

अर्धचन्द्रं तथा शुभ्रं केयूरान् सर्वबाहुषु ।
नूपुरौ विमलौ तद्वद् ग्रैवेयकमनुत्तमम् ॥

ardhacandraṃ tathā śubhraṃ keyūrān sarva bāhuṣu |
nūpurau vimalau tadvad graiveyakamanuttamam ||

- 27 -

अङ्गुलीयकरत्नानि समस्तास्वङ्गुलीषु च ।
विश्वकर्मा ददौ तस्यै परशुं चातिनिर्मलम् ॥

aṅgulīyakaratnāni samastā svaṅgulīṣu ca |
viśvakarmā dadau tasyai paraśuṃ cātinirmalam ||

25-27. The Ocean of Pure Thoughts gave a necklace of excellent gems and garments, which never lose their luster, and donated earrings, a divine crest and bangles, and a halo of light. The Radiant Half-Moon gave bracelets for Her arms, aṇklets for Her feet, a beautiful neck ornament, and rings of precious stones for Her fingers.And the Universal Doer gave His extremely holy axe of good actions.

- 28 -

अस्त्राण्यनेकरूपाणि तथाभेद्यं च दंशनम् ।
अम्लानपङ्कजां मालां शिरस्युरसि चापराम् ॥

astrāṇya neka rūpāṇi tathābhedyaṃ ca daṃśanam |
amlānapaṅkajāṃ mālāṃ śirasyurasi cāparām ||

All manner of weapons and impenetrable armor were presented to protect Her head and breast, and from True Wealth, a garland of lotuses was given that would never lose its luster.

- 29 -

अददज्जलधिस्तस्यै पङ्कजं चातिशोभनम् ।
हिमवान् वाहनं सिंहं रत्नानि विविधानि च ॥

adadajjaladhis tasyai paṅkajaṃ cātiśobhanam |
himavān vāhanaṃ siṃhaṃ ratnāni vividhāni ca ||

The Sea presented a beautiful lotus, the blessing of peace, and the Himalayas gave the jewel of the lion of courage upon which to ride.

- 30 -

ददावशून्यं सुरया पानपात्रं धनाधिपः ।

शेषश्च सर्वनागेशो महामणिविभूषितम् ॥

dadāvaśūnyaṃ surayā pānapātraṃ dhanādhipaḥ |

śeṣaścasarvanāgeśo mahāmaṇi vibhūṣitam ||

- 31 -

नागहारं ददौ तस्यै धत्ते यः पृथिवीमिमाम् ।

अन्यैरपि सुरैर्देवी भूषणैरायुधैस्तथा ॥

nāgahāraṃ dadau tasyai dhatte yaḥ pṛthivīmimām |

anyairapi surair devī bhūṣanair āyudhaistathā ||

30-31. The Lord of Wealth gave a drinking vessel constantly full of intoxicating spirit, and the Ultimate, Lord of all serpents of energy by which the earth is sustained, gave great jewels that shine luminously in a necklace of serpents. Other Gods, too, bestowed ornaments and weapons upon the Goddess.

- 32 -

सम्मानिता ननादोच्चैः साट्टहासं मुहुर्मुहुः ।

तस्या नादेन घोरेण कृत्स्नमापूरितं नभः ॥

sammānitā nanādoccaiḥ sāttahāsaṃ muhur muhuḥ |

tasyā nādena ghoreṇa kṛtsnamāpūritaṃ nabhaḥ ||

After being worshipped, again and again She laughed and roared in a high tone, and Her dreadful sound resounded through the ether.

- 33 -

अमायतातिमहता प्रतिशब्दो महानभूत् ।

चुक्षुभुः सकला लोकाः समुद्राश्च चकम्पिरे ॥

amāyatātimahatā prati śabdo mahānabhūt |

cukṣubhuḥ sakalā lokāḥ samudrāśca cakampire ||

The Goddess caused such an excessive noise that caused all the worlds to quake and the oceans to rage.

\- 34 -

चचाल वसुधा चेलुः सकलाश्च महीधराः ।

जयेति देवाश्च मुदा तामूचुः सिंहवाहिनीम् ॥

cacāla vasudhā celuḥ sakalāśca mahī dharāḥ |
jayeti devāśca mudā tāmūcuḥ siṃha vāhinīm ||

The earth rocked and the mountains shook, and the Gods were extremely pleased and joyfully cried out to the lion rider, "Victory be yours!"

\- 35 -

तुष्टुवुर्मुनयश्चैनां भक्तिनम्रात्ममूर्तयः ।

दृष्ट्वा समस्तं संक्षुब्धं त्रैलोक्यममरारयः ॥

tuṣṭuvur munayaścainām bhakti namrātma mūrtayaḥ |
dṛṣṭvā samastaṃ saṃkṣubdhaṃ
trailokyamamarārayaḥ ||

And with great satisfaction, the wise people praised the image of their worship, bowing with devotion. Seeing the three worlds in such a commotion,

\- 36 -

संन्नद्धाखिलसैन्यास्ते समुत्तस्थुरुदायुधाः ।

आः किमेतदिति क्रोधादाभाष्य महिषासुरः ॥

saṃnaddhākhila sainyāste samuttasthu rudāyudhāḥ |
āḥ kimetaditi krodhād ābhāṣya mahiṣāsuraḥ ||

the army of thoughts adorned their armor, took up their weapons, and stood together. The Great Ego, in excessive anger, exclaimed, "Ah, what is this?"

\- 37 -

अभ्यधावत तं शब्दमशेषैरसुरैर्वृतः ।

स ददर्श ततो देवीं व्याप्तलोकत्रयां त्विषा ॥

abhyadhāvata taṃ śabdam aśeṣair asurair vṛtaḥ |
sa dadarśa tato devīṃ vyāpta loka trayāṃ tviṣā ||

Then along with all the thoughts that had assembled ready to attack, he ran towards that ultimate sound and saw the Goddess illuminating the three worlds.

- 38 -

पादाक्रान्त्या नतभुवं किरीटोल्लिखिताम्बराम् ।
क्षोभिताशेषपातालां धनुर्ज्यानिःस्वनेन ताम् ॥

pādākrāntyā natabhuvaṃ kirīṭollikhitāmbarām |
kṣobhitāśeṣa pātālāṃ dhanurjyāniḥ svanena tām ||

Her feet stood upon the earth, and Her crown touched the furthest reaches of the atmosphere. The twang of Her bow string sent fear through the seven regions of hell!

- 39 -

दिशो भुजसहस्रेण समन्ताद् व्याप्य संस्थिताम् ।
ततः प्रववृते युद्धं तया देव्या सुरद्विषाम् ॥

diśo bhuja sahasreṇa samantād vyāpya saṃsthitām |
tataḥ pravavṛte yuddhaṃ tayā devyā suradviṣām ||

The thousand arms of this Goddess covered all the directions. And then began the battle between the Goddess and the Thoughts.

- 40 -

शस्त्रास्त्रैर्बहुधा मुक्तैरादीपितदिगन्तरम् ।
महिषासुरसेनानीश्चिक्षुराख्यो महासुरः ॥

śastrāstrair bahudhā muktair ādīpitadigantaram |
mahiṣāsurasenānīścikṣurākhyo mahāsuraḥ ||

Many kinds of weapons illuminated the entire atmosphere in flight. And a very powerful general of the Great Ego, Devoid of Clear Understanding, rose to do battle.

- 41 -

युयुधे चामरश्चान्यैश्चतुरङ्गबलान्वितः ।
रथानामयुतैः षड्भिरुदग्राख्यो महासुरः ॥

yuyudhe cāmaraścānyaiś caturaṅga balānvitaḥ |
rathānāma yutaiḥ ṣadbhir udagrākhyo mahāsuraḥ ||

Fickleness waged battle with his four divisions of horses, elephants, chariots, and infantry of great strength, and Haughtiness joined in the fray with sixty thousand chariots.

- 42 -

अयुध्यतायुतानां च सहस्रेण महाहनुः ।
पञ्चाशद्भिश्च नियुतैरसिलोमा महासुरः ॥

ayudhyatāyutānāṃ ca sahasreṇa mahāhanuḥ |
pañcā śadbhiśca niyutair asilomā mahāsuraḥ ||

With hundreds of thousands, the Great Deceiver, and with his army of ten million foot soldiers, Want of Resolution, a great thought, came to the battle.

- 43 -

अयुतानां शतैः षड्भिर्बाष्कलो युयुधे रणे ।
गजवाजिसहस्रौघैरनेकैः परिवारितः ॥

ayutānāṃ śataiḥ śaḍbhir bāṣkalo yuyudhe raṇe |
gajavāji sahasraughair anekaiḥ parivāritaḥ ||

With six million soldiers Memories entered the battlefield, and with thousands of elephants and horses, Wandering To and Fro.

- 44 -

वृतो रथानां कोट्या च युद्धे तस्मिन्नयुध्यत ।
बिडालाख्योऽयुतानां च पञ्चाशद्भिरथायुतैः ॥

vṛto rathānāṃ koṭyā ca yuddhe tasminnayudhyata |
biḍālākhyo-yutānāṃ ca pañcāśadbhi rathāyutaiḥ ||

Hypocrisy joined in the fighting with five thousand million chariots assembled, and, moreover, tens of thousands of great thoughts on elephants and horses.

- 45 -

युयुधे संयुगे तत्र रथानां परिवारितः ।
अन्ये च तत्रायुतशो रथनागहयैर्वृताः ॥

yuyudhe saṃyuge tatra rathānāṃ parivāritaḥ |
anye ca tatrā yutaśo ratha nāgahayair vṛtāḥ ||

Wandering To and Fro fought on in that battle with his chariots racing about, and others too continued to fight; their chariots and elephants kept coming.

- 46 -

युयुधुः संयुगे देव्या सह तत्र महासुराः ।
कोटिकोटिसहस्रैस्तु रथानां दन्तिनां तथा ॥

yuyudhuḥ saṃyuge devyā saha tatra mahāsurāḥ I
koṭi koṭi sahasraistu rathānāṃ dantināṃ tathā II

The great thoughts fought and fought in that battle with the Goddess. Uncountable thousands of warriors and chariots, horses and elephants, accumulated there.

- 47 -

हयानां च वृतो युद्धे तत्राभून्महिषासुरः ।
तोमरैर्भिन्दिपालैश्च शक्तिभिर्मुसलैस्तथा ॥

hayānāṃ ca vṛto yuddhe tatrā bhūn mahiṣāsuraḥ I
tomarair bhindipālaiś ca śaktibhir musalais tathā II

The Great Ego himself joined in the battle with his large javelin, his small javelin, his energy, and his mace.

- 48 -

युयुधुः संयुगे देव्या खड्गैः परशुपट्टिशैः ।
केचिच्च चिक्षिपुः शक्तीः केचित्पाशांस्तथापरे ॥

yuyudhuḥ saṃyuge devyā khaḍgaiḥ paraśu paṭṭiśaiḥ I
kecicca cikṣipuḥ śaktīḥ kecit pāśāṃstathāpare II

Other thoughts fought and fought in that battle and tried to strike the Goddess with their swords, with all of their energies, and to bind Her with their nets.

- 49 -

देवीं खड्गप्रहारैस्तु ते तां हन्तुं प्रचक्रमुः ।
सापि देवी ततस्तानि शस्त्राण्यस्त्राणि चण्डिका ॥

devīṃ kaḍgaprahāraistu
te tāṃ hantuṃ pracakramuḥ I
sāpi devī tatastāni śastrāṇya strāṇi caṇḍikā II

They were trying to kill the Goddess with their swords. And the Goddess, She Who Tears Apart Thought, attacked them with Her own weapons.

- 50 -

लीलयैव प्रचिच्छेद निजशस्त्रास्त्रवर्षिणी ।
अनायस्तानना देवी स्तूयमाना सुरर्षिभिः ॥

līlayaiva praciccheda nija śastrā stravarṣiṇī |
anāyastānanā devī stūyamānā surarṣibhiḥ ||

Playfully the Goddess rained upon Her attackers a shower of Her own weapons and mantras, which cut all their weapons to pieces, while Gods and Seers praised Her with hymns and minds of divinity.

- 51 -

मुमोचासुरदेहेषु शस्त्राण्यस्त्राणि चेश्वरी ।
सोऽपि क्रुद्धो धुतसटो देव्या वाहनकेसरी ॥

mumocāsura deheṣu śastrāṇyastrāṇi ceśvarī |
so-pi kruddho dhutasaṭo devyā vāhanakesarī ||

- 52 -

चचारासुरसैन्येषु वनेष्विव हुताशनः ।
निःश्वासान् मुमुचे यांश्च युध्यमाना रणेऽम्बिका ॥

cacārāsura sainyeṣu vaneṣviva hutāśanaḥ |
niḥśvāsān mumuce yāṃśca
yudhyamānā raṇe-mbikā ||

51-52. In Her face was not the slightest exertion as the Empress of the Universe hurled weapon after weapon upon the bodies of the attackers. And the lion of the Goddess, shaking its mane in rage, strolled through the army of thoughts like a forest conflagration. Each expiration of the breath of the Mother of the Universe manifested there as Her army,

- 53 -

त एव सद्यः सम्भूता गणाः शतसहस्रशः ।
युयुधुस्ते परशुभिर्भिन्दिपालासिपट्टिशैः ॥

ta eva sadyaḥ sambhūtā gaṇāḥ śatasahasraśaḥ |
yuyudhuste paraśubhir bhindipālāsi paṭṭiśaiḥ ||

numbering in hundreds and thousands, fighting in the battle with the axe, javelin, sword and spear.

- 54 -

नाशयन्तोऽसुरगणान् देवीशक्त्युपबृंहिताः ।
अवादयन्त पटहान् गणाः शङ्खांस्तथापरे ॥

nāśayanto-suragaṇān devīśaktyupa bṛṃhitāḥ |
avādayanta paṭahān gaṇāḥ śaṅkhāṃstathāpare ||

The Goddess and Her immense energy destroyed numbers of thoughts while beating on the drum and sounding the conch.

- 55 -

मृदङ्गांश्च तथैवान्ये तस्मिन् युद्धमहोत्सवे ।
ततो देवी त्रिशूलेन गदया शक्तिवृष्टिभिः ॥

mṛdaṅgāṃśca tathaivānye tasmin yuddhamahotsave |
tato devī triśūlena gadayā śakti vṛṣṭibhiḥ ||

Playing cymbals and swinging the club and trident, and raining energy in that festival of battle.

- 56 -

खड्गादिभिश्च शतशो निजघान महासुरान् ।
पातयामास चैवान्यान् घण्टास्वनविमोहितान् ॥

khaḍgādibhiśca śataśo nijaghāna mahāsurān |
pātayāmāsa caivānyān ghaṇṭā svanavimohitān ||

the terrible noise of Her bell stunned the great thoughts to unconsciousness, while She cut them with Her sword. How many thousands fell to their death!

- 57 -

असुरान् भुवि पाशेन बद्ध्वा चान्यानकर्षयत् ।
केचिद् द्विधा कृतास्तीक्ष्णैः खड्गपातैस्तथापरे ॥

asurān bhuvi pāśena baddhvā cānyānakarṣayat |
kecid dvidhā kṛtāstīkṣnaiḥ khaḍgapātaistathāpare ||

Many thoughts were bound by the net and dragged to the earth. Many thoughts were cut into two by the sharp edge of Her sword.

- 58 -

विपोथिता निपातेन गदया भुवि शेरते ।

वेमुश्च केचिद्रुधिरं मुसलेन भृशं हताः ॥

vipothitā nipātena gadayā bhuvi śerate |
vemuśca kecidrudhiraṃ musalena bhṛśaṃ hatāḥ ||

How many thoughts fell wounded to the earth from the impact of the club. How many were struck by the mace and became extremely injured.

- 59 -

केचिन्निपतिता भूमौ भिन्नाः शूलेन वक्षसि ।

निरन्तराः शरौघेण कृताः केचिद्रणाजिरे ॥

kecinnipatitā bhūmau bhinnāḥ śūlena vakṣasi |
nirantarāḥ śaraugheṇa kṛtāḥ kecidraṇājire ||

Some thoughts pierced in the breast by the pike fell to the earth in a heap. How many thoughts in that battlefield struck by a rain of arrows were cut apart.

- 60 -

श्येनानुकारिणः प्राणान् मुमुचुस्त्रिदशार्दनाः ।

केषांचिद् बाहवश्छिन्नाश्छिन्नग्रीवास्तथापरे ॥

śyenānu kāriṇaḥ prāṇān mumucustridaśārdanāḥ |
keṣāṃcid bāhavaśchinnāś chinnagrīvās tathāpare ||

- 61 -

शिरांसि पेतुरन्येषामन्ये मध्ये विदारिताः ।

विच्छिन्नजङ्घास्त्वपरे पेतुरुर्व्यां महासुराः ॥

śirāṃsi peturanyeṣāmanye madhye vidāritāḥ |
vicchinna jaṅghāstvapare petururvyāṃ mahāsurāḥ ||

- 62 -

एकबाह्वक्षिचरणाः केचिद्देव्या द्विधा कृताः ।

छिन्नेऽपि चान्ये शिरसि पतिताः पुनरुत्थिताः ॥

ekabāhvakṣicaraṇāḥ kecid devyā dvidhā kṛtāḥ |
chinne-pi cānye śirasi patitāḥ punarutthitāḥ ||

- 63 -

कबन्धा युयुधुर्देव्या गृहीतपरमायुधाः ।
ननृतुश्चापरे तत्र युद्धे तूर्यलयाश्रिताः ॥

kabandhā yuyudhur devyā gṛhītaparamāyudhāḥ |
nanṛtuścāpare tatra yuddhe tūrya layāśritāḥ ||

- 64 -

कबन्धाश्छिन्नशिरसः खड्गशक्त्यृष्टिपाणयः ।
तिष्ठ तिष्ठेति भाषन्तो देवीमन्ये महासुराः ॥

kabandhāśchinna śirasaḥ khaḍga śaktyṛṣṭi pāṇayaḥ |
tiṣṭha tiṣṭheti bhāṣanto devīmanye mahāsurāḥ ||

- 65 -

पातितै रथनागाश्वैरसुरैश्च वसुन्धरा ।
अगम्या साभवत्तत्र यत्राभूत्स महारणः ॥

pātitai ratha nāgāśvair asuraiśca vasundharā |
agamyā sābhavat tatra yatrā bhūtsa mahā raṇaḥ ||

- 66 -

शोणितौघा महानद्यः सद्यस्तत्र प्रसुस्रुवुः ।
मध्ये चासुरसैन्यस्य वारणासुरवाजिनाम् ॥

śoṇitaughā mahānadyaḥ sadyas tatra prasusruvuḥ |
madhye cāsura sainyasya vāraṇāsura vājinām ||

60-66. Several of the number of thoughts who had tormented the Gods relinquished their vital breath. Many others lost their arms or necks and were reduced to dust. How many fell with their heads cut, how many with their bodies divided at the mid-section! Many cut from the hips fell. Many lost a limb, or an eye, or were torn into two pieces. Many thoughts, with their heads severed, rose again as headless bodies in a terrible form to take up their arms and continue to battle with the Goddess. Other headless torsos danced to the rhythmic music of the battle. And many without heads raced about with their swords and energies and other weapons and shouted at the Goddess, "Stop! Stop!" Where that terrible encounter took place, the earth was covered with chariots, elephants, horses, and thoughts that the

Goddess had caused to fall, so that there was no possibility to find a path by which to come and go. From the army of thoughts, and from their elephants and horses, poured forth so much blood as to create a great river.

- 67 -

क्षणेन तन्महासैन्यमसुराणां तथाम्बिका ।
निन्ये क्षयं यथा वह्निस्तृणदारुमहाचयम् ॥

kṣaṇena tanmahā sainyam asurāṇāṃ tathāmbikā |
ninye kṣayaṃ yathā vahnis tṛṇadāru mahācayam ||

Within an instant that gigantic army of thoughts perished before the Mother of the Universe, just as grass and timber are reduced to ashes in a moment by a great fire.

- 68 -

स च सिंहो महानादमुत्सृजन्धुतकेसरः ।
शरीरेभ्योऽमरारीणामसूनिव विचिन्वति ॥

sa ca siṃho mahānādam utsṛjandhuta kesaraḥ |
śarīrebhyo-marārīṇāmasūniva vicinvati ||

And that lion, shaking its mane to and fro and roaring loudly, extracted the life force from many thoughts.

- 69 -

देव्या गणैश्च तैस्तत्र कृतं युद्धं महासुरैः ।
यथैषां तुतुषुर्देवाः पुष्पवृष्टिमुचो दिवि ॥

devyā gaṇaiśca taistatra
kṛtaṃ yuddhaṃ mahāsuraiḥ |
yathaiṣāṃ tutuṣur devāḥ puṣpa vṛṣṭimuco divi ||

Thus the Goddess and Her army waged battle with the multitude of the great thoughts, as the Gods in heaven were extremely joyous and showered the earth with flowers.

ॐ

oṃ

तृतीयोऽध्यायः
tṛtīyo-dhyāyaḥ
Chapter Three

ध्यानम्
dhyānam
Meditation

ॐ उद्यद्भानुसहस्रकान्तिमरुणक्षौमां शिरोमालिकां
रक्तालिप्तपयोधरां जपवटीं विद्यामभीतिं वरम् ।
हस्ताब्जैर्दधतीं त्रिनेत्रविलसद्वक्त्रारविन्दश्रियं
देवीं बद्धहिमांशुरत्नमुकुटां वन्देऽरविन्दस्थिताम् ॥

oṃ udyad bhānu sahasra kāntim
aruṇakṣaumāṃ śiromālikāṃ
raktāliptapayodharāṃ
japavaṭīṃ vidyāmabhītiṃ varam ।
hastābjairdadhatīṃ trinetra
vilasad vaktrāravindaśriyaṃ
devīṃ baddhahimāṃśu ratna
mukuṭāṃ vande-ravindasthitām ॥

The radiant body of the Mother of the Universe has the magnificence of a thousand rising suns. She is draped in a sarree of red silk. Around Her neck is a garland of red skulls. Her two breasts have been colored with red sandal- paste. In Her four lotus-like hands She holds a rosary and shows the mudrās of Knowledge, Fearlessness, and Granting of Boons. Her three eyes are shining and Her budlike mouth is extremely beautiful. Upon Her head sits a crown of jewels in which the moon is situated, and She is resting upon a lotus seat. With unlimited devotion I bow down to this Goddess.

- 1 -

ॐ ऋषिरुवाच ॥

oṃ ṛṣi ruvāca ||

Oṃ The Ṛṣi said:

- 2 -

निहन्यमानं तत्सैन्यमवलोक्य महासुरः ।

सेनानीश्चिक्षुरः कोपाद्ययौ योद्धुमथाम्बिकाम् ॥

nihanyamānaṃ tat sainyam avalokya mahāsuraḥ |
senānīścikṣuraḥ kopādyayau yoddhumathāmbikām ||

When the great thoughts thus saw their forces being destroyed, that heroic general, Devoid of Clear Understanding, in great anger proceeded to battle with the Mother of the Universe.

- 3 -

स देवीं शरवर्षेण ववर्ष समरेऽसुरः ।

यथा मेरुगिरेः शृङ्गं तोयवर्षेण तोयदः ॥

sa devīṃ śaravarṣeṇa vavarṣa samare-suraḥ |
yathā meru gireḥ śṛṅgaṃ toyavarṣeṇa toyadaḥ ||

That thought rained upon the Goddess a cloud of the arrows of various doubts as plentiful as the waters that fall from a cloud upon Mount Meru.

- 4 -

तस्यच्छित्त्वा ततो देवी लीलयैव शरोत्करान् ।

जघान तुरगान् बाणैर्यन्तारं चैव वाजिनाम् ॥

tasyac chittvā tato devī līlayaiva śarotkarān |
jaghānaturagān bāṇair yantāraṃ caiva vājinām ||

Then the Goddess fired such a multitude of arrows that cut his arrows into pieces, and also killed his horses and his charioteer.

- 5 -

चिच्छेद च धनुः सद्यो ध्वजं चातिसमुच्छ्रितम् ।

विव्याध चैव गात्रेषु छिन्नधन्वानमाशुगैः ॥

ciccheda ca dhanuḥ sadyo
dhvajaṃ cātisamucchritam |
vivyādha caiva gātreṣu chinnadhanvānamā śugaiḥ ||

With this She also cut his bow and his exceedingly high banner. After cutting his bow, She pierced his body with Her arrows.

\- 6 -

सच्छिन्नधन्वा विरथो हताश्वो हतसारथिः ।

अभ्यधावत तां देवीं खड्गचर्मधरोऽसुरः ॥

sacchinnadhanvā viratho hatāśvo hatasārathiḥ |
abhyadhāvata tāṃ devīṃ
khaḍga carma dharo-suraḥ ||

Losing his bow, chariot, horses, and charioteer, that thought took up his sword and shield, and ran after the Goddess.

\- 7 -

सिंहमाहत्य खड्गेन तीक्ष्णधारेण मूर्धनि ।

आजघान भुजे सव्ये देवीमप्यतिवेगवान् ॥

siṃha māhatya khaḍgena tīkṣṇadhāreṇa mūrdhani |
ājaghāna bhuje savye devī mapyati vegavān ||

With the sharp edge of his sword he struck the lion on the head, and with great speed he gave a blow to the Goddess on Her left arm.

\- 8 -

तस्याः खड्गो भुजं प्राप्य पफाल नृपनन्दन ।

ततो जग्राह शूलं स कोपादरुणलोचनः ॥

tasyāḥ khaḍgo bhujaṃ prāpya paphāla nṛpanandana |
tato jagrāha śūlaṃ sa kopādaruṇa locanaḥ ||

When that sword touched Her body, it broke into pieces, and that angry thought of many considerations took a pike in his hands.

\- 9 -

चिक्षेप च ततस्तत्तु भद्रकाल्यां महासुरः ।

जाज्वल्यमानं तेजोभी रविबिम्बमिवाम्बरात् ॥

cikṣepa ca tatas tattu bhadra kālyāṃ mahāsuraḥ |
jājvalyamānaṃ tejobhī ravibimba mivāmbarāt ||
And that great thought threw that glaring pike at the Excellent One Beyond Time, just as the Sun fills the heavens with dazzling luster.

- 10 -

दृष्ट्वा तदापतच्छूलं देवी शूलममुञ्चत ।
तच्छूलं शतधा तेन नीतं स च महासुरः ॥

dṛṣṭvā tadā patac chūlaṃ devī śūlamamuñcata |
tacchūlaṃ śatadhā tena nītaṃ sa ca mahāsuraḥ ||
When the Goddess saw that pike coming at Her, She, too, let loose Her pike, which split his weapon into numerous pieces, and Devoid of Clear Understanding gave up his life.

- 11 -

हते तस्मिन्महावीर्ये महिषस्य चमूपतौ ।
आजगाम गजारूढश्चामरस्त्रिदशार्दनः ॥

hate tasmin mahāvīrye mahiṣasya camūpatau |
ājagāma gajā rūḍhaś cāmarastri daśārdanaḥ ||
After the death of that valiant general in the army of the Great Ego, Devoid of Clear Understanding, who had been the source of affliction to many Gods, Fickleness approached mounted on an elephant.

- 12 -

सोऽपि शक्तिं मुमोचाथ देव्यास्तामम्बिका द्रुतम् ।
हुंकाराभिहतां भूमौ पातयामास निष्प्रभाम् ॥

so-pi śaktiṃ mumocātha devyāstāmambikā drutam |
huṃkārābhihatāṃ bhūmau pātayāmāsa niṣprabhām ||
He attacked the Goddess from above with his energy, but the Mother of the Universe, with the shout of Her mantra "Huṃ," wounded him and, deprived of light, the energy fell to the earth.

- 13 -

भग्नां शक्तिं निपतितां दृष्ट्वा क्रोधसमन्वितः ।
चिक्षेप चामरः शूलं बाणैस्तदपि साच्छिनत् ॥

bhagnāṃ śaktiṃ nipatitāṃ
dṛṣṭvā krodha samanvitaḥ |
cikṣepa cāmaraḥ śūlaṃ bāṇaistadapi sācchinat ||
When he found that his energy was broken, Fickleness became intensely angry. Now he threw his pike at Her, but the Goddess cut it with Her arrows.

- 14 -

ततः सिंहः समुत्पत्य गजकुम्भान्तरे स्थितः ।
बाहुयुद्धेन युयुधे तेनोच्चैस्त्रिदशारिणा ॥

tataḥ siṃhaḥ samutpatya gajakumbhāntare sthitaḥ |
bāhuyuddhena yuyudhe tenoc caistridaśāriṇā ||
In all of this the lion of the Goddess jumped upon the head of the elephant and began an intensive battle with that thought.

- 15 -

युद्ध्यमानौ ततस्तौ तु तस्मान्नागान्महीं गतौ ।
युयुधातेऽतिसंरब्धौ प्रहारैरतिदारुणैः ॥

yuddhyamānau tatastau tu
tasmān nāgān mahīṃ gatau |
yuyudhāte-tisaṃrabdhau prahārairatidāruṇaiḥ ||
Those two fought and fought, and the elephant fell to the ground. Then they rose in excessive rage and began to fight again with fierce blows.

- 16 -

ततो वेगात् खमुत्पत्य निपत्य च मृगारिणा ।
करप्रहारेण शिरश्चामरस्य पृथक्कृतम् ॥

tato vegāt khamutpatya nipatya ca mṛgāriṇā |
karaprahāreṇa śiraś cāmarasya pṛthak kṛtam ||
Thereafter with great speed the lion leaped into the atmosphere, and falling from the sky, severed the head of Fickleness from his body.

- 17 -

उदग्रश्च रणे देव्या शिलावृक्षादिभिर्हतः ।
दन्तमुष्टितलैश्चैव करालश्च निपातितः ॥

udagraśca raṇe devyā śilāvṛkṣā dibhirhataḥ |
dantamuṣṭi talaiścaiva karālaśca nipātitaḥ ||

Haughtiness was slain by the Goddess with stones and trees in that battlefield, and striking with his paws and biting with his teeth, the lion brought down Disbelief.

- 18 -

देवी क्रुद्धा गदापातैश्चूर्णयामास चोद्धतम् ।
बाष्कलं भिन्दिपालेन बाणैस्ताम्रं तथान्धकम् ॥

devī kruddhā gadāpātaiś cūrṇayāmāsa coddhatam |
bāṣkalaṃ bhindipālena
bāṇaistāmraṃ tathāndhakam ||

Striking angrily with Her club, the Goddess reduced Arrogance to powder. Memories was cut by the sword, and Anxiety and Blindness by Her arrows.

- 19 -

उग्रास्यमुग्रवीर्यं च तथैव च महाहनुम् ।
त्रिनेत्रा च त्रिशूलेन जघान परमेश्वरी ॥

ugrāsyam ugravīryaṃ ca tathaiva ca mahāhanum |
trinetrā ca triśūlena jaghāna parameśvarī ||

Violent Temper and Passion and the Great Deceiver, too, were slain by the three-eyed Seer of All.

- 20 -

बिडालस्यासिना कायात्पातयामास वै शिरः ।
दुर्धरं दुर्मुखं चोभौ शरैर्निन्ये यमक्षयम् ॥

biḍālasyāsinā kāyāt pātayāmāsa vai śiraḥ |
durdharaṃ durmukhaṃ cobhau
śarairninye yamakṣayam ||

Hypocrisy's head was cut by the sword, and Irresistible Temptation and Foul Mouth were both sent to the Kingdom of Death by Her arrows.

- 21 -

एवं संक्षीयमाणे तु स्वसैन्ये महिषासुरः ।
माहिषेण स्वरूपेण त्रासयामास तान् गणान् ॥

evaṃ saṃkṣīyamāṇe tu svasainye mahiṣāsuraḥ |
māhiṣeṇa svarūpeṇa trāsayāmāsa tān gaṇān ||

Seeing his army thus being destroyed, the Great Ego assumed the form of a buffalo, and he himself began to terrify the troops of the Goddess.

- 22 -

कांश्चित्तुण्डप्रहारेण खुरक्षेपैस्तथापरान् ।
लाङ्गूलताडितांश्चान्याञ्छृङ्गाभ्यां च विदारितान् ॥

kāṃścit tuṇḍa prahāreṇa khurakṣepais tathāparān |
lāṅgūlatāḍitaṃścānyāñ chṛṅgābhyāṃ ca vidāritān ||

- 23 -

वेगेन कांश्चिदपरान्नादेन भ्रमणेन च ।
निःश्वासपवनेनान्यान् पातयामास भूतले ॥

vegena kāṃścidaparān nādena bhramaṇena ca |
niḥśvāsapavanenānyān pātayāmāsa bhūtale ||

22-23. Sometimes he fought with his snout, sometimes kicking with his hooves into the air, sometimes hitting with his tail, sometimes whirling around while ripping with his horns. With great speed and a great war cry, his breath puffing in exertion, he scattered the troops over the ground.

- 24 -

निपात्य प्रमथानीकमभ्यधावत सोऽसुरः ।
सिंहं हन्तुं महादेव्याः कोपं चक्रे ततोऽम्बिका ॥

nipātya pramathānīkam abhyadhāvata so-suraḥ |
siṃhaṃ hantuṃ mahādevyāḥ
kopaṃ cakre tato-mbikā ||

Having laid low the troops of Her army, that thought advanced to kill the lion of the Goddess. Then the Mother of the Universe became very angry.

- 25 -

सोऽपि कोपान्महावीर्यः खुरक्षुण्णमहीतलः ।
शृङ्गाभ्यां पर्वतानुच्चांश्चिक्षेप च ननाद च ॥

so-pi kopān mahāvīryaḥ khurakṣuṇṇamahītalaḥ |
śriṅgābhyāṃ parvatanuccāṃściksepa ca nanāda ca ||

That great evil one, the Great Ego, also became very angry. He kicked the earth with his hooves, and raised large mountains with his horns and threw them aside as he roared.

- 26 -

वेगभ्रमणविक्षुण्णा मही तस्य व्यशीर्यत ।
लाङ्गूलेनाहतश्चाब्धिः प्लावयामास सर्वतः ॥

vegabhramaṇa vikṣuṇṇā mahī tasya vyaśīryata |
lāṅgūlenā hataścābdhiḥ plāvayāmāsa sarvataḥ ||

With the great speed of this thought, the earth split in fear; his tail lashed the sea of desire, causing the waters to flood the earth.

- 27 -

धुतशृङ्गविभिन्नाश्च खण्डं खण्डं ययुर्घनाः ।
श्वासानिलास्ताः शतशो निपेतुर्नभसोऽचलाः ॥

dhutaśṛṅgavibhinnāśca
khaṇḍaṃ khaṇḍaṃ yayurghanāḥ |
śvāsānilāstāḥ śataśo nipetur nabhaso-calāḥ ||

Tossing about his horns, he dashed and split the clouds to pieces, and cast up by the violent speed of his breath winds, mountains fell from the sky.

- 28 -

इति क्रोधसमाध्मातमापतन्तं महासुरम् ।
दृष्ट्वा सा चण्डिका कोपं तद्वधाय तदाकरोत् ॥

iti krodha samādhmātamāpatantaṃ mahāsuram |
dṛṣṭvā sā caṇḍikā kopaṃ tadvadhāya tadākarot ||

And waging battle in this great anger, the great thought advanced towards Her, while She Who Tears Apart Thought assumed anger and prepared to slay him.

- 29 -

सा क्षिप्त्वा तस्य वै पाशं तं बबन्ध महासुरम् ।
तत्याज माहिषं रूपं सोऽपि बद्धो महामृधे ॥

sā kṣiptvā tasya vai pāśaṃ
taṃ babandha mahāsuram |
tatyāja māhiṣaṃ rūpaṃ so-pi baddho mahāmṛdhe ||
Throwing Her net, She bound that great thought. After being bound in that great encounter, he left his form as a buffalo.

- 30 -

ततः सिंहोऽभवत्सद्यो यावत्तस्याम्बिका शिरः ।
छिनत्ति तावत्पुरुषः खड्गपाणिरदृश्यत ॥

tataḥ siṃho-bhavatsadyo yāvat tasyāmbikā śiraḥ |
chinatti tāvat puruṣaḥ khaḍga pāṇiradṛśyata ||
Thereafter he manifested in the form of a lion. In this condition the Mother of the Universe was prepared to cut off his head, but somehow he changed his form again to that of a man bearing a sword.

- 31 -

तत एवाशु पुरुषं देवी चिच्छेद सायकैः ।
तं खड्गचर्मणा सार्द्धं ततः सोऽभून्महागजः ॥

tata evāśu puruṣaṃ devī ciccheda sāyakaiḥ |
taṃ khaḍgacarmaṇā sārddhaṃ
tataḥ so-bhūnmahāgajaḥ ||
Then the Goddess instantly rained upon him a shower of arrows, and with sword and shield, She was ready to pierce him. Just then he took the form of the King of Elephants.

- 32 -

करेण च महासिंहं तं चकर्ष जगर्ज च ।
कर्षतस्तु करं देवी खड्गेन निरकृन्तत ॥

kareṇa ca mahāsiṃhaṃ taṃ cakarṣa jagarja ca |
karṣatastu karaṃ devī khaḍgena nirakṛntata ||
With his trunk he began to pull the huge lion of the Goddess and to roar, but as he was pulling, She cut the trunk with Her sword.

- 33 -

ततो महासुरो भूयो माहिषं वपुरास्थितः ।
तथैव क्षोभयामास त्रैलोक्यं सचराचरम् ॥

tato mahāsuro bhūyo māhiṣaṃ vapurāsthitaḥ |
tathaiva kṣobhayāmāsa trailokyaṃ sacarācaram ||

Then that great thought again wore the body of a buffalo, and in the manner as before with the inhalation and exhalation of his breath, he shook the three worlds with all that moves and moves not.

- 34 -

ततः क्रुद्धा जगन्माता चण्डिका पानमुत्तमम् ।
पपौ पुनः पुनश्चैव जहासारुणलोचना ॥

tataḥ kruddhā jaganmātā caṇḍikā pānamuttamam |
papau punaḥ punaścaiva jahāsāruṇa locanā ||

In great rage the Mother of the Perceivable World, She Who Tears Apart Thought, again and again drank an excellent spirit and with red eyes began to laugh.

- 35 -

ननर्द चासुरः सोऽपि बलवीर्यमदोद्धतः ।
विषाणाभ्यां च चिक्षेप चण्डिकां प्रति भूधरान् ॥

nanarda cāsuraḥ so-pi balavīryamadoddhataḥ |
viṣāṇābhyāṃ ca cikṣepa caṇḍikāṃ prati bhūdharān ||

There in the strength and boldness of that wild ecstasy, that evil demon roared, and with his horns, threw mountains at She Who Tears Apart Thought.

- 36 -

सा च तान् प्रहितांस्तेन चूर्णयन्ती शरोत्करैः ।
उवाच तं मदोद्धूतमुखरागाकुलाक्षरम् ॥

sā ca tān prahitāṃstena cūrṇayantī śarotkaraiḥ |
uvāca taṃ madoddhūta mukha rāgā kulākṣaram ||

She began to pulverize those mountains with Her arrows of Speech. Speaking in the ecstasy of spirit, Her mouth became red and Her tongue was stuttering.

- 37 -

देव्युवाच ॥

devyuvāca ||

The Goddess said:

- 38 -

गर्ज गर्ज क्षणं मूढ मधु यावत्पिबाम्यहम् ।
मया त्वयि हतेऽत्रैव गर्जिष्यन्त्याशु देवताः ॥

garja garja kṣaṇaṃ muḍha
madhu yāvat pibāmyaham ।
mayā tvayi hate-traiva garjiṣyantyāśu devatāḥ ॥

"Roar and roar, you fool! For so long as I drink this spirit, roar so much as you like. Your death is in my hands, and when I have finished drinking, soon the Gods will be roaring!"

- 39 -

ऋषिरुवाच ॥

ṛṣi ruvāca ॥

The Ṛṣi said:

- 40 -

एवमुक्त्वा समुत्पत्य साऽऽरूढा तं महासुरम् ।
पादेनाक्रम्य कण्ठे च शूलेनैनमताडयत् ॥

evamuktvā samutpatya sā--rūḍhā taṃ mahāsuram ।
pādenākramya kaṇṭhe ca śūlenainamatāḍayat ॥

Thus speaking, the Goddess leaped and ascended above that great thought. Pressing down upon him and holding him with Her foot, She struck him in the throat with Her pike.

- 41 -

ततः सोऽपि पदाऽऽक्रान्तस्तया निजमुखात्ततः ।
अर्धनिष्क्रान्त एवासीद् देव्या वीर्येण संवृतः ॥

tataḥ so-pi padā--krāntas tayā nijamukhāt tataḥ ।
ardhaniṣkrānta evāsīd devyā vīryeṇa saṃvṛtaḥ ॥

The Great Ego again, hit by the foot of the Goddess, changed his form from his mouth, but was able to free only half of his body. And with Her great strength the Goddess restrained that as well.

- 42 -

अर्धनिष्क्रान्त एवासौ युध्यमानो महासुरः ।
तया महासिना देव्या शिरश्छित्त्वा निपातितः ॥

ardhaniṣkrānta evāsau yudhyamāno mahāsuraḥ |
tayā mahāsinā devyā śiraśchittvā nipātitaḥ ||

Even with the half of his body coming out, the great thought waged battle with the Goddess. Then the Goddess cut off his head with a great double-edged sword.

- 43 -

ततो हाहाकृतं सर्वं दैत्यसैन्यं ननाश तत् ।
प्रहर्षं च परं जग्मुः सकला देवतागणाः ॥

tato hāhākṛtaṃ sarvaṃ daitya sainyaṃ nanāśa tat |
praharṣaṃ ca paraṃ jagmuḥ sakalā devatāgaṇāḥ ||

Shrieking and crying the remaining thoughts of that army ran away, and all the Gods became exceedingly joyous!

- 44 -

तुष्टुवुस्तां सुरा देवीं सह दिव्यैर्महर्षिभिः ।
जगुर्गन्धर्वपतयो ननृतुश्चाप्सरोगणाः ॥

tuṣṭuvustāṃ surā devīṃ saha divyair maharṣibhiḥ |
jagur gandharva patayo nanṛtuścāp sarogaṇāḥ ||

In great satisfaction the Gods joined the great seers in hymns of praise to the Goddess, while the celestial chorus and nymphs sang and danced with joy!

ॐ

oṃ

चतुर्थोऽध्यायः
caturtho-dhyāyaḥ
Chapter Four

ध्यानम्
dhyānam
Meditation

ॐ कालाभ्राभां कटाक्षैररिकुलभयदां मौलिबद्धेन्दुरेखां
शङ्खं चक्रं कृपाणं त्रिशिखमपि करैरुद्वहन्तीं त्रिनेत्राम् ।
सिंहस्कन्धाधिरूढां त्रिभुवनमखिलं तेजसा पूरयन्तीं
ध्यायेद् दुर्गां जयाख्यां त्रिदशपरिवृतां सेवितां सिद्धिकामैः ॥

oṃ kālābhrābhāṃ kaṭākṣairarikulabhayadāṃ
maulibaddhendurekhāṃ
śaṅkhaṃ cakraṃ kṛpāṇaṃ
triśikhamapikarairudvahantīṃ trinetrām ।
siṃhaskandhādhirūḍhāṃ
tribhuvanam akhilaṃ tejasā pūrayantīṃ
dhyāyed durgāṃ jayākhyāṃ
tridaśaparivṛtāṃ sevitāṃ siddhi kāmaiḥ ॥

We meditate on She who is constantly served by all men desiring the Ultimate Perfection, who is surrounded on all sides by Gods, the Goddess Who Removes Difficulties, who is named Jayā-Victory. Her beautiful body is splendidly dark like a black cloud. With Her side looks She instills fear into multitudes of enemies. A digit of the moon has been fastened upon Her head where it shines. In Her hands She holds a conch, discus, small sword or scimitar, and trident. She has three eyes. She stands leaning upon the shoulders of a lion, and Her radiant illumination has completely filled the three worlds.

- 1 -

ॐ ऋषिरुवाच ॥

oṃ ṛṣi ruvāca ||

Oṃ The Ṛṣi said:

- 2 -

शक्रादयः सुरगणा निहतेऽतिवीर्ये
तस्मिन्दुरात्मनि सुरारिबले च देव्या ।
तां तुष्टुवुः प्रणतिनम्रशिरोधरांसा
वाग्भिः प्रहर्षपुलकोद्गमचारुदेहाः ॥

śakrādayaḥ suragaṇā nihate-tivīrye
tasminduratmani surāribale ca devyā |
tāṃ tuṣṭuvuḥ praṇati namra śiro dharāṃsā
vāgbhiḥ praharṣa pulakodgamacārudehāḥ ||

After the death of that excessively forceful and evil thought, the Great Ego, and the destruction of his army of perturbations by the hand of the Divine Goddess, the Rule of the Pure, along with other divine ones, with their heads bowed in reverence, began to sing a hymn of praise to the Supreme Empress. Their beautiful bodies were filled with excessive delight and pleasurable excitement.

- 3 -

देव्या यया ततमिदं जगदात्मशक्त्या
निश्शेषदेवगणशक्तिसमूहमूर्त्या ।
तामम्बिकामखिलदेवमहर्षिपूज्यां
भक्त्या नताः स्म विदधातु शुभानि सा नः ॥

devyā yayā tatam idaṃ jagadāt maśaktyā
niśśeṣa devagaṇa śakti samūhamūrtyā |
tāmambikām akhila deva maharṣipūjyāṃ
bhaktyā natāḥ sma vidadhātu śubhāni sā naḥ ||

Her intrinsic nature is the aggregate energy of all the Gods; with Her energy She pervades the entire universe. She is the most highly regarded by all the Gods and Seers of sacred

Wisdom. To the Mother of the Universe, with the greatest intensity of devotion, we give reverence unto Her. May She grant us all welfare.

\- 4 -

यस्याः प्रभावमतुलं भगवाननन्तो
ब्रह्मा हरश्च न हि वक्तुमलं बलं च ।
सा चण्डिकाखिलजगत्परिपालनाय
नाशाय चाशुभभयस्य मतिं करोतु ॥

yasyāḥ prabhāvam atulaṃ bhagavān ananto
brahmā haraśca na hi vaktumalaṃ balaṃ ca |
sā caṇḍikākhila jagat pari pālanāya
nāśāya cāśubha bhayasya matiṃ karotu ||

Whose incomparable greatness and strength the Lord of the Universe (masculine) who creates, preserves, and dissolves the creation is incapable to extol, may that Supreme Empress, She Who Tears Apart Thought, think to protect the entire gross world and destroy fear and impurity.

\- 5 -

या श्रीः स्वयं सुकृतिनां भवनेष्वलक्ष्मीः
पापात्मनां कृतधियां हृदयेषु बुद्धिः ।
श्रद्धा सतां कुलजनप्रभवस्य लज्जा
तां त्वां नताः स्म परिपालय देवि विश्वम् ॥

yā śrīḥ svayaṃ sukṛtināṃ bhavaneṣvalakṣmīḥ
pāpātmanāṃ kṛtadhiyāṃ hṛdayeṣu buddhiḥ |
śraddhā satāṃ kulajana prabhavasya lajjā
tāṃ tvāṃ natāḥ sma paripālaya devi viśvam ||

She is the Goddess of True Wealth in the homes of virtuous souls and is the misery of those who perform evil. She is Intelligence in the hearts of the pure minded, Faith to the truthful, and Humility to the truly noble. To that Divine Goddess we bow in reverence. Please protect the entire universe.

\- 6 -

किं वर्णयाम तव रूपमचिन्त्यमेतत्
किं चातिवीर्यमसुरक्षयकारि भूरि ।
किं चाहवेषु चरितानि तवाद्भुतानि
सर्वेषु देव्यसुरदेवगणादिकेषु ॥

kiṃ varṇayāma tava rūpam acintyam etat
kiṃ cātivīryam asurakṣaya kāri bhūri |
kiṃ cāhaveṣu caritāni tavād bhutāni
sarveṣu devyasura deva gaṇādikeṣu ||

How can we describe your inconceivable form or your uncanny behavior displayed in the battle between all the Gods and thoughts, how you valiantly slew the thoughts and other evil ones?

\- 7 -

हेतुः समस्तजगतां त्रिगुणापि दोषै-
र्न ज्ञायसे हरिहरादिभिरप्यपारा ।
सर्वाश्रयाखिलमिदं जगदंशभूत-
मव्याकृता हि परमा प्रकृतिस्त्वमाद्या ॥

hetuḥ samasta jagatāṃ triguṇāpi doṣair
na jñāyase hariharādibhirapya pārā |
sarvāśrayākhilamidaṃ jagadaṃ śabhūtam
avyākṛtā hi paramā prakṛtis tvamādyā ||

In the origin of all perceivable existence you are the cause. Within you are the three qualities of Nature: conception, activity, and rest. These three exist in you, but you have no connection with any of their defects. You are beyond the conception of the Supreme Consciousness and the Great God and other Gods. You are the support of all. This entire perceivable universe is only a portion of your being because you are the imperceptible Primordial Being, the Supreme Nature.

- 8 -

यस्याः समस्तसुरता समुदीरणेन
तृप्तिं प्रयाति सकलेषु मखेषु देवि ।
स्वाहासि वै पितृगणस्य च तृप्तिहेतु-
रुच्चार्यसे त्वमत एव जनैः स्वधा च ॥

yasyāḥ samasta suratā samudīraṇena
tṛptiṃ prayāti sakaleṣu makheṣu devi |
svāhāsi vai pitṛgaṇasya ca tṛpti hetur
uccāryase tvamata eva janaiḥ svadhā ca ||

Oh Divine Goddess, in all sacrifices you are the word Svāhā, I am One with God, by whose pronunciation all Gods win contentment. Moreover, you are performed by all people as Oblations of Ancestral Praise, Svadhā, the cause of satisfaction to the ancestors.

- 9 -

या मुक्तिहेतुरविचिन्त्यमहाव्रता त्व-
मभ्यस्यसे सुनियतेन्द्रियतत्त्वसारैः ।
मोक्षार्थिभिर्मुनिभिरस्तसमस्तदोषै-
र्विद्यासि सा भगवती परमा हि देवि ॥

yā mukti heturavi cintya mahāvratā tvam
abhyasyase suniyatendriya tattva sāraiḥ |
mokṣārthibhir munibhirasta samasta doṣair
vidyāsi sā bhagavatī paramā hi devi ||

Oh Goddess, for those who seek realization, the inculcation of absolute freedom, inconceivable are the great austerities to be performed to be devoid of all defects, having the senses subdued, complying with the essence of the principles of Truth. Oh Supreme Empress, the wise who practice yearning for liberation, that, Ultimate Knowledge of Realization is you.

- 10 -

शब्दात्मिका सुविमलर्ग्यजुषां निधान-
मुद्गीथरम्यपदपाठवतां च साम्नाम् ।
देवी त्रयी भगवती भवभावनाय
वार्त्ता च सर्वजगतां परमार्त्तिहन्त्री ॥

śabdātmikā suvimalargya juṣāṃ nidhānam
udgītharamya padapāṭhavatāṃ ca sāmnām |
devī trayī bhagavatī bhavabhāvanāya
vārttā ca sarva jagatāṃ paramārtti hantrī ||

You are the intrinsic nature of sound and exceedingly pure as the Ṛg Veda, the Yājur Veda, and as the Sāma Veda with the special mode of pronunciation of songs in praise of the Divine. You are the foundation. You are the three Vedas and the Supreme Empress. The generation and protection of the universe is the activity that you manifest. You are the Destroyer of Fear and Torment in the entire perceivable universe.

- 11 -

मेधासि देवि विदिताखिलशास्त्रसारा
दुर्गासि दुर्गभवसागरनौरसङ्गा ।
श्रीः कैटभारिहृदयैककृताधिवासा
गौरी त्वमेव शशिमौलिकृतप्रतिष्ठा ॥

medhāsi devi viditākhila śāstrasārā
durgāsi durgabhava sāgara naurasaṅgā |
śrīḥ kaiṭabhāri hṛdayai kakṛtādhivāsā
gaurī tvameva śaśimauli kṛta pratiṣṭhā ||

Oh Goddess, you are the energy of intelligence by which the essence of all scriptures is understood. As the Goddess Who Relieves Afflictions, you are the boat that takes aspirants across the difficult sea of worldly thoughts unbound by attachment. You manifest as the Goddess of Wealth in the heart of Consciousness to do battle with the desires of want, and as the Goddess of Light to Lord Śiva, who wears the moon as a diadem.

- 12 -

ईषत्सहासममलं परिपूर्णचन्द्र-
बिम्बानुकारि कनकोत्तमकान्तिकान्तम् ।
अत्यद्भुतं प्रहृतमात्तरुषा तथापि
वक्त्रं विलोक्य सहसा महिषासुरेण ॥

īṣat sahāsamamalaṃ pari pūrṇa candra
bimbānu kāri kanakottama kānti kāntam |
atyadbhutaṃ prahṛtamāttaruṣā tathāpi
vaktraṃ vilokya sahasā mahiṣāsureṇa ||

The smile on your face shines pure like the splendor of the full moon's reflection, or like excellent gold desirable as beauty enhanced by love. Yet still, after seeing that beauty, the Great Ego struck out in anger; this is a greatly incomprehensible act.

- 13 -

दृष्ट्वा तु देवि कुपितं भ्रुकुटीकराल-
मुद्यच्छशाङ्कसदृशच्छवि यन्न सद्यः ।
प्राणान्मुमोच महिषस्तदतीव चित्रं
कैर्जीव्यते हि कुपितान्तकदर्शनेन ॥

dṛṣṭvā tu devi kupitaṃ bhrukuṭīkarālam
udyac chaśāṅka sadṛśac chavi yanna sadyaḥ |
prāṇān mumoca mahiṣas tadatīva citraṃ
kairjīvyate hi kupitān takadarśanena ||

Oh Goddess, it is even more incredulous still that the Great Ego did not quit his life immediately upon seeing your wrathful face, terrible with brows knit, and of reddish hue like the rising moon; for who can maintain his individual self upon seeing the Ruler of Dissolution?

- 14 -

देवि प्रसीद परमा भवती भवाय
सद्यो विनाशयसि कोपवती कुलानि ।
विज्ञातमेतदधुनैव यदस्तमेत-
न्नीतं बलं सुविपुलं महिषासुरस्य ॥

devi prasīda paramā bhavatī bhavāya
sadyo vināśayasi kopavatī kulāni |
vijñātametadadhunaiva yadastametan
nītaṃ balaṃ suvipulaṃ mahiṣāsurasya ||

Oh Goddess, be gracious. When you are pleased as the intrinsic nature of the Universal Soul, the entire world enjoys welfare and prosperity. And when your anger is known, immediately the entire families of enmity are destroyed, as we have verified the moment when the Great Ego with his extensive forces met his demise.

- 15 -

ते सम्मता जनपदेषु धनानि तेषां
तेषां यशांसि न च सीदति धर्मवर्गः ।
धन्यास्त एव निभृतात्मजभृत्यदारा
येषां सदाभ्युदयदा भवती प्रसन्ना ॥

te sammatā janapadeṣu dhanāni teṣāṃ
teṣāṃ yaśāṃsi na ca sīdati dharma vargaḥ |
dhanyāsta eva nibhṛtāt majabhṛtyadārā
yeṣaṃ sadābhyudayadā bhavatī prasannā ||

Oh you who are the Grantor of all Welfare, those with whom you are pleased are certainly respected in their country. They are endowed with welfare, and their acts of Wisdom and Harmony do not perish. They are blessed by the devotion of their children, wives, and servants.

- 16 -

धर्म्याणि देवि सकलानि सदैव कर्मा-
ण्यत्यादृतः प्रतिदिनं सुकृती करोति ।
स्वर्गं प्रयाति च ततो भवतीप्रसादा-
ल्लोकत्रयेऽपि फलदा ननु देवि तेन ॥

dharmyāṇi devi sakalāni sadaiva karmāṇ
yatyādṛtaḥ pratidinaṃ sukṛtī karoti |
svargaṃ prayāti ca tato bhavatī prasādāl
lokatraye-pi phaladā nanu devi tena ||

By your grace, Oh Goddess, the meritorious souls perform every day all the actions of spiritual discipline and righteous conduct with the greatest of faith and devotion, and thereby attain to heavenly perception. Are you not therefore the grantor of all fruit in the three worlds?

- 17 -

दुर्गे स्मृता हरसि भीतिमशेषजन्तोः
स्वस्थैः स्मृता मतिमतीव शुभां ददासि ।
दारिद्र्यदुःखभयहारिणि का त्वदन्या
सर्वोपकारकरणाय सदाऽऽर्द्रचित्ता ॥

durgę smṛtā harasi bhītima śeṣa jantoḥ
svasthaiḥ smṛtā matimatīva śubhāṃ dadāsi |
dāridrya duḥkha bhayahāriṇi kā tvadanyā
sarvopakāra karaṇāya sadā--rdracittā ||

Oh Reliever of Difficulties, remembering you the fear of all living beings is dispelled. When remembered by those individuals in the harmony of spiritual growth, you increase their welfare and intelligence. Who is like you, Oh Dispeller of Poverty, Pain, and Fear, whose sympathetic demeanor always extends compassionate assistance to everyone?

- 18 -

एभिर्हतैर्जगदुपैति सुखं तथैते
कुर्वन्तु नाम नरकाय चिराय पापम् ।
संग्राममृत्युमधिगम्य दिवं प्रयान्तु
मत्वेति नूनमहितान् विनिहंसि देवि ॥

ebhir hatair jagad upaiti sukhaṃ tathai te
kurvantu nāma narakāya cirāya pāpam |
saṃgrāmamṛtyum adhigamya divaṃ prayāntu
matveti nūnamahitān vinihaṃsi devi ||

The entire cosmos is pleased by the destruction of this enmity, and even though these ill-advised beings committed sins sufficient to warrant an infinite suffering in hell, nevertheless let them attain to the realms of heaven by meeting their demise in the battle with me. Thinking thus, Oh Goddess, certainly you destroy all enmity.

- 19 -

दृष्ट्वैव किं न भवती प्रकरोति भस्म
सर्वासुरानरिषु यत्प्रहिणोषि शस्त्रम् ।
लोकान् प्रयान्तु रिपवोऽपि हि शस्त्रपूता
इत्थं मतिर्भवति तेष्वपि तेऽतिसाध्वी ॥

dṛṣṭvaiva kiṃ na bhavatī prakaroti bhasma
sarvā surānariṣu yatprahiṇoṣi śastram |
lokān prayāntu ripavo-pi hi śastra pūtā
itthaṃ matirbhavati teṣvapi te-tisādhvī ||

Why is it that your one glance does not reduce all thoughts to ashes? So that being purified by the weapons these thoughts may be raised to the higher worlds. You are so benevolent that you think for the welfare of even your enemies.

- 20 -

खड्गप्रभानिकरविस्फुरणैस्तथोग्रैः
शूलाग्रकान्तिनिवहेन दृशोऽसुराणाम् ।
यन्नागता विलयमंशुमदिन्दुखण्ड-
योग्याननं तव विलोकयतां तदेतत् ॥

khaḍga prabhānikara visphuraṇais tathograiḥ
śūlāgra kānti nivahena dṛśo-surāṇām ।
yannāgatā vilaya maṃśumad indu khaṇḍa
yogyānanaṃ tava vilokayatāṃ tadetat ॥

If your sword's light and the foremost dazzling radiance from your pike did not blind the eyes of the thoughts, the reason was that they also saw the rays of light like the glow of the moon, the Giver of Bliss, in perceiving the vision of your beautiful face.

- 21 -

दुर्वृत्तवृत्तशमनं तव देवि शीलं
रूपं तथैतदविचिन्त्यमतुल्यमन्यैः ।
वीर्यं च हन्तृ हृतदेवपराक्रमाणां
वैरिष्वपि प्रकटितैव दया त्वयेत्थम् ॥

durvṛtta vṛtta śamanaṃ tava devi śīlaṃ
rūpaṃ tathaitada vicintyam atulyamanyaiḥ ।
vīryaṃ ca hantṛ hṛtadeva parākramāṇāṃ
vairiṣvapi prakaṭitaiva dayā tvayettham ॥

Oh Goddess, your inclination is to eradicate the faulty conduct of the wicked. With the vision of your form, no other concept may be contemplated, as no other similar exists. Hence your strength and prowess in slaying these thoughts who were destroying the power of the Gods. Thus you manifest your compassion to the enemies.

- 22 -

केनोपमा भवतु तेऽस्य पराक्रमस्य
रूपं च शत्रुभयकार्यतिहारि कुत्र ।
चित्ते कृपा समरनिष्ठुरता च दृष्टा
त्वय्येव देवि वरदे भुवनत्रयेऽपि ॥

kenopamā bhavatu te-sya parākramasya
rūpaṃ ca śatru bhaya kārya ti hāri kutra |
citte kṛpā samaraniṣṭhuratā ca dṛṣṭā
tvayyeva devi varade bhuvana traye-pi ||

Oh Goddess, Grantor of Wishes! With what can your valor be compared? You give fear to enemies with your excessive beauty. Where is a form beyond your own? Kindness in the heart and severity in battle; in all the three worlds these two can only be seen in you.

- 23 -

त्रैलोक्यमेतदखिलं रिपुनाशनेन
त्रातं त्वया समरमूर्धनि तेऽपि हत्वा ।
नीता दिवं रिपुगणा भयमप्यपास्त-
मस्माकमुन्मदसुरारिभवं नमस्ते ॥

trailokyam etadakhilaṃ ripunāśanena
trātaṃ tvayā samaramūrdhani te-pi hatvā |
nītā divaṃ ripugaṇā bhayam apyapāstam
asmākamunmadasurāri bhavaṃ namaste ||

In slaying these enemies, you have protected the entire three worlds. By dying on the battlefield, these enemies have arrived in heaven, and you have dispelled all our fears of thoughts. We bow to you!

- 24 -

शूलेन पाहि नो देवि पाहि खड्गेन चाम्बिके ।
घण्टास्वनेन नः पाहि चापज्यानिःस्वनेन च ॥

śūlena pāhi no devi pāhi khaḍgena cāmbike |
ghaṇṭā svanena naḥ pāhi cāpajyāniḥ svanena ca ||

Oh Goddess, protect us with your spear; Mother of the Universe, protect us with your sword. Protect us with the sound of your bell, and protect us with the twang of your bow string.

- 25 -

प्राच्यां रक्ष प्रतीच्यां च चण्डिके रक्ष दक्षिणे ।
भ्रामणेनात्मशूलस्य उत्तरस्यां तथेश्वरि ॥

prācyāṃ rakṣa pratīcyāṃ ca caṇḍike rakṣa dakṣiṇe |
bhrāmaṇenātmaśūlasya uttarasyāṃ tatheśvari ||

Protect us in the East, protect us in the West; Oh you Who Tear Apart Thought, protect us in the South. Then rotate your spear and protect us in the North.

- 26 -

सौम्यानि यानि रूपाणि त्रैलोक्ये विचरन्ति ते ।
यानि चात्यर्थघोराणि तै रक्षास्मांस्तथा भुवम् ॥

saumyāni yāni rūpāṇi trailokye vicaranti te |
yāni cātyarthaghorāṇi tai rakṣāsmāṃs tathā bhuvam ||

In the three worlds there are forms of your exquisite beauty and others exceedingly frightful that are conceived. With all of them protect us and protect the world.

- 27 -

खड्गशूलगदादीनि यानि चास्त्राणि तेऽम्बिके ।
करपल्लवसङ्गीनि तैरस्मान् रक्ष सर्वतः ॥

khaḍga śūla gadādīni yāni cāstrāṇi te-mbike |
karapallavasaṅgīni tairasmān rakṣa sarvataḥ ||

Oh Mother of the Universe, protect us everywhere and every time with your sword, your spear, your club; protect us on every side with every weapon that is in your lovely hands.

- 28 -

ऋषिरुवाच ॥

ṛṣi ruvāca ||

The Ṛṣi said:

- 29 -

एवं स्तुता सुरैर्दिव्यैः कुसुमैर्नन्दनोद्भवैः ।

अर्चिता जगतां धात्री तथा गन्धानुलेपनैः ॥

evaṃ stutā surairdivyaiḥ
kusumair nandanod bhavaiḥ |
arcitā jagatāṃ dhātrī tathā gandhānulepanaiḥ ||

Thus the Gods sang praise to the Creator of the Perceivable Universe and worshipped Her with flowers and perfume and other items of the garden of delight.

- 30 -

भक्त्या समस्तैस्त्रिदशैर्दिव्यैर्धूपैस्तु धूपिता ।

प्राह प्रसादसुमुखी समस्तान् प्रणतान् सुरान् ॥

bhaktyā samastais tridaśair
divyair dhūpaistu dhūpitā |
prāha prasādasumukhī samastān praṇatān surān ||

When all united in the fullest heavenly devotion and offered incense, fragrances, and food, then they all bowed to the Goddess in obeisance, and in serene countenance She spoke to them.

- 31 -

देव्युवाच ॥

devyuvāca ||

The Goddess said:

- 32 -

व्रियतां त्रिदशाः सर्वे यदस्मत्तोऽभिवाञ्छितम् ॥

vriyatāṃ tridaśāḥ sarve yadasmatto-bhivāñchitam ||

I will grant you the fulfillment of your desire.

- 33 -

देवा ऊचुः ॥

devā ūcuḥ ||

The Gods said:

- 34 -

भगवत्या कृतं सर्वं न किञ्चिदवशिष्यते ॥

bhagavatyā kṛtaṃ sarvaṃ na kiñcid avaśiṣyate ||

The Supreme Empress has fulfilled our every desire and there is nothing that remains undone.

- 35 -

यदयं निहतः शत्रुरस्माकं महिषासुरः ।
यदि चापि वरो देयस्त्वयास्माकं महेश्वरि ॥

yadayaṃ nihataḥ śatrur asmākaṃ mahiṣāsuraḥ |
yadi cāpi varo deyas tvayāsmākaṃ maheśvari ||

- 36 -

संस्मृता संस्मृता त्वं नो हिंसेथाः परमापदः ।
यश्च मर्त्यः स्तवैरेभिस्त्वां स्तोष्यत्यमलानने ॥

saṃsmṛtā saṃsmṛtā tvaṃ no
hiṃsethāḥ paramāpadaḥ |
yaśca martyaḥ stavairebhis
tvaṃ stoṣyatyamalānane ||

- 37 -

तस्य वित्तर्द्धिविभवैर्धनदारादि सम्पदाम् ।
वृद्धयेऽस्मत्प्रसन्ना त्वं भवेथाः सर्वदाम्बिके ॥

tasya vittarddhivibhavair dhana dārādi sampadām |
vṛddhaye-smatprasannā tvaṃ
bhavethāḥ sarvadāmbike ||

35-37. Our enemy the Great Ego has been slain. Oh Great Seer of All, beyond that you desire to grant us a boon? Then whenever we will remember you, then and there you will give us intuitive vision and remove our greatest distress. And, Oh Mother of the Universe, what ever humans praise you with these verses may you increase their knowledge, prosperity, and greatness, as well as their other possessions in life. Oh Mother! Always be pleased with us and grant us welfare and prosperity.

- 38 -

ऋषिरुवाच ॥

ṛṣi ruvāca ||

The Ṛṣi said:

- 39 -

इति प्रसादिता देवैर्जगतोऽर्थे तथाऽऽत्मनः ।

तथेत्युक्त्वा भद्रकाली बभूवान्तर्हिता नृप ॥

iti prasāditā devair jagator-the tathā--tmanaḥ |
tathet yuktvā bhadrakālī babhūvāntarhitā nṛpa ||

Oh King, when the Gods prayed for the welfare of themselves and the world, the Excellent One Beyond Time was pleased, and saying, "Let it be so," vanished from sight.

- 40 -

इत्येतत्कथितं भूप सम्भूता सा यथा पुरा ।

देवी देवशरीरेभ्यो जगत्त्रयहितैषिणी ॥

ityetatkathitaṃ bhūpa sambhūtā sā yathā purā |
devī devaśarīrebhyo jagat traya hitaiṣiṇī ||

Your Highness, I have told you the story of how in times of old the Goddess who desires the welfare of the three worlds was manifested from the bodies of the Gods.

- 41 -

पुनश्च गौरीदेहात्सा समुद्भूता यथाभवत् ।

वधाय दुष्टदैत्यानां तथा शुम्भनिशुम्भयोः ॥

punaśca gaurīdehātsā samudbhūtā yathābhavat |
vadhāya duṣṭa daityānāṃ
tathā śumbha niśumbhayoḥ ||

- 42 -

रक्षणाय च लोकानां देवानामुपकारिणी ।

तच्छृणुश्व मयाऽऽख्यातं यथावत्कथयामि ते ॥

rakṣaṇāya ca lokānāṃ devānām upakāriṇī |

tacchṛnuśva mayā-khyātaṃ yathā vatkathayāmi te ||

41-42. And now, oh Virtuous Soul, in like manner I shall narrate to you of Her appearance from the body of the Goddess of Light, the slayer of the vicious thoughts Self-Conceit and Self-Deprecation, and the Giver of Assistance to the Gods in order to protect all the worlds. Please listen to this entire episode being narrated by me.

ह्रीं ॐ

hrīṃ oṃ

पञ्चमोऽध्यायः
pañcamo-dhyāyaḥ
Chapter Five

विनियोगः
viniyogaḥ
Application

ॐ अस्य श्री उत्तरचरित्रस्य रुद्रऋषिः महासरस्वती देवता अनुष्टुप् छन्दः भीमा शक्तिः भ्रामरी बीजं सूर्यस्तत्त्वं सामवेदः स्वरूपं महासरस्वती प्रीत्यर्थे उत्तरचरित्रपाठे विनियोगः ।

oṃ asya śrī uttara caritrasya rudra ṛṣiḥ mahāsarasvatī devatā anuṣṭup chandaḥ bhīmā śaktiḥ bhrāmarī bījaṃ sūryas tattvaṃ sāmavedaḥ svarūpaṃ mahāsarasvatī prītyarthe uttara caritra pāṭhe viniyogaḥ ।

Oṃ Presenting the concluding episode: the Reliever from Suffering is the Seer, the Great Goddess of All-Pervading Knowledge is the deity, Anuṣṭup (32 syllables to the verse) is the meter, Bhīmā is the energy, Bhrāmarī is the seed, Sun is the principle, Sāma Veda is the intrinsic nature, and for the satisfaction of the Great Goddess of All-Pervading Knowledge this last episode is being applied in recitation.

ध्यानम्

dhyānam

Meditation

घण्टाशूलहलानि शङ्खमुसले चक्रं धनुः सायकं
हस्ताब्जैर्दधतीं घनान्तविलसच्छीतांशुतुल्यप्रभाम् ।
गौरीदेहसमुद्भवां त्रिजगतामाधारभूतां महा-
पूर्वामत्र सरस्वतीमनुभजे शुम्भादिदैत्यार्दिनीम् ॥

ghaṇṭā śūla halāni śaṅkha
musale cakraṃ dhanuḥ sāyakaṃ
hastābjair dadhatīṃ ghanānta
vilasacchītāṃ śutulya prabhām |
gaurīdeha samudbhavāṃ
trijagatām ādhārabhūtāṃ mahā-
pūrvāmatra sarasvatīm anubhaje
śumbhādi daityārdinīm ||

Bearing in Her lotus hands the bell of continuous tone, the pike of concentration, the plow sowing the seeds of the Way of Truth to Wisdom, the conch of vibrations, the pestle of refinement, the discus of revolving time, the bow of determination, and the arrow of speech, whose radiance is like the moon in autumn, whose appearance is most beautiful, who is manifested from the body of She Who is Rays of Light, and is the support of the three worlds, that Great Goddess of All-Pervading Knowledge, who destroyed Self-Conceit and other thoughts, I worship.

- 1 -

ॐ क्लीं ऋषिरुवाच ॥

oṃ klīṃ ṛṣi ruvāca ||

Oṃ Klīṃ The Ṛṣi said:

- 2 -

पुरा शुम्भनिशुम्भाभ्यामसुराभ्यां शचीपतेः ।
त्रैलोक्यं यज्ञभागाश्च हृता मदबलाश्रयात् ॥

purā śumbha niśumbhābhyām
asurābhyāṃ śacīpateḥ |
trailokyaṃ yajña bhāgāśca hṛtā madabalāśrayāt ||

In olden days there were two thoughts, Self-Conceit and Self-Deprecation, who, with the abundance of their excessive self-conceit, robbed the Rule of the Pure, the husband of the Power That Rules and master of the three worlds, of a portion of sacrifice.

- 3 -

तावेव सूर्यतां तद्वदधिकारं तथैन्दवम् ।
कौबेरमथ याम्यं च चक्राते वरुणस्य च ॥

tāveva sūryatāṃ tadvad adhikāraṃ tathaindavam |
kauberamatha yāmyaṃ ca cakrāte varuṇasya ca ||

- 4 -

तावेव पवनर्द्धिं च चक्रतुर्वह्निकर्म च ।
ततो देवा विनिर्धूता भ्रष्टराज्याः पराजिताः ॥

tāveva pavanarddhiṃ ca cakraturvahni karma ca |
tato devā vinirdhūtā bhraṣṭa rājyāḥ parājitāḥ ||

- 5 -

हृताधिकारास्त्रिदशास्ताभ्यां सर्वे निराकृताः ।
महासुराभ्यां तां देवीं संस्मरन्त्यपराजिताम् ॥

hṛtādhikārāstridaśās tābhyāṃ sarve nirākṛtāḥ |
mahāsurābhyāṃ tāṃ devīṃ
saṃsmarantya parājitām ||

- 6 -

तयास्माकं वरो दत्तो यथाऽऽपत्सु स्मृताखिलाः ।
भवतां नाशयिष्यामि तत्क्षणात्परमापदः ॥

tayāsmākaṃ varo datto yathā--patsu smṛtākhilāḥ |
bhavatāṃ nāśayiṣyāmi tatkṣaṇāt paramāpadaḥ ||

3-6. Those two assumed the dominions of the Light of Wisdom and Devotion, the Lord of Wealth, the Power of Control, and the Lord of Equilibrium, and made them subservient. The effects of Emancipation and the Light of Meditation were also removed. These two defeated the Gods, assumed their authority, and spoiled the kingdom, and with disrespect all the Gods were put out of heaven. Having been thus insulted by the two great thoughts, the Gods remembered the Invincible Goddess and thought of the boon the Mother of the Universe gave to them. In any time of adversity if you remember Me, then and there I will eradicate your every distress.

- 7 -

इति कृत्वा मतिं देवा हिमवन्तं नगेश्वरम् ।
जग्मुस्तत्र ततो देवीं विष्णुमायां प्रतुष्टुवुः ॥

iti kṛtvā matiṃ devā himavantaṃ nageśvaram |
jagmustatra tato devīṃ viṣṇumāyāṃ pratuṣṭuvuḥ ||

Thinking thus, the Gods went to the King of Mountains, Himalayas, and there began to extol the Goddess, the Supreme Lord, the Great Measurement of the Consciousness that Pervades All.

- 8 -

देवा ऊचुः ॥

devā ūcuḥ ||

The Gods said:

- 9 -

नमो देव्यै महादेव्यै शिवायै सततं नमः ।
नमः प्रकृत्यै भद्रायै नियताः प्रणताः स्म ताम् ॥

namo devyai mahādevyai śivāyai satataṃ namaḥ |
namaḥ prakṛtyai bhadrāyai
niyatāḥ praṇatāḥ sma tām ||

We bow to the Goddess, to the Great Goddess, to the Energy of Infinite Goodness at all times we bow. We bow to Nature, to the Excellent One, with discipline we have bowed down.

- 10 -

रौद्रायै नमो नित्यायै गौर्यै धात्र्यै नमो नमः ।
ज्योत्स्नायै चेन्दुरूपिण्यै सुखायै सततं नमः ॥

raudrāyai namo nityāyai
gauryai dhātryai namo namaḥ |
jyotsnāyai cendurūpiṇyai sukhāyai satataṃ namaḥ ||

To the Reliever of Sufferings we bow, to the Eternal, to the
Embodiment of Rays of Light, to the Creatress, to She Who
Manifests Light, to the form of Devotion, to Happiness contin-
ually we bow.

- 11 -

कल्याण्यै प्रणतां वृद्ध्यै सिद्ध्यै कुर्मो नमो नमः ।
नैर्ऋत्यै भूभृतां लक्ष्म्यै शर्वाण्यै ते नमो नमः ॥

kalyāṇyai praṇatāṃ vṛddhyai
siddhyai kurmo namo namaḥ |
nairṛtyai bhūbhṛtāṃ lakṣmyai
śarvāṇyai te namo namaḥ ||

To the Welfare of those who bow, we bow; to Change, to
Perfection, to Dissolution, to the Wealth that sustains the earth,
to the Wife of Consciousness, to you, we bow, we bow.

- 12 -

दुर्गायै दुर्गपारायै सारायै सर्वकारिण्यै ।
ख्यात्यै तथैव कृष्णायै धूम्रायै सततं नमः ॥

durgāyai durgapārāyai sārāyai sarvakāriṇyai |
khyātyai tathaiva kṛṣṇāyai
dhūmrāyai satataṃ namaḥ ||

To She Who Removes Difficulties, to She Who Removes
Beyond All Difficulties, to the Essence, to the Cause of All; to
Perception, and to the Doer of All, to the Unknowable One,
continually we bow.

- 13 -

अतिसौम्यातिरौद्रायै नतास्तस्यै नमो नमः ।
नमो जगत्प्रतिष्ठायै देव्यै कृत्यै नमो नमः ॥

atisaumyāti raudrāyai natāstasyai namo namaḥ |
namo jagat pratiṣṭhāyai devyai kṛtyai namo namaḥ ||

To the extremely beautiful and to the extremely fierce, we bow to Her, we bow, we bow. We bow to the Establisher of the Perceivable Universe, to the Goddess, to All Action, we bow, we bow.

- 14 -

या देवी सर्वभूतेषु विष्णुमायेति शब्दिता । नमस्तस्यै ॥
15. नमस्तस्यै ॥ 16. नमस्तस्यै नमो नमः ॥

yā devī sarva bhūteṣu viṣṇu māyeti śabditā |
namastasyai || namastasyai || namastasyai namo namaḥ ||

To the Divine Goddess in all existence who is addressed as the Perceivable Form of the Consciousness That Pervades All, we bow to Her; we bow to Her; we bow to Her, continually we bow, we bow.

- 17 -

या देवी सर्वभूतेषु चेतनेत्यभिधीयते । नमस्तस्यै ॥
18. नमस्तस्यै ॥ 19. नमस्तस्यै नमो नमः ॥

yā devī sarva bhūteṣu cetanetyabhi dhīyate |
namastasyai || namastasyai || namastasyai namo namaḥ ||

To the Divine Goddess in all existence who resides all throughout the Consciousness and is known by the reflections of mind, we bow to Her; we bow to Her; we bow to Her, continually we bow, we bow.

- 20 -

या देवी सर्वभूतेषु बुद्धिरूपेण संस्थिता । नमस्तस्यै ॥
21. नमस्तस्यै ॥ 22. नमस्तस्यै नमो नमः ॥

yā devī sarva bhūteṣu buddhi rūpeṇa saṃsthitā |
namastasyai || namastasyai || namastasyai namo namaḥ ||

To the Divine Goddess who resides in all existence in the form of Intelligence, we bow to Her; we bow to Her; we bow to Her, continually we bow, we bow.

\- 23 -

या देवी सर्वभूतेषु निद्रारूपेण संस्थिता । नमस्तस्यै ॥

24\. नमस्तस्यै ॥ 25. नमस्तस्यै नमो नमः ॥

yā devī sarva bhūteṣu nidrā rūpeṇa saṃsthitā | namastasyai || namastasyai || namastasyai namo namaḥ ||

To the Divine Goddess who resides in all existence in the form of Sleep, we bow to Her; we bow to Her; we bow to Her, continually we bow, we bow.

\- 26 -

या देवी सर्वभूतेषु क्षुधारूपेण संस्थिता । नमस्तस्यै ॥

27\. नमस्तस्यै ॥ 28. नमस्तस्यै नमो नमः ॥

yā devī sarva bhūteṣu kṣudhā rūpeṇa saṃsthitā | namastasyai || namastasyai || namastasyai namo namaḥ ||

To the Divine Goddess who resides in all existence in the form of Hunger, we bow to Her; we bow to Her; we bow to Her, continually we bow, we bow.

\- 29 -

या देवी सर्वभूतेषु छायारूपेण संस्थिता । नमस्तस्यै ॥

30\. नमस्तस्यै ॥ 31. नमस्तस्यै नमो नमः ॥

yā devī sarva bhūteṣu chāyā rūpeṇa saṃsthitā | namastasyai || namastasyai || namastasyai namo namaḥ ||

To the Divine Goddess who resides in all existence in the form of Appearance, we bow to Her; we bow to Her; we bow to Her, continually we bow, we bow.

\- 32 -

या देवी सर्वभूतेषु शक्तिरूपेण संस्थिता । नमस्तस्यै ॥

33\. नमस्तस्यै ॥ 34. नमस्तस्यै नमो नमः ॥

yā devī sarva bhūteṣu śakti rūpeṇa saṃsthitā | namastasyai || namastasyai || namastasyai namo namaḥ ||

To the Divine Goddess who resides in all existence in the form of Energy, we bow to Her; we bow to Her; we bow to Her, continually we bow, we bow.

- 35 -

या देवी सर्वभूतेषु तृष्णारूपेण संस्थिता । नमस्तस्यै ॥

36. नमस्तस्यै ॥ 37. नमस्तस्यै नमो नमः ॥

yā devī sarva bhūteṣu tṛṣṇā rūpeṇa saṃsthitā I namastasyai II namastasyai II namastasyai namo namaḥ II

To the Divine Goddess who resides in all existence in the form of Desire, we bow to Her; we bow to Her; we bow to Her, continually we bow, we bow.

- 38 -

या देवी सर्वभूतेषु क्षान्तिरूपेण संस्थिता । नमस्तस्यै ॥

39. नमस्तस्यै ॥ 40. नमस्तस्यै नमो नमः ॥

yā devī sarva bhūteṣu kṣānti rūpeṇa saṃsthitā I namastasyai II namastasyai II namastasyai namo namaḥ II

To the Divine Goddess who resides in all existence in the form of Patient Forgiveness, we bow to Her; we bow to Her; we bow to Her, continually we bow, we bow.

- 41 -

या देवी सर्वभूतेषु जातिरूपेण संस्थिता । नमस्तस्यै ॥

42. नमस्तस्यै ॥ 43. नमस्तस्यै नमो नमः ॥

yā devī sarva bhūteṣu jāti rūpeṇa saṃsthitā I namastasyai II namastasyai II namastasyai namo namaḥ II

To the Divine Goddess who resides in all existence in the form of All Living Beings, we bow to Her; we bow to Her; we bow to Her, continually we bow, we bow.

- 44 -

या देवी सर्वभूतेषु लज्जारूपेण संस्थिता । नमस्तस्यै ॥

45. नमस्तस्यै ॥ 46. नमस्तस्यै नमो नमः ॥

yā devī sarva bhūteṣu lajjā rūpeṇa saṃsthitā | namastasyai || namastasyai || namastasyai namo namaḥ ||

To the Divine Goddess who resides in all existence in the form of Humility, we bow to Her; we bow to Her; we bow to Her, continually we bow, we bow.

- 47 -

या देवी सर्वभूतेषु शान्तिरूपेण संस्थिता । नमस्तस्यै ॥

48. नमस्तस्यै ॥ 49. नमस्तस्यै नमो नमः ॥

yā devī sarva bhūteṣu śānti rūpeṇa saṃsthitā | namastasyai || namastasyai || namastasyai namo namaḥ ||

To the Divine Goddess who resides in all existence in the form of Peace, we bow to Her; we bow to Her; we bow to Her, continually we bow, we bow.

- 50 -

या देवी सर्वभूतेषु श्रद्धारूपेण संस्थिता । नमस्तस्यै ॥

51. नमस्तस्यै ॥ 52. नमस्तस्यै नमो नमः ॥

yā devī sarva bhūteṣu śraddhā rūpeṇa saṃsthitā | namastasyai || namastasyai || namastasyai namo namaḥ ||

To the Divine Goddess who resides in all existence in the form of Faith, we bow to Her; we bow to Her; we bow to Her, continually we bow, we bow.

- 53 -

या देवी सर्वभूतेषु कान्तिरूपेण संस्थिता । नमस्तस्यै ॥

54. नमस्तस्यै ॥ 55. नमस्तस्यै नमो नमः ॥

yā devī sarva bhūteṣu kānti rūpeṇa saṃsthitā | namastasyai || namastasyai || namastasyai namo namaḥ ||

To the Divine Goddess who resides in all existence in the form of Beauty Enhanced by Love, we bow to Her; we bow to Her; we bow to Her, continually we bow, we bow.

\- 56 -

या देवी सर्वभूतेषु लक्ष्मीरूपेण संस्थिता । नमस्तस्यै ॥

57\. नमस्तस्यै ॥ 58. नमस्तस्यै नमो नमः ॥

yā devī sarva bhūteṣu lakṣmī rūpeṇa saṃsthitā | namastasyai || namastasyai || namastasyai namo namaḥ ||

To the Divine Goddess who resides in all existence in the form of True Wealth, we bow to Her; we bow to Her; we bow to Her, continually we bow, we bow.

\- 59 -

या देवी सर्वभूतेषु वृत्तिरूपेण संस्थिता । नमस्तस्यै ॥

60\. नमस्तस्यै ॥ 61. नमस्तस्यै नमो नमः ॥

yā devī sarva bhūteṣu vṛtti rūpeṇa saṃsthitā | namastasyai || namastasyai || namastasyai namo namaḥ ||

To the Divine Goddess who resides in all existence in the form of Activity, we bow to Her; we bow to Her; we bow to Her, continually we bow, we bow.

\- 62 -

या देवी सर्वभूतेषु स्मृतिरूपेण संस्थिता । नमस्तस्यै ॥

63\. नमस्तस्यै ॥ 64. नमस्तस्यै नमो नमः ॥

yā devī sarva bhūteṣu smṛti rūpeṇa saṃsthitā | namastasyai || namastasyai || namastasyai namo namaḥ ||

To the Divine Goddess who resides in all existence in the form of Recollection, we bow to Her; we bow to Her; we bow to Her, continually we bow, we bow.

\- 65 -

या देवी सर्वभूतेषु दयारूपेण संस्थिता । नमस्तस्यै ॥

66\. नमस्तस्यै ॥ 67. नमस्तस्यै नमो नमः ॥

yā devī sarva bhūteṣu dayā rūpeṇa saṃsthitā | namastasyai || namastasyai || namastasyai namo namaḥ ||

To the Divine Goddess who resides in all existence in the form of Compassion, we bow to Her; we bow to Her; we bow to Her, continually we bow, we bow.

\- 68 -

या देवी सर्वभूतेषु तुष्टिरूपेण संस्थिता । नमस्तस्यै ॥

69. नमस्तस्यै ॥ 70. नमस्तस्यै नमो नमः ॥

yā devī sarva bhūteṣu tuṣṭi rūpeṇa saṃsthitā | namastasyai || namastasyai || namastasyai namo namaḥ ||

To the Divine Goddess who resides in all existence in the form of Satisfaction, we bow to Her; we bow to Her; we bow to Her, continually we bow, we bow.

\- 71 -

या देवी सर्वभूतेषु मातृरूपेण संस्थिता । नमस्तस्यै ॥

72. नमस्तस्यै ॥ 73. नमस्तस्यै नमो नमः ॥

yā devī sarva bhūteṣu mātṛ rūpeṇa saṃsthitā | namastasyai || namastasyai || namastasyai namo namaḥ ||

To the Divine Goddess who resides in all existence in the form of Mother, we bow to Her; we bow to Her; we bow to Her, continually we bow, we bow.

\- 74 -

या देवी सर्वभूतेषु भ्रान्तिरूपेण संस्थिता । नमस्तस्यै ॥

75. नमस्तस्यै ॥ 76. नमस्तस्यै नमो नमः ॥

yā devī sarva bhūteṣu bhrānti rūpeṇa saṃsthitā | namastasyai || namastasyai || namastasyai namo namaḥ ||

To the Divine Goddess who resides in all existence in the form of Confusion, we bow to Her; we bow to Her; we bow to Her, continually we bow, we bow.

\- 77 -

इन्द्रियाणामधिष्ठात्री भूतानां चाखिलेषु या ।

भूतेषु सततं तस्यै व्याप्तिदेव्यै नमो नमः ॥

indriyāṇāmadhiṣṭhātrī bhūtānāṃ cākhileṣu yā |
bhūteṣu satataṃ tasyai vyāptidevyai namo namaḥ ||

Presiding over the senses of all beings and pervading all existence, to the Omnipresent Goddess who individualizes creation we bow, we bow.

\- 78 -

चितिरूपेण या कृत्स्नमेतद् व्याप्य स्थिता जगत् ।
नमस्तस्यै ॥ 79. नमस्तस्यै ॥ 80. नमस्तस्यै नमो नमः ॥

citirūpeṇa yā kṛtsnametad vyāpya sthitā jagat |
namastasyai || namastasyai || namastasyai namo namaḥ ||

In the form of Consciousness She distinguishes the individual phenomena of the perceivable universe. We bow to Her; we bow to Her; we bow to Her, continually we bow, we bow.

\- 81 -

स्तुता सुरैः पूर्वमभीष्टसंश्रयात्तथा सुरेन्द्रेण दिनेषु सेविता ।
करोतु सा नः शुभहेतुरीश्वरी शुभानि भद्राण्यभिहन्तु चापदः ॥

stutā suraiḥ pūrvamabhīṣṭa saṃśrayāt
tathā surendreṇa dineṣu sevitā |
karotu sā naḥ śubha hetur īśvarī
śubhāni bhadrāṇyabhi hantu cāpadaḥ ||

In days of old, all of the Gods, led by Indra, the Rule of the Pure, sang these verses of praise for the purpose of accomplishing their desired objective of surrendering the ego in the Light of Wisdom, and for many days that service was rendered. May She, the Seer of All, the Lord of All, the Source of All Good, perform similarly for us all auspicious things by putting an end to all distress.

\- 82 -

या साम्प्रतं चोद्धतदैत्यतापितैरस्माभिरीशा च सुरैर्नमस्यते ।
या च स्मृता तत्क्षणमेव हन्ति नः सर्वापदो भक्ति विनम्रमूर्तिभिः ॥

yā sāmpratam̱ coddhata daitya tāpitair
asmābhi rīśā ca surair namasyate |
yā ca smṛtā tat kṣaṇameva hanti naḥ
sarvāpado 'bhakti vinamra mūrtibhiḥ ||

We Gods have been harassed by arrogant thoughts in the manner of humans, and at this time all of us Gods bow to the Seer of All, who, when bowed to with devotion, and remembered in a physical image, immediately terminates our every adversity.

- 83 -

ऋषिरुवाच ॥

ṛṣi ruvāca ||

The Ṛṣi said:

- 84 -

एवं स्तवादियुक्तानां देवानां तत्र पार्वती ।
स्नातुमभ्याययौ तोये जाह्नव्या नृपनन्दन ॥

evam̱ stavādi yuktānām̱ devānām̱ tatra pārvatī |
snātumabhyāyayau toye jāhnavyā nṛpanandana ||

Your Highness, just as the Gods were singing that hymn of praise, the Goddess of Nature came there to bathe in the Ganges.

- 85 -

साब्रवीत्तान् सुरान् सुभ्रूर्भवद्भिः स्तूयतेऽत्र का ।
शरीरकोशतश्चास्याः समुद्भूताब्रवीच्छिवा ॥

sābravīttān surān subhrūr bhavadbhiḥ stūyate-tra kā |
śarīra kośataścāsyāḥ samud bhūtā bravīcchivā ||

That Supreme Empress with beautiful eyebrows asked the Gods, "Whose praise is being sung here?" Then from within Herself an auspicious form manifested and said:

- 86 -

स्तोत्रं ममैतत् क्रियते शुम्भदैत्यनिराकृतैः ।
देवैः समेतैः समरे निशुम्भेन पराजितैः ॥

stotram̱ mamaitat kriyate śumbhadaityanirākṛtaiḥ |
devaiḥ sametaiḥ samare niśumbhena parājitaiḥ ||

"Self-Conceit and Self-Deprecation, two terrible thoughts, have defeated the Gods and insulted them, and so all the Gods have collected here and are singing my praise."

- 87 -

शरीरकोशाद्यत्तस्याः पार्वत्या निःसृताम्बिका ।

कौशिकीति समस्तेषु ततो लोकेषु गीयते ॥

śarīra kośādyat tasyāḥ pārvatyā nihsṛtāmbikā |

kauśitkīti samasteṣu tato lokeṣu gīyate ||

And as the Mother of the Universe emerged from within the Goddess of Nature, She is known in all the worlds as She Who Comes From Within.

- 88 -

तस्यां विनिर्गतायां तु कृष्णाभूत्सापि पार्वती ।

कालिकेति समाख्याता हिमाचलकृताश्रया ॥

tasyāṃ vinirgatāyāṃ tu kṛṣṇā bhūtsāpi pārvatī |

kāliketi samākhyātā himācala kṛtāśrayā ||

After the manifestation of She Who Comes From Within, the body of Nature became dark, and consequently became a Goddess who dwells in the Himalayas, distinguished as the Remover of Darkness.

- 89 -

ततोऽम्बिकां परं रूपं बिभ्राणां सुमनोहरम् ।

ददर्श चण्डो मुण्डश्च भृत्यौ शुम्भनिशुम्भयोः ॥

tato-mbikāṃ paraṃ rūpaṃ bibhrāṇāṃ sumanoharam |

dadarśa caṇḍo muṇḍaśca

bhṛtyau śumbha niśumbhayoḥ ||

Thereafter two servants of Self-Conceit and Self-Deprecation, named Passion and Anger, came and saw the extremely beautiful form worn by the Mother of the Universe.

- 90 -

ताभ्यां शुम्भाय चाख्याता अतीव सुमनोहरा ।

काप्यास्ते स्त्री महाराज भासयन्ती हिमाचलम् ॥

tābhyāṃ śumbhāya cākhyātā atīva sumanoharā |

kāpyāste strī mahārāja bhāsayantī himācalam ||

Then Self-Conceit was told by them, "Oh Great King, there is an excessively beautiful woman whose heavenly beauty is illuminating the Himalayas.

- 91 -

नैव तादृक् क्वचिद्रूपं दृष्टं केनचिदुत्तमम् ।
ज्ञायतां काप्यसौ देवी गृह्यतां चासुरेश्वर ॥

naiva tādṛk kvacidrūpaṃ dṛṣṭaṃ kenaciduttamam |
jñāyatāṃ kāpyasau devī gṛhyatāṃ cāsureśvara ||

Such an excellent form no one has ever before beheld. Oh Lord of Thought, please find out who that Goddess is and take Her.

- 92 -

स्त्रीरत्नमतिचार्वङ्गी द्योतयन्ती दिशस्त्विषा ।
सा तु तिष्ठति दैत्येन्द्र तां भवान् द्रष्टुमर्हति ॥

strī ratnamati cārvaṅgī dyotayantī diśastviṣā |
sā tu tiṣṭhati daityendra tāṃ bhavān draṣṭu marhati ||

Of all women She is a jewel. Her every limb is very beautiful, and the radiant splendor of Her body is illuminating all the directions. She is present there. You should see Her!

- 93 -

यानि रत्नानि मणयो गजाश्वादीनि वै प्रभो ।
त्रैलोक्ये तु समस्तानि साम्प्रतं भान्ति ते गृहे ॥

yāni ratnāni maṇayo gajāśvādīni vai prabho |
trailokye tu samastāni sāmpratam bhānti te gṛhe ||

Lord, of the three worlds, jewels, gems, elephants, horses, the best all shine in your house.

- 94 -

ऐरावतः समानीतो गजरत्नं पुरन्दरात् ।
पारिजाततरुश्चायं तथैवोच्चैःश्रवा हयः ॥

airāvataḥ samānīto gajaratnaṃ purandarāt |
pārijāta taruścāyaṃ tathaivoc caiḥ śravā hayaḥ ||

Of elephants you have the jewel, Love for All, taken from the Rule of the Pure; of trees the Tree of Life; of horses, the horse of Wisdom.

- 95 -

विमानं हंससंयुक्तमेतत्तिष्ठति तेऽङ्गणे ।
रत्नभूतमिहानीतं यदासीद्वेधसोऽद्भुतम् ॥

vimānaṃ haṃsa saṃyuktam etattiṣṭhati te-ṅgaṇe |
ratnabhūtamihānītaṃ yadāsīd vedhaso-dbhutam ||

The most wonderful carrier, yoked to the swans of union through the control of breath, which before was with the Lord of Creation, now has been brought here and shines in your court-yard, the jewel of its kind.

- 96 -

निधिरेष महापद्मः समानीतो धनेश्वरात् ।
किञ्जल्किनीं ददौ चाब्धिर्मालामम्लानपङ्कजाम् ॥

nidhireṣa mahāpadmaḥ samānīto dhaneśvarāt |
kiñjalkinīṃ dadau cābdhir mālāmamlā napañkajām ||

Of the nine treasures of the Lord of Wealth, you have taken the Great Lotus of Peace, and the ocean has given you a garland of fine lotuses that never lose their luster.

- 97 -

छत्रं ते वारुणं गेहे काञ्चनस्रावि तिष्ठति ।
तथायं स्यन्दनवरो यः पुराऽऽसीत् प्रजापतेः ॥

chatraṃ te vāruṇaṃ gehe kāñcanasrāvi tiṣṭhati |
tathāyaṃ syandanavaro yaḥ purā--sīt prajāpateḥ ||

The umbrella of the Lord of Equilibrium, which causes gold to flow, stands in your house, and also the chosen chariot that belonged to the Creator of Beings.

- 98 -

मृत्योरुत्क्रान्तिदा नाम शक्तिरीश त्वया हृता ।
पाशः सलिलराजस्य भ्रातुस्तव परिग्रहे ॥

mṛtyorutkrāntidā nāma śaktirīśa tvayā hṛtā |
pāśaḥ salilarājasya bhrātustava parigrahe ||

From Death you have taken the Supreme Energy known as "Moving Beyond," and your brother has taken possession of the shining net of the Lord of Fluctuation.

- 99 -

निशुम्भस्याब्धिजाताश्च समस्ता रत्नजातयः ।
वह्निरपि ददौ तुभ्यमग्निशौचे च वाससी ॥

niśumbhasyābdhi jātāśca samastā ratnajātayaḥ |
vahnirapi dadau tubhyam agni śauce ca vāsasī ||

And of the beings born of the sea, Self-Deprecation has taken the most excellent jewels. The Divine Fire himself purified two garments and presented them to you.

- 100 -

एवं दैत्येन्द्र रत्नानि समस्तान्याहृतानि ते ।
स्त्रीरत्नमेषा कल्याणी त्वया कस्मान्न गृह्यते ॥

evaṃ daityendra ratnāni samastān yāhṛtāni te |
strīratnameṣa kalyāṇī tvayā kasmānna gṛhyate ||

And so, Oh Lord of Thought, of all jewels you have taken the best and most excellent. And of all women the finest jewel is the Goddess of Welfare. Why don't you bring Her to your house?"

- 101 -

ऋषिरुवाच ॥

ṛṣi ruvāca ||

The Ṛṣi said:

- 102 -

निशम्येति वचः शुम्भः स तदा चण्डमुण्डयोः ।
प्रेषयामास सुग्रीवं दूतं देव्या महासुरम् ॥

niśamyeti vacaḥ śumbhaḥ sa tadā caṇḍa muṇḍayoḥ |
preṣayāmāsa sugrīvaṃ dūtaṃ devyā mahāsuram ||

After hearing the words of Passion and Anger, Self-Conceit sent He Who Appears to be a Friend, a great thought, as an ambassador to the Goddess.

- 103 -

इति चेति च वक्तव्या सा गत्वा वचनान्मम ।
यथा चाभ्येति सम्प्रीत्या तथा कार्यं त्वया लघु ॥

iti ceti ca vaktavyā sā gatvā vacanān mama |
yathā cābhyeti samprītya tathā kāryaṃ tvayā laghu ||
He commanded him: "Explain all this to Her with sweet words so that, being pleased, She will quickly come."

- 104 -

स तत्र गत्वा यत्रास्ते शैलोद्देशेऽति शोभने ।
सा देवी तां ततः प्राह श्लक्ष्णं मधुरया गिरा ॥

sa tatra gatvā yatrāste śailod deśe-ti śobhane |
sā devī tāṃ tataḥ prāha ślakṣṇaṃ madhurayā girā ||
Then the ambassador went to that very beautiful area in the mountains where the Goddess was seated, and spoke in tender, honey-like words.

- 105 -

दूत उवाच ॥

dūta uvāca ||
The Ambassador said:

- 106 -

देवि दैत्येश्वरः शुम्भस्त्रैलोक्ये परमेश्वरः ।
दूतोऽहं प्रेषितस्तेन त्वत्सकाशमिहागतः ॥

devi daityeśvaraḥ śumbhastrailokye parameśvaraḥ |
dūto-haṃ preṣitastena tvat sakāśamihāgataḥ ||
"Oh Goddess, the King of Thought, Self-Conceit, is the Lord of the three worlds. I have been sent as his ambassador to come to you.

- 107 -

अव्याहताज्ञः सर्वासु यः सदा देवयोनिषु ।
निर्जिताखिलदैत्यारिः स यदाह शृणुश्व तत् ॥

avyāhatājñaḥ sarvāsu yaḥ sadā devayoniṣu |
nirjitākhiladaityāriḥ sa yadāha śṛṇuśva tat ||
All of the Gods have been defeated by him, and all obey his commands. No one can violate his order. Listen to the message he sends to you.

- 108 -

मम त्रैलोक्यमखिलं मम देवा वशानुगाः ।

यज्ञभागानहं सर्वानुपाश्नामि पृथक् पृथक् ॥

mama trailokyamakhilaṃ mama devā vaśānugāḥ |

yajñabhāgānahaṃ sarvānupāśnāmi pṛthak pṛthak ||

'The entire three worlds are under my authority, and all the Gods obey my every command. I personally enjoy the share of every sacrifice.

- 109 -

त्रैलोक्ये वररत्नानि मम वश्यान्यशेषतः ।

तथैव गजरत्नं च हृत्वा देवेन्द्रवाहनम् ॥

trailokye vararatnāni mama vaśyān yaśeṣataḥ |

tathaiva gajaratnaṃ ca hṛtvā devendra vāhanam ||

All the finest jewels in the three worlds are under my authority, and I have taken the jewel of elephants, the carrier of the God, the Rule of the Pure.

- 110 -

क्षीरोदमथनोद्भूतमश्वरत्नं ममामरैः ।

उच्चैःश्रवससंज्ञं तत्प्रणिपत्य समर्पितम् ॥

kṣīrodamathanod bhūtam aśvaratnaṃ mamāmaraiḥ |

uccaiḥ śravasasaṃjñaṃ tat praṇipatya samarpitam ||

The jewel of horses, the horse of Wisdom, which was produced from the beginning of creation, the Gods have surrendered at my feet.

- 111 -

यानि चान्यानि देवेषु गन्धर्वेषूरगेषु च ।

रत्नभूतानि भूतानि तानि मय्येव शोभने ॥

yāni cānyāni deveṣu gandarveṣū rageṣu ca |

ratna bhūtāni bhūtāni tāni mayyeva śobhane ||

Oh Beautiful One, beyond that, as many beautiful jewels that belonged to the Gods or to the heavenly beings or to the swift-ly proceeding, they all shine with me.

- 112 -

स्त्रीरत्नभूतां त्वां देवि लोके मन्यामहे वयम् ।
सा त्वमस्मानुपागच्छ यतो रत्नभुजो वयम् ॥

strī ratna bhūtāṃ tvāṃ devi
loke manyāmahe vayam |
sā tvamasmānupāgaccha yato ratna bhujo vayam ||

Oh Goddess, we consider you to be the jewel of all women in the creation; therefore you come to us because we are the enjoyers of all jewels.

- 113 -

मां वा ममानुजं वापि निशुम्भमुरुविक्रमम् ।
भज त्वं चञ्चलापाङ्गि रत्नभूतासि वै यतः ॥

māṃ vā mamānujaṃ vāpi niśumbha muruvikramam |
bhaja tvaṃ cañcalāpāṅgi ratna bhūtāsi vai yataḥ ||

You of inconstant gaze, come and serve me and my extremely valiant brother, Self-Deprecation, because you are the very essence of jewels.

- 114 -

परमैश्वर्यमतुलं प्राप्स्यसे मत्परिग्रहात् ।
एतद् बुद्ध्या समालोच्य मत्परिग्रहतां व्रज ॥

paramaiśvaryamatulaṃ prāpsyase mat parigrahāt |
etad buddhyā samālocya matparigrahatāṃ vraja ||

By fulfilling my wish you will achieve great glory. Now, use your intelligence to decide if you want to be my wife.'"

- 115 -

ऋषिरुवाच ॥

ṛṣi ruvāca ||

The Ṛṣi said:

- 116 -

इत्युक्ता सा तदा देवी गम्भीरान्तः स्मिता जगौ ।
दुर्गा भगवती भद्रा ययेदं धार्यते जगत् ॥

ityuktā sā tadā devī gambhīrāntaḥ smitāḥ jagau |
durgā bhagavatī bhadrā yayedaṃ dhāryate jagat ||

Then the Goddess, the Excellent Supreme Empress, She Who Removes Difficulties, thoughtfully, tranquilly, gently smiling, gave Her reply.

\- 117 -

देव्युवाच ॥

devyuvāca ||

The Goddess said:

\- 118 -

सत्यमुक्तं त्वया नात्र मिथ्या किञ्चित्त्वयोदितम् ।
त्रैलोक्याधिपतिः शुम्भो निशुम्भश्चापि तादृशः ॥

satyamuktaṃ tvayā nātra mithyā kiñcittvayoditam |
trailokyādhipatiḥ śumbho niśumbhaścāpi tādṛśaḥ ||

All that you have said is true without a particle of falsehood. Self-Conceit is the Master of the three worlds, as is equally the valiant Self-Deprecation.

\- 119 -

किं त्वत्र यत्प्रतिज्ञातं मिथ्या तत्क्रियते कथम् ।
श्रूयतामल्पबुद्धित्वात्प्रतिज्ञा या कृता पुरा ॥

kiṃ tvatra yat pratijñātaṃ mithyā tat kriyate katham |
śrūyatām alpa buddhitvāt pratijñā yā kṛtā purā ||

But in this matter, because of my small intelligence, I have already undertaken an oath to which I cannot be untrue. Please listen:

\- 120 -

यो मां जयति संग्रामे यो मे दर्पं व्यपोहति ।
यो मे प्रतिबलो लोके स मे भर्ता भविष्यति ॥

yo māṃ jayati saṅgrāme yo me darpaṃ vyapohati |
yo me prati balo loke sa me bhartā bhaviṣyati ||

Whoever will defeat me in the battle, whoever will lose his self-conceit in me, whoever will see all the force of the universe in me, he will be my husband.

\- 121 -

तदागच्छतु शुम्भोऽत्र निशुम्भो वा महासुरः ।
मां जित्वा किं चिरेणात्र पाणिं गृह्णातु मे लघु ॥

tadāgacchatu śumbho-tra niśumbho vā mahāsuraḥ |
mām jitvā kiṃ cireṇātra pāṇiṃ gṛhṇātu me laghu ||
So you return to Self-Conceit and Self-Deprecation, great thoughts. When they conquer me, I will marry. What is the necessity of delay?

- 122 -

दूत उवाच ॥
dūta uvāca ||
The Ambassador said:

- 123 -

अवलिप्तासि मैवं त्वं देवि ब्रूहि ममाग्रतः ।
त्रैलोक्ये कः पुमांस्तिष्ठेदग्रे शुम्भनिशुम्भयोः ॥
avaliptāsi maivaṃ tvaṃ devi brūhi mamāgrataḥ |
trailokye kaḥ pumāṃstiṣṭhe
dagre śumbha niśumbhayoḥ ||
Goddess, your pride is very great to speak like that to me. In the three worlds there is not a man who can stand against Self-Conceit and Self-Deprecation.

- 124 -

अन्येषामपि दैत्यानां सर्वे देवा न वै युधि ।
तिष्ठन्ति सम्मुखे देवि किं पुनः स्त्री त्वमेकिका ॥
anyeṣāmapi daityānāṃ sarve devā na vai yudhi |
tiṣṭhanti sammukhe devi kiṃ punaḥ strī tvamekikā ||
Goddess, all of the Gods cannot challenge the thoughts in battle. What merit have you as you are alone and a woman?

- 125 -

इन्द्राद्याः सकला देवास्तस्थुर्येषां न संयुगे ।
शुम्भादीनां कथं तेषां स्त्री प्रयास्यसि सम्मुखम् ॥
indrādyāḥ sakalā devās tasthuryeṣāṃ na saṃyuge |
śumbhādīnāṃ kathaṃ teṣāṃ
strī prayāsyasi sammukham ||
If the Rule of the Pure and all the other Gods could not stand up to Self-Conceit in battle, how will you, a woman, go forth to battle?

- 126 -

सा त्वं गच्छ मयैवोक्ता पार्श्वं शुम्भनिशुम्भयोः ।
केशाकर्षणनिर्धूतगौरवा मा गमिष्यसि ॥

sā tvaṃ gaccha mayaivoktā
pārśvaṃ śumbha niśumbhayoḥ I
keśākarṣaṇanirdhūta gauravā mā gamiṣyasi II

Therefore go to Self-Conceit and Self-Deprecation because of what I have said. In this way you will protect your dignity. Otherwise, when you are grabbed by the hair and dragged, you will lose your honor.

- 127 -

देव्युवाच ॥

devyuvāca II

The Goddess said:

- 128 -

एवमेतद् बली शुम्भो निशुम्भश्चातिवीर्यवान् ।
किं करोमि प्रतिज्ञा मे यदनालोचिता पुरा ॥

evametad balī śumbho niśumbhaś cāti vīryavān I
kiṃ karomi pratijñā me yadanalocitā purā II

What you say is correct. Self-Conceit iṣ very strong and Self-Deprecation too is a valiant warrior. But what can I do? Without thinking, I have made this promise.

- 129 -

स त्वं गच्छ मयोक्तं ते यदेतत्सर्वमादृतः ।
तदाचक्ष्वासुरेन्द्राय स च युक्तं करोतु तत् ॥

sa tvaṃ gaccha mayoktaṃ te yadetatsarvamādṛtaḥ I
tadā cakṣvāsurendrāya sa ca yuktaṃ karotu tat II

Now you go and, just as I have told you, explain fully to the King of Thought. Then let him do what he thinks is proper.

ॐ

oṃ

षष्ठोऽध्यायः
ṣaṣṭho-dhyāyaḥ
Chapter Six

ध्यानम्
dhyānam
Meditation

ॐ नागाधीश्वरविष्टरां फणिफणोत्तंसोरुरत्नावली-
भास्वद्देहलतां दिवाकरनिभां नेत्रत्रयोद्भासिताम् ।
मालाकुम्भकपालनीरजकरां चन्द्रार्धचूडां परां
सर्वज्ञेश्वरभैरवाङ्कनिलयां पद्मावतीं चिन्तये ॥

oṃ nāgādhīśvara viṣṭarāṃ
phaṇi phaṇottaṃsoru ratnāvalī-
bhāsvaddehalatāṃ divākaranibhāṃ
netra trayodbhāsitām |
mālā kumbhakapāla nīrajakarāṃ
candrārdhacūḍāṃ parāṃ
sarva jñeśvara bhairavāṅkanilayāṃ
padmāvatīṃ cintaye ||

I think of the Ultimate Goddess, Padmāvatī, who resides in the Eyes of the Lord of All Wisdom, Bhairava. Her tender body is effulgent with the brilliance of the multitude of jewels on the hoods of the King of Snakes upon whom She is reclining. Her luster is like that of the sun, and Her three eyes are brilliant. In Her hands She holds a rosary, a gourd, a skull, and a lotus, and the radiant half-moon is the shining crown upon Her head.

- 1 -

ॐ ऋषिरुवाच ॥
oṃ ṛṣi ruvāca ||
Oṃ The Ṛṣi said:

- 2 -

इत्याकर्ण्य वचो देव्याः स दूतोऽमर्षपूरितः ।
समाचष्ट समागम्य दैत्यराजाय विस्तरात् ॥

ityākarṇya vaco devyāḥ sa dūto-marṣa pūritaḥ I
samācaṣṭa samāgamya daitya rājāya vistarāt II

After listening to the words of the Goddess, the Ambassador became very angry, and returning to the King of Thought, gave a detailed explanation.

- 3 -

तस्य दूतस्य तद्वाक्यमाकर्ण्यासुरराट् ततः ।
सक्रोधः प्राह दैत्यानामधिपं धूम्रलोचनम् ॥

tasya dūtasya tadvākyam ākarṇyāsurarāṭ tataḥ I
sakrodhaḥ prāha daityānām
adhipaṃ dhūmralocanam II

Hearing the report of the ambassador, the King of Thought became very indignant, and in great anger he called a thought named Sinful Eyes.

- 4 -

हे धूम्रलोचनाशु त्वं स्वसैन्यपरिवारितः ।
तामानय बलाद् दुष्टां केशाकर्षणविह्वलाम् ॥

he dhūmralocanāśu tvaṃ svasainya parivāritaḥ I
tāmānaya balād duṣṭāṃ keśākarṣaṇa vihvalām II

Hey Sinful Eyes! Go quickly, taking your army and grabbing that naughty one by the hair, drag Her here!

- 5 -

तत्परित्राणदः कश्चिद्यदि वोत्तिष्ठतेऽपरः ।
स हन्तव्योऽमरो वापि यक्षो गन्धर्व एव वा ॥

tatparitrāṇadaḥ kaścidyadi vottiṣṭhate-paraḥ I
sa hantavyo-maro vāpi yakṣo gandharva eva vā II

And if anyone stands up to defend Her, be he God, semi-divine being, or celestial being, certainly you will kill him!

- 6 -

ऋषिरुवाच ॥

ṛṣi ruvāca ||

The Ṛṣi said:

- 7 -

तेनाज्ञप्तस्ततः शीघ्रं स दैत्यो धूम्रलोचनः ।

वृतः षष्ट्या सहस्राणामसुराणां द्रुतं ययौ ॥

tenājñaptastataḥ śīghraṃ sa daityo dhūmralocanaḥ |

vṛtaḥ ṣaṣṭyā sahasrāṇām asurāṇāṃ drutaṃ yayau ||

Receiving the command from Self-Conceit, Sinful Eyes, along with an army of sixty thousand thoughts, immediately proceeded.

- 8 -

स दृष्ट्वा तां ततो देवीं तुहिनाचलसंस्थिताम् ।

जगादोच्चैः प्रयाहीति मूलं शुम्भनिशुम्भयोः ॥

sa dṛṣṭvā tāṃ tato devīṃ tuhinācala saṃsthitām |

jagādoccaiḥ prayāhīti mūlaṃ śumbha niśumbhayoḥ ||

- 9 -

न चेत्प्रीत्याद्य भवती मद्भर्तारमुपैष्यति ।

ततो बलान्नयाम्येष केशाकर्षणविह्वलाम् ॥

na cet prītyādya bhavatī madbhartāram upaiṣyati |

tato balān nayāmyeṣa keśākarṣaṇa vihvalām ||

8-9. Arriving there he saw the Goddess seated upon the Himalayas, and defiantly shouted, "Enemy! Go to Self-Conceit and Self-Deprecation! If you won't go lovingly to the side of my master right now, then I will grab you by the hair and forcibly drag you there!"

- 10 -

देव्युवाच ॥

devyuvāca ||

The Goddess said:

- 11 -

दैत्येश्वरेण प्रहितो बलवान् बलसंवृतः ।

बलान्नयसि मामेवं ततः किं ते करोम्यहम् ॥

daityeśvareṇa prahito balavān balasaṃvṛtaḥ |

balānnayasi māmevaṃ tataḥ kiṃ te karomyaham ||

You have been sent by the King of Thought, and you yourself are extremely mighty. Along with you is a great army. In this condition, if you take me by force, then what can I do?

- 12 -

ऋषिरुवाच ॥

ṛṣi ruvāca ||

The Ṛṣi said:

- 13 -

इत्युक्तः सोऽभ्यधावत्तामसुरो धूम्रलोचनः ।

हुंकारेणैव तं भस्म सा चकाराम्बिका ततः ॥

ityuktaḥ so-bhyadhā vattām asuro dhūmralocanaḥ |

huṃkāreṇaiva taṃ bhasma sā cakārāmbikā tataḥ ||

After the Goddess answered thus, that thought, Sinful Eyes attacked, and with the pronunciation of the mantra, "Huṃ!" the Mother of the Universe reduced him to ashes.

- 14 -

अथ क्रुद्धं महासैन्यमसुराणां तथाम्बिका ।

ववर्ष सायकैस्तीक्ष्णैस्तथा शक्तिपरश्वधैः ॥

atha kruddhaṃ mahāsainyamasurāṇāṃ tathāmbikā |

vavarṣa sāyakaistīkṣṇais tathā śakti paraśvadhaiḥ ||

Then in great anger that immense army of thoughts and the Mother of the Universe began to exchange a rain of arrows, energies, and battle axes.

- 15 -

ततो धुतसटः कोपात्कृत्वा नादं सुभैरवम् ।

पपातासुरसेनायां सिंहो देव्याः स्ववाहनः ॥

tato dhutasaṭaḥ kopāt kṛtvā nādaṃ subhairavam |

papātāsurasenāyāṃ siṃho devyāḥ svavāhanaḥ ||

In all of this the carrier of the Goddess, the lion, shaking his mane in excessive rage, with a frightful roar, jumped into the army of thoughts.

- 16 -

कांश्चित् करप्रहारेण दैत्यानास्येन चापरान् ।

आक्रम्य चाधरेणान्यान् स जघान महासुरान् ॥

kāṃścit karaprahāreṇa daityā nāsyena cāparān |

ākramya cādhareṇānyān sa jaghāna mahā surān ||

Some thoughts died from the striking of his paws, others from his jaws. Still other great thoughts were trampled by his hind legs and died from their wounds.

- 17 -

केषांचित्पाटयामास नखैः कोष्ठानि केसरी ।

तथा तलप्रहारेण शिरांसि कृतवान् पृथक् ॥

keṣāṃcitpāṭayāmāsa nakhaiḥ koṣṭhāni kesarī |

tathā talaprahāreṇa śirāṃsi kṛtavān pṛthak ||

Striking with his claws, he struck so many in the stomach, and by the sword, so many heads he severed.

- 18 -

विच्छिन्नबाहुशिरसः कृतास्तेन तथापरे ।

पपौ च रुधिरं कोष्ठादन्येषां धुतकेसरः ॥

vicchinnabāhu śirasaḥ kṛtāstena tathāpare |

papau ca rudhiraṃ koṣṭhādanyeṣāṃ dhutakesaraḥ ||

Shaking his mane, the lion cut so many arms and heads. Striking the stomachs of some thoughts, that lion caused their blood to flow.

- 19 -

क्षणेन तद्बलं सर्वं क्षयं नीतं महात्मना ।

तेन केसरिणा देव्या वाहनेनातिकोपिना ॥

kṣaṇena tadbalaṃ sarvaṃ

kṣayaṃ nītaṃ mahātmanā |

tena kesariṇā devyā vāhanenāti kopinā ||

Excessively angry, the carrier of the Goddess, that extremely forceful lion, in but a moment annihilated that entire army of thoughts.

- 20 -

श्रुत्वा तमसुरं देव्या निहतं धूम्रलोचनम् ।

बलं च क्षयितं कृत्स्नं देवीकेसरिणा ततः ॥

śrutvā tamasuraṃ devyā nihataṃ dhūmralocanam |

balaṃ ca kṣayitaṃ kṛtsnaṃ devī kesariṇā tataḥ ||

- 21 -

चुकोप दैत्याधिपतिः शुम्भः प्रस्फुरिताधरः ।

आज्ञापयामास च तौ चण्डमुण्डौ महासुरौ ॥

cukopa daityādhipatiḥ śumbhaḥ prasphuritādharaḥ |

ājñāpayāmāsa ca tau caṇḍa muṇḍau maha surau ||

20-21. When the King of Thought heard that the Goddess killed Sinful Eyes, and that Her lion eradicated the entire army, he became very angry. His lower lip trembled with rage. Then he gave a command to Passion and Anger.

- 22 -

हे चण्ड हे मुण्ड बलैर्बहुभिः परिवारितौ ।

तत्र गच्छत गत्वा च सा समानीयतां लघु ॥

he caṇḍa he muṇḍa balair bahubhiḥ parivāritau |

tatra gacchata gatvā ca sā samānīyatāṃ laghu ||

- 23 -

केशेष्वाकृष्य बद्ध्वा वा यदि वः संशयो युधि ।

तदाशेषायुधैः सर्वैरसुरैर्विनिहन्यताम् ॥

keśeṣvākṛṣya baddhvā vā yadi vaḥ saṃśayo yudhi |

tadāśeṣāyudaiḥ sarvair asurair vinihanyatām ||

22-23. Hey Passion! Hey Anger! Take a great army and grab that Goddess by the hair, and binding Her, quickly bring Her here. And if there is any doubt in bringing Her, then fight with all your weapons and with the entire army of thoughts and wound Her.

- 24 -

तस्यां हतायां दुष्टायां सिंहे च विनिपातिते ।

शीघ्रमागम्यतां बद्ध्वा गृहीत्वा तामथाम्बिकाम् ॥

tasyāṃ hatāyāṃ duṣṭāyāṃ siṃhe ca vinipātite |
śīghramāgamyatāṃ baddhvā
gṛhītvā tāmathāmbikām ||

And after wounding that naughty one and Her lion, bind that Mother of the Universe and return with Her quickly.

ॐ

oṃ

सप्तमोऽध्यायः
saptamo-dhyāyaḥ
Chapter Seven

ध्यानम्
dhyānam
Meditation

ॐ ध्यायेयं रत्नपीठे शुककलपठितं शृण्वतीं श्यामलाङ्गीं
न्यस्तैकाङ्घ्रिं सरोजे शशिशकलधरां वल्लकीं वादयन्तीम् ।
कह्लाराबद्धमालां नियमितविलसच्चोलिकां रक्तवस्त्रां
मातङ्गीं शङ्खपात्रां मधुरमधुमदां चित्रकोद्भासिभालाम् ॥

oṃ dhyāyeyaṃ ratnapīṭhe śukakalapaṭhitaṃ
śṛṇvatīṃ śyāmalāṅgīṃ
nyastaikāṅghriṃ saroje śaśi śakaladharāṃ
vallakīṃ vādayantīm |
kahlārābaddhamālāṃ niyamitavilasac
colikāṃ raktavastrāṃ
mātaṅgīṃ śankhapātrāṃ madhuramadhumadāṃ
citrakodbhāsibhālām ||

I meditate upon the Goddess Mātaṇgī, the Embodiment of the Mother. Sitting upon a throne of jewels, She is listening to the sweet sounds of parrots. The color of Her body is dark. She has one foot resting upon a lotus, and She wears a half-moon upon Her head. Wearing a garland of flower buds, She plays the strings of a vīṇā. She covers Her body with a blouse and a red-colored ṣari. In Her hand is a cup made of a conch shell. From Her face comes a slight sweet scent that causes intoxication, and a brilliant spot of vermillion shines on Her forehead.

- 1 -

ॐ ऋषिरुवाच ॥

oṃ ṛṣi ruvāca ||

Oṃ The Ṛṣi said:

- 2 -

आज्ञप्तास्ते ततो दैत्याश्चण्डमुण्डपुरोगमाः ।
चतुरङ्गबलोपेता ययुरभ्युद्यतायुधाः ॥

ājñaptāste tato daityāś caṇḍa muṇḍa purogamāḥ |
caturaṅga balopetā yayurabhyudyatāyudhāḥ ||

In adherence to the command of Self-Conceit, Passion and Anger set forth with four divisions of their army of thoughts, well adorned with weapons and armor.

- 3 -

ददृशुस्ते ततो देवीमीषद्धासां व्यवस्थिताम् ।
सिंहस्योपरि शैलेन्द्रशृङ्गे महति काञ्चने ॥

dadṛśuste tato devīmīṣaddhāsāṃ vyavasthitām |
siṃhasyopari śailendra śṛṅge mahati kāñcane ||

On a high peak in the golden mountains, they saw the Goddess sitting on Her lion, smiling with delight.

- 4 -

ते दृष्ट्वा तां समादातुमुद्यमं चक्रुरुद्यताः ।
आकृष्टचापासिधरास्तथान्ये तत्समीपगाः ॥

te dṛṣṭvā tāṃ samādātumudyamaṃ cakrurudyatāḥ |
ākṛṣṭa cāpāsidharās tathānye tat samīpagāḥ ||

Seeing Her, the thoughts made ready to capture Her. Some took up their bows, some raised their swords, some collected around the Goddess to begin the fight.

- 5 -

ततः कोपं चकारोच्चैरम्बिका तानरीन् प्रति ।
कोपेन चास्या वदनं मषीवर्णमभूत्तदा ॥

tataḥ kopaṃ cakāroccair ambikā tānarīn prati |
kopena cāsya vadanaṃ maṣīvarṇama bhūttadā ||

Then the Mother of the Universe became very angry with those attackers, and Her face turned dark with rage.

- 6 -

भ्रुकुटीकुटिलात्तस्या ललाटफलकाद् द्रुतम् ।
काली करालवदना विनिष्क्रान्तासिपाशिनी ॥

bhrukuṭī kuṭilāt tasyā lalāṭa phalakād drutam |
kālī karālavadanā viniṣkrāntāsipāśinī ||

The eyebrows were scowling, and from Her frowning forehead appeared the Remover of Darkness with a terribly frightening face, who was holding a sword and a net in Her hands.

- 7 -

विचित्रखट्वाङ्गधरा नरमालाविभूषणा ।
द्वीपिचर्मपरीधाना शुष्कमांसातिभैरवा ॥

vicitra khaṭvāṅgadharā naramālā vibhūṣaṇā |
dvīpicarmaparīdhānā śuṣkamāṃsāti bhairavā ||

She wore a leopard skin garment and a garland of human skulls. Her flesh had withered, and She appeared as a skeleton of bones and very fierce. She displayed fantastic missiles of consciousness.

- 8 -

अतिविस्तारवदना जिह्वाललनभीषणा ।
निमग्नारक्तनयना नादापूरितदिङ्मुखा ॥

ativistāravadanā jihvālalanabhīṣaṇā |
nimagnā rakta nayanā nādāpūrita diṅmukhā ||

Her mouth was immense, and She brandished Her tongue as a sword that caused great fear. Her eyes were penetrating and somewhat red, and Her fearful roar was humming in all directions.

- 9 -

सा वेगेनाभिपतिता घातयन्ती महासुरान् ।
सैन्ये तत्र सुरारीणामभक्षयत तद्बलम् ॥

sā vegenābhipatitā ghātayantī mahāsurān |
sainye tatra surārīṇām abhakṣayata tadbalam ||

The Remover of Darkness killed many great thoughts and, after destroying an army of thoughts in great haste, She began to eat them all.

- 10 -

पार्ष्णिग्राहाङ्कुशग्राहियोधघण्टासमन्वितान् ।
समादायैकहस्तेन मुखे चिक्षेप वारणान् ॥

pārṣṇigrāhāṅkuśagrāhi yodha ghaṇṭā samanvitān |
samādāyaikahastena mukhe cikṣepa vāraṇān ||

She picked up elephants with one hand and put them into Her mouth together with their protectors, the driver with his goad, soldiers, and bells.

- 11 -

तथैव योधं तुरगै रथं सारथिना सह ।
निक्षिप्य वक्त्रे दशनैश्चर्वयन्त्यतिभैरवम् ॥

tathaiva yodhaṃ turagai rathaṃ sārathinā saha |
nikṣipya vaktre daśanaiś carvayantyati bhairavam ||

In the same way She took warriors, horses, chariots with their charioteers, and the entire cavalry of thoughts, She put them into Her mouth, and hideously began to chew.

- 12 -

एकं जग्राह केशेषु ग्रीवायामथ चापरम् ।
पादेनाक्रम्य चैवान्यमुरसान्यमपोथयत् ॥

ekaṃ jagrāha keśeṣu grīvāyāmatha cāparam |
pādenākramya caivānyam urasānyamapothayat ||

Some thoughts She grabbed by the hair, others She crushed at the throat; still others She trampled with Her feet, and others She killed by a stroke to the breast.

- 13 -

तैर्मुक्तानि च शस्त्राणि महास्त्राणि तथासुरैः ।
मुखेन जग्राह रुषा दशनैर्मथितान्यपि ॥

tairmuktāni ca śastrāṇi mahāstrāṇi tathāsuraiḥ |
mukhena jagrāha ruṣā daśanair mathitānyapi ||

She picked up the great weapons of that army in Her mouth, and in fearful anger She ground them with Her teeth.

- 14 -

बलिनां तद् बलं सर्वमसुराणां दुरात्मनाम् ।

ममर्दाभक्षयच्चान्यानन्यांश्चाताडयत्तथा ॥

balināṃ tad balaṃ sarvam asurāṇāṃ durātmanām |
mamardābhakṣayac cānyān anyāṃścātāḍayat tathā ||

She trampled that entire army of mighty and wicked thoughts and ate them all, and others She fiercely beat.

- 15 -

असिना निहिताः केचित्केचित्खट्वाङ्गताडिताः ।

जग्मुर्विनाशमसुरा दन्ताग्राभिहतास्तथा ॥

asinā nihitāḥ kecit kecit khaṭvāṅga tāḍitāḥ |
jagmurvināśam asurā dantā grābhi hatāstathā ||

Some fell by the blade of Her sword, some were beaten by the missiles of consciousness, and some were crushed to death by Her formidable teeth.

- 16 -

क्षणेन तद् बलं सर्वमसुराणां निपातितम् ।

दृष्ट्वा चण्डोऽभिदुद्राव तां कालीमतिभीषणाम् ॥

kṣaṇena tad balaṃ sarvam asurāṇāṃ nipātitam |
dṛṣṭvā caṇḍo-bhidudrāva tāṃ kālīmati bhīṣaṇām ||

In this way that entire mighty army of thoughts was killed in a moment. Seeing this, Passion attacked that excessively fearful Remover of Darkness.

- 17 -

शरवर्षैर्महाभीमैर्भीमाक्षीं तां महासुरः ।

छादयामास चक्रैश्च मुण्डः क्षिप्तैः सहस्रशः ॥

śaravarṣair mahā bhīmair
bhīmākṣīṃ tāṃ mahāsuraḥ |
chādayāmāsa cakraiśca
muṇḍaḥ kṣiptaiḥ sahasraśaḥ ||

Also that great thought, Anger, rained his extremely terrible arrows and hurled a thousand discuses against the fearful-eyed Goddess.

- 18 -

तानि चक्राण्यनेकानि विशमानानि तन्मुखम् ।
बभुर्यथार्कबिम्बानि सुबहूनि घनोदरम् ॥

tāni cakrāṇyanekāni viśamānāni tanmukham |
babhuryathārka bimbāni subahūni ghanodaram ||

Those discuses entering into Her mouth shone as a halo of light of the sun absorbed in many clouds.

- 19 -

ततो जहासातिरुषा भीमं भैरवनादिनी ।
काली करालवक्त्रान्तर्दुर्दर्शदशनोज्ज्वला ॥

tato jahāsātiruṣā bhīmaṃ bhairava nādinī |
kālī karāla vaktrāntar durdarśa daśanojjvalā ||

Then with a fearful roar, the Remover of Darkness laughed furiously, Her teeth radiantly gleaming in Her fierce mouth.

- 20 -

उत्थाय च महासिंहं देवी चण्डमधावत ।
गृहीत्वा चास्य केशेषु शिरस्तेनासिनाच्छिनत् ॥

utthāya ca mahāsiṃhaṃ devī caṇḍa madhāvata |
gṛhītvā cāsya keśeṣu śirastenāṣinācchinat ||

Then the Goddess, mounting upon the lion, seized Passion by the hair, and with a broad sword, She cut off his head.

- 21 -

अथ मुण्डोऽभ्यधावत्तां दृष्ट्वा चण्डं निपातितम् ।
तमप्यपातयद्भूमौ सा खड्गाभिहतं रुषा ॥

atha muṇḍo-bhyadhāvattāṃ
dṛṣṭvā caṇḍaṃ nipātitam |
tamapyapātayad bhūmau sā khaḍgābhihataṃ ruṣā ||

Seeing the death of Passion, Anger attacked the Goddess. Then in terrible anger, stabbing him with Her sword, She laid him to rest on the ground.

- 22 -

हतशेषं ततः सैन्यं दृष्ट्वा चण्डं निपातितम् ।
मुण्डं च सुमहावीर्यं दिशो भेजे भयातुरम् ॥

hataśeṣaṃ tataḥ sainyaṃ dṛṣṭvā caṇḍaṃ nipātitam |
muṇḍaṃ ca sumahāvīryaṃ diśo bheje bhayāturam ||

The remaining army, seeing the death of the terribly valiant Passion and Anger, were overcome with fear and ran away.

- 23 -

शिरश्चण्डस्य काली च गृहीत्वा मुण्डमेव च ।
प्राह प्रचण्डाट्टहासमिश्रमभ्येत्य चण्डिकाम् ॥

śiraś caṇḍasya kālī ca gṛhītvā muṇḍameva ca |
prāha pracaṇḍāṭṭahāsa miśramabhyetya caṇḍikām ||

Thereafter the Remover of Darkness took the heads of Passion and Anger in Her hands and brought them to She Who Ṭears Apart Thought, and spoke to Her with a great laugh.

- 24 -

मया तवात्रोपहृतौ चण्डमुण्डौ महापशू ।
युद्धयज्ञे स्वयं शुम्भं निशुम्भं च हनिष्यसि ॥

mayā tavātropahṛtau caṇḍa muṇḍau mahā paśū |
yuddhayajñe svayaṃ śumbhaṃ
niśumbhaṃ ca haniṣyasi ||

"I present to you two great beasts, Passion and Anger. Now in the war of sacrifice, you yourself will kill Self-Conceit and Self-Deprecation."

- 25 -

ऋषिरुवाच ॥

ṛṣi ruvāca ||

The Ṛṣi said:

- 26 -

तावानीतौ ततो दृष्ट्वा चण्डमुण्डौ महासुरौ ।
उवाच कालीं कल्याणी ललितं चण्डिका वचः ॥

tāvānītau tato dṛṣṭvā caṇḍa muṇḍau mahāsurau |
uvāca kālīṃ kalyāṇī lalitaṃ caṇḍikā vacaḥ ||
Seeing the heads of the two great thoughts, Passion and Anger, brought there, the Goddess of Welfare, She Who Tears Apart Thought, in sweet words said to the Remover of Darkness:

- 27 -

यस्माच्चण्डं च मुण्डं च गृहीत्वा त्वमुपागता ।
चामुण्डेति ततो लोके ख्याता देवि भविष्यसि ॥

yasmāccaṇḍaṃ ca muṇḍaṃ ca gṛhītvā tvamupāgatā |
cāmuṇḍeti tato loke khyātā devi bhaviṣyasi ||
Since you have brought me the heads of Passion and Anger, henceforth you will be known in all the worlds as the Slayer of Passion and Anger.

ॐ

oṃ

अष्टमोऽध्यायः
aṣṭamo-dhyāyaḥ
Chapter Eight

ध्यानम्
dhyānam
Meditation

ॐ अरुणां करुणातरङ्गिताक्षीं
धृतपाशाङ्कुशबाणचापहस्ताम् ।
अणिमादिभिरावृतां मयूखैर-
हमित्येव विभावये भवानीम् ॥

oṃ aruṇāṃ karuṇātaraṅgitākṣīṃ
dhṛta pāśāṅkuśa bāṇa cāpa hastām |
aṇimādibhirāvṛtāṃ mayūkhair
ahamityeva vibhāvaye bhavānīm ||

I meditate upon Bhavānī, the Embodiment of Existence, the Grantor of Perfection, who is surrounded by rays of light and other subtle energies. Her body is of red hue. Her three eyes are exuberant with compassion. In Her hands are the net, the curved sword, bow, and arrow.

- 1 -

ॐ ऋषिरुवाच ॥

oṃ ṛṣi ruvāca ||

Oṃ The Ṛṣi said:

- 2 -

चण्डे च निहते दैत्ये मुण्डे च विनिपातिते ।
बहुलेषु च सैन्येषु क्षयितेष्वसुरेश्वरः ॥

caṇḍe ca nihate daitye muṇḍe ca vinipātite |
bahuleṣu ca sainyeṣu kṣayiteṣva sureśvaraḥ ||

When the Lord of Thought became aware of the death of Passion and Anger and many of their army,

- 3 -

ततः कोपपराधीनचेताः शुम्भः प्रतापवान् ।
उद्योगं सर्वसैन्यानां दैत्यानामादिदेश ह ॥

tataḥ kopaparādhīna cetāḥ śumbhaḥ pratāpavān |
udyogaṃ sarva sainyānāṃ daityānām ādideśa ha ||

then excessive anger filled the mind of the infamous Self-Conceit, and he ordered all the armies of thought to march to war.

- 4 -

अद्य सर्वबलैर्दैत्याः षडशीतिरुदायुधाः ।
कम्बूनां चतुरशीतिर्निर्यान्तु स्वबलैर्वृताः ॥

adya sarva balair daityāḥ ṣaḍaśītir udāyudhāḥ |
kambūnāṃ caturaśītir niryāntu svabalair vṛtāḥ ||

"Today let all thoughts of strength arise. Let the eighty-six Plunderers of Peace holding weapons and eighty-four Without Restraint assemble with all their forces.

- 5 -

कोटिवीर्याणि पञ्चाशदसुराणां कुलानि वै ।
शतं कुलानि धौम्राणां निर्गच्छन्तु ममाज्ञया ॥

koṭivīryāṇi pañcāśad asurāṇāṃ kulāni vai |
śataṃ kulāni dhaumrāṇāṃ
nirgacchantu mamājñayā ||

I order five hundred million heroic warriors of the family of thoughts to assemble, and the assemblage of hundreds of the family of vices. Let them march off to war.

- 6 -

कालका दौर्हृदा मौर्याः कालकेयास्तथासुराः ।
युद्धाय सज्जा निर्यान्तु आज्ञया त्वरिता मम ॥

kālakā daurhṛdā mauryāḥ kālakeyās tathāsurāḥ |
yuddhāya sajjā niryāntu ājñayā tvaritā mama ||

And let the thoughts born of calamity and thoughts born of perplexed hearts, and recurring thoughts and fears of the unknown, be ready for war and immediately set forth at my command."

- 7 -

इत्याज्ञाप्यासुरपतिः शुम्भो भैरवशासनः ।
निर्जगाम महासैन्यसहस्रैर्बहुभिर्वृतः ॥

**ityājñāpyāsurapatiḥ śumbho bhairavaśāsanaḥ |
nirjagāma mahāsainya sahasrair bahubhirvṛtaḥ ||**

After the command, the fearful King of Thought, Self-Conceit, the terrible ruler, marched to battle surrounded by thousands of warriors.

- 8 -

आयान्तं चण्डिका दृष्ट्वा तत्सैन्यमतिभीषणम् ।
ज्यास्वनैः पूरयामास धरणीगगनान्तरम् ॥

**āyāntaṃ caṇḍikā dṛṣṭvā tat sainyam atibhīṣaṇam |
jyāsvanaiḥ pūrayāmāsa dharaṇīgaganāntaram ||**

When She saw that exceedingly terrible army approaching, She Who Tears Apart Thought made the twang of Her bow string hum from the earth to the sky.

- 9 -

ततः सिंहो महानादमतीव कृतवान् नृप ।
घण्टास्वनेन तन्नादमम्बिका चोपबृंहयत् ॥

**tataḥ siṃho mahānādam atīva kṛtavān nṛpa |
ghaṇṭā svanena tannādam ambikā copabṛṃhayat ||**

Oh King, then the lion of the Goddess began to roar extremely loudly, and the Mother of the Universe increased the noise with the sound of Her bell.

- 10 -

धनुर्ज्यासिंहघण्टानां नादापूरितदिङ्मुखा ।
निनादैर्भीषणैः काली जिग्ये विस्तारितानना ॥

**dhanurjyā siṃha ghaṇṭānāṃ nādā pūritadiṅmukhā |
ninādair bhīṣaṇaiḥ kālī jigye vistāritānanā ||**

With the twang of the bowstring, the roar of the lion, and the sound of the bell, the hum of sound rose in all directions. From the tremendous mouth of the Remover of Darkness came a dreadful sound, even greater than the others.

- 11 -

तं निनादमुपश्रुत्य दैत्यसैन्यैश्चतुर्दिशम् ।
देवी सिंहस्तथा काली सरोषैः परिवारिताः ॥

taṃ ninādam upaśrutya daitya sainyaiścaturdiśam |
devī siṃhas tathā kālī saroṣaiḥ parivāritāḥ ||

Having heard that tumultuous sound in all four directions, the warriors in the army of thought angrily surrounded the Goddess, the lion, and the Remover of Darkness.

- 12 -

एतस्मिनन्तरे भूप विनाशाय सुरद्विषाम् ।
भवायामरसिंहानामतिवीर्यबलान्विताः ॥

etasminantare bhūpa vināśāya suradviṣām |
bhavāyāmara siṃhānām ativīrya balānvitāḥ ||

- 13 -

ब्रह्मेशगुहविष्णूनां तथेन्द्रस्य च शक्तयः ।
शरीरेभ्यो विनिष्क्रम्य तद्रूपैश्चण्डिकां ययुः ॥

brahmeśa guha viṣṇūnāṃ tathendrasya ca śaktayaḥ |
śarīrebhyo viniṣkramya tadrūpaiścaṇḍikāṃ yayuḥ ||

12-13. Your Highness, at this time in order to slay the thoughts and to raise the Gods back to heaven, from the bodies of the Creative Capacity, the Consciousness of Infinite Goodness and the Consciousness That Pervades All, and also from the Rule of the Pure and other Gods as well, energies emerged in forms that possessed extreme valor and tremendous strength, and these forms joined in the battle with She Who Tears Apart Thought.

- 14 -

यस्य देवस्य यद्रूपं यथा भूषणवाहनम् ।
तद्वदेव हि तच्छक्तिरसुरान् योद्धुमाययौ ॥

yasya devasya yadrūpaṃ yathā bhūṣaṇavāhanam |
tadvadeva hi tacchaktir asurān yoddhumāyayau ||

In the same dress and ornaments, and with the same carriers as the Gods possess, in that same appearance their energies came to fight in the war with the thoughts.

- 15 -

हंसयुक्तविमानाग्रे साक्षसूत्रकमण्डलुः ।
आयाता ब्रह्मणः शक्तिर्ब्रह्माणी साभिधीयते ॥

haṃsayukta vimānāgre sākṣasūtra kamaṇḍaluḥ I
āyātā brahmaṇaḥ śaktir brahmāṇī sābhidhīyate II

Seated upon a carrier yoked to the swans of vital breath, displaying a rosary and a begging bowl, came the energy of the Creative Capacity called Creative Energy.

- 16 -

माहेश्वरी वृषारूढा त्रिशूलवरधारिणी ।
महाहिवलया प्राप्ता चन्द्ररेखाविभूषणा ॥

māheśvarī vṛṣārūḍhā triśūla varadhāriṇī I
mahāhivalayā prāptā candra rekhāvibhūṣaṇā II

The Energy of the Great Seer of All arrived riding upon the bull of discipline, bearing the trident of unity, and wearing bracelets of great serpents of energy with a digit of the moon of devotion shining on Her forehead.

- 17 -

कौमारी शक्तिहस्ता च मयूरवरवाहना ।
योद्धुमभ्याययौ दैत्यानम्बिका गुहरूपिणी ॥

kaumārī śakti hastā ca mayūra varavāhanā I
yoddhumabhyāyayau daityān ambikā guharūpiṇī II

The Energy of the Ever Pure One, the Mother of the Universe, who is the form of Consciousness, holding the weapon of energy, arrived there carried by the peacock of beauty to fight with the thoughts in the battle.

- 18 -

तथैव वैष्णवी शक्तिर्गरुडोपरि संस्थिता ।
शङ्खचक्रगदाशार्ङ्गखड्गहस्ताभ्युपाययौ ॥

tathaiva vaiṣṇavī śaktir garuḍopari saṃsthitā I
śaṅkhacakra gadāśārṅga khaḍgahastābhyupāyayau II

And the Energy of the Consciousness That Pervades All arrived sitting upon the great bird of Brilliancy with the conch of vibrations, discus of revolving time, club of articulation, bow of determination, and sword of worship in Her hands with which to fight.

- 19 -

यज्ञवाराहमतुलं रूपं या बिभ्रतो हरेः ।

शक्तिः साप्यायययौ तत्र वाराहीं बिभ्रती तनुम् ॥

yajña vārāhamatulaṃ rūpaṃ yā bibhrato hareḥ I
śaktiḥ sāpyāyayau tatra vārāhīṃ bibhratī tanum II

The Energy of the incomparable He Who Pervades All, the Most Excellent Desire of Union, also wore the form of a boar and presented Herself.

- 20 -

नारसिंही नृसिंहस्य बिभ्रती सदृशं वपुः ।

प्राप्ता तत्र सटाक्षेपक्षिप्तनक्षत्रसंहतिः ॥

nārasiṃhī nṛsiṃhasya bibhratī sadṛśaṃ vapuḥ I
prāptā tatra saṭākṣepakṣipta nakṣatra saṃhatiḥ II

The Energy of the illustrious Man-Lion of Courageous Fortitude took the same form and arrived. From Her fearful roar and the toss of Her hair, the stars were scattered about the sky.

- 21 -

वज्रहस्ता तथैवैन्द्री गजराजोपरि स्थिता ।

प्राप्ता सहस्रनयना यथा शक्रस्तथैव सा ॥

vajrahastā tathaivaindrī gajarājopari sthitā I
prāptā sahasranayanā yathā śakras tathaiva sā II

Mounted upon the King of Elephants, the Energy of the Rule of the Pure arrived with the thunderbolt of illumination in Her hand. She had a thousand eyes just as He.

- 22 -

ततः परिवृतस्ताभिरीशानो देवशक्तिभिः ।

हन्यन्तामसुराः शीघ्रं मम प्रीत्याऽऽह चण्डिकाम् ॥

tathaḥ parivṛtastābhir īśāno devaśaktibhiḥ I
hanyantām aṣurāḥ śīghraṃ
mama prītyā--ha caṇḍikām II

After all the energies of the Gods had collected, the Great God said to She Who Tears Apart Thought: "I will be pleased if you will quickly slay all those thoughts."

- 23 -

ततो देवीशरीरात्तु विनिष्क्रान्तातिभीषणा ।

चण्डिकाशक्तिरत्युग्रा शिवाशतनिनादिनी ॥

tato devī śarīrāttu viniṣkrāntātibhīṣaṇā |

caṇḍikā śaktir atyugrā śivā śataninādinī ||

Then from the body of the Goddess manifested the excessively fearful and extremely terrific energy, known as She Who Tears Apart Thought, who made noise in the manner of numerous jackals.

- 24 -

सा चाह धूम्रजटिलमीशानमपराजिता ।

दूत त्वं गच्छ भगवन् पार्श्वं शुम्भनिशुम्भयोः ॥

sā cāha dhūmrajaṭilam īśānam aparājitā |

dūta tvaṃ gaccha bhagavan

pārśvaṃ śumbha niśumbhayoḥ ||

That invincible Goddess said to the One of dark matted hair, the Great God, "Supreme Lord, please go to Self-Conceit and Self-Deprecation as my ambassador.

- 25 -

ब्रूहि शुम्भं निशुम्भं च दानवावतिगर्विंतौ ।

ये चान्ये दानवास्तत्र युद्धाय समुपस्थिताः ॥

brūhi śumbhaṃ niśumbhaṃ ca dānavāvatigarvitau |

ye cānye dānavās tatra yuddhāya samupasthitāḥ ||

Tell those two extremely conceited ones, Self-Conceit and Self-Deprecation and any other thoughts there ready to wage battle, this order:

- 26 -

त्रैलोक्यमिन्द्रो लभतां देवाः सन्तु हविर्भुजः ।

यूयं प्रयात पातालं यदि जीवितुमिच्छथ ॥

trailokyam indro labhatāṃ devāḥ santu havir bhujaḥ |
yūyaṃ prayāta pātālaṃ yadi jīvitumicchatha ||
If you want to live, then return to the lower worlds. Let the Rule of the Pure be the King of the three worlds, and let the Gods enjoy their portion of sacrifice.

\- 27 -

बलावलेपादथ चेद्भवन्तो युद्धकाङ्क्षिणः ।
तदागच्छत तृप्यन्तु मच्छिवाः पिशितेन वः ॥

balāvalepādatha ced bhavanto yuddhakāṅkṣiṇaḥ |
tadā gacchata tṛpyantu macchivāḥ piśitena vaḥ ||
But if in the strength of your collected pride you still desire to fight, then come. My manifestations will be pleased to enjoy your flesh!"

\- 28 -

यतो नियुक्तो दौत्येन तया देव्या शिवः स्वयम् ।
शिवदूतीति लोकेऽस्मिंस्ततः सा ख्यातिमागता ॥

yato niyukto dautyena tayā devyā śivaḥ svayam |
śivadūtīti loke-smiṃs tataḥ sā khyātimāgatā ||
Because this Goddess sent Consciousness himself as Her ambassador to the thoughts, She has become known in the world as She for Whom Consciousness is Emissary.

\- 29 -

तेऽपि श्रुत्वा वचो देव्याः शर्वाख्यातं महासुराः ।
अमर्षापूरिता जग्मुर्यत्र कात्यायनी स्थिता ॥

te-pi śrutvā vaco devyāḥ śarvākhyātaṃ mahāsurāḥ |
amarṣāpūritā jagmur yatra kātyāyanī sthitā ||
Those great thoughts, hearing the words of the Goddess from the mouth of Consciousness, in great anger went to where the Ever Pure One was brilliantly shining.

\- 30 -

ततः प्रथममेवाग्रे शरशक्त्यृष्टिवृष्टिभिः ।
ववर्षुरुद्धतामर्षास्तां देवीममरारयः ॥

tataḥ prathamam evāgre śara śaktyṛṣṭi vṛṣṭibhiḥ |
vavarṣurud dhatāmarṣās tāṃ devī mamarārayaḥ ||
Then from above, the wrath of the thoughts caused a rain of arrows, energies, spears, and other weapons upon the Goddess.

- 31 -

सा च तान् प्रहितान् बाणाञ्छूलशक्तिपरश्वधान् ।
चिच्छेद लीलयाऽऽध्मातधनुर्मुक्तैर्महेषुभिः ॥

sā ca tān prahitān bāṇāñ chūlaśakti paraśvadhān |
ciccheda līlayā--dhmātadhanurmuktairmaheṣubhiḥ ||
She playfully cut to pieces the arrows, pikes, energies, weapons, and battle axes hurled at Her by the enemy thoughts with the great arrows let loose with the twang of Her bow-string.

- 32 -

तस्याग्रतस्तथा काली शूलपातविदारितान् ।
खट्वाङ्गपोथितांश्चारीन् कुर्वती व्यचरत्तदा ॥

tasyāgratas tathā kālī śūlapāta vidāritān |
khaṭvāṅga pothitāṃścārīn kurvatī vyacarattadā ||
Then the Remover of Darkness went in front of those enemies and, striking with Her pike, began to kill them. With the missiles of consciousness, She reduced them to powder on that battlefield.

- 33 -

कमण्डलुजलाक्षेपहतवीर्यान् हतौजसः ।
ब्रह्माणी चाकरोच्छत्रून् येन येन स्म धावति ॥

kamaṅḍalu jalākṣepa hatavīryān hataujasaḥ |
brahmāṇī cākarocchatrūn yena yena sma dhāvati ||
Creative Energy sprinkled water from Her begging bowl on groups of thoughts, and on whomever the water fell, his vitality and valor were destroyed.

- 34 -

माहेश्वरी त्रिशूलेन तथा चक्रेण वैष्णवी ।
दैत्याञ्जघान कौमारी तथा शक्त्यातिकोपना ॥

māheśvarī triśūlena tathā cakreṇa vaiṣṇavī |
daityāñ jaghāna kaumārī tathā śaktyātikopanā ||
The Energy of the Great Seer, with Her trident; the Energy of the Consciousness That Pervades All, with Her discus; and the Ever Pure One, with Her energy, battled with the thoughts in fierce rage.

- 35 -

ऐन्द्रीकुलिशपातेन शतशो दैत्यदानवाः ।
पेतुर्विदारिताः पृथ्व्यां रुधिरौघप्रवर्षिणः ॥
aindrī kuliśapātena śataśo daitya dānavāḥ |
peturvidāritāḥ pṛthvyāṃ rudhiraughapravarṣiṇaḥ ||
The Energy of the Rule of the Pure struck with Her thunderbolt, killing hundreds of thoughts and confusions, who fell to the ground with blood flowing.

- 36 -

तुण्डप्रहारविध्वस्ता दंष्ट्राग्रक्षतवक्षसः ।
वाराहमूर्त्या न्यपतंश्चक्रेण च विदारिताः ॥
tuṇḍaprahāra vidhvastā daṃṣṭrāgra kṣatavakṣasaḥ |
vārāha mūrtyā nyapataṃś cakreṇa ca vidāritāḥ ||
The Energy of the Most Excellent Desire of Union killed many with the blows of Her snout. Many chests She punctured with Her prominent tusks, and many thoughts fell to their death from the blows of Her discus.

- 37 -

नखैर्विदारितांश्चान्यान् भक्षयन्ती महासुरान् ।
नारसिंही चचाराजौ नादापूर्णदिगम्बरा ॥
nakhairvidāritāṃś cānyān bhakṣayantī mahāsurān |
nārasiṃhī cacārājau nādāpūrṇa digambarā ||
The Energy of the illustrious Man-Lion killed many great thoughts with Her claws and devoured them. She filled the sky above the battlefield with the hum of Her roar.

- 38 -

चण्डाट्टहासैरसुराः शिवदूत्यभिदूषिताः ।
पेतुः पृथिव्यां पतितांस्तांश्चखादाथ सा तदा ॥

caṇḍāṭṭahāsairasurāḥ śiva dūtyabhi dūṣitāḥ |
petuḥ pṛthivyāṃ patitāṃstāṃś cakhādātha sā tadā ||

Many of the thoughts fell to the ground from fear of the excessively furious laugh of She for Whom Consciousness is Emissary, and She relished their taste in Her mouth.

\- 39 -

इति मातृगणं क्रुद्धं मर्दयन्तं महासुरान् ।
दृष्ट्वाभ्युपायैर्विविधैर्नेशुर्देवारिसैनिकाः ॥

iti mātṛgaṇaṃ kruddhaṃ mardayantaṃ mahāsurān |
dṛṣṭvā bhyupāyair vividhair neśurdevārisainikāḥ ||

Seeing the multitude of Mothers slaying such great thoughts in various ways, the army of thoughts began to run away.

\- 40 -

पलायनपरान् दृष्ट्वा दैत्यान् मातृगणार्दितान् ।
योद्धुमभ्याययौ क्रुद्धो रक्तबीजो महासुरः ॥

palāyanaparān dṛṣṭvā daityān mātṛ gaṇārditān |
yoddhumabhyāyayau kruddho raktabījo mahāsuraḥ ||

Seeing those oppressed thoughts fleeing from the forces of the Mothers, the Seed of Desire, a great thought of bounteous strength, entered to fight in excessive rage.

\- 41 -

रक्तबिन्दुर्यदा भूमौ पतत्यस्य शरीरतः ।
समुत्पतति मेदिन्यां तत्प्रमाणस्तदासुरः ॥

raktabindur yadā bhūmau patatyasya śarīrataḥ |
samutpatati medinyāṃ tat pramāṇas tadāsuraḥ ||

When a drop of blood from his body touches the ground, another great thought with the same intensity is born in that very place.

\- 42 -

युयुधे स गदापाणिरिन्द्रशक्त्या महासुरः ।
ततश्चैन्द्री स्ववज्रेण रक्तबीजमताडयत् ॥

yuyudhe sa gadā pāṇir indra śaktyā mahāsuraḥ |
tataścaindrī svavajreṇa raktabījam atāḍayat ||

The Energy of the Rule of the Pure began to fight with this great thought who held a club in his hand. Then She smote the Seed of Desire with Her thunderbolt.

- 43 -

कुलिशेनाहतस्याशु बहु सुस्राव शोणितम् ।
समुत्तस्थुस्ततो योधास्तद्रूपास्तत्पराक्रमाः ॥

kuliśenāhatasyāśu bahu susrāva śoṇitam |
samuttasthus tato yodhās tadrūpāstat parākramāḥ ||

Wounded by the thunderbolt, blood poured forth from his body, and for every drop of blood that touched the ground there appeared the same form, and equally fierce.

- 44 -

यावन्तः पतितास्तस्य शरीराद्रक्तबिन्दवः ।
तावन्तः पुरुषा जातास्तद्वीर्यबलविक्रमाः ॥

yāvantaḥ pati tāstasya śarīrād rakta bindavaḥ |
tāvantaḥ puruṣā jātās tadvīrya balavikramāḥ ||

For as many drops of blood that poured forth from the wounds of the Seed of Desire, just so many warriors manifested, all equally valiant, equally strong, and equally fierce.

- 45 -

ते चापि युयुधुस्तत्र पुरुषा रक्तसम्भवाः ।
समं मातृभिरत्युग्रशस्त्रपातातिभीषणम् ॥

te cāpi yuyudhus tatra puruṣā rakta sambhavāḥ |
samaṃ mātṛbhir atyugra śastra pātāti bhīṣaṇam ||

Those warriors born of the Seed of Desire possessed extremely fearful weapons, and they began a violent battle with the multitude of Mothers.

- 46 -

पुनश्च वज्रपातेन क्षतमस्य शिरो यदा ।
ववाह रक्तं पुरुषास्ततो जाताः सहस्रशः ॥

punaśca vajra pātena kṣatamasya śiro yadā |
vavāha raktaṃ puruṣās tato jātāḥ sahasraśaḥ ||

When he was wounded on the head by that meritorious thunderbolt, and the blood began to flow, then from it thousands of warriors were born.

- 47 -

वैष्णवी समरे चैनं चक्रेणाभिजघान ह ।

गदया ताडयामास ऐन्द्री तमसुरेश्वरम् ॥

vaiṣṇavī samare cainaṃ cakreṇābhi jaghāna ha |
gadayā tāḍayāmāsa aindrī tamasureśvaram ||

The Energy of the Consciousness That Pervades All struck the Seed of Desire with Her discus; the Energy of the Rule of the Pure smote that general of the armies of thought with Her club.

- 48 -

वैष्णवीचक्रभिन्नस्य रुधिरस्रावसम्भवैः ।

सहस्रशो जगद्व्याप्तं तत्प्रमाणैर्महासुरैः ॥

vaiṣṇavī cakrabhinnasya rudhirasrāva sambhavaiḥ |
sahasraśo jagadvyāptaṃ tatpramāṇair mahāsuraiḥ ||

Wounded by the discus of the Energy of the Consciousness That Pervades All, profuse blood poured forth, manifesting in thousands of great thoughts, so that soon the entire gross world was pervaded by the Seeds of Desire.

- 49 -

शक्त्या जघान कौमारी वाराही च तथासिना ।

माहेश्वरी त्रिशूलेन रक्तबीजं महासुरम् ॥

śaktyā jaghāna kaumārī vārāhī ca tathāsinā |
māheśvarī triśūlena raktabījaṃ mahā suram ||

The Ever Pure One struck that great thought, the Seed of Desire, with Her energy, and the Energy of the Most Excellent Desire of Union, with Her sword, and the Great Seer of All, with Her pike.

- 50 -

स चापि गदया दैत्यः सर्वा एवाहनत् पृथक् ।

मातॄः कोपसमाविष्टो रक्तबीजो महासुरः ॥

sa cāpi gadayā daityaḥ sarvā evāhanat pṛthak |
mātṝḥ kopa samāviṣṭo raktabījo mahā suraḥ ||

In great anger that great thought, the Seed of Desire, himself struck with his club at all the energies of the Mothers.

\- 51 -

तस्याहतस्य बहुधा शक्तिशूलादिभिर्भुवि ।
पपात यो वै रक्तौघस्तेनासञ्छतशोऽसुराः ॥

tasyāhatasya bahudhā śaktiśūlādibhir bhuvi |
papāta yo vai raktau ghastenāsañ chataśo-surāḥ ||

Wounded by the energies, pikes, and other weapons, the blood poured forth from his body as a river, and certainly there were uncountable thoughts born from it.

\- 52 -

तैश्चासुरासृक्सम्भूतैरसुरैः सकलं जगत् ।
व्याप्तमासीत्ततो देवा भयमाजग्मुरुत्तमम् ॥

taiś cāsurā sṛksambhūtair asuraiḥ sakalaṃ jagat |
vyāptam āsīt tato devā bhayamājagmuruttamam ||

In this way the thoughts born of the Seed of Desire pervaded the entire perceivable universe, and the Gods became greatly frightened.

\- 53 -

तान् विषण्णान् सुरान् दृष्ट्वा चण्डिका प्राह सत्वरा ।
उवाच कालीं चामुण्डे विस्तीर्णं वदनं कुरु ॥

tān viṣaṇṇān surān dṛṣṭvā caṇḍikā prāha satvarā |
uvāca kālīṃ cāmuṇḍe vistīrṇaṃ vadanaṃ kuru ||

Seeing the Gods' dejection, She Who Tears Apart Thought promptly told the Remover of Darkness, "Hey Slayer of Passion and Anger! Expand your mouth.

\- 54 -

मच्छस्त्रपातसम्भूतान् रक्तबिन्दून्महासुरान् ।
रक्तबिन्दोः प्रतीच्छ त्वं वक्त्रेणानेन वेगिना ॥

macchastra pāta sambhūtān
raktabindhūn mahāsurān |
raktabindoḥ pratīccha tvaṃ vaktreṇānena veginā ||

Quickly eat all these Seeds of Desire and all these great thoughts that come from the Seed of Deșire when he is struck with the blows of my weapons.

- 55 -

भक्षयन्ती चर रणे तदुत्पन्नान्महासुरान् ।
एवमेष क्षयं दैत्यः क्षीणरक्तो गमिष्यति ॥

bhakṣayantī cara raṇe tadutpannān mahāsurān |
evameṣa kṣayaṃ daityaḥ kṣīṇarakto gamiṣyati ||

Stroll about the battlefield and eat all of the great thoughts born of that blood, and as all of the blood is wasted, he will soon destroy himself.

- 56 -

भक्ष्यमाणास्त्वया चोग्रा न चोत्पत्स्यन्ति चापरे ।
इत्युक्त्वा तां ततो देवी शूलेनाभिजघान तम् ॥

bhakṣyamāṇās tvayā cogrā na cotpatsyanti cāpare |
ityuktvā tāṃ tato devī śūlenābhi jaghāna tam ||

When you will eat those fearful thoughts, then new thoughts will not be born." Thus saying, the Goddess Who Tears Apart Thought struck the Seed of Desire with Her pike.

- 57 -

मुखेन काली जगृहे रक्तबीजस्य शोणितम् ।
ततोऽसावाजघानाथ गदया तत्र चण्डिकाम् ॥

mukhena kālī jagṛhe raktabījasya śoṇitam |
tato-sāvājaghānātha gadayā tatra caṇḍikām ||

And the Remover of Darkness took his blood in Her mouth. Then he struck She Who Tears Apart Thought with his club.

- 58 -

न चास्या वेदनां चक्रे गदापातोऽल्पिकामपि ।
तस्याहतस्य देहात्तु बहु सुस्राव शोणितम् ॥

na cāsyā vedanāṃ cakre gadāpāto-lpikāmapi |
tasyāhatasya dehāttu bahu susrāva śoṇitam ||

But the Goddess felt no pain from the blow of the club. Still the blood continued to flow from his wounds.

- 59 -

यतस्ततस्तद्वक्त्रेण चामुण्डा सम्प्रतीच्छति ।

मुखे समुद्गता येऽस्या रक्तपातान्महासुराः ॥

yatas tatas tad vaktreṇa cāmuṇḍā sampratīcchati I
mukhe samudgatā ye-syā rakta pātān mahā surāḥ II

- 60 -

तांश्चखादाथ चामुण्डा पपौ तस्य च शोणितम् ।

देवी शूलेन वज्रेण बाणैरसिभिर्ऋष्टिभिः ॥

tāṃś cakhādātha cāmuṇḍā papau tasya ca śoṇitam I
devī śūlena vajreṇa bāṇairasibhir ṛṣṭibhiḥ II

- 61 -

जघान रक्तबीजं तं चामुण्डापीतशोणितम् ।

स पपात महीपृष्ठे शस्त्रसङ्घसमाहतः ॥

jaghāna raktabījam tam cāmuṇḍāpīta śoṇitam I
sa papāta mahīpṛṣṭhe śastra saṅgha samāhataḥ II

- 62 -

नीरक्तश्च महीपाल रक्तबीजो महासुरः ।

ततस्ते हर्षमतुलमवापुस्त्रिदशा नृप ॥

nīraktaśca mahīpāla raktabījo mahāsuraḥ I
tataste harṣamatulam avāpustridaśā nṛpa II

59-62. But whatever blood fell, the Slayer of Passion and Anger took in Her mouth. As many great thoughts as were born from that blood, She instantly took into Her mouth, and She also drank the blood. Then the Goddess fought with the Seed of Desire with Her pike, thunderbolt, bow, sword, and spear, while the Slayer of Passion and Anger drank the blood. Oh King, the Seed of Desire was wounded by that great collection of weapons, and deprived of blood, that great thought fell to the ground. The Gods attained inconceivable bliss!

- 63 -

तेषां मातृगणो जातो ननर्तासृङ्मदोद्धतः ॥

teṣāṃ mātṛgaṇo jāto nanartāsṛṅ madoddhataḥ ॥

The multitude of the Mothers, delighted from the drink of his blood, danced vigorously with joy!

ॐ

oṃ

नवमोऽध्यायः
navamo-dhyāyaḥ
Chapter Nine

ध्यानम्
dhyānam
Meditation

ॐ बन्धूककाञ्चननिभं रुचिराक्षमालां
पाशाङ्कुशौ च वरदां निजबाहुदण्डैः ।
बिभ्राणमिन्दुशकलाभरणं त्रिनेत्र-
मर्धाम्बिकेशमनिशं वपुराश्रयामि ॥
oṃ bandhū kakāñcananibhaṃ rucirākṣa mālāṃ
pāśāṅkuśau ca varadāṃ nijabāhudaṇḍaiḥ |
bibhrāṇamindu śakalābharaṇaṃ trinetram
ardhāmbike śamaniśaṃ vapurāśrayāmi ||
I take refuge in the Supremely Divided One, the Lord who is both male and female continuously without end. Her color is like flowers (*Pentapetes Phoenicea*) or excellent gold with a red and yellow mixture. In Her beautiful hands She holds a rosary, a net, and curved sword, and shows the mudrā giving blessings. The radiant half-moon is Her ornament, and She has three eyes.

- 1 -

ॐ राजोवाच ॥
oṃ rājovāca ||
Oṃ The King said:

- 2 -

विचित्रमिदमाख्यातं भगवन् भवता मम ।
देव्याश्चरितमाहात्म्यं रक्तबीजवधाश्रितम् ॥

vicitramidamākhyātaṃ bhagavan bhavatā mama |
devyāś carita māhātmyaṃ raktabīja vadhāśritam ||

Oh Divine Being, this narrative you have told me of the death of the Seed of Desire and the greatness of the Goddess is wonderful indeed.

- 3 -

भूयश्चेच्छाम्यहं श्रोतुं रक्तबीजे निपातिते ।
चकार शुम्भो यत्कर्म निशुम्भश्चातिकोपनः ॥

bhūyaścec chāmyahaṃ śrotuṃ raktabīje nipātite |
cakāra śumbho yatkarma niśumbhaścāti kopanaḥ ||

Self-Conceit and Self-Deprecation must have been very angry at his death. I wish to hear how they reacted.

- 4 -

ऋषिरुवाच ॥

ṛṣi ruvāca ||

The Ṛṣi said:

- 5 -

चकार कोपमतुलं रक्तबीजे निपातिते ।
शुम्भासुरो निशुम्भश्च हतेष्वन्येषु चाहवे ॥

cakāra kopam atulaṃ raktabīje nipātite |
śumbhāsuro niśumbhaśca hateṣvanyeṣu cāhave ||

After the death of the Seed of Desire and other thoughts in the battle, there was no limit to the anger of Self-Conceit and Self-Deprecation.

- 6 -

हन्यमानं महासैन्यं विलोक्यामर्षमुद्वहन् ।
अभ्यधावन्निशुम्भोऽथ मुख्ययासुरसेनया ॥

hanyamānaṃ mahāsainyaṃ vilokyāmarṣamudvahan |
abhyadhāvanniśumbho-tha mukhyayāsura senayā ||

Seeing that his extensive army was being killed in this way, Self-Deprecation, along with his foremost soldiers, in great anger ran towards the Goddess.

\- 7 -

तस्याग्रतस्तथा पृष्ठे पार्श्वयोश्च महासुराः ।
संदष्टौष्ठपुटाः क्रुद्धा हन्तुं देवीमुपाययुः ॥

tasyāgratas tathā pṛṣṭhe pārśvayośca mahāsurāḥ |
saṃdaṣṭauṣṭha puṭāḥ kruddhā
hantuṃ devīmupāyayuḥ ||

In front of him and behind him, and also on both flanks, were great thoughts, who expressed anger by biting their lips, and they came to kill the Goddess.

\- 8 -

आजगाम महावीर्यः शुम्भोऽपि स्वबलैर्वृतः ।
निहन्तुं चण्डिकां कोपात्कृत्वा युद्धं तु मातृभिः ॥

ājagāma mahāvīryaḥ śumbho-pi svabalair vṛtaḥ |
nihantuṃ caṇḍikāṃ kopāt
kṛtvā yuddhaṃ tu mātṛbhiḥ ||

The extremely violent Self-Conceit also came in great anger, along with his army, to do battle with the multitude of Mothers, and to kill She Who Tears Apart Thought.

\- 9 -

ततो युद्धमतीवासीद्देव्या शुम्भनिशुम्भयोः ।
शरवर्षमतीवोग्रं मेघयोरिव वर्षतोः ॥

tato yuddhamatīvāsīd devyā śumbha niśumbhayoḥ |
śaravarṣamatīvograṃ meghayoriva varṣatoḥ ||

Then Self-Conceit and Self-Deprecation began a violent fight with the Goddess. Those two thoughts, in the manner of clouds, caused a fearful shower of arrows.

\- 10 -

चिच्छेदास्ताञ्छरांस्ताभ्यां चण्डिका स्वशरोत्करैः ।
ताडयामास चाङ्गेषु शस्त्रौघैरसुरेश्वरौ ॥

cicchedāstāñcharāṃstābhyāṃ
caṇḍikā svaśarot karaiḥ |
tāḍayāmāsa cāṅgeṣu śastraughair asureśvarau ||

Those hurled arrows were immediately cut in flight by the mass of arrows from the bow of She Who Tears Apart Thought, and the multitude of other weapons She rained upon the two Kings of Thought wounded their bodies.

- 11 -

निशुम्भो निशितं खड्गं चर्म चादाय सुप्रभम् ।
अताडयन्मूर्ध्नि सिंहं देव्या वाहनमुत्तमम् ॥

niśumbho niśitaṃ khaḍgaṃ
carma cādāya suprabham |
atāḍayanmūrdhni siṃhaṃ devyā vāhanamuttamam ||

Self-Deprecation took a sharp sword and shining shield, and struck the Goddess's carrier, the lion, upon the head.

- 12 -

ताडिते वाहने देवी क्षुरप्रेणासिमुत्तमम् ।
निशुम्भस्याशु चिच्छेद चर्म चाप्यष्टचन्द्रकम् ॥

tāḍite vāhane devī kṣurapreṇāsimuttamam |
niśumbhasyāśu ciccheda
carma cāpyaṣṭa candrakam ||

After Her carrier was wounded, the Goddess immediately cut that sword of Self-Deprecation into pieces with Her arrows, and also his shield, which was inlaid with eight moons.

- 13 -

छिन्ने चर्मणि खड्गे च शक्तिं चिक्षेप सोऽसुरः ।
तामप्यस्य द्विधा चक्रे चक्रेणाभिमुखागताम् ॥

chinne carmaṇi khaḍge ca śaktiṃ cikṣepa so-suraḥ |
tāmapyasya dvidhā cakre cakreṇābhimukhāgatām ||

When his sword and shield were torn in pieces, that thought thrust his energy, but the Goddess cut it also into pieces by Her discus.

- 14 -

कोपाध्मातो निशुम्भोऽथ शूलं जग्राह दानवः ।
आयातं मुष्टिपातेन देवी तच्चाप्यचूर्णयत् ॥

kopādhmāto niśumbho-tha śūlaṃ jagrāha dānavaḥ |
āyātaṃ muṣṭipātena devī taccāpya cūrṇayat ||
His temper flaring, Self-Deprecation took his pike to fight with the Goddess, but She instantly pulverized it with a blow of Her fist.

- 15 -

आविध्याथ गदां सोऽपि चिक्षेप चण्डिकां प्रति ।
सापि देव्या त्रिशूलेन भिन्ना भस्मत्वमागता ॥

āvidhyātha gadāṃ so-pi cikṣepa caṇḍikāṃ prati |
sāpi devyā triśūlena bhinnā bhasmatvamāgatā ||
Then he grabbed a club and hurled it at the Goddess, but that, too, She Who Tears Apart Thought cut by Her trident and reduced it to ashes.

- 16 -

ततः परशुहस्तं तमायान्तं दैत्यपुङ्गवम् ।
आहत्य देवी बाणौघैरपातयत भूतले ॥

tataḥ paraśu hastaṃ tamāyāntaṃ daityapuṅgavam |
āhatya devī bāṇaughair apātayata bhūtale ||
Thereafter that King of Thought, Self Deprecation, took a battle axe in his hands, but seeing him coming, the Goddess let loose a multitude of arrows and, having wounded him, She put him to rest on the earth.

- 17 -

तस्मिन्निपतिते भूमौ निशुम्भे भीमविक्रमे ।
भ्रातर्यतीव संक्रुद्धः प्रययौ हन्तुमम्बिकाम् ॥

tasmin nipatite bhūmau niśumbhe bhīmavikrame |
bhrātaryatīva saṃkruddhaḥ
prayayau hantum ambikām ||
After Self-Deprecation was laid to rest on the earth, his extremely fierce brother was greatly agitated, and he approached to kill the Mother of the Universe.

- 18 -

स रथस्थस्तथात्युच्चैर्गृहीतपरमायुधैः ।
भुजैरष्टाभिरतुलैर्व्याप्याशेषं बभौ नभः ॥

sa rathasthas tathāt yuccair gṛhītaparamāyudhaiḥ |
bhujair aṣṭābhir atulair
vyāpyāśeṣaṃ babhau nabhaḥ ||

Seated on his chariot, he was displaying magnificent weapons in his eight mighty arms, and he covered the entire atmosphere with his wonderful brilliance.

- 19 -

तमायान्तं समालोक्य देवी शङ्खमवादयत् ।
ज्याशब्दं चापि धनुषश्चकारातीव दुःसहम् ॥

tamāyāntaṃ samālokya devī śaṅkham avādayat |
jyāśabdaṃ cāpi dhanuṣaścakārātīva duḥsaham ||

Seeing him approaching, the Goddess sounded Her conch and made an excessively unbearable noise along with the twang of Her bowstring.

- 20 -

पूरयामास ककुभो निजघण्टास्वनेन च ।
समस्तदैत्यसैन्यानां तेजोवधविधायिना ॥

pūrayāmāsa kakubho nijaghaṇṭā svanena ca |
samasta daitya sainyānāṃ tejo vadhavidhāyinā ||

The sound of Her bell, which destroys the splendor of all thoughts, pervaded in all directions.

- 21 -

ततः सिंहो महानादैस्त्याजितेभमहामदैः ।
पूरयामास गगनं गां तथैव दिशो दश ॥

tataḥ siṃho mahānādais tyājitebha mahāmadaiḥ |
pūrayāmāsa gaganaṃ gāṃ tathaiva diśo daśa ||

Thereafter the lion gave a roar, hearing which even the greatest kings of elephants lost their pride, and the hum of the roar filled the earth, the atmosphere, and the ten directions.

- 22 -

ततः काली समुत्पत्य गगनं क्ष्मामताडयत् ।

कराभ्यां तन्निनादेन प्राक्स्वनास्ते तिरोहिताः ॥

tataḥ kālī samutpatya gaganaṃ kṣmāmatāḍayat |
karābhyāṃ tanni nādena prāksvanāste tirohitāḥ ||

Then the Remover of Darkness leaped into the atmosphere and, with Her two hands, She slapped the earth. From this there was such an excessive noise that the preceding sounds became quiet.

- 23 -

अट्टाट्टहासमशिवं शिवदूती चकार ह ।

तैः शब्दैरसुरास्त्रेसुः शुम्भः कोपं परं ययौ ॥

aṭṭāṭṭahāsamaśivaṃ śivadūtī cakāra ha |
taiḥ śabdairasurāstresuḥ
śumbhaḥ kopaṃ paraṃ yayau ||

Thereafter She for Whom Consciousness is Emissary gave a great horse-laugh, to the displeasure of the thoughts, and hearing this, all the thoughts began to shudder. Self-Conceit was greatly agitated.

- 24 -

दुरात्मंस्तिष्ठ तिष्ठेति व्याजहाराम्बिका यदा ।

तदा जयेत्यभिहितं देवैराकाशसंस्थितैः ॥

durātmaṃstiṣṭha tiṣṭheti vyājahārāmbikā yadā |
tadā jayetyabhihitaṃ devairākāśa saṃsthitaiḥ ||

The Goddess said to Self-Conceit: "Oh Wicked One, stand fast!" And then the voice of the Gods rose in the atmosphere, "VICTORY TO YOU!"

- 25 -

शुम्भेनागत्य या शक्तिर्मुक्ता ज्वालातिभीषणा ।

आयान्ती वह्निकूटाभा सा निरस्ता महोल्कया ॥

śumbhenāgatya yā śaktir muktā jvālātibhīṣaṇā |
āyāntī vahni kūṭābhā sā nirastā maholkayā ||

As Self-Conceit was advancing, he thrust an extremely fearful luminous energy, which was coming like a mountain of fire, and the Goddess, with a great flame of fire, put it away.

- 26 -

सिंहनादेन शुम्भस्य व्याप्तं लोकत्रयान्तरम् ।
निर्घातनिःस्वनो घोरो जितवानवनीपते ॥

siṃhanādena śumbhasya vyāptaṃ lokatrayāntaram |
nirghātaniḥ svano ghoro jitavāna vanīpate ||

The atmosphere of the three worlds was pervaded by the lion-like cry of Self-Conceit, but of even greater volume was the frightful clap of thunder that conquered all other sounds.

- 27 -

शुम्भमुक्ताञ्छरान्देवी शुम्भस्तत्प्रहिताञ्छरान् ।
चिच्छेद स्वशरैरुग्रैः शतशोऽथ सहस्रशः ॥

śumbha muktāñ charāndevī
śumbhastat prahitāñ charān |
ciccheda svaśarairugraiḥ śataśo-tha sahasraśaḥ ||

Self-Conceit and the Goddess cut one another's arrows in hundreds and thousands.

- 28 -

ततः सा चण्डिका क्रुद्धा शूलेनाभिजघान तम् ।
स तदाभिहतो भूमौ मूर्च्छितो निपपात ह ॥

tataḥ sā caṇḍikā kruddhā śūlenābhi jaghāna tam |
sa tadābhihato bhūmau mūrcchito nipapāta ha ||

Then the enraged She Who Tears Apart Thought struck him with the pike, and, wounded, he fell to the ground senseless.

- 29 -

ततो निशुम्भः सम्प्राप्य चेतनामात्तकार्मुकः ।
आजघान शरैर्देवीं कालीं केसरिणं तथा ॥

tato niśumbhaḥ samprāpya cetanāmātta kārmukaḥ |
ājaghāna śarair devīṃ kālīṃ kesariṇaṃ tathā ||

Then Self-Deprecation, regaining consciousness, took his bow and struck the Goddess the Remover of Darkness and the lion with arrows.

- 30 -

पुनश्च कृत्वा बाहूनामयुतं दनुजेश्वरः ।

चक्रायुधेन दितिजश्छादयामास चण्डिकाम् ॥

punaśca kṛtvā bāhūnām ayutaṃ danujeśvaraḥ ।

cakrāyudhena ditijaś chādayāmāsa caṇḍikām ॥

Again the Lord of Confusion, the son of earthly concepts, extending ten thousand arms, attacked She Who Tears Apart Thought with a discus.

- 31 -

ततो भगवती क्रुद्धा दुर्गा दुर्गार्तिनाशिनी ।

चिच्छेद तानि चक्राणि स्वशरैः सायकांश्च तान् ॥

tato bhagavatī kruddhā durgā durgārti nāśinī ।

ciccheda tāni cakrāṇi svaśaraiḥ sāyakāṃśca tān ॥

Then the Supreme Lord, the Destroyer of Troubles and Afflictions, grew angry and cut those discuses and arrows with Her own arrows.

- 32 -

ततो निशुम्भो वेगेन गदामादाय चण्डिकाम् ।

अभ्यधावत वै हन्तुं दैत्यसेनासमावृतः ॥

tato niśumbho vegena gadāmādāya caṇḍikām ।

abhyadhāvata vai hantuṃ daityasenā samāvṛtaḥ ॥

Self-Deprecation swiftly took his club and, accompanied by an army of thoughts, rushed forward to kill She Who Tears Apart Thought.

- 33 -

तस्यापतत एवाशु गदां चिच्छेद चण्डिका ।

खड्गेन शितधारेण स च शूलं समाददे ॥

tasyāpatata evāśu gadāṃ ciccheda caṇḍikā ।

khaḍgena śitadhāreṇa sa ca śūlaṃ samādade ॥

As he was approaching, She Who Tears Apart Thought cut his club with a sharp-edged sword, whereupon he seized a pike.

- 34 -

शूलहस्तं समायान्तं निशुम्भममरार्दनम् ।
हृदि विव्याध शूलेन वेगाविद्धेन चण्डिका ॥

śūla hastaṃ samāyāntaṃ niśumbhamamarārdanam |
hṛdi vivyādha śūlena vegāviddhena caṇḍikā ||

As Self-Deprecation, the afflictor of Gods, approached with pike in hand, She Who Tears Apart Thought swiftly pierced him in the heart with Her own pike.

- 35 -

भिन्नस्य तस्य शूलेन हृदयान्निःसृतोऽपरः ।
महाबलो महावीर्यस्तिष्ठेति पुरुषो वदन् ॥

bhinnasya tasya śūlena hṛdayān niḥsṛto-paraḥ |
mahābalo mahāvīryas tiṣṭheti puruṣo vadan ||

Emerging from the heart pierced by the pike came a spirit of great strength and valor crying, "Stop!"

- 36 -

तस्य निष्क्रामतो देवी प्रहस्य स्वनवत्ततः ।
शिरश्चिच्छेद खड्गेन ततोऽसावपतद्भुवि ॥

tasya niṣkrāmato devī prahasya svanavat tataḥ |
śiraściccheda khaḍgena tato-sāvapatadbhuvi ||

With loud laughter, the Goddess severed his head with Her sword, and he fell to the ground.

- 37 -

ततः सिंहश्चखादोग्रं दंष्ट्राक्षुण्णशिरोधरान् ।
असुरांस्तांस्तथा काली शिवदूती तथापरान् ॥

tataḥ siṃhaś cakhādograṃ
daṃṣṭrākṣuṇṇa śirodharān |
asurāṃstāṃstathā kālī śivadūtī tathā parān ||

Then the lion crushed the necks of many thoughts with his fierce teeth and ate them, while the Remover of Darkness, and She for Whom Consciousness is Emissary, devoured others.

- 38 -

कौमारीशक्तिनिर्भिन्नाः केचिन्नेशुर्महासुराः ।
ब्रह्माणीमन्त्रपूतेन तोयेनान्ये निराकृताः ॥

kaumārī śakti nirbhinnāḥ kecin neśur mahāsurāḥ |
brahmāṇī mantra pūtena toyenānye nirākṛtāḥ ||

Some great thoughts perished, being pierced by the energy of the Ever Pure One, while others were repulsed, being sprinkled by the water sanctified by the incantation of Creative Energy.

- 39 -

माहेश्वरीत्रिशूलेन भिन्नाः पेतुस्तथापरे ।
वाराहीतुण्डघातेन केचिच्चूर्णीकृता भुवि ॥

māheśvarī triśūlena bhinnāḥ petustathāpare |
vārāhī tuṇḍa ghātena kecic cūrṇīkṛtā bhuvi ||

Others were cut by the trident of the Energy of the Great Seer of All and fell, while others were ground to powder by the snout of the Most Excellent Desire of Union.

- 40 -

खण्डं खण्डं च चक्रेण वैष्णव्या दानवाः कृताः ।
वज्रेण चैन्द्रीहस्ताग्रविमुक्तेन तथापरे ॥

khaṇḍaṃ khaṇḍaṃ ca cakreṇa
vaiṣṇavyā dānavāḥ kṛtāḥ |
vajreṇa caindrī hastāgra vimuktena tathāpare ||

Confusions were cut to pieces by the discus of the Energy of the Consciousness That Pervades All, and others by the thunderbolt hurled from the palm of the hand of the Energy of the Rule of the Pure.

- 41 -

केचिद्विनेशुरसुराः केचिन्नष्टा महाहवात् ।
भक्षिताश्चापरे काली शिवदूतीमृगाधिपैः ॥

kecid vineśurasurāḥ kecinnaṣṭā mahāhavāt I
bhakṣitāścāpare kālī śivadūtī mṛgādhipaiḥ II

Some thoughts perished and other thoughts fled from the battle, while still others were eaten by the Remover of Darkness, She for Whom Consciousness is Emissary, and the King of Beasts.

ॐ

oṃ

दशमोऽध्यायः
daśamo-dhyāyaḥ
Chapter Ten

ध्यानम्
dhyānam
Meditation

ॐ उत्तप्तहेमरुचिरां रविचन्द्रवह्नि-
नेत्रां धनुश्शरयुताङ्कुशपाशशूलम् ।
रम्यैर्भुजैश्च दधतीं शिवशक्तिरूपां
कामेश्वरीं हृदि भजामि धृतेन्दुलेखाम् ॥
oṃ uttaptahema rucirāṃ ravi candra vahni
netrāṃ dhanuś śarayutāṅkuśa pāśa śūlam |
ramyair bhujaiśca dadhatīṃ śiva śakti rūpāṃ
kāmeśvarīṃ hṛdi bhajāmi dhṛtendulekhām ||
With the fullness of my heart, I think of the female Lord of All, Kāmeśvarī, the Ruler of Desire, who unites the intrinsic nature of Śiva and Śakti, of consciousness and energy, who wears the radiant half-moon on Her head. Her luster is as beautiful as excellent gold. The sun, moon, and fire are Her three eyes, and in Her lovely hands She holds a bow and arrow, curved sword, net, and spear.

\- 1 -

ॐ ऋषिरुवाच ॥
oṃ ṛṣi ruvāca ||
The Ṛṣi said:

\- 2 -

निशुम्भं निहतं दृष्ट्वा भ्रातरं प्राणसम्मितम् ।
हन्यमानं बलं चैव शुम्भः क्रुद्धोऽब्रवीद्वचः ॥

niśumbhaṃ nihataṃ dṛṣṭvā
bhrātaraṃ prāṇasammitam |
hanyamānaṃ balaṃ caiva
śumbhaḥ kruddho-bravīd vacaḥ ||

Seeing his brother, Self-Deprecation, who was dear as his own life, slain, and his strong forces being conquered, Self-Conceit spoke these words in anger:

- 3 -

बलावलेपाद्दुष्टे त्वं मा दुर्गे गर्वमावह ।
अन्यासां बलमाश्रित्य युद्ध्यसे यातिमानिनी ॥

balāvalepād duṣṭe tvaṃ mā durge garvamāvaha |
anyāsāṃ balamāśritya yuddhyase yātimāninī ||

"Oh Reliever of Difficulties, wicked and proud of your strength! Do not show your pride to me. You fight by means of the strength of others."

- 4 -

देव्युवाच ॥

devyuvāca ||

The Goddess said:

- 5 -

एकैवाहं जगत्यत्र द्वितीया का ममापरा ।
पश्यैता दुष्ट मय्येव विशन्त्यो मद्विभूतयः ॥

ekaivāhaṃ jagatyatra dvitīyā kā mamāparā |
paśyaitā duṣṭa mayyeva viśantyo madvibhūtayaḥ ||

I am the only One here in the perceivable world. No other exists beyond me. Oh wicked one, see as these manifestations of my energy enter into myself.

- 6 -

ततः समस्तास्ता देव्यो ब्रह्माणीप्रमुखा लयम् ।
तस्या देव्यास्तनौ जग्मुरेकैवासीत्तदाम्बिका ॥

tataḥ samastāstā devyo brahmāṇīpramukhā layam |
tasyā devyās tanau jagmur ekaivāsīt tadāmbikā ||

Then all the Goddesses, led by the Creative Energy, dissolved into the Being of the Goddess, and there was only ONE EXISTENCE in the perceivable world - THE MOTHER OF THE UNIVERSE!

- 7 -

देव्युवाच ॥

devyuvāca ||

The Goddess said:

- 8 -

अहं विभूत्या बहुभिरिह रूपैर्यदास्थिता ।
तत्संहृतं मयैकैव तिष्ठाम्याजौ स्थिरो भव ॥

ahaṃ vibhūtyā bahubhir iha rūpair yadā sthitā |
tat saṃhṛtaṃ mayaikaiva tiṣṭhāmyājau sthiro bhava ||

I resided here in many forms, which were manifestations of my energy. These have all been withdrawn by me, and now I stand alone. Stand up to fight!

- 9 -

ऋषिरुवाच ॥

ṛṣi ruvāca ||

The Ṛṣi said:

- 10 -

ततः प्रववृते युद्धं देव्याः शुम्भस्य चोभयोः ।
पश्यतां सर्वदेवानामसुराणां च दारुणम् ॥

tataḥ pravavṛte yuddhaṃ
devyāḥ śumbhasya cobhayoḥ |
paśyatāṃ sarva devānāṃ asurāṇāṃ ca dāruṇam ||

Then the Goddess and Self-Conceit began a dreadful battle while the Gods and thoughts looked on.

- 11 -

शरवर्षैः शितैः शस्त्रैस्तथास्त्रैश्चैव दारुणैः ।
तयोर्युद्धमभूद्भूयः सर्वलोकभयङ्करम् ॥

śaravarṣaiḥ śitaiḥ śastrais tathā straiścaiva dāruṇaiḥ |
tayor yuddham abhūdbhūyaḥ
sarva lokabhayaṅkaram ||

With showers of arrows, sharp weapons, and incredible missiles, the combat that engaged them was frightful to all the worlds.

- 12 -

दिव्यान्यस्त्राणि शतशो मुमुचे यान्यथाम्बिका ।
बभञ्ज तांनि दैत्येन्द्रस्तत्प्रतीघातकर्तृभिः ॥

divyānyastrāṇi śataśo mumuce yānyathāmbikā |
babhañja tāni daityendras tatpratīghāta kartṛbhiḥ ||

The Mother of the Universe discharged hundreds of divine missiles, which were cut by the Lord of Thought by his defensive weapons.

- 13 -

मुक्तानि तेन चास्त्राणि दिव्यानि परमेश्वरी ।
बभञ्ज लीलयैवोग्रहुङ्कारोच्चारणादिभिः ॥

muktāni tena cāstrāṇi divyāni parameśvarī |
babhañja līlayaivogra huṅkāroc cāraṇādibhiḥ ||

And as many excellent missiles as were hurled by him were playfully cut by the Supreme Sovereign with fierce incantations of "Huṃ!" and other mantras.

- 14 -

ततः शरशतैर्देवीमाच्छादयत सोऽसुरः ।
सापि तत्कुपिता देवी धनुश्चिच्छेद चेषुभिः ॥

tataḥ śaraśatair devīmācchādayata so-suraḥ |
sāpi tat kupitā devī dhanuś ciccheda ceṣubhiḥ ||

Then that thought covered the Goddess with hundreds of arrows, and the Goddess, in anger, cut his bow with Her arrows.

- 15 -

छिन्ने धनुषि दैत्येन्द्रस्तथा शक्तिमथाददे ।
चिच्छेद देवी चक्रेण तामप्यस्य करे स्थिताम् ॥

chinne dhanuṣi daityendras tathā śaktimathādade |
ciccheda devī cakreṇa tāmapyasya kare sthitām ||

With his bow broken, the Lord of Thought took up his energy, but that was cut by the Goddess with Her discus while it was still in his hand.

- 16 -

ततः खड्गमुपादाय शतचन्द्रं च भानुमत् ।
अभ्यधावत्तदा देवीं दैत्यानामधिपेश्वरः ॥

tataḥ khaḍgamupādāya śatacandraṃ ca bhānumat |
abhyadhāvattadā devīṃ daityānāma dhipeśvaraḥ ||

Then the Supreme Lord of Thought took his brilliant sword and shield, bearing a hundred moons, and rushed toward the Goddess.

- 17 -

तस्यापतत एवाशु खड्गं चिच्छेद चण्डिका ।
धनुर्मुक्तैः शितैर्बाणैश्चर्म चार्ककरामलम् ॥

tasyāpatata evāśu khaḍgaṃ ciccheda caṇḍikā |
dhanurmuktaiḥ śitair bāṇaiś
carma cārka karāmalam ||

As he was approaching, She Who Tears Apart Thought cut his sword with sharp arrows from Her bow, and also his shield as bright as the rays of the sun.

- 18 -

हताश्वः स तदा दैत्यश्छिन्नधन्वा विसारथिः ।
जग्राह मुद्गरं घोरमम्बिका निधनोद्यतः ॥

hatāśvaḥ sa tadā daityaś chinnadhanvā visārathiḥ |
jagrāha mudgaraṃ ghoramambikā nidhanodyataḥ ||

With his horses slain, his bow cut, and without a charioteer, that thought seized a fierce mace, trying to kill the Mother of the Universe.

- 19 -

चिच्छेदापततस्तस्य मुद्गरं निशितैः शरैः ।
तथापि सोऽभ्यधावत्तां मुष्टिमुद्यम्य वेगवान् ॥

ciccheda patatastasya mudgaraṃ niśitaiḥ śaraiḥ I
tathāpi so-bhyadhāvattāṃ muṣṭimudyamya vegavān II
As he approached, She cut his mace with Her sharp arrows, whereupon he continued towards Her with great speed to strike Her with his fist.

- 20 -

स मुष्टिं पातयामास हृदये दैत्यपुङ्गवः ।
देव्यास्तं चापि सा देवी तलेनोरस्यताडयत् ॥

sa muṣṭiṃ pātayāmāsa hṛdaye daitya puṅgavaḥ I
devyāstaṃ cāpi sā devī talenorasya tāḍayat II
That renowned thought brought his fist down on the heart of the Goddess, while the Goddess struck him on the chest with Her palm.

- 21 -

तलप्रहाराभिहतो निपपात महीतले ।
स दैत्यराजः सहसा पुनरेव तथोत्थितः ॥

talaprahārābhihato nipapāta mahītale I
sa daitya rājaḥ sahasā punareva tathotthitaḥ II
Struck by the blow of the palm, he fell to the ground, but the King of Thought immediately rose again.

- 22 -

उत्पत्य च प्रगृह्योच्चैर्देवीं गगनमास्थितः ।
तत्रापि सा निराधारा युयुधे तेन चण्डिका ॥

utpatya ca pragṛhyoccair devīṃ gaganamāsthitaḥ I
tatrāpi sā nirādhārā yuyudhe tena caṇḍikā II
Then seizing the Goddess, he rose up into the atmosphere, and there also She Who Tears Apart Thought waged battle with him without any support.

- 23 -

नियुद्धं खे तदा दैत्यश्चण्डिका च परस्परम् ।
चक्रतुः प्रथमं सिद्धमुनिविस्मयकारकम् ॥

niyuddhaṃ khe tadā daityaścaṇḍikā ca parasparam I
cakratuḥ prathamaṃ siddhamunivismaya kārakam II

Then that thought and She Who Tears Apart Thought began to fight in the atmosphere as never before, causing astonishment to adepts and men of wisdom.

- 24 -

ततो नियुद्धं सुचिरं कृत्वा तेनाम्बिका सह ।

उत्पात्य भ्रामयामास चिक्षेप धरणीतले ॥

tato niyuddhaṃ suciraṃ kṛtvā tenāmbikā saha |

utpātya bhrāmayā māsa cikṣepa dharaṇītale ||

After a long close encounter, the Mother of the Universe raised him above, spun him around, and threw him to the earth.

- 25 -

स क्षिप्तो धरणीं प्राप्य मुष्टिमुद्यम्य वेगितः ।

अभ्यधावत दुष्टात्मा चण्डिकानिधनेच्छया ॥

sa kṣipto dharaṇīṃ prāpya muṣṭim udyamya vegitaḥ |

abhyadhāvata duṣṭātmā caṇḍikā nidhanec chayā ||

Thus thrown to the earth, he hastily got up and, raising his fist, that wicked one rushed forward to kill She Who Tears Apart Thought.

- 26 -

तमायान्तं ततो देवी सर्वदैत्यजनेश्वरम् ।

जगत्यां पातयामास भित्त्वा शूलेन वक्षसि ॥

tamāyāntaṃ tato devī sarva daitya janeśvaram |

jagatyāṃ pātayāmāsa bhittvā śūlena vakṣasi ||

Seeing the approach of the Sovereign of All Thoughts, the Goddess pierced him in the chest with Her pike and threw him again to the earth.

- 27 -

स गतासुः पपातोर्व्यां देवीशूलाग्रविक्षतः ।

चालयन् सकलां पृथ्वीं साब्धिद्वीपां सपर्वताम् ॥

sa gatāsuḥ papātorvyāṃ devī śūlāgravikṣataḥ |

cālayan sakalāṃ pṛthvīṃ

sābdhi dvīpaṃ saparvatām ||

Pierced by the sharp point of the Goddess's pike, he fell dead upon the ground, shaking the entire earth with its oceans, islands, and mountains.

- 28 -

ततः प्रसन्नमखिलं हते तस्मिन् दुरात्मनि ।
जगत्स्वास्थ्यमतीवाप निर्मलं चाभवन्नभः ॥

tataḥ prasannamakhilaṃ hate tasmin durātmani |
jagatsvāsthyamatīvāpa nirmalaṃ cābhavannabhaḥ ||

When that evil one was killed, the entire perceivable universe was pleased, all was at Peace, and the sky became clear.

- 29 -

उत्पातमेघाः सोल्का ये प्रागासंस्ते शमं ययुः ।
सरितो मार्गवाहिन्यस्तथासंस्तत्र पातिते ॥

utpātameghāḥ solkā ye prāgāsaṃste śamaṃ yayuḥ |
sarito mārga vāhinyas tathā saṃstatra pātite ||

The flaming clouds of symptomatic confusion became tranquil after his fall, and the rivers flowed in their courses.

- 30 -

ततो देवगणाः सर्वे हर्षनिर्भरमानसाः ।
बभूवुर्निहते तस्मिन् गन्धर्वा ललितं जगुः ॥

tato devagaṇāḥ sarve harṣanirbhara mānasāḥ |
babhūvurnihate tasmin gandharvā lalitaṃ jaguḥ ||

On his death the minds of the multitude of Gods became overjoyed, and the celestial minstrels began to sing sweet songs.

- 31-

अवादयंस्तथैवान्ये ननृतुश्चाप्सरोगणाः ।
ववुः पुण्यास्तथा वाताः सुप्रभोऽभूद्दिवाकरः ॥

avādayaṃs tathaivānye nanṛtuścāpsaro gaṇāḥ |
vavuḥ puṇyāstathā vātāḥ suprabho-bhūddivākaraḥ ||

Other celestial minstrels played their instruments while the heavenly maidens danced. A gentle breeze began to blow and the sun shined radiantly above.

- 32 -

जज्वलुश्चाग्नयः शान्ताः शान्ता दिग्जनितस्वनाः ॥

jajvaluścāgnayaḥ śāntāḥ śāntā digjanitasvanāḥ ||

The sacred fires burned brilliantly in Peace, and Peaceful became the fearful sounds that had filled all the directions.

ॐ

oṃ

एकादशोऽध्यायः
ekādaśo-dhyāyaḥ
Chapter Eleven

ध्यानम्
dhyānam
Meditation

ॐ बालरविद्युतिमिन्दुकिरीटां तुङ्गकुचां नयनत्रययुक्ताम् ।
स्मेरमुखीं वरदाङ्कुशपाशाभीतिकरां प्रभजे भुवनेशीम् ॥

oṃ bālaravidyutim indu kirīṭāṃ
tuṅgakucāṃ nayanatrayayuktām |
smeramukhīṃ varadāṅkuśa pāśābhītikarāṃ
prabhaje bhuvaneśīm ||

I meditate on the Goddess Bhuvaneśvarī, the Ruler of the Earth. The brilliancy of Her body is like sunrise in the morning. The moon is a crown upon Her head. Her swelling breasts overflow, and Her three eyes are in union. Upon Her face shines Her radiant smile, and Her hands show the mudrā granting boons, the curved sword, net, and the mudrā granting fearlessness.

- 1 -

ॐ ऋषिरुवाच ॥
oṃ ṛṣi ruvāca ||
Oṃ The Ṛṣi said:

- 2 -

देव्या हते तत्र महासुरेन्द्रे
सेन्द्राः सुरा वह्निपुरोगमास्ताम् ।
कात्यायनीं तुष्टुवुरिष्टलाभाद्
विकाशिवक्त्राब्जविकाशिताशाः ॥

devyā hate tatra mahāsurendre
sendrāḥ surā vahni purogamāstām |
kātyāyanīṃ tuṣṭuvuriṣṭa lābhād
vikāśi vaktrāb javikāśi tāśāḥ ||

When the Great Lord of Thought was slain by the Goddess, the Gods with the Rule of the Pure, led by the Light of Meditation, illuminating the quarters with their cheerful faces because of the fulfillment of their desire, praised the Ever Pure One.

- 3 -

देवि प्रपन्नार्तिहरे प्रसीद
प्रसीद मातर्जगतोऽखिलस्य ।
प्रसीद विश्वेश्वरि पाहि विश्वं
त्वमीश्वरी देवि चराचरस्य ॥

devi prapannārti hare prasīda
prasīda mātar jagato-khilasya |
prasīda viśveśvari pāhi viśvaṃ
tvamīśvarī devi carācarasya ||

Oh Goddess, you who remove the distress of all who take refuge in you, be pleased. Be pleased, Oh Mother of the entire Perceivable World. Be pleased, Oh Supreme of the Universe; protect the universe. Oh Goddess, you are Supreme over all that moves and does not move.

- 4 -

आधारभूता जगतस्त्वमेका
महीस्वरूपेण यतः स्थितासि ।
अपां स्वरूपस्थितया त्वयैत-
दाप्यायते कृत्स्नमलङ्घ्यवीर्ये ॥

ādhārabhūtā jagatas tvamekā
mahīsvarūpeṇa yataḥ sthitāsi |
apāṃ svarūpa sthitayā tvayaita
dāpyāyate kṛtsnamalaṅghyavīrye ||

Because you exist as the intrinsic nature of the earth, you alone are the sole support of the material world. Oh Goddess of unchallengeable valor, you reside as the intrinsic nature of water (in the form of its container), whereby you gratify this All.

- 5 -

त्वं वैष्णवी शक्तिरनन्तवीर्या
विश्वस्य बीजं परमासि माया ।
सम्मोहितं देवि समस्तमेतत्
त्वं वै प्रसन्ना भुवि मुक्तिहेतुः ॥

tvaṃ vaiṣṇavī śaktir anantavīryā
viśvasya bījaṃ paramāsi māyā |
sammohitaṃ devi samastametat
tvaṃ vai prasannā bhuvi mukti hetuḥ ||

You are the Energy of The Consciousness That Pervades All, of infinite valor, the Seed of the Universe, that which is beyond limitation. By you, Oh Goddess, all is deluded by attachment, and if you are gracious, you are the cause of liberation in this world.

- 6 -

विद्याः समस्तास्तव देवि भेदाः
स्त्रियः समस्ताः सकला जगत्सु ।
त्वयैकया पूरितमम्बयैतत्
का ते स्तुतिः स्तव्यपरा परोक्तिः ॥

vidyāḥ samastāstava devi bhedāḥ
striyaḥ samastāḥ sakalā jagatsu |
tvayaikayā pūritamambayaitat
kā te stutiḥ stavyaparā paroktiḥ ||

Oh Goddess, all that is knowable are your various distinctions, and all women in the world reflect your capacity entirely. By you, Oh Mother, this world is filled. For you who are beyond praise, how can we sing of your glory?

- 7 -

सर्वभूता यदा देवी स्वर्गमुक्तिप्रदायिनी ।

त्वं स्तुता स्तुतये का वा भवन्तु परमोक्तयः ॥

sarva bhūtā yadā devī svarga mukti pradāyinī |

tvaṃ stutā stutaye kā vā bhavantu paramoktayaḥ ||

Oh Goddess, Bestower of Heaven and Liberation, you are all existence. When you have been thus extolled, what else can be sung of your glory?

- 8 -

सर्वस्य बुद्धिरूपेण जनस्य हृदि संस्थिते ।

स्वर्गापवर्गदे देवि नारायणि नमोऽस्तु ते ॥

sarvasya buddhirūpeṇa janasya hṛdi saṃsthite |

svargā pavargade devi nārāyaṇi namo-stu te ||

You reside in the hearts of all living beings in the form of Intelligence. You bestow upon your devotees heaven and liberation. Oh Goddess, Exposer of Consciousness, we bow to you.

- 9 -

कलाकाष्ठादिरूपेण परिणामप्रदायिनि ।

विश्वस्योपरतौ शक्ते नारायणि नमोऽस्तु ते ॥

kalākāṣṭhādi rūpeṇa pariṇāma pradāyini |

viśvasyo paratau śakte nārāyaṇi namo-stu te ||

In the form of divisions of Time, you bring about change. To the Energy that exists after the dissolution of the universe, Exposer of Consciousness, we bow to you.

- 10 -

सर्वमङ्गलमङ्गल्ये शिवे सर्वार्थसाधिके ।

शरण्ये त्र्यम्बके गौरि नारायणि नमोऽस्तु ते ॥

sarva maṅgala maṅgalye śive sarvārtha sādhike |

śaraṇye tryambake gauri nārāyaṇi namo-stu te ||

To the Auspicious of all Auspiciousness, to the Good, to the Accomplisher of all Objectives, to the Source of Refuge, to the Mother of the Three Worlds, to the Goddess Who is Rays of Light, Exposer of Consciousness, we bow to you.

\- 11 -

सृष्टिस्थितिविनाशानां शक्तिभूते सनातनि ।

गुणाश्रये गुणमये नारायणि नमोऽस्तु ते ॥

sṛṣṭi sthiti vināśānāṃ śakti bhūte sanātani |

guṇāśraye guṇamaye nārāyaṇi namo-stu te ||

You are the Eternal Energy of Creation, Preservation, and Destruction in all existence; that upon which all qualities depend, that which limits all qualities, Exposer of Consciousness, we bow to you.

\- 12 -

शरणागतदीनार्तपरित्राणपरायणे ।

सर्वस्यार्त्तिहरे देवि नारायणि नमोऽस्तु ते ॥

śaraṇāgata dīnārta paritrāṇa parāyaṇe |

sarvasyārtti hare devi nārāyaṇi namo-stu te ||

Those who are devoted to you and take refuge in you, even though lowly and humble, you save them from all discomfort and unhappiness. All worry you take away, Oh Goddess, Exposer of Consciousness, we bow to you.

\- 13 -

हंसयुक्तविमानस्थे ब्रह्माणीरूपधारिणि ।

कौशाम्भःक्षरिके देवि नारायणि नमोऽस्तु ते ॥

haṃsayukta vimānasthe brahmāṇī rūpa dhāriṇi |

kauśāmbhaḥkṣarike devi nārāyaṇi namo-stu te ||

Wearing the form of Creative Energy, sitting upon the carrier yoked to the swans of vital breath, sprinkling water with the sanctity of kuśa grass, Oh Goddess, Exposer of Consciousness, we bow to you.

\- 14 -

त्रिशूलचन्द्राहिधरे महावृषभवाहिनि ।

माहेश्वरीस्वरूपेण नारायणि नमोऽस्तु ते ॥

triśūla candrāhidhare mahāvṛṣabha vāhini |

māheśvarīśvarūpeṇa nārāyaṇi namo-stu te ||

In the form of the Energy of the Great Seer of All, displaying the trident of unity, the moon of devotion, and the serpents of Energy, mounted upon the great bull of discipline, Exposer of Consciousness, we bow to you.

- 15 -

मयूरकुक्कुटवृते महाशक्तिधरेऽनघे ।
कौमारीरूपसंस्थाने नारायणि नमोऽस्तु ते ॥

mayūra kukkuṭavṛte mahāśakti dhare-naghe |
kaumārīrūpa saṃsthāne nārāyaṇi namo-stu te ||

Appearing in the form of the Ever Pure One, accompanied by the cock of regularity and the peacock of beauty, wielding the great energy, sinless, Exposer of Consciousness, we bow to you.

- 16 -

शङ्खचक्रगदाशार्ङ्गगृहीतपरमायुधे ।
प्रसीद वैष्णवीरूपे नारायणि नमोऽस्तु ते ॥

śaṅkha cakra gadā śārṅga gṛhīta paramāyudhe |
prasīda vaiṣṇavī rūpe nārāyaṇi namo-stu te ||

Be gracious in the form of the Energy of the Consciousness That Pervades All, you who bear the conch of vibrations, the discus of revolving time, the club of articulation and the bow of determination. Exposer of Consciousness, we bow to you.

- 17 -

गृहीतोग्रमहाचक्रे दंष्ट्रोद्धृतवसुंधरे ।
वराहरूपिणि शिवे नारायणि नमोऽस्तु ते ॥

gṛhītogra mahācakre daṃṣṭroddhṛta vasuṃdhare |
varāharūpiṇi śive nārāyaṇi namo-stu te ||

In the form of the Most Excellent Desire of Union, you raised the earth with your tusks of perseverance, wielding the great discus of revolving time for the Good. Exposer of Consciousness, we bow to you.

- 18 -

नृसिंहरूपेणोग्रेण हन्तुं दैत्यान् कृतोद्यमे ।
त्रैलोक्यत्राणसहिते नारायणि नमोऽस्तु ते ॥

nṛsiṃharūpeṇogreṇa hantuṃ daityān kṛtodyame |
trailokya trāṇa sahite nārāyaṇi namo-stu te ||
In the form of the Man-Lion of Courageous Fortitude, you engaged in slaying thoughts, protecting the three worlds. Exposer of Consciousness, we bow to you.

\- 19 -

किरीटिनि महावज्रे सहस्रनयनोज्ज्वले ।
वृत्रप्राणहरे चैन्द्रि नारायणि नमोऽस्तु ते ॥

kirīṭini mahāvajre sahasra nayanojjvale |
vṛtra prāṇa hare caindri nārāyaṇi namo-stu te ||
Possessing a crown, the great thunderbolt of illumination, and a thousand radiant eyes, and taking the life of confusion, Exposer of Consciousness, we bow to you.

\- 20 -

शिवदूतीस्वरूपेण हतदैत्यमहाबले ।
घोररूपे महारावे नारायणि नमोऽस्तु ते ॥

śivadūtī svarūpeṇa hata daitya mahābale |
ghorarūpe mahārāve nārāyaṇi namo-stu te ||
The intrinsic nature of She for Whom Consciousness is Emissary, who conquered the mighty armies of thought, of fearful form and intense sound, Exposer of Consciousness, we bow to you.

\- 21 -

दंष्ट्राकरालवदने शिरोमालाविभूषणे ।
चामुण्डे मुण्डमथने नारायणि नमोऽस्तु ते ॥

daṃṣṭrā karālavadane śiro mālā vibhūṣaṇe |
cāmuṇḍe muṇḍa mathane nārāyaṇi namo-stu te ||
With great teeth in your mouth, displaying a garland of heads of evil thoughts, Oh Slayer of Passion and Anger, Exposer of Consciousness, we bow to you.

\- 22 -

लक्ष्मि लज्जे महाविद्ये श्रद्धे पुष्टि स्वधे ध्रुवे ।
महारात्रि महामाये नारायणि नमोऽस्तु ते ॥

lakṣmi lajje mahā vidye
śraddhe puṣṭi svadhe dhruve |
mahārātri mahāmāye nārāyaṇi namo-stu te ||
To True Wealth, Humility, Great Knowledge, Faith, Nourishment, Self-Sustenance, Constancy, the Great Night of Ignorance, and the Great Measurement of Consciousness, Exposer of Consciousness, we bow to you.

- 23 -

मेधे सरस्वति वरे भूति बाभ्रवि तामसि ।
नियते त्वं प्रसीदेशे नारायणि नमोऽस्तु ते ॥

medhe sarasvati vare bhūti bābhravi tāmasi |
niyate tvaṃ prasīdeśe nārāyaṇi namo-stu te ||
The Intellect of Love, the Spirit of All-Pervading Knowledge, the Best, All Existence, Nature, Unknowable One, fully occupied with self-restraint, Oh Supreme, be pleased. Exposer of Consciousness, we bow to you.

- 24 -

सर्वस्वरूपे सर्वेशे सर्वशक्तिसमन्विते ।
भयेभ्यस्त्राहि नो देवि दुर्गे देवि नमोऽस्तु ते ॥

sarva svarūpe sarveśe sarva śakti samanvite |
bhayebhyastrāhi no devi durge devi namo-stu te ||
The Intrinsic Nature of All, the Supreme of All, and the Energy of All as well; you remove all fear from us, Oh Goddess; Reliever of Difficulties, Oh Goddess, we bow to you.

- 25 -

एतत्ते वदनं सौम्यं लोचनत्रयभूषितम् ।
पातु नः सर्वभीतिभ्यः कात्यायनि नमोऽस्तु ते ॥

etatte vadanaṃ saumyaṃ locana trayabhūṣitam |
pātu naḥ sarvabhītibhyaḥ kātyāyani namo-stu te ||
May this beautiful face, displaying three eyes, protect us from all existence. Ever Pure One, we bow to you.

- 26 -

ज्वालाकरालमत्युग्रमशेषासुरसूदनम् ।
त्रिशूलं पातु नो भीतेर्भद्रकालि नमोऽस्तु ते ॥

jvālākarālamatyugram aśeṣāsura sūdanam |
triśūlaṃ pātu no bhīter bhadrakāli namo-stu te ||

With intensive brilliance, exceedingly sharp, the fierce destroyer of all thoughts, may your trident protect us from all fear. Oh Excellent She Who is Beyond All Time, we bow to you.

- 27 -

हिनस्ति दैत्यतेजांसि स्वनेनापूर्य या जगत् ।
सा घण्टा पातु नो देवि पापेभ्योऽनः सुतानिव ॥

hinasti daitya tejāṃsi svanenāpūrya yā jagat |
sā ghaṇṭā pātu no devi pāpebhyo-naḥ sutāniva ||

Oh Goddess, the loud sound of your bell fills the perceivable world, destroying the prowess of all thoughts, and protecting us from evil as a Mother protects Her children.

- 28 -

असुरासृग्वसापङ्कचर्चितस्ते करोज्ज्वलः ।
शुभाय खड्गो भवतु चण्डिके त्वां नता वयम् ॥

asurāsṛg vasāpaṅka carcitaste karojjvalaḥ |
śubhāya khaḍgo bhavatu caṇḍike tvāṃ natā vayam ||

May the brilliant sword of worship in your hands, smeared with the blood and fat of thoughts, act for our welfare. Oh you Who Tear Apart Thought, we bow down to you.

- 29 -

रोगानशेषानपहंसि तुष्टा
रुष्टा तु कामान् सकलानभीष्टान् ।
त्वामाश्रितानां न विपन्नराणां
त्वमाश्रिता ह्याश्रयतां प्रयान्ति ॥

rogānaśeṣā napahaṃsi tuṣṭā
ruṣṭā tu kāmān sakalān abhīṣṭān |
tvāmāśritānāṃ na vipannarāṇāṃ
tvamāśritā hyāśrayatāṃ prayānti ||

When you are pleased, you destroy all infirmities, and when you are displeased, you frustrate all desires. No calamity befalls those who take refuge in you, and those who take refuge in you invariably become a refuge to others.

\- 30 -

एतत्कृतं यत्कदनं त्वयाद्य
धर्मद्विषां देवि महासुराणाम् ।
रूपैरनेकैर्बहुधाऽऽत्ममूर्तिं
कृत्वाम्बिके तत्प्रकरोति कान्या ॥

etat kṛtaṃ yat kadanaṃ tvayādya
dharma dviṣāṃ devi mahāsurāṇām |
rūpairanekair bahudhā-tma mūrtiṃ
kṛtvāmbike tat prakaroti kānyā ||

Who else could do this that you have now performed, slaughtering the great thoughts, enemies of the Way of Truth to Wisdom, by manifesting the One form of the Mother of the Universe into many?

\- 31 -

विद्यासु शास्त्रेषु विवेकदीपे-
ष्वाद्येषु वाक्येषु च का त्वदन्या ।
ममत्वगर्तेऽतिमहान्धकारे
विभ्रामयत्येतदतीव विश्वम् ॥

vidyāsu śāstreṣu vivekadīpeṣ
vādyeṣu vākyeṣu ca kā tvadanyā |
mamatvagarte-timahāndhakāre
vibhrāmayatye tada tīva viśvam ||

Who other than you is spoken of in knowledge, in scriptures, in discourses, in all sound, as the Light of Discrimination? You throw the universe into the great blinding darkness of Egotism and Attachment, and make it whirl.

- 32 -

रक्षांसि यत्रोग्रविषाश्च नागा
यत्रारयो दस्युबलानि यत्र ।
दावानलो यत्र तथाब्धिमध्ये
तत्र स्थिता त्वं परिपासि विश्वम् ॥

rakṣāṃsi yatro graviṣāśca nāgā
yatrārayo dasyubalāni yatra I
dāvānalo yatra tathābdhimadhye
tatra sthitā tvaṃ paripāsi viśvam II

Where there are demons of confused thoughts, serpents of dreadful poison, where there are foes and mighty hosts of robbers, where there is a great conflagration, in the midst of the sea of objects and their relationships, you stand and save the universe.

- 33 -

विश्वेश्वरि त्वं परिपासि विश्वं
विश्वात्मिका धारयसीति विश्वम् ।
विश्वेशवन्द्या भवती भवन्ति
विश्वाश्रया ये त्वयि भक्तिनम्राः ॥

viśveśvari tvaṃ paripāsi viśvaṃ
viśvātmikā dhārayasīti viśvam I
viśveśavandyā bhavatī bhavanti
viśvāśrayā ye tvayi bhakti namrāḥ II

You are the Sovereign of the universe. You protect the universe. The soul of the universe, you support the universe. Those who bow to you with devotion become the refuge of the universe.

- 34 -

देवि प्रसीद परिपालय नोऽरिभीते
र्नित्यं यथासुरवधादधुनैव सद्यः ।
पापानि सर्वजगतां प्रशमं नयाशु
उत्पातपाकजनितांश्च महोपसर्गान् ॥

devi prasīda paripālaya no-ribhiter
nityaṃ yathāsura vadhādadhunaiva sadyaḥ ।
pāpāni sarva jagatāṃ praśamaṃ nayāśu
utpātapāka janitāṃśca mahopasargān ॥

Oh Goddess, please be pleased. As you have just now saved us by slaying thoughts, in like manner always save us from fear of foes. Eradicate all evil from all the worlds, as well as all confusion and disturbance.

- 35 -

प्रणतानां प्रसीद त्वं देवि विश्वार्तिहारिणि ।
त्रैलोक्यवासिनामीड्ये लोकानां वरदा भव ॥

praṇatānāṃ prasīda tvaṃ devi viśvārtihāriṇi ।
trailokya vāsinā mīḍye lokānāṃ varadā bhava ॥

Oh Goddess, Remover of the sufferings and calamities of the universe, be gracious to us who bow down to you. You who are worthy of praise by the inhabitants of the three worlds, grant the best to all the worlds.

- 36 -

देव्युवाच ॥

devyuvāca ॥

The Goddess said:

- 37 -

वरदाहं सुरगणा वरं यन्मनसेच्छथ ।
तं वृणुध्वं प्रयच्छामि जगतामुपकारकम् ॥

varadāhaṃ surāgaṇā varaṃ yanmana secchatha ।
taṃ vṛṇudhvaṃ prayacchāmi jagatāmupakārakam ॥

Oh Gods, I shall give you a blessing. Whatever blessing be your mind's desire for the benefit of the world, that blessing I shall certainly give.

- 38 -

देवा ऊचुः ॥

devā ūcuḥ ||

The Gods said:

- 39 -

सर्वाबाधाप्रशमनं त्रैलोक्यस्याखिलेश्वरि ।

एवमेव त्वया कार्यमस्मद्वैरिविनाशनम् ॥

sarvā bādhā praśamanaṃ trailokyasyākhileśvari |
evameva tvayā kāryam asmad vairivināśanam ||

Oh Spirit of the Supreme Sovereign, terminate all disturbance in the three worlds, and in like manner, remove from us all hostility.

- 40 -

देव्युवाच ॥

devyuvāca ||

The Goddess said:

- 41 -

वैवस्वतेऽन्तरे प्राप्ते अष्टाविंशतिमे युगे ।

शुम्भो निशुम्भश्चैवान्यावुत्पत्स्येते महासुरौ ॥

vaivasvate-ntare prāpte aṣṭā viṃśatime yuge |
śumbho niśumbhaścaivānyāvutpatsyete mahāsurau ||

In the fourteenth part of a day of the Infinite ruled by the Universal Light, in the twenty-eighth period for manifestation, two great thoughts, Self-Conceit and Self-Deprecation, will manifest again.

- 42 -

नन्दगोपगृहे जाता यशोदागर्भसम्भवा ।

ततस्तौ नाशयिष्यामि विन्ध्याचलनिवासिनी ॥

nanda gopa gṛhe jātā yaśodā garbha sambhavā |
tatastau nāśayiṣyāmi vindhyācalanivāsinī ||

Then I shall be born from the womb of welfare in the house of the Guardian of Delight, and residing in the mountains of Knowledge, I shall slay them.

- 43 -

पुनरप्यतिरौद्रेण रूपेण पृथिवीतले ।
अवतीर्य हनिष्यामि वैप्रचित्तांस्तु दानवान् ॥

punarapyatiraudreṇa rūpeṇa pṛthivītale I
avatīrya haniṣyāmi vaipracittāṃstu dānavān II

Again I shall incarnate on earth in a ferocious form and slay the confusions of Agitated Awareness.

- 44 -

भक्षयन्त्याश्च तानुग्रान् वैप्रचित्तान्महासुरान् ।
रक्ता दन्ता भविष्यन्ति दाडिमीकुसुमोपमाः ॥

bhakṣayantyāśca tānugrān vaipracittān mahāsurān I
raktā dantā bhaviṣyanti dāḍimīkusumopamāḥ II

And when I devour those great thoughts of Agitated Awareness, my teeth will become as red as a pomegranate flower.

- 45 -

ततो मां देवताः स्वर्गे मर्त्यलोके च मानवाः ।
स्तुवन्तो व्याहरिष्यन्ति सततं रक्तदन्तिकाम् ॥

tato māṃ devatāḥ svarge martyaloke ca mānavāḥ I
stuvanto vyāhariṣyanti satataṃ rakta dantikām II

Then the Gods in the heavens and the men of the world of mortals will continually sing my praise as "She With Red Teeth."

- 46 -

भूयश्च शतवार्षिक्यामनावृष्ट्यामनम्भसि ।
मुनिभिः संस्तुता भूमौ संभविष्याम्ययोनिजा ॥

bhūyaśca śatavārṣikyāmanā vṛṣṭyāmanambhasi I
munibhiḥ saṃstutā bhūmau saṃbhaviṣyāmya yonijā II

And when rain shall cease for a hundred years and the earth will be devoid of water, praised by those who have wisdom, I shall manifest on earth, but not taking birth in a womb.

- 47 -

ततः शतेन नेत्राणां निरीक्षिष्यामि यन्मुनीन् ।
कीर्तयिष्यन्ति मनुजाः शताक्षीमिति मां ततः ॥

tataḥ śatena netrāṇāṃ nirīkṣiṣyāmi yanmunīn |
kīrtayiṣyanti manujāḥ śatākṣīmiti māṃ tataḥ ||

Then I shall look at the wise people with a hundred eyes, whereupon the descendants of the incarnation of wisdom shall sing my praise as "She with a Hundred Eyes."

- 48 -

ततोऽहमखिलं लोकमात्मदेहसमुद्भवैः ।
भरिष्यामि सुराः शाकैरावृष्टेः प्राणधारकैः ॥

tato-hamakhilaṃ lokam ātmadeha samudbhavaiḥ |
bhariṣyāmi surāḥ śākair āvṛṣṭeḥ prāṇadhārakaiḥ ||

Then, Oh Gods, I shall nourish and maintain the entire world and preserve living beings with vegetables from my body until the rain comes.

- 49 -

शाकम्भरीति विख्यातिं तदा यास्याम्यहं भुवि ।
तत्रैव च वधिष्यामि दुर्गमाख्यं महासुरम् ॥

śākambharīti vikhyātiṃ tadā yāsyāmyahaṃ bhuvi |
tatraiva ca vadhiṣyāmi durgamākhyaṃ mahāsuram ||

Then I shall be famed on earth as "She Who Nourishes With Vegetables." Also at that time I shall slay the great thought Impossible.

- 50 -

दुर्गादेवीति विख्यातं तन्मे नाम भविष्यति ।
पुनश्चाहं यदा भीमं रूपं कृत्वा हिमाचले ॥

durgā devīti vikhyātaṃ tanme nāma bhaviṣyati |
punaścāhaṃ yadā bhīmaṃ rūpaṃ kṛtvā himācale ||

- 51 -

रक्षांसि भक्षयिष्यामि मुनीनां त्राणकारणात् ।
तदा मां मुनयः सर्वे स्तोष्यन्त्यानम्रमूर्तयः ॥

rakṣāṃsi bhakṣayiṣyāmi munīnāṃ trāṇakāraṇāt |
tadā māṃ munayaḥ sarve
stoṣyantyā namra mūrtayaḥ ||

50-51. Then my name shall become renowned as Durgā, She Who Removes Difficulties. Again I shall present a fearful form to protect the people of wisdom in the Himālayas, and I will eat confusions, whereupon all those who are wise will sing my praise bowing to my manifested image.

- 52 -

भीमा देवीति विख्यातं तन्मे नाम भविष्यति ।
यदारुणाख्यस्त्रैल्लोक्ये महाबाधां करिष्यति ॥

bhīmā devīti vikhyātaṃ tanme nāma bhaviṣyati |
yadāruṇākhyas trailokye mahābādhāṃ kariṣyati ||

Then my name will become famous as the Goddess of Fearful Form. When Perplexity will create great oppressions in the three worlds,

- 53 -

तदाहं भ्रामरं रूपं कृत्वाऽसंख्येयषट्पदम् ।
त्रैलोक्यस्य हितार्थाय वधिष्यामि महासुरम् ॥

tadāhaṃ bhrāmaraṃ rūpaṃ
kṛtvā-saṃkhyeyaṣaṭpadam |
trailokyasya hitārthāya vadhiṣyāmi mahāsuram ||

then I shall take the form of innumerable bees with six legs, and for the benefit of the three worlds, I shall slay that great thought.

- 54 -

भ्रामरीति च मां लोकास्तदा स्तोष्यन्ति सर्वतः ।
इत्थं यदा यदा बाधा दानवोत्था भविष्यति ॥

bhrāmarīti ca māṃ lokāstadā stoṣyanti sarvataḥ |
itthaṃ yadā yadā bādhā dānavotthā bhaviṣyati ||

- 55 -

तदा तदावतीर्याहं करिष्याम्यरिसंक्षयम् ॥

tadā tadā vatīryāhaṃ kariṣyāmyari saṃkṣayam ||

54-55. Then everywhere people will offer me praise as "She Who has a Bee-like Nature." Thus whenever oppression arises from confused thought, I shall manifest to destroy the foes.

ॐ

oṃ

द्वादशोऽध्यायः
dvādaśo-dhyāyaḥ
Chapter Twelve

ध्यानम्
dhyānam
Meditation

ॐ विद्युद्दामसमप्रभां मृगपतिस्कन्धस्थितां भीषणां
कन्याभिः करवालखेटविलसद्धस्ताभिरासेविताम् ।
हस्तैश्चक्रगदासिखेटविशिखांश्चापं गुणं तर्जनीं
बिभ्राणामनलात्मिकां शशिधरां दुर्गां त्रिनेत्रां भजे ॥

oṃ vidyud dāmasamaprabhāṃ
mṛgapati skandhasthitāṃ bhīṣaṇāṃ
kanyābhiḥ karavālakheṭa
vilasaddhastābhirā sevitām ।
hastaiścakra gadāsi kheṭa
viśikhāṃścāpaṃ guṇaṃ tarjanīṃ
bibhrāṇāmanalātmikāṃ śaśidharāṃ
durgāṃ trinetrāṃ bhaje ॥

I meditate upon the three-eyed Goddess, Durgā, the Reliever of Difficulties; the luster of Her beautiful body is like lightning. She sits upon the shoulders of a lion and appears very fierce. Many maidens, holding the double-edged sword and shield in their hands, are standing at readiness to serve Her. She holds in Her hands the discus, club, double-edged sword, shield, arrow, bow, net, and the mudrā connecting the thumb and the pointer finger, with the other three fingers extended upwards, indicating the granting of wisdom. Her intrinsic nature is fire, and upon her head She wears the moon as a crown.

- 1 -

ॐ देव्युवाच ॥

oṃ devyuvāca ||

Oṃ The Goddess said:

- 2 -

एभिः स्तवैश्च मां नित्यं स्तोष्यते यः समाहितः ।

तस्याहं सकलां बाधां नाशयिष्याम्यसंशयम् ॥

ebhiḥ stavaiśca māṃ nityaṃ stoṣyate yaḥ samāhitaḥ |
tasyāhaṃ sakalāṃ bādhāṃ
nāśayiṣyāmya saṃśayam ||

Whoever will constantly recite these hymns of praise to me with a concentrated mind, I shall without doubt put an end to their every difficulty.

- 3 -

मधुकैटभनाशं च महिषासुरघातनम् ।

कीर्तयिष्यन्ति ये तद्वद् वधं शुम्भनिशुम्भयोः ॥

madhu kaiṭabha nāśaṃ ca mahiṣāsura ghātanam |
kīrtayiṣyanti ye tadvad
vadhaṃ śumbha niśumbhayoḥ ||

Whoever will sing of the destruction of Too Much and Too Little, the slaughter of the Great Ego, and the death of Self-Conceit and Self-Deprecation;

- 4 -

अष्टम्यां च चतुर्दश्यां नवम्यां चैकचेतसः ।

श्रोष्यन्ति चैव ये भक्त्या मम माहात्म्यमुत्तमम् ॥

aṣṭamyāṃ ca caturdaśyāṃ navamyāṃ caikacetasaḥ |
śroṣyanti caiva ye bhaktyā
mama māhātmyamuttamam ||

whoever, with one-pointed attention and devotion, will listen to this presentation of my excellent glory on the eighth, fourteenth, and ninth days of the lunar fortnight;

- 5 -

न तेषां दुष्कृतं किञ्चिद् दुष्कृतोत्था न चापदः ।
भविष्यति न दारिद्र्यं न चैवेष्टवियोजनम् ॥

na teṣāṃ duṣkṛtaṃ kiñcid duṣkṛtotthā na cāpadaḥ |
bhaviṣyati na dāridryaṃ na caiveṣṭa viyojanam ||

to them neither will anything bad occur nor will misfortunes arise out of inauspicious events. Neither will poverty arise, nor separation from beloved ones.

- 6 -

शत्रुतो न भयं तस्य दस्युतो वा न राजतः ।
न शस्त्रानलतोयौघात्कदाचित्सम्भविष्यति ॥

śatruto na bhayaṃ tasya dasyuto vā na rājataḥ |
na śastrānalatoyaughāt kadācitsam bhaviṣyati ||

No fear will ever come to them from enemies, robbers, or kings, nor from weapon, fire, or floods.

- 7 -

तस्मान्ममैतन्माहात्म्यं पठितव्यं समाहितैः ।
श्रोतव्यं च सदा भक्त्या परं स्वस्त्ययनं हि तत् ॥

tasmān mamai tanmāhātmyaṃ
paṭhitavyaṃ samāhitaiḥ |
śrotavyaṃ ca sadā bhaktyā
paraṃ svastyayanaṃ hi tat ||

Therefore this presentation of my glories should be recited with full attention and should be constantly listened to with devotion, as it is one's own path to self-realization.

- 8 -

उपसर्गानशेषांस्तु महामारीसमुद्भवान् ।
तथा त्रिविधमुत्पातं माहात्म्यं शमयेन्मम ॥

upasargānaśeṣāṃstu mahāmārī samudbhavān |
tathā trividhamutpātaṃ māhātmyaṃ śamayenmama ||

This presentation of my glories, the Great Destroyer of all Disturbances, will bring peace to the threefold nature of confusion (physical, mental, and spiritual; or myself, others, and acts of God).

- 9 -

यत्रैतत्पठ्यते सम्यङ् नित्यमायतने मम ।

सदा न तद्विमोक्ष्यामि सांनिध्यं तत्र मे स्थितम् ॥

yatraitat paṭhyate samyaṅ nityamāyatane mama I
sadā na tadvimokṣyāmi
sāṃnidhyaṃ tatra me sthitam II

I shall never forsake the place where this narration is well recited; there my presence will constantly abide.

- 10 -

बलिप्रदाने पूजायामग्निकार्ये महोत्सवे ।

सर्वं ममैतच्चरितमुच्चार्यं श्राव्यमेव च ॥

bali pradāne pūjāyām agnikārye mahotsave I
sarvaṃ mamaitaccaritamuccāryaṃ śrāvyameva ca II

When offerings are made during worship, in the fire sacrifice at great festive occasions, this presentation of my glory should be completely recited and listened to.

- 11 -

जानताऽजानता वापि बलिपूजां तथा कृताम् ।

प्रतीच्छिष्याम्यहं प्रीत्या वह्निहोमं तथा कृतम् ॥

jānatā-jānatā vāpi bali pūjāṃ tathā kṛtām I
pratīc chiṣyāmyahaṃ prītyā
vahni homaṃ tathā kṛtam II

I will accept with love all acts of worship, offerings, and fire sacrifices, whether performed with understanding or without it.

- 12 -

शरत्काले महापूजा क्रियते या च वार्षिकी ।

तस्यां ममैतन्माहात्म्यं श्रुत्वा भक्तिसमन्वितः ॥

śaratkāle mahāpūjā kriyate yā ca vārṣikī I
tasyāṃ mamai tan māhātmyaṃ
śrutvā bhakti samanvitaḥ II

In the great periods when yearly worship is performed in the autumn season, this presentation of my glories should be listened to with devotion and full attention.

- 13 -

सर्वाबाधाविनिर्मुक्तो धनधान्यसुतान्वितः ।
मनुष्यो मत्प्रसादेन भविष्यति न संशयः ॥

sarvā bādhā vinir mukto dhanadhānya sutānvitaḥ |
manuṣyo matprasādena bhaviṣyati na saṃśayaḥ ||

People will become liberated from all troubles and, without doubt, will be blessed with wealth, food, and beautiful children.

- 14 -

श्रुत्वा ममैतन्माहात्म्यं तथा चोत्पत्तयः शुभाः ।
पराक्रमं च युद्धेषु जायते निर्भयः पुमान् ॥

śrutvā mamaitan māhātmyaṃ
tathā cotpattayaḥ śubhāḥ |
parākramaṃ ca yuddheṣu jāyate nirbhayaḥ pumān ||

Listening to this presentation of my glories, of my auspicious manifestations, and my heroic conquering in the battles, people become fearless.

- 15 -

रिपवः संक्षयं यान्ति कल्याणं चोपपद्यते ।
नन्दते च कुलं पुंसां माहात्म्यं मम शृण्वताम् ॥

ripavaḥ saṃkṣayaṃ yānti kalyāṇaṃ copapadyate |
nandate ca kulaṃ puṃsāṃ
māhātmyaṃ mama śṛṇvatām ||

Enemies perish and welfare is generated for those who listen to this narrative of my glories, and their families rejoice.

- 16 -

शान्तिकर्मणि सर्वत्र तथा दुःस्वप्नदर्शने ।
ग्रहपीडासु चोग्रासु माहात्म्यं शृणुयान्मम ॥

śānti karmaṇi sarvatra tathā duḥsvapna darśane |
grahapīḍāsu cogrāsu māhātmyaṃ śṛṇuyānmama ||

Let my glories be heard everywhere, in functions of Peace, upon seeing a bad dream, or to alleviate the adverse effects of positions of the planets.

\- 17 -

उपसर्गाः शमं यान्ति ग्रहपीडाश्च दारुणाः ।

दुःस्वप्नं च नृभिर्दृष्टं सुस्वप्नमुपजायते ॥

upasargāḥ śamaṃ yānti grahapīḍāśca dāruṇāḥ I

duḥsvapnaṃ ca nṛbhirdṛṣṭaṃ susvapnamupajāyate II

Troubles subside as well as the afflicting influences of the planets. The bad dream seen by people becomes a good dream.

\- 18 -

बालग्रहाभिभूतानां बालानां शान्तिकारकम् ।

संघातभेदे च नृणां मैत्रीकरणमुत्तमम् ॥

bālagrahābhi bhūtānāṃ bālānāṃ śānti kārakam I

saṃghātabhede ca nṛṇāṃ maitrī karaṇamuttamam II

It pacifies children affected by the existence of adverse planetary influences, and it is the best cause of friendship when associations of people have divided.

\- 19 -

दुर्वृत्तानामशेषाणां बलहानिकरं परम् ।

रक्षोभूतपिशाचानां पठनादेव नाशनम् ॥

durvṛttānāmaśeṣāṇāṃ balahānikaraṃ param I

rakṣobhūta piśācānāṃ paṭhanādeva nāśanam II

It annihilates the strength of evil doers, and its recitation destroys demons, ghosts, and ungodly spirits.

\- 20 -

सर्वं ममैतन्माहात्म्यं मम सन्निधिकारकम् ।

पशुपुष्पार्घ्यधूपैश्च गन्धदीपैस्तथोत्तमैः ॥

sarvaṃ mamaitan māhātmyaṃ

mama sannidhi kārakam I

paśupuṣpārghyadhūpaiśca

gandha dīpais tathottamaiḥ II

- 21 -

विप्राणां भोजनैर्होमैः प्रोक्षणीयैरहर्निशम् ।

अन्यैश्च विविधैर्भोगैः प्रदानैर्वत्सरेण या ॥

viprāṇāṃ bhojanairhomaiḥ prokṣaṇīyairaharniśam |

anyaiśca vividhairbhogaiḥ pradānairvatsareṇa yā ||

- 22 -

प्रीतिर्मे क्रियते सास्मिन् सुकृत्सुचरिते श्रुते ।

श्रुतं हरति पापानि तथाऽऽरोग्यं प्रयच्छति ॥

prītirme kriyate sāsmin sukṛt sucarite śrute |

śrutaṃ harati pāpāni tathā--rogyaṃ prayacchati ||

20-22. This entire narration of my glories makes my presence manifest. With the same satisfaction with which I receive one year of worship with offerings of your animalistic nature, flowers, objects of value, incense, perfumes, lights, the feeding of wise people, fire offerings, daily sprinkling of consecrated waters, and the offering of other objects of enjoyment, similar is my gratification for those who, with love for me, recite this excellent narration or listen to it but once. Hearing removes sin and gives freedom from infirmities.

- 23 -

रक्षां करोति भूतेभ्यो जन्मनां कीर्तनं मम ।

युद्धेषु चरितं यन्मे दुष्टदैत्यनिबर्हणम् ॥

rakṣāṃ karoti bhūtebhyo janmanāṃ kīrtanaṃ mama |

yuddheṣu caritaṃ yanme duṣṭadaitya nibarhaṇam ||

Those who sing the praise of my births are protected from evil spirits, and the narration of my heroic acts in battle renders evil confusions without strength.

- 24 -

तस्मिञ्छ्रुते वैरिकृतं भयं पुंसां न जायते ।

युष्माभिः स्तुतयो याश्च याश्च ब्रह्मर्षिभिः कृताः ॥

tasmiñchrute vairikṛtaṃ bhayaṃ puṃsāṃ na jāyate |

yuṣmābhiḥ stutayo yāśca yāśca brahmarṣibhiḥ kṛtāḥ ||

After listening to this, fear of enemies is lost. The hymns of praise made by you Gods and Seers of Divinity,

- 25 -

ब्रह्मणा च कृतास्तास्तु प्रयच्छन्ति शुभां मतिम् ।
अरण्ये प्रान्तरे वापि दावाग्निपरिवारितः ॥

brahmaṇā ca kṛtāstāstu prayacchanti śubhāṃ matim |
araṇye prāntare vāpi dāvāgni parivāritaḥ ||

and by the Creative Capacity, and others as well, will bestow auspicious thoughts. On a lonely path in the forest, surrounded by a raging fire,

- 26 -

दस्युभिर्वा वृतः शून्ये गृहीतो वापि शत्रुभिः ।
सिंहव्याघ्रानुयातो वा वने वा वनहस्तिभिः ॥

dasyubhirvā vṛtaḥ śūnye gṛhīto vāpi śatrubhiḥ |
siṃhavyāghrānuyāto vā vane vā vanahastibhiḥ ||

encircled by robbers in a lonely place, captured by enemies, pursued by a lion, tiger, or wild elephants in the jungle;

- 27 -

राज्ञा क्रुद्धेन चाज्ञप्तो वध्यो बन्धगतोऽपि वा ।
आघूर्णितो वा वातेन स्थितः पोते महार्णवे ॥

rājñā kruddhena cājñapto vadhyo bandha gato-pi vā |
āghūrṇito vā vātena sthitaḥ pote mahārṇave ||

or under orders of an angry king imprisoned or condemned to death, or tossed about by turbulent winds in a boat on the great sea;

- 28 -

पतत्सु चापि शस्त्रेषु संग्रामे भृशदारुणे ।
सर्वाबाधासु घोरासु वेदनाभ्यर्दितोऽपि वा ॥

patatsu cāpi śastreṣu saṃgrāme bhṛśadāruṇe |
sarvābādhāsu ghorāsu vedanābhyardito-pi vā ||

or in an intensive battle under heavy fire from opposing weapons; in all terrible afflictions and moments of distress,

- 29 -

स्मरन्ममैतच्चरितं नरो मुच्येत सङ्कटात् ।

मम प्रभावात्सिंहाद्या दस्यवो वैरिणस्तथा ॥

smaran mamaitac caritaṃ naro mucyeta saṅkaṭāt |
mama prabhāvāt siṃhādyā dasyavo vairiṇas tatha ||

- 30 -

दूरादेव पलायन्ते स्मरतश्चरितं मम ॥

dūrādeva palāyante smarataś caritaṃ mama ||

29-30. people who remember my glory will be freed from calamity and anguish. By my power lions, robbers, and enemies flee to a distance from one who remembers this narration of my glory.

- 31 -

ऋषिरुवाच ॥

ṛṣi ruvāca ||

The Ṛṣi said:

- 32 -

इत्युक्त्वा सा भगवती चण्डिका चण्डविक्रमा ॥

ityuktvā sā bhagavatī caṇḍikā caṇḍa vikramā ||

Thus having spoken, the Supreme She Who Tears Apart Thought, of fierce prowess,

- 33 -

पश्यतामेव देवानां तत्रैवान्तरधीयत ।

तेऽपि देवा निरातङ्काः स्वाधिकारान् यथा पुरा ॥

paśyatāmeva devānāṃ tatraivāntaradhīyata |
te-pi devā nirātaṅkāḥ svādhikārān yathā purā ||

disappeared from there while all the Gods watched Her. Their enemies having been slain, all the Gods were freed from disruption of the mind.

- 34 -

यज्ञभागभुजः सर्वे चक्रुर्विनिहतारयः ।

दैत्याश्च देव्या निहते शुम्भे देवरिपौ युधि ॥

yajña bhāgabhujaḥ sarve cakrur vinihatārayaḥ |
daityāśca devyā nihate śumbhe devaripau yudhi ||

- 35 -

जगद्विध्वंसिनि तस्मिन् महोग्रेऽतुलविक्रमे ।
निशुम्भे च महावीर्ये शेषाः पातालमाययुः ॥

jagad vidhvaṃsini tasmin mahogre-tulavikrame |
niśumbhe ca mahāvīrye śeṣāḥ pātālamāyayuḥ ||

34-35. They all began to enjoy their shares of sacrifices and to exercise their divine authority as before. When those thoughts, enemies of the Gods, and afflictors of the world, Self-Conceit, greatly fierce and of unequalled prowess, and Self-Deprecation, of great valor, were slain in battle by the Goddess, the remaining thoughts entered the lower worlds.

- 36 -

एवं भगवती देवी सा नित्यापि पुनः पुनः ।
सम्भूय कुरुते भूप जगतः परिपालनम् ॥

evaṃ bhagavatī devī sā nityāpi punaḥ punaḥ |
sambhūya kurute bhūpa jagataḥ paripālanam ||

Thus, Oh King, the Supreme Goddess, although Eternal, again and again manifests Herself for the protection of the worlds.

- 37 -

तयैतन्मोह्यते विश्वं सैव विश्वं प्रसूयते ।
सा याचिता च विज्ञानं तुष्टा ऋद्धिं प्रयच्छति ॥

tayaitanmohyate viśvaṃ saiva viśvaṃ prasūyate |
sā yācitā ca vijñānaṃ tuṣṭā ṛddhiṃ prayacchati ||

The universe is deluded by Her, and it is She who creates the universe. Satisfied by prayer, She grants Wisdom and Perfection.

- 38 -

व्याप्तं तयैतत्सकलं ब्रह्माण्डं मनुजेश्वर ।
महाकाल्या महाकाले महामारीस्वरूपया ॥

vyāptaṃ tayaitat sakalaṃ
brahmāṇḍaṃ manujeśvara |
mahākālyā mahākāle mahāmārī svarūpayā ||

Oh Sovereign of thinking beings, the entire cosmos is pervaded by Her, the Great Goddess who is the intrinsic nature of the Great Remover of Darkness and the Great Destroyer.

- 39 -

सैव काले महामारी सैव सृष्टिर्भवत्यजा ।
स्थितिं करोति भूतानां सैव काले सनातनी ॥

saiva kāle mahāmārī saiva sṛṣṭir bhavatyajā |
sthitiṃ karoti bhūtānāṃ saiva kāle sanātanī ||

Sometimes She is the Great Destroyer, sometimes She, the unborn, becomes the creation; sometimes She, the Eternal, preserves all beings.

- 40 -

भवकाले नृणां सैव लक्ष्मीर्वृद्धिप्रदा गृहे ।
सैवाभावे तथाऽलक्ष्मीर्विनाशायोपजायते ॥

bhavakāle nṛṇāṃ saiva lakṣmīr vṛddhipradā gṛhe |
saivā bhāve tathā-lakṣmīr vināśāyopajāyate ||

During the time of welfare, She is the Goddess of True Wealth in the homes of men granting increase. In times of misfortune, She Herself is calamity and brings about ruin.

- 41 -

स्तुता सम्पूजिता पुष्पैर्धूपगन्धादिभिस्तथा ।
ददाति वित्तं पुत्रांश्च मतिं धर्मे गतिं शुभाम् ॥

stutā sampūjitā puṣpair dhūpa gandhādibhis tathā |
dadāti vittaṃ putrāṃśca
matiṃ dharme gatiṃ śubhām ||

Praised and worshipped with flowers, perfumes, incense and other offerings, She bestows understanding, wealth, offspring, and a beautiful mind in the Way of Truth to Wisdom.

ॐ

oṃ

त्रयोदशोऽध्यायः

trayodaśo-dhyāyaḥ

Chapter Thirteen

ध्यानम्

dhyānam

Meditation

ॐ बालार्कमण्डलाभासां चतुर्बाहुं त्रिलोचनाम् ।
पाशाङ्कुशवराभीतीर्धारयन्तीं शिवां भजे ॥

oṃ bālārkamaṇḍalābhāsāṃ caturbāhuṃ trilocanām ।
pāśāṅkuśavarābhītīr dhārayantīṃ śivāṃ bhaje ॥

I meditate upon that Goddess who wears beauty comparable to the regions of the sun at sunrise, who has four hands and three eyes, and who holds in Her hands the net, the curved sword, and the mudrās granting boons and fearlessness. She is Śivā, the Energy of Infinite Goodness.

- 1 -

ॐ ऋषिरुवाच ॥

oṃ ṛṣi ruvāca ॥

Oṃ The Ṛṣi said:

- 2 -

एतत्ते कथितं भूप देवीमाहात्म्यमुत्तमम् ।
एवंप्रभावा सा देवी ययेदं धार्यते जगत् ॥

etatte kathitaṃ bhūpa devī māhātmyam uttamam ।
evaṃ prabhāvā sā devī yayedaṃ dhāryate jagat ॥

Thus, Oh King, I have narrated the excellent glory of the Goddess. Such power has this Goddess that She sustains the world.

- 3 -

विद्या तथैव क्रियते भगवद्विष्णुमायया ।
तया त्वमेष वैश्यश्च तथैवान्ये विवेकिनः ॥

vidyā tathaiva kriyate bhagavad viṣṇu māyayā |
tayā tvameṣa vaiśyaśca tathaivānye vivekinaḥ ||

- 4 -

मोह्यन्ते मोहिताश्चैव मोहमेष्यन्ति चापरे ।
तामुपैहि महाराज शरणं परमेश्वरीम् ॥

mohyante mohitāścaiva mohameṣyanti cāpare |
tāmupaihi mahārāja śaraṇaṃ parameśvarīm ||

3-4. Knowledge is conferred by Her, the Perceivable Form of the Consciousness That Pervades All, and by Her you, this businessman, and others of discrimination are being deluded, have been deluded, and will be deluded. Oh Great King, take refuge in Her, the Supreme Sovereign.

- 5 -

आराधिता सैव नृणां भोगस्वर्गापवर्गदा ॥

ārādhitā saiva nṛṇāṃ bhogasvargā pavargadā ||

When She is pleased, She bestows upon mankind enjoyment, heaven, and liberation.

- 6 -

मार्कण्डेय उवाच ॥

mārkaṇḍeya uvāca ||

Mārkaṇḍeya said:

- 7 -

इति तस्य वचः श्रुत्वा सुरथः स नराधिपः ॥

iti tasya vacaḥ śrutvā surathaḥ sa narādhipaḥ ||

- 8 -

प्रणिपत्य महाभागं तमृषिं शंसितव्रतम् ।
निर्विण्णोऽतिममत्वेन राज्यापहरणेन च ॥

praṇipatya mahābhāgaṃ tamṛṣiṃ śaṃsitavratam |
nirviṇṇo-timamatvena rājyā paharaṇena ca ||

7-8. Thus hearing the words of that very eminent seer who had performed severe penances, Good Thoughts, The King of Men, despondent over his excessive egotism and attachment to the loss of his kingdom, bowed down to that seer.

- 9 -

जगाम सद्यस्तपसे स च वैश्यो महामुने ।

संदर्शनार्थमम्बाया नदीपुलिनसंस्थितः ॥

jagāma sadyas tapase sa ca vaiśyo mahāmune I
saṃdarśanārtham ambāyā nadī pulina saṃsthitaḥ II

He and the very wise businessman set forth to practice disciplined meditation. With the object of obtaining the complete intuitive vision of the Mother, they stayed on the sand bank of the river.

- 10 -

स.च वैश्यस्तपस्तेपे देवीसूक्तं परं जपन् ।

तौ तस्मिन् पुलिने देव्याः कृत्वा मूर्तिं महीमयीम् ॥

sa ca vaiśyas tapastepe devī sūktaṃ paraṃ japan I
tau tasmin puline devyāḥ kṛtvā mūrtiṃ mahīmayīm II

- 11 -

अर्हणां चक्रतुस्तस्याः पुष्पधूपाग्नितर्पणैः ।

निराहारौ यताहारौ तन्मनस्कौ समाहितौ ॥

arhaṇāṃ cakratustasyāḥ puṣpa dhūpāgni tarpaṇaiḥ I
nirāhārau yatāhārau tanmanaskau samāhitau II

10-11. He and the businessman in the radiant illumination of disciplined meditation continually recited the verses of praise to the Goddess. They prepared an earthen image of the Goddess on the river bank, which was worshipped in turns. With their minds fully concentrated, with the offering of flowers, incense, and fire, they remained without food or with limited food.

- 12 -

ददतुस्तौ बलिं चैव निजगात्रासृगुक्षितम् ।

एवं समाराधयतोस्त्रिभिर्वर्षैर्यतात्मनोः ॥

dadatustau baliṃ caiva nijagātrā sṛgukṣitam I
evaṃ samārādhayatos tribhir varṣair yatātmanoḥ II

- 13 -

परितुष्टा जगद्धात्री प्रत्यक्षं प्राह चण्डिका ॥

paritușțā jagaddhātrī pratyakṣaṃ prāha caṇḍikā ||

12-13. They gave the offering sprinkled in blood taken from their own bodies. Thus they propitiated Her for three years with concentrated minds, whereupon the Sustainer of the World was extremely pleased, and She Who Tears Apart Thought spoke to them in a perceivable form.

- 14 -

देव्युवाच ॥

devyuvāca ||

The Goddess said:

- 15 -

यत् प्रार्थ्यते त्वया भूप त्वया च कुलनन्दन ।

मत्तस्तत्प्राप्यतां सर्वं परितुष्टा ददामि तत् ॥

yat prārthyate tvayā bhūpa tvayā ca kulanandana |

matastatprāpyatāṃ sarvaṃ paritușțā dadāmi tat ||

Oh King, and you Businessman, delight of your family: you have attained to extreme bliss, and I am completely satisfied. I shall give to you whatever you pray for.

- 16 -

मार्कण्डेय उवाच ॥

mārkaṇḍeya uvāca ||

Mārkaṇḍeya said:

- 17 -

ततो वव्रे नृपो राज्यमविभ्रंश्यन्यजन्मनि ।

अत्रैव च निजं राज्यं हतशत्रुबलं बलात् ॥

tato vavre nṛpo rājyam avibhraṃśyanyajanmani |

atraiva ca nijaṃ rājyaṃ hata śatru balaṃ balāt ||

Then the King chose an imperishable kingdom, which will remain with him even in another life, and also the return of his own kingdom, which was forcibly taken from him by his mighty enemies.

- 18 -

सोऽपि वैश्यस्ततो ज्ञानं वव्रे निर्विण्णमानसः ।
ममेत्यहमिति प्राज्ञः सङ्गविच्युतिकारकम् ॥

so-pi vaiśyas tato jñānaṃ vavre nirviṇṇamānasaḥ |
mametyahamiti prājñaḥ saṅga vicyuti kārakam ||

Then the wise businessman, whose mind was filled with indifference to worldly objects, asked for the wisdom that removes the attachments of egotism and possession.

- 19 -

देव्युवाच ॥

devyuvāca ||

The Goddess said:

- 20 -

स्वल्पैरहोभिर्नृपते स्वं राज्यं प्राप्स्यते भवान् ॥

svalpairahobhir nṛpate
svaṃ rājyaṃ prāpsyate bhavān ||

Oh King, within a few days your kingdom will be returned to you.

- 21 -

हत्वा रिपूनस्खलितं तव तत्र भविष्यति ॥

hatvā ripūnas khalitaṃ tava tatra bhaviṣyati ||

After having slain your enemies, you will remain there firm and unshaken.

- 22 -

मृतश्च भूयः सम्प्राप्य जन्म देवाद्विवस्वतः ॥

mṛtaśca bhūyaḥ samprāpya
janma devād vivasvataḥ ||

After your death, you shall take birth from the God of Universal Light.

- 23 -

सावर्णिको नाम मनुर्भवान् भुवि भविष्यति ॥

sāvarṇiko nāma manur bhavān bhuvi bhaviṣyati ||

The Manifestation of Wisdom, He Who Belongs to All Colors, Tribes, and Castes will be the name by which you will be known on earth.

- 24 -

वैश्यवर्य त्वया यश्च वरोऽस्मत्तोऽभिवाञ्छितः ॥

vaiśyavarya tvayā yaśca varo-smatto-bhivāñchitaḥ ||

Oh Best of Businessmen, I grant to you the blessing that you desire of me.

- 25 -

तं प्रयच्छामि संसिद्धयै तव ज्ञानं भविष्यति ॥

taṃ prayacchāmi saṃsiddhyai
tava jñānaṃ bhaviṣyati ||

I bestow upon you the fullest attainment, and you will remain in the highest wisdom by which you will attain liberation.

- 26 -

मार्कण्डेय उवाच ॥

mārkaṇḍeya uvāca ||

Mārkaṇḍeya said:

- 27 -

इति दत्त्वा तयोर्देवी यथाभिलषितं वरम् ॥

iti dattvā tayordevī yathā bhilaṣitaṃ varam ||

Having thus granted the blessing as each desired,

- 28 -

बभूवान्तर्हिता सद्यो भक्त्या ताभ्यामभिष्टुता ।
एवं देव्या वरं लब्ध्वा सुरथः क्षत्रियर्षभः ॥

babhūvāntarhitā sadyo bhaktyā tābhyāmabhiṣṭutā |
evaṃ devyā varaṃ labdhvā suratha kṣatriyarṣabhaḥ ||

the Goddess vanished, having been praised with devotion. Having obtained the blessing from the Goddess, Good Thoughts, the best of warriors,

- 29 -

सूर्याज्जन्म समासाद्य सावर्णिर्भविता मनुः ॥

sūryājjanma samāsādya sāvarṇir bhavitā manuḥ ||

will take his birth from the Light of Wisdom, and will become the Manifestation of Wisdom, He Who Belongs to All Colors, Tribes, and Castes.

- 30 -

एवं देव्या वरं लब्ध्वा सुरथः क्षत्रियर्षभः ।

सूर्याज्जन्म समासाद्य सावर्णिर्भविता मनुः ॥

evaṃ devyā varaṃ labdhvā

surathaḥ kṣatri yarṣabhaḥ |

sūryājjanma samāsādya sāvarṇir bhavitā manuḥ ||

Having obtained the blessing from the Goddess, Good Thoughts, the best of warriors, will take his birth from the Light of Wisdom, and will become the Manifestation of Wisdom, He Who Belongs to All Colors, Tribes, and Castes.

क्लीं ॐ

klīṃ oṃ

शापोद्धार मन्त्रः

śāpoddhāra mantraḥ

The mantra that removes the curses

ॐ ह्रीं क्लीं श्रीं क्रां क्रीं चण्डिकादेव्यै
शापनाशानुग्रहं कुरु कुरु स्वाहा ॥

oṃ hrīṃ klīṃ śrīṃ krāṃ krīṃ caṇḍikā devyai
śāpanāśānugrahaṃ kuru kuru svāhā ||

Repeat eleven times

Oṃ All existence, transformation, Increase, the Cause of Dissolution in the Gross Body, the Cause of Dissolution in the Causal Body, to the Goddess, She Who Tears Apart Thoughts, take away the curse, take away the curse, I am One with God!

उत्कीलन मन्त्रः

utkīlana mantraḥ

The mantra that opens the pin

ॐ श्रीं क्लीं ह्रीं सप्तशति चण्डिके
उत्कीलनं कुरु कुरु स्वाहा ॥

oṃ śrīṃ klīṃ hrīṃ saptaśati caṇḍike
utkīlanaṃ kuru kuru svāhā ||

Repeat twenty-one times

Oṃ Increase, transformation, all existence, the seven hundred verses of the Chaṇḍī, remove the pin, remove the pin, I am One with God!

मृतसंजीवनी मन्त्रः

mṛtasaṃjīvanī mantraḥ

The mantra that bestows life from death

ॐ ह्रीं ह्रीं वं वं ऐं ऐं मृतसंजीवनि विद्ये
मृतमुत्थापयोत्थापय क्रीं ह्रीं ह्रीं वं स्वाहा ॥

oṃ hrīṃ hrīṃ vaṃ vaṃ aiṃ aiṃ
mṛtasaṃjīvani vidye mṛtamutthāpayot
thāpaya krīṃ hrīṃ hrīṃ vaṃ svāhā ||

Repeat eleven times

Oṃ all existence, all existence, vibrations, vibrations, wisdom, wisdom, Oh knowledge that bestows life from death, raise from death, transformation, all existence, all existence, vibrations, I am One with God!

शापविमोचनमन्त्रः

śāpavimocana mantraḥ

The mantra that removes the curses

ॐ श्रीं श्रीं क्लीं हूं ॐ ऐं क्षोभय मोहय
उत्कीलय उत्कीलय उत्कीलय ठं ठं ॥

oṃ śrīṃ śrīṃ klīṃ hūṃ oṃ aiṃ kṣobhaya
mohaya utkīlaya utkīlaya utkīlaya ṭhaṃ ṭhaṃ ||

Repeat eleven times

Oṃ Increase, increase, transformation, cut the ego! Erase the fears of ignorance, remove the pin, remove, remove, devotion, devotion.

अथ नवार्णविधिः

atha navārṇa vidhiḥ

And now, The System of Worship
with the Nine Lettered Mantra

श्रीगणपतिर्जयति

śrī gaṇapatir jayati

May the Lord of Wisdom be Victorious.

ॐ अस्य श्रीनवार्णमन्त्रस्य ब्रह्मविष्णुरुद्रा ऋषयः
गायत्र्युष्णिगनुष्टुभश्छन्दांसि श्रीमहाकालीमहालक्ष्मीमहा
सरस्वत्यो देवताः ऐं बीजम् ह्रीं शक्तिः क्लीं कीलकम्
श्रीमहाकालीमहालक्ष्मीमहासरस्वती प्रीत्यर्थे नवार्णसिद्धयर्थे
जपे विनियोगः ।

oṃ asya śrī navārṇa mantrasya brahma viṣṇu rudrā ṛṣayaḥ gāyatryuṣṇig anuṣṭubhaś chandāṃsi śrī mahākālī mahālakṣmī mahāsarasvatyo devatāḥ aiṃ bījam hrīṃ śaktiḥ klīṃ kīlakam śrī mahākālī mahālakṣmī mahāsarasvatī prītyarthe navārṇa siddhyarthe jape viniyogaḥ |

Oṃ. Presenting the Highly Efficacious Mantra of Nine Letters. The Lords of Creation, Preservation, and Destruction are the Seers; Gāyatrī, Uṣṇig, and Anuṣṭup (24, 28, and 32 syllables to the verse) are the Meters; the Great Remover of Darkness, the Great Goddess of True Wealth, and the Great Goddess of All-Pervading Knowledge are the Deities; Aiṃ is the Seed; Hrīṃ is the Energy; Klīṃ is the Pin; for the Satisfaction of the Great Remover of Darkness, the Great Goddess of True Wealth, and the Great Goddess of All-Pervading Knowledge, this System is applied in recitation.

ऋष्यादिन्यासः

ṛṣyādi nyāsaḥ
Establishment of the Seers

ॐ ब्रह्मविष्णुरुद्रऋषिभ्यो नमः

oṃ brahma viṣṇu rudra ṛṣibhyo namaḥ *head*
I bow to the Seers, the Lords of Creation, Preservation, and Destruction

गायत्र्युष्णिगनुष्टुप् छन्दोभ्यो नमः

gāyatryuṣṇig anuṣṭup chandobhyo namaḥ *mouth*
I bow to the Meters Gāyatrī, Uṣṇig, and Anuṣṭup

महाकालीमहालक्ष्मीमहासरस्वतीदेवताभ्यो नमः

mahākālī mahālakṣmī mahāsarasvatī devatābhyo namaḥ *heart*
I bow to the Deities, the Remover of Darkness, the Great Goddess of True Wealth, and the Great Goddess of All-Pervading Knowledge

ऐं बीजाय नमः

aiṃ bījāya namaḥ *anus*
I bow to the Seed Aiṃ

ह्रीं शक्तये नमः

hrīṃ śaktaye namaḥ *feet*
I bow to the Energy Hrīṃ

क्लीं कीलकाय नमः

klīṃ kīlakāya namaḥ *navel*
I bow to the Pin Klīṃ

ॐ ऐं ह्रीं क्लीं चामुण्डायै विच्चे

oṃ aiṃ hrīṃ klīṃ cāmuṇḍāyai vicce
Oṃ Aiṃ Hrīṃ Klīṃ Cāmuṇḍāyai Vicce

करन्यासः

kara nyāsaḥ

Establishment in the Hands

ॐ ऐं अङ्गुष्ठाभ्यां नमः

oṃ aiṃ aṅguṣṭhābhyāṃ namaḥ *thumb-forefinger*

Oṃ I bow to Aiṃ in the thumb

ॐ ह्रीं तर्जनीभ्यां स्वाहा

oṃ hrīṃ tarjanībhyāṃ svāhā *thumb-forefinger*

Oṃ I bow to Hrīṃ in the forefinger, I Am One With God!

ॐ क्लीं मध्यमाभ्यां वषट्

oṃ klīṃ madhyamābhyāṃ vaṣaṭ *thumb-middle finger*

Oṃ I bow to Klīṃ in the middle finger, Purify!

ॐ चामुण्डायै अनामिकाभ्यां हुम्

oṃ cāmuṇḍāyai anāmikābhyāṃ huṃ *thumb-ring finger*

Oṃ I bow to Cāmuṇḍā in the ring finger, Cut The Ego!

ॐ विच्चे कनिष्ठिकाभ्यां वौषट्

oṃ vicce kaniṣṭhikābhyāṃ vauṣaṭ *thumb-little finger*

Oṃ I bow to Vicce in the little finger, Ultimate Purity!

ॐ ऐं ह्रीं क्लीं चामुण्डायै विच्चे
करतलकरपृष्ठाभ्यां अस्त्राय फट्

oṃ aiṃ hrīṃ klīṃ cāmuṇḍāyai vicce
karatalakara pṛṣṭhābhyāṃ astrāya phaṭ
(roll hand over hand front and back and clap)
Oṃ Aiṃ Hrīṃ Klīṃ Cāmuṇḍāyai Vicce
with the weapon of Virtue

ॐ ऐं ह्रीं क्लीं चामुण्डायै विच्चे

oṃ aiṃ hrīṃ klīṃ cāmuṇḍāyai vicce
Oṃ Aiṃ Hrīṃ Klīṃ Cāmuṇḍāyai Vicce

हृदयादिन्यासः

hṛdayādi nyāsaḥ
Establishment in the Heart

ॐ ऐं हृदयाय नमः

oṃ aiṃ hṛdayāya namaḥ *touch heart*
Oṃ I bow to Aiṃ in the heart

ॐ ह्रीं शिरसे स्वाहा

oṃ hrīṃ śirase svāhā *top of head*
Oṃ I bow to Hrīṃ on top of the head, I am One with God!

ॐ क्लीं शिखायै वषट्

oṃ klīṃ śikhāyai vaṣaṭ *back of head*
Oṃ I bow to Klīṃ on the back of the head, Purify!

ॐ चामुण्डायै कवचाय हुम्

oṃ cāmuṇḍāyai kavacāya huṃ *cross arms*
Oṃ I bow to Cāmuṇḍā crossing both arms, Cut the Ego!

ॐ विच्चे नेत्रत्रयाय वौषट्

oṃ vicce netratrayāya vauṣaṭ *touch three eyes*
Oṃ I bow to Vicce on the three eyes, Ultimate Purity!

ॐ ऐं ह्रीं क्लीं चामुण्डायै विच्चे
करतलकरपृष्ठाभ्यां अस्त्राय फट्
oṃ aiṃ hrīṃ klīṃ cāmuṇḍāyai vicce
karatalakara pṛṣṭhābhyāṃ astrāya phaṭ
(roll hand over hand front and back and clap)
Oṃ Aiṃ Hrīṃ Klīṃ Cāmuṇḍāyai Vicce
with the weapon of Virtue.

ॐ ऐं ह्रीं क्लीं चामुण्डायै विच्चे
oṃ aiṃ hrīṃ klīṃ cāmuṇḍāyai vicce
Oṃ Aiṃ Hrīṃ Klīṃ Cāmuṇḍāyai Vicce

अक्षरन्यासः
akṣaranyāsaḥ
Establishment of the letters

ॐ ऐं नमः
oṃ aiṃ namaḥ *top of head*
Oṃ I bow to Aiṃ

ॐ ह्रीं नमः
oṃ hrīṃ namaḥ *right eye*
Oṃ I bow to Hrīṃ

ॐ क्लीं नमः
oṃ klīṃ namaḥ *left eye*
Oṃ I bow to Klīṃ

ॐ चां नमः
oṃ cāṃ namaḥ *right ear*
Oṃ I bow to Cāṃ

ॐ मुं नमः
oṃ muṃ namaḥ *left ear*
Oṃ I bow to muṇ

ॐ डां नमः

oṃ ḍāṃ namaḥ *right nostril*
Oṃ I bow to ḍāṃ

ॐ यैं नमः

oṃ yaiṃ namaḥ *left nostril*
Oṃ I bow to yaiṃ

ॐ विं नमः

oṃ viṃ namaḥ *mouth*
Oṃ I bow to viṃ

ॐ चें नमः

oṃ ceṃ namaḥ *anus*
Oṃ I bow to ceṃ

ॐ ऐं ह्रीं क्लीं चामुण्डायै विच्चे

oṃ aiṃ hrīṃ klīṃ cāmuṇḍāyai vicce
Oṃ Aiṃ Hrīṃ Klīṃ Cāmuṇḍāyai Vicce

दिङ्न्यासः

diṅ nyāsaḥ

Establishment in the Directions

ॐ ऐं उदीच्यै नमः

oṃ aiṃ udīcyai namaḥ *north*

Oṃ I bow to Aiṃ in the North

ॐ ह्रीं प्राच्यै नमः

oṃ hrīṃ prācyai namaḥ *east*

Oṃ I bow to Hrīṃ in the East

ॐ क्लीं दक्षिणायै नमः

oṃ klīṃ dakṣiṇāyai namaḥ *south*

Oṃ I bow to Klīṃ in the South

ॐ चामुण्डायै प्रतीच्यै नमः

oṃ cāmuṇḍāyai pratīcyai namaḥ *west*

Oṃ I bow to Cāmuṇḍā in the West

ॐ विच्चे वायव्यै नमः

oṃ vicce vāyavyai namaḥ *northwest*

Oṃ I bow to Vicce in the Northwest

ॐ ऐं ऐशान्यै नमः

oṃ aiṃ aiśānyai namaḥ *northeast*

Oṃ I bow to Aiṃ in the Northeast

ॐ ह्रीं आग्नेय्यै नमः

oṃ hrīṃ āgneyyai namaḥ *southeast*

Oṃ I bow to Hrīṃ in the Southeast

ॐ क्लीं नैर्ऋत्यै नमः

oṃ klīṃ nairṛtyai namaḥ *southwest*

Oṃ I bow to Klīṃ in the Southwest

ॐ चामुण्डायै ऊर्ध्वायै नमः

oṃ cāmuṇḍāyai ūrdhvāyai namaḥ *up*

Oṃ I bow to Cāmuṇḍā, looking up

ॐ विच्चे भूम्यै नमः

oṃ vicce bhūmyai namaḥ *down*

Oṃ I bow to Vicce, looking down

ॐ ऐं ह्रीं क्लीं चामुण्डायै विच्चे

oṃ aiṃ hrīṃ klīṃ cāmuṇḍāyai vicce ten directions

Oṃ Aiṃ Hrīṃ Klīṃ Cāmuṇḍāyai Vicce

ध्यानम्

dhyānam

Meditation

खड्गं चक्रगदेषुचापपरिघाञ्छूलं भुशुण्डीं शिरः
शङ्खं संदधतीं करैस्त्रिनयनां सर्वाङ्गभूषावृताम् ।
नीलाश्मद्युतिमास्यपाददशकां सेवे महाकालिकां
यामस्तौत्स्वपिते हरौ कमलजो हन्तुं मधुं कैटभम् ॥

khaḍgaṃ cakra gadeṣu cāpa
parighāñ chūlaṃ bhuśuṇḍīṃ śiraḥ
śaṅkhaṃ saṃdadhatīṃ karai
strinayanāṃ sarvāṅga bhūṣāvṛtām |
nīlāśmadyutimāsya pāda
daśakāṃ seve mahākālikāṃ
yāmastaut svapite harau kamalajo
hantuṃ madhuṃ kaiṭabham ||

Bearing in Her ten hands the sword of worship, the discus of revolving time, the club of articulation, the bow of determination, the iron bar of restraint, the pike of attention, the sling, the head of egotism, and the conch of vibrations, She has three eyes and displays ornaments on all Her limbs. Shining like a blue gem, She has ten faces. I worship that Great Remover of Darkness whom the lotus-born Creative Capacity praised in order to slay Too Much and Too Little when the Supreme Consciousness was in sleep.

अक्षस्रक्परशुं गदेषुकुलिशं पद्मं धनुः कुण्डिकां
दण्डं शक्तिमसिं च चर्म जलजं घण्टां सुराभाजनम् ।
शूलं पाशसुदर्शने च दधतीं हस्तैः प्रसन्नाननां
सेवे सैरिभमर्दिनीमिह महालक्ष्मीं सरोजस्थिताम् ॥

akṣasrak paraśuṃ gadeṣu kuliśaṃ
padmaṃ dhanuḥ kuṇḍikāṃ
daṇḍaṃ śaktim asiṃ ca carma
jalajaṃ ghaṇṭāṃ surābhājanam |
śūlaṃ pāśa sudarśane ca
dadhatīṃ hastaiḥ prasannānanāṃ
seve sairibha mardinīmiha
mahālakṣmīṃ sarojasthitām ||

She with the beautiful face, the Destroyer of the Great Ego, is seated upon the lotus of peace. In Her hands She holds the rosary of alphabets, the battle axe of good actions, the club of articulation, the arrow of speech, the thunderbolt of illumination, the lotus of peace, the bow of determination, the water pot of purification, the staff of discipline, energy, the sword of worship, the shield of faith, the conch of vibrations, the bell of continuous tone, the wine cup of joy, the pike of concentration, the net of unity, and the discus of revolving time, named Excellent Intuitive Vision. I worship that Great Goddess of True Wealth.

घण्टाशूलहलानि शङ्खमुसले चक्रं धनुः सायकं
हस्ताब्जैर्दधतीं घनान्तविलसच्छीतांशुतुल्यप्रभाम् ।
गौरीदेहसमुद्भवां त्रिजगतामाधारभूतां महा-
पूर्वामत्र सरस्वतीमनुभजे शुम्भादिदैत्यार्दिनीम् ॥

ghaṇṭā śūla halāni śaṅkha
musale cakraṃ dhanuḥ sāyakaṃ
hastābjair dadhatīṃ ghanānta
vilasacchītāṃśutulya prabhām |
gaurīdeha samudbhavāṃ
trijagatām ādhārabhūtāṃ mahā-
pūrvāmatra sarasvatīm anubhaje
śumbhādi daityārdinīm ||

Bearing in Her lotus hands the bell of continuous tone, the pike of concentration, the plow sowing the seeds of the Way of Truth to Wisdom, the conch of vibrations, the pestle of refinement, the discus of revolving time, the bow of determination, and the arrow of speech; whose radiance is like the moon in autumn; whose appearance is most beautiful; who is manifested from the body of She Who is Rays of Light; and is the support of the three worlds, that Great Goddess of All-Pervading Knowledge, who destroyed Self-Conceit and other thoughts, I worship.

ॐ ऐं ह्रीं अक्षमालिकायै नमः

oṃ aiṃ hrīṃ akṣa mālikāyai namaḥ

Oṃ Aiṃ Hrīṃ I bow to the Rosary of Letters

ॐ मां माले महामाये सर्वशक्तिस्वरूपिणि ।
चतुर्वर्गस्त्वयि न्यस्तस्तस्मान्मे सिद्धिदा भव ॥

oṃ māṃ māle mahāmāye sarva śakti svarūpiṇi |
catur vargas tvayi nyastas
tasmān me siddhidā bhava ||

Oṃ My Rosary, the Great Measurement of Consciousness, containing all energy within as your intrinsic nature, give to me the attainment of your Perfection, fulfilling the four objectives of life.

ॐ अविघ्नं कुरु माले त्वं गृह्णामि दक्षिणे करे ।
जपकाले च सिद्ध्यर्थं प्रसीद मम सिद्धये ॥

oṃ avighnaṃ kuru māle tvaṃ gṛhṇāmi dakṣiṇe kare |
japakāle ca siddhyarthaṃ prasīda mama siddhaye ||
Oṃ Rosary, You please remove all obstacles. I hold you in my right hand. At the time of recitation be pleased with me. Allow me to attain the Highest Perfection.

ॐ अक्षमालाधिपतये सुसिद्धिं देहि देहि सर्वमन्त्रार्थसाधिनि
साधय साधय सर्वसिद्धिं परिकल्पय परिकल्पय मे स्वाहा ॥
oṃ akṣa mālā dhipataye susiddhiṃ dehi dehi sarva mantrārtha sādhini sādhaya sādhaya sarva siddhiṃ parikalpaya parikalpaya me svāhā ||
Oṃ Rosary of rudrākṣa seeds, my Lord, give to me excellent attainment. Give to me, give to me. Illuminate the meanings of all mantras, illuminate, illuminate! Fashion me with all excellent attainments, fashion me! I am One with God!

ॐ ऐं ह्रीं क्लीं चामुण्डायै विच्चे
oṃ aiṃ hrīṃ klīṃ cāmuṇḍāyai vicce 108 times
Oṃ Aiṃ Hrīṃ Klīṃ Cāmuṇḍāyai Vicce

ॐ गुह्यातिगुह्यगोप्त्री त्वं गृहाणास्मत्कृतं जपम् ।
सिद्धिर्भवतु मे देवि त्वत्प्रसादान्महेश्वरि ॥
oṃ guhyātiguhyagoptrī tvaṃ
gṛhāṇās matkṛtaṃ japam |
siddhir bhavatu me devi tvat prasādān maheśvari ||
Oh Goddess, You are the Protector of the most secret of mystical secrets. Please accept the recitation that I have offered and grant to me the attainment of Perfection.

ध्यानम्

dhyānam

Meditation

ॐ विद्युद्दामसमप्रभां मृगपतिस्कन्धस्थितां भीषणां
कन्याभिः करवालखेटविलसद्धस्ताभिरासेविताम् ।
हस्तैश्चक्रगदासिखेटविशिखांश्चापं गुणं तर्जनीं
बिभ्राणामनलात्मिकां शशिधरां दुर्गां त्रिनेत्रां भजे ॥

oṃ vidyud dāmasamaprabhāṃ
mṛgapati skandhasthitāṃ bhīṣaṇāṃ
kanyābhiḥ karavālakheṭa
vilasaddhastābhirā sevitām ।
hastaiścakra gadāsi kheṭa
viśikhāṃścāpaṃ guṇaṃ tarjanīṃ
bibhrāṇāmanalātmikāṃ śaśidharāṃ
durgāṃ trinetrāṃ bhaje ॥

I meditate upon the three-eyed Goddess, Durgā, the Reliever of Difficulties; the luster of Her beautiful body is like lightning. She sits upon the shoulders of a lion and appears very fierce. Many maidens holding the double-edged sword and shield in their hands are standing at readiness to serve Her. She holds in Her hands the discus, club, double-edged sword, shield, arrow, bow, net, and the mudrā connecting the thumb and the pointer finger, with the other three fingers extended upwards, indicating the granting of wisdom. Her intrinsic nature is fire, and upon her head She wears the moon as a crown.

ॐ

oṃ

ऋग्वेदोक्तं देवीसूक्तम्

ṛgvedoktaṃ devī sūktam

The Vedic Praise of the Goddess

- 1 -

ॐ अहं रुद्रेभिर्वसुभिश्चराम्यहमादित्यैरुत विश्वदेवैः ।
अहं मित्रावरुणोभा बिभर्म्यहमिन्द्राग्नी अहमश्विनोभा ॥

aham rudrebhir vasubhiś carāmyaham
ādityai ruta viśva devaiḥ |
ahaṃ mitrā varuṇobhā bibharmyaham
indrāgnī ahamaśvinobhā ||

I travel with the Relievers of Suffering, with the Finders of the Wealth, with the Sons of Enlightenment as also with All Gods. I hold aloft Friendship and Equanimity, the Rule of the Pure, the Light of Meditation, and the Divine Urge to Union.

- 2 -

अहं सोममाहनसं बिभर्म्यहं त्वष्टारमुत पूषणं भगम् ।
अहं दधामि द्रविणं हविष्मते सुप्राव्ये यजमानाय सुन्वते ॥

ahaṃ somamāhanasaṃ bibharmyahaṃ
tvaṣṭāramuta pūṣaṇaṃ bhagam |
ahaṃ dadhāmi draviṇaṃ haviṣmate
suprāvye yajamānāya sunvate ||

I perform the functions of Great Devotion, Creative Intelligence, Searchers for Truth, and the Wealth of Realization. I give the wealth to the sacrificer who presses out the offering of devotion with attention.

- 3 -

अहं राष्ट्री संगमनी वसूनां चिकितुषी प्रथमा यज्ञियानाम् ।
तां मा देवा व्यदधुः पुरुत्रा भूरिस्थात्रां भूर्य्यावेशयन्तीम् ॥

ahaṃ rāṣṭrī saṅgamanī vasūnāṃ
cikituṣī prathamā yajñiyānām |
tāṃ mā devā vyadadhuḥ purutrā
bhūristhātrāṃ bhūryyāveśayantīm ||

I am the Queen, the united mind of the Guardians of the Treasure, the Supreme Consciousness of those who are offered sacrifice. Thus the Gods have established me in the manifold existence, the All-Pervading Soul of the Abundant Being.

- 4 -

मया सो अन्नमत्ति यो विपश्यति यः प्राणिति य ईं शृणोत्युक्तम् ।
अमन्तवो मां त उप क्षियन्ति श्रुधि श्रुत श्रद्धिवं ते वदामि ॥

mayā so annamatti yo vipaśyati
yaḥ prāṇiti ya īṃ śṛṇotyuktam |
amantavo māṃ ta upa kṣiyanti
śrudhi śruta śraddhivaṃ te vadāmi ||

Through me alone all eat, all see, all breathe, all hear. They know me not, but yet they dwell beside me. Hear from me the truth of Faith as I speak to you.

- 5 -

अहमेव स्वयमिदं वदामि जुष्टं देवेभिरुत मानुषेभिः ।
यं कामये तं तमुग्रं कृणोमि तं ब्रह्माणं तमृषिं तं सुमेधाम् ॥

ahameva svayamidaṃ vadāmi juṣṭaṃ
devebhiruta mānuṣebhiḥ |
yaṃ kāmaye taṃ tamugraṃ kṛṇomi
taṃ brahmāṇaṃ tamṛṣiṃ taṃ sumedhām ||

Only I, myself, of my own volition, speak this, which is loved by Gods and men. Whosoever I love I give him strength and make him a Knower of Divinity, a Seer, one of loving intellect.

- 6 -

अहं रुद्राय धनुरा तनोमि ब्रह्मद्विषे शरवे हन्तवा उ ।
अहं जनाय समदं कृणोम्यहं द्यावापृथिवी आ विवेश ॥

ahaṃ rudrāya dhanurā tanomi
brahmadviṣe śarave hantavā u |
ahaṃ janāya samadaṃ kṛṇomyahaṃ
dyāvā pṛthivī ā viveśa ||

I, the Preserving Energy, bend the bow for the Reliever of Suffering to slay the enemies of the Creative Consciousness by the arrows of speech. I give the people zealous fervor. I pervade throughout heaven and earth.

- 7 -

अहं सुवे पितरमस्य मूर्द्धन्मम योनिरप्स्वन्तः समुद्रे ।
ततो वि तिष्ठे भुवनानु विश्वोतामूं द्यां वर्ष्मणोप स्पृशामि ॥

ahaṃ suve pitaramasya mūrddhanmama
yonirapsvantaḥ samudre |
tato vi tiṣṭhe bhuvanānu viśvo
tāmūṃ dyāṃ varṣmaṇopa spṛśāmi ||

I give birth to the Supreme Father of this All. My creative energy is in the waters of the inner ocean. From thence I extend through all the worlds of the Universe and touch the summit of heaven with my greatness.

- 8 -

अहमेव वात इव प्रवाम्यारभमाणा भुवनानि विश्वा ।
परो दिवा पर एना पृथिव्यैतावती महिना संबभूव ॥

ahameva vāta iva pravāmyārabhamāṇā
bhuvanāni viśvā |
paro divā para enā pṛthivyai
tāvatī mahinā saṃbabhūva ||

I blow intensely all beings of the Universe like the wind. Beyond the heavens and beyond the earth to such an extent has my greatness altogether extended.

Devi 26

अथ तन्त्रोक्तं देवीसूक्तम्

atha tantroktaṃ devī sūktam

The Tantric Praise of the Goddess

\- 1 -

नमो देव्यै महादेव्यै शिवायै सततं नमः ।

नमः प्रकृत्यै भद्रायै नियताः प्रणताः स्म ताम् ॥

namo devyai mahādevyai śivāyai satataṃ namaḥ |
namaḥ prakṛtyai bhadrāyai
niyatāḥ praṇatāḥ sma tām ||

We bow to the Goddess, to the Great Goddess, to the Energy of Infinite Goodness at all times we bow. We bow to Nature, to the Excellent One, with discipline we have bowed down.

\- 2 -

रौद्रायै नमो नित्यायै गौर्यै धात्र्यै नमो नमः ।

ज्योत्स्नायै चेन्दुरूपिण्यै सुखायै सततं नमः ॥

raudrāyai namo nityāyai
gauryai dhātryai namo namaḥ |
jyotsnāyai cendurūpiṇyai sukhāyai satataṃ namaḥ ||

To the Reliever of Sufferings we bow, to the Eternal, to the Embodiment of Rays of Light, to the Creatress, to She Who Manifests Light, to the form of Devotion, to Happiness continually we bow.

\- 3 -

कल्याण्यै प्रणतां वृद्ध्यै सिद्ध्यै कुर्मो नमो नमः ।

नैर्ऋत्यै भूभृतां लक्ष्म्यै शर्वाण्यै ते नमो नमः ॥

kalyāṇyai praṇatāṃ vṛddhyai
siddhyai kurmo namo namaḥ |
nairṛtyai bhūbhṛtāṃ lakṣmyai
śarvāṇyai te namo namaḥ ||

To the Welfare of those who bow, we bow; to Change, to Perfection, to Dissolution, to the Wealth that sustains the earth, to the Wife of Consciousness, to you, we bow, we bow.

- 4 -

दुर्गायै दुर्गपारायै सारायै सर्वकारिण्यै ।

ख्यात्यै तथैव कृष्णायै धूम्रायै सततं नमः ॥

durgāyai durgapārāyai sārāyai sarvakāriṇyai |
khyātyai tathaiva kṛṣṇāyai
dhūmrāyai satatam namaḥ ||

To She Who Removes Difficulties, to She Who Removes Beyond All Difficulties, to the Essence, to the Cause of All; to Perception, and to the Doer of All, to the Unknowable One, continually we bow.

- 5 -

अतिसौम्यातिरौद्रायै नतास्तस्यै नमो नमः ।

नमो जगत्प्रतिष्ठायै देव्यै कृत्यै नमो नमः ॥

atisaumyāti raudrāyai natāstasyai namo namaḥ |
namo jagat pratiṣṭhāyai devyai kṛtyai namo namaḥ ||

To the extremely beautiful and to the extremely fierce, we bow to Her, we bow, we bow. We bow to the Establisher of the Perceivable Universe, to the Goddess, to All Action, we bow, we bow.

- 6 -

या देवी सर्वभूतेषु विष्णुमायेति शब्दिता ।

नमस्तस्यै ॥ नमस्तस्यै ॥ नमस्तस्यै नमो नमः ॥

yā devī sarva bhūteṣu viṣṇu māyeti śabditā |
namastasyai || namastasyai || namastasyai namo namaḥ ||

To the Divine Goddess in all existence who is addressed as the Perceivable Form of the Consciousness That Pervades All, we bow to Her; we bow to Her; we bow to Her, continually we bow, we bow.

- 7 -

या देवी सर्वभूतेषु चेतनेत्यभिधीयते ।

नमस्तस्यै ॥ नमस्तस्यै ॥ नमस्तस्यै नमो नमः ॥

yā devī sarva bhūteṣu cetanetyabhi dhīyate |
namastasyai || namastasyai || namastasyai namo namaḥ ||

To the Divine Goddess in all existence who resides all throughout the Consciousness and is known by the reflections of mind, we bow to Her; we bow to Her; we bow to Her, continually we bow, we bow.

\- 8 -

या देवी सर्वभूतेषु बुद्धिरूपेण संस्थिता ।
नमस्तस्यै ॥ नमस्तस्यै ॥ नमस्तस्यै नमो नमः ॥

yā devī sarva bhūteṣu buddhi rūpeṇa saṃsthitā |
namastasyai || namastasyai || namastasyai namo namaḥ ||

To the Divine Goddess who resides in all existence in the form of Intelligence, we bow to Her; we bow to Her; we bow to Her, continually we bow, we bow.

\- 9 -

या देवी सर्वभूतेषु निद्रारूपेण संस्थिता ।
नमस्तस्यै ॥ नमस्तस्यै ॥ नमस्तस्यै नमो नमः ॥

yā devī sarva bhūteṣu nidrā rūpeṇa saṃsthitā |
namastasyai || namastasyai || namastasyai namo namaḥ ||

To the Divine Goddess who resides in all existence in the form of Sleep, we bow to Her; we bow to Her; we bow to Her, continually we bow, we bow.

\- 10 -

या देवी सर्वभूतेषु क्षुधारूपेण संस्थिता ।
नमस्तस्यै ॥ नमस्तस्यै ॥ नमस्तस्यै नमो नमः ॥

yā devī sarva bhūteṣu kṣudhā rūpeṇa saṃsthitā
namastasyai || namastasyai || namastasyai namo namaḥ ||

To the Divine Goddess who resides in all existence in the form of Hunger, we bow to Her; we bow to Her; we bow to Her, continually we bow, we bow.

- 11 -

या देवी सर्वभूतेषु छायारूपेण संस्थिता ।

नमस्तस्यै ॥ नमस्तस्यै ॥ नमस्तस्यै नमो नमः ॥

yā devī sarva bhūteṣu chāyā rūpeṇa saṃsthitā । namastasyai ॥ namastasyai ॥ namastasyai namo namaḥ ॥

To the Divine Goddess who resides in all existence in the form of Appearance, we bow to Her; we bow to Her; we bow to Her, continually we bow, we bow.

- 12 -

या देवी सर्वभूतेषु शक्तिरूपेण संस्थिता ।

नमस्तस्यै ॥ नमस्तस्यै ॥ नमस्तस्यै नमो नमः ॥

yā devī sarva bhūteṣu śakti rūpeṇa saṃsthitā । namastasyai ॥ namastasyai ॥ namastasyai namo namaḥ ॥

To the Divine Goddess who resides in all existence in the form of Energy, we bow to Her; we bow to Her; we bow to Her, continually we bow, we bow.

- 13 -

या देवी सर्वभूतेषु तृष्णारूपेण संस्थिता ।

नमस्तस्यै ॥ नमस्तस्यै ॥ नमस्तस्यै नमो नमः ॥

yā devī sarva bhūteṣu tṛṣṇā rūpeṇa saṃsthitā । namastasyai ॥ namastasyai ॥ namastasyai namo namaḥ ॥

To the Divine Goddess who resides in all existence in the form of Desire, we bow to Her; we bow to Her; we bow to Her, continually we bow, we bow.

- 14 -

या देवी सर्वभूतेषु क्षान्तिरूपेण संस्थिता ।

नमस्तस्यै ॥ नमस्तस्यै ॥ नमस्तस्यै नमो नमः ॥

yā devī sarva bhūteṣu kṣānti rūpeṇa saṃsthitā । namastasyai ॥ namastasyai ॥ namastasyai namo namaḥ ॥

To the Divine Goddess who resides in all existence in the form of Patient Forgiveness, we bow to Her; we bow to Her; we bow to Her, continually we bow, we bow.

- 15 -

या देवी सर्वभूतेषु जातिरूपेण संस्थिता ।

नमस्तस्यै ॥ नमस्तस्यै ॥ नमस्तस्यै नमो नमः ॥

yā devī sarva bhūteṣu jāti rūpeṇa saṃsthitā |
namastasyai || namastasyai || namastasyai namo namaḥ ||

To the Divine Goddess who resides in all existence in the form of All Living Beings, we bow to Her; we bow to Her; we bow to Her, continually we bow, we bow.

- 16 -

या देवी सर्वभूतेषु लज्जारूपेण संस्थिता ।

नमस्तस्यै ॥ नमस्तस्यै ॥ नमस्तस्यै नमो नमः ॥

yā devī sarva bhūteṣu lajjā rūpeṇa saṃsthitā |
namastasyai || namastasyai || namastasyai namo namaḥ ||

To the Divine Goddess who resides in all existence in the form of Humility, we bow to Her; we bow to Her; we bow to Her, continually we bow, we bow.

- 17 -

या देवी सर्वभूतेषु शान्तिरूपेण संस्थिता ।

नमस्तस्यै ॥ नमस्तस्यै ॥ नमस्तस्यै नमो नमः ॥

yā devī sarva bhūteṣu śānti rūpeṇa saṃsthitā |
namastasyai || namastasyai || namastasyai namo namaḥ ||

To the Divine Goddess who resides in all existence in the form of Peace, we bow to Her; we bow to Her; we bow to Her, continually we bow, we bow.

- 18 -

या देवी सर्वभूतेषु श्रद्धारूपेण संस्थिता ।

नमस्तस्यै ॥ नमस्तस्यै ॥ नमस्तस्यै नमो नमः ॥

yā devī sarva bhūteṣu śraddhā rūpeṇa saṃsthitā |
namastasyai || namastasyai || namastasyai namo namaḥ ||

To the Divine Goddess who resides in all existence in the form of Faith, we bow to Her; we bow to Her; we bow to Her. continually we bow, we bow.

- 19 -

या देवी सर्वभूतेषु कान्तिरूपेण संस्थिता ।

नमस्तस्यै ॥ नमस्तस्यै ॥ नमस्तस्यै नमो नमः ॥

yā devī sarva bhūteṣu kānti rūpeṇa saṃsthitā |
namastasyai || namastasyai || namastasyai namo namaḥ ||

To the Divine Goddess who resides in all existence in the form of Beauty Enhanced by Love, we bow to Her; we bow to Her; we bow to Her, continually we bow, we bow.

- 20 -

या देवी सर्वभूतेषु लक्ष्मीरूपेण संस्थिता ।

नमस्तस्यै ॥ नमस्तस्यै ॥ नमस्तस्यै नमो नमः ॥

yā devī sarva bhūteṣu lakṣmī rūpeṇa saṃsthitā |
namastasyai || namastasyai || namastasyai namo namaḥ ||

To the Divine Goddess who resides in all existence in the form of True Wealth, we bow to Her; we bow to Her; we bow to Her, continually we bow, we bow.

- 21 -

या देवी सर्वभूतेषु वृत्तिरूपेण संस्थिता ।

नमस्तस्यै ॥ नमस्तस्यै ॥ नमस्तस्यै नमो नमः ॥

yā devī sarva bhūteṣu vṛtti rūpeṇa saṃsthitā |
namastasyai || namastasyai || namastasyai namo namaḥ ||

To the Divine Goddess who resides in all existence in the form of Activity, we bow to Her; we bow to Her; we bow to Her, continually we bow, we bow.

- 22 -

या देवी सर्वभूतेषु स्मृतिरूपेण संस्थिता ।

नमस्तस्यै ॥ नमस्तस्यै ॥ नमस्तस्यै नमो नमः ॥

yā devī sarva bhūteṣu smṛti rūpeṇa saṃsthitā I namastasyai II namastasyai II namastasyai namo namaḥ II

To the Divine Goddess who resides in all existence in the form of Recollection, we bow to Her; we bow to Her; we bow to Her, continually we bow, we bow.

- 23 -

या देवी सर्वभूतषु दयारूपेण संस्थिता ।

नमस्तस्यै ॥ नमस्तस्यै ॥ नमस्तस्यै नमो नमः ॥

yā devī sarva bhūteṣu dayā rūpeṇa saṃsthitā I namastasyai II namastasyai II namastasyai namo namaḥ II

To the Divine Goddess who resides in all existence in the form of Compassion, we bow to Her; we bow to Her; we bow to Her, continually we bow, we bow.

- 24 -

या देवी सर्वभूतेषु तुष्टिरूपेण संस्थिता ।

नमस्तस्यै ॥ नमस्तस्यै ॥ नमस्तस्यै नमो नमः ॥

yā devī sarva bhūteṣu tuṣṭi rūpeṇa saṃsthitā I namastasyai II namastasyai II namastasyai namo namaḥ II

To the Divine Goddess who resides in all existence in the form of Satisfaction, we bow to Her; we bow to Her; we bow to Her, continually we bow, we bow.

- 25 -

या देवी सर्वभूतेषु मातृरूपेण संस्थिता ।

नमस्तस्यै ॥ नमस्तस्यै ॥ नमस्तस्यै नमो नमः ॥

yā devī sarva bhūteṣu mātṛ rūpeṇa saṃsthitā I namastasyai II namastasyai II namastasyai namo namaḥ II

To the Divine Goddess who resides in all existence in the form of Mother, we bow to Her; we bow to Her; we bow to Her, continually we bow, we bow.

\- 26 -

या देवी सर्वभूतेषु भ्रान्तिरूपेण संस्थिता ।

नमस्तस्यै ॥ नमस्तस्यै ॥ नमस्तस्यै नमो नमः ॥

yā devī sarva bhūteṣu bhrānti rūpeṇa saṃsthitā |

namastasyai || namastasyai || namastasyai namo namaḥ ||

To the Divine Goddess who resides in all existence in the form of Confusion, we bow to Her; we bow to Her; we bow to Her, continually we bow, we bow.

\- 27 -

इन्द्रियाणामधिष्ठात्री भूतानां चाखिलेषु या ।

भूतेषु सततं तस्यै व्याप्तिदेव्यै नमो नमः ॥

indriyāṇāmadhiṣṭhātrī bhūtānāṃ cākhileṣu yā |

bhūteṣu satataṃ tasyai vyāptidevyai namo namaḥ ||

Presiding over the senses of all beings and pervading all existence, to the Omnipresent Goddess who individualizes creation we bow, we bow.

\- 28 -

चितिरूपेण या कृत्स्नमेतद् व्याप्य स्थिता जगत् ।

नमस्तस्यै ॥ नमस्तस्यै ॥ नमस्तस्यै नमो नमः ॥

citirūpeṇa yā kṛtsnametad vyāpya sthitā jagat |

namastasyai || namastasyai || namastasyai namo namaḥ ||

In the form of Consciousness She distinguishes the individual phenomena of the perceivable universe. We bow to Her; we bow to Her; we bow to Her, continually we bow, we bow.

\- 29 -

स्तुता सुरैः पूर्वमभीष्टसंश्रयात्तथा सुरेन्द्रेण दिनेषु सेविता ।

करोतु सा नः शुभहेतुरीश्वरी शुभानि भद्राण्यभिहन्तु चापदः ॥

stutā suraiḥ pūrvamabhīṣṭa saṃśrayāt
tathā surendreṇa dineṣu sevitā |
karotu sā naḥ śubha hetur īśvarī
śubhāni bhadrāṇyabhi hantu cāpadaḥ ||

In days of old, all of the Gods, led by Indra, the Rule of the Pure, sang these verses of praise for the purpose of accomplishing their desired objective of surrendering the ego in the Light of Wisdom, and for many days that service was rendered. May She, the Seer of All, the Lord of All, the Source of All Good, perform similarly for us all auspicious things by putting an end to all distress.

- 30 -

या साम्प्रतं चोद्धतदैत्यतापितैर-
स्माभिरीशा च सुरैर्नमस्यते ।
या च स्मृता तत्क्षणमेव हन्ति नः
सर्वापदो भक्तिविनम्रमूर्त्तिभिः ॥

yā sāmpratam coddhata daitya tāpitair
asmābhi rīśā ca surair namasyate |
yā ca smṛtā tat kṣaṇameva hanti naḥ
sarvāpado bhakti vinamra mūrtibhiḥ ||

We Gods have been harassed by arrogant thoughts in the manner of humans, and at this time all of us Gods bow to the Seer of All, who, when bowed to with devotion, and remembered in a physical image, immediately terminates our every adversity.

ॐ

oṃ

अथ प्राधानिकं रहस्यम्

atha prādhānikaṃ rahasyam

And Now, The Most Preeminent Secret

Dev. 27

ॐ अस्य श्रीसप्तशतीरहस्यत्रयस्य नारायण ऋषिरनुष्टुप्
छन्दः महाकालीमहालक्ष्मीमहासरस्वत्यो देवता
यथोक्तफलावाप्त्यर्थं जपे विनियोगः ।

**oṃ asya śrī saptaśatī rahasya trayasya nārāyaṇa
ṛṣir anuṣṭup chandaḥ mahākālī mahālakṣmī
mahāsarasvatyo devatā yathokta phalāvāptyartham
jape viniyogaḥ |**

Presenting the three secrets of the Seven Hundred Verses. Nārāyaṇa is the Seer, Anuṣṭup (32 syllables to the verse) is the meter, the Great Remover of Darkness, the Great Goddess of True Wealth, and the Great Spirit of All-Pervading Knowledge are the deities. The application of the recitation of these mantras is to inculcate the qualities of this scripture.

राजोवाच

rājovāca

The King said:

- 1 -

भगवन्नवतारा मे चण्डिकायास्त्वयोदिताः ।
एतेषां प्रकृतिं ब्रह्मन् प्रधानं वक्तुमर्हसि ॥

**bhagavannavatārā me caṇḍikāyās tvayoditāḥ |
eteṣāṃ prakṛtiṃ brahman
pradhānaṃ vaktu marhasi ||**

Lord, you have explained to me the manifestations of the Energy That Tears Apart Thought. Oh Knower of Wisdom, now please describe the principal characteristics of their nature.

- 2 -

आराध्यं यन्मया देव्याः स्वरूपं येन च द्विज ।
विधिना ब्रूहि सकलं यथावत्प्रणतस्य मे ॥

ārādhyaṃ yanmayā devyāḥ svarūpaṃ yena ca dvija |
vidhinā brūhi sakalaṃ yathāvat praṇatasya me ||
Oh Twice-born, I bow to you. Please tell me which intrinsic natures are to be worshipped and by which systems of worship they will be pleased.

ऋषिरुवाच

ṛṣi ruvāca
The Ṛṣi said:

\- 3 -

इदं रहस्यं परममनाख्येयं प्रचक्ष्यते ।
भक्तोऽसीति न मे किञ्चित्तवावाच्यं नराधिप ॥

idaṃ rahasyaṃ paramam anākhyeyaṃ pracakṣyate |
bhakto-sīti na me kiñcat tavāvācyaṃ narādhipa ||
Oh King, this secret is extremely esoteric, and it is said that it should not be readily divulged. But you are devoted to me, and I find no cause not to tell you all.

\- 4 -

सर्वस्याद्या महालक्ष्मीस्त्रिगुणा परमेश्वरी ।
लक्ष्यालक्ष्यस्वरूपा सा व्याप्य कृत्स्नं व्यवस्थिता ॥

sarvasyādyā mahālakṣmīs triguṇā parameśvarī |
lakṣyā lakṣyasvarūpā sā
vyāpya kṛtsnaṃ vyavasthitā ||
The Supreme Sovereign, the Great Goddess of True Wealth, who is comprised of the three qualities, is the first and foremost of all causes. Her intrinsic nature is both definable and undefinable, and having distinguished all the individual phenomena of the universe, She resides within.

\- 5 -

मातुलिङ्गं गदां खेटं पानपात्रं च बिभ्रती ।
नागं लिङ्गं च योनिं च बिभ्रती नृप मूर्द्धनि ॥

mātuliṅgaṃ gadāṃ kheṭaṃ pāna pātraṃ ca bibhratī |
nāgaṃ liṅgaṃ ca yoniṃ ca bibhratī nṛpa mūrddhani ||

Oh King, She holds in Her hands a pomegranate (symbolizing the unity of creation), the club, the shield, and a drinking vessel, and on Her uppermost part, She bears the snake and liṅgaṃ, which unites the male principle (Consciousness) with the female principle (energy).

- 6 -

तप्तकाञ्चनवर्णाभा तप्तकाञ्चनभूषणा ।
शून्यं तदखिलं स्वेन पूरयामास तेजसा ॥

taptakāñcana varṇābhā taptakāñcana bhūṣaṇā |
śūnyaṃ tadakhilaṃ svena pūrayāmāsa tejasā ||

Her beauty is comparable with melted gold, and Her ornaments shine like melted gold. She filled the entire Nothingness with Her radiant Light.

- 7 -

शून्यं तदखिलं लोकं विलोक्य परमेश्वरी ।
बभार परमं रूपं तमसा केवलेन हि ॥

śūnyaṃ tadakhilaṃ lokaṃ vilokya parameśvarī |
babhāra paramaṃ rūpaṃ tamasā kevalena hi ||

Seeing the entire Nothingness, the Supreme Sovereign, by the quality of Darkness, assumed another excellent form.

- 8 -

सा भिन्नाञ्जनसंकाशा दंष्ट्राङ्कितवरानना ।
विशाललोचना नारी बभूव तनुमध्यमा ॥

sā bhinnāñjana saṃkāśā daṃṣṭrāṅkitavarānanā |
viśāla locanā nārī babhūva tanumadhyamā ||

That form became a beautiful woman whose radiant body was black like soot. Her finely shaped mouth had large, protruding teeth, Her eyes were large and Her waist thin.

- 9 -

खड्गपात्रशिरःखेटैरलंकृतचतुर्भुजा ।
कबन्धहारं शिरसा बिभ्राणा हि शिरःस्रजम् ॥

khaḍgapātraśiraḥ kheṭair alaṃkṛta caturbhujā |
kabandhahāraṃ śirasā bibhrāṇā hi śiraḥ srajam ||

In Her four hands She displayed the sword, the drinking cup, a severed head, and a shield, with decapitated body parts forming a necklace, and a garland of skulls worn over Her head.

- 10 -

सा प्रोवाच महाल्क्ष्मीं तामसी प्रमदोत्तमा ।

नाम कर्म च मे मातर्देहि तुभ्यं नमो नमः ॥

sā provāca mahā lakṣmīṃ tāmasī pramadottamā |
nāma karma ca me mātar
dehi tubhyaṃ namo namaḥ ||

Having thus appeared, that manifestation of Darkness, excellent among women, said to the Great Goddess of True Wealth, "Mother, again and again I bow to you. Give to me my names and describe the actions I am to perform."

- 11 -

तां प्रोवाच महाल्क्ष्मीस्तामसीं प्रमदोत्तमाम् ।

ददामि तव नामानि यानि कर्माणि तानि ते ॥

tāṃ provāca mahālakṣmīstāmasīṃ pramadottamām |
dadāmi tava nāmāni yāni karmāṇi tāni te ||

Then the Great Goddess of True Wealth said to the Excellent Lady of Darkness, "I give to you your names and the various actions that you will perform.

- 12 -

महामाया महाकाली महामारी क्षुधा तृषा ।

निद्रा तृष्णा चैकवीरा कालरात्रिर्दुरत्यया ॥

mahā māyā mahā kālī mahā mārī kṣudhā tṛṣā |
nidrā tṛṣṇā caikavīrā kālarātrir duratyayā ||

The Great Measurement of Consciousness, the Great Remover of Darkness, the Great Destroyer, Hunger and Thirst, Sleep, Desire, Solely attentive to the Battle, the Dark Night, the Impassable.

- 13 -

इमानि तव नामानि प्रतिपाद्यानि कर्मभिः ।

एभिः कर्माणि ते ज्ञात्वा योऽधीते सोऽश्नुते सुखम् ॥

imāni tava nāmāni pratipādyāni karmabhiḥ I
ebhiḥ karmāṇi te jñātvā yo-dhīte so-śnute sukham II
These are your names, indicative of the actions that you perform. One who knows your activity by meditating upon these names, attains the highest happiness."

- 14 -

तामित्युक्त्वा महालक्ष्मीः स्वरूपमपरं नृप ।
सत्त्वाख्येनातिशुद्धेन गुणेनेन्दुप्रभं दधौ ॥

tāmityuktvā mahālakṣmīḥ svarūpamaparaṃ nṛpa I
sattvākhyenāti śuddhena
guṇenendu prabhaṃ dadau II
Oh King, thus having spoken, the Great Goddess of True Wealth, by means of Her extremely pure quality of Light, assumed another form with radiant luster like the moon.

- 15 -

अक्षमालाङ्कुशधरा वीणापुस्तकधारिणी ।
सा बभूव वरा नारी नामान्यस्यै च सा ददौ ॥

akṣamālāṅkuśadharā vīṇā pustaka dhāriṇī I
sā babhūva varā nārī nāmānyasyai ca sā dadau II
This supreme woman held in Her hands the rosary of alphabets, the curved sword, the lute or vina, and a book, and She, too, was given names.

- 16 -

महाविद्या महावाणी भारती वाक् सरस्वती ।
आर्या ब्राह्मी कामधेनुर्वेदगर्भा च धीश्वरी ॥

mahā vidyā mahā vāṇī bhāratī vāk sarasvatī I
āryā brāhmī kāmadhenur vedagarbhā ca dhīśvarī II
The Great Knowledge, the Great Vibration, the Light of Wisdom, Sound, the Spirit of All-Pervading Knowledge, She Who Purifies with Wisdom, Creative Energy, the Cow Who Fulfills all Desires, the Womb of Wisdom, and the Lord of the Mind.

- 17 -

अथोवाच महालक्ष्मीर्महाकालीं सरस्वतीम् ।
युवां जनयतां देव्यौ मिथुने स्वानुरूपतः ॥

athovāca mahālakṣmīr mahā kālīṃ sarasvatīm |
yuvāṃ janayatāṃ devyau mithune svānurūpataḥ ||

Then the Great Goddess of True Wealth said to the Great Remover of Darkness and the Spirit of All-Pervading Knowledge, "Goddesses, you both produce pairs, male and female, according to your natures."

- 18 -

इत्युक्त्वा ते महालक्ष्मीः ससर्ज मिथुनं स्वयम् ।
हिरण्यगर्भौ रुचिरौ स्त्रीपुंसौ कमलासनौ ॥

ityuktvā te mahālakṣmīḥ sasarja mithunaṃ svayam |
hiraṇyagarbhau rucirau strī puṃsau kamalāsanau ||

Thus having instructed them, the Great Goddess of True Wealth first produced Her own pair, a male and a female of beautiful appearance seated upon the lotus seat, having come forth from the Golden Womb (the first spark of creation also known as *bindu*).

- 19 -

ब्रह्मन् विधे विरिञ्चेति धातरित्याह तं नरम् ।
श्रीः पद्मे कमले लक्ष्मीत्याह माता च तां स्त्रियम् ॥

brahman vidhe viriñceti dhātarityāha taṃ naram |
śrīḥ padme kamale lakṣmīt
yāha mātā ca tāṃ striyam ||

Then the Mother, the Great Goddess of True Wealth, said to the male, "Knower of Consciousness, Systematic Worship, Shining One, Creator." And again to the female, "Ultimate Prosperity, Lotus Blossom, Goddess of Wealth," and in this way gave their names.

- 20 -

महाकाली भारती च मिथुने सृजतः सह ।
एतयोरपि रूपाणि नामानि च वदामि ते ॥

mahākālī bhāratī ca mithune sṛjataḥ saha |
etayorapi rūpāṇi nāmāni ca vadāmi te ||
The Great Remover of Darkness and the Light of Wisdom also produced pairs. I am telling you their names and forms.

- 21 -

नीलकण्ठं रक्तबाहुं श्वेताङ्गं चन्द्रशेखरम् ।
जनयामास पुरुषं महाकाली सितां स्त्रियम् ॥

nīlakaṇṭhaṃ raktabāhuṃ
śvetāṅgaṃ candraśekharam |
janayāmāsa puruṣaṃ mahākālī sitāṃ striyam ||
The Great Remover of Darkness gave birth to a male who had a blue throat, red arms, a white body, and who wore a digit of the moon on his forehead, and also to a white female.

- 22 -

स रुद्रः शङ्करः स्थाणुः कपर्दी च त्रिलोचनः ।
त्रयी विद्या कामधेनुः सा स्त्री भाषाक्षरा स्वरा ॥

sa rudraḥ śaṅkaraḥ sthāṇuḥ kapardī ca trilocanaḥ |
trayī vidyā kāmadhenuḥ sā strī bhāṣākṣarā svarā ||
He is known as the Reliever of Suffering, the Cause of Peace, the Permanent Resident, of Matted Hair, with Three Eyes, while the female is called the Three, Knowledge, the Cow Fulfilling Desires, Language, Letters, and Melody.

- 23 -

सरस्वती स्त्रियं गौरीं कृष्णं च पुरुषं नृप ।
जनयामास नामानि तयोरपि वदामि ते ॥

sarasvatī striyaṃ gaurīṃ kṛṣṇaṃ ca puruṣaṃ nṛpa |
janayāmāsa nāmāni tayorapi vadāmi te ||
Oh King, the Spirit of All-Pervading Knowledge brought forth a female of bright color and also a male who is dark. I am telling you their names.

- 24 -

विष्णुः कृष्णो हृषीकेशो वासुदेवो जनार्दनः ।
उमा गौरी सती चण्डी सुन्दरी सुभगा शिवा ॥

viṣṇuḥ kṛṣṇo hṛṣīkeśo vāsudevo janārdanaḥ |
umā gaurī satī caṇḍī sundarī subhagā śivā ||

The names Consciousness That Pervades All, the Doer of All, Ruler of the Senses, the God of True Wealth, and the Lord of Existence apply to the male. The Nourishing Mother, She Who is Rays of Light, Truth, the Energy That Tears Apart Thought, the Beautiful, Excellent Fortune, and the Energy of Infinite Goodness apply to the female.

\- 25 -

एवं युवतयः सद्यः पुरुषत्वं प्रपेदिरे ।
चक्षुष्मन्तो नु पश्यन्ति नेतरेऽतद्विदो जनाः ॥

evaṃ yuvatayaḥ sadyaḥ puruṣatvaṃ prapedire |
cakṣuṣmanto nu paśyanti netare-tadvido janāḥ ||

In this way the three young ladies immediately gave the form to the males. This fact those who see with the eye of wisdom may understand. Other uninitiated people may not understand the esoteric meaning of this secret.

\- 26 -

ब्रह्मणे प्रददौ पत्नीं महालक्ष्मीर्नृप त्रयीम् ।
रुद्राय गौरीं वरदां वासुदेवाय च श्रियम् ॥

brahmaṇe pradadau patnīṃ
mahā lakṣmīr nṛpa trayīm |
rudrāya gaurīṃ varadāṃ vāsudevāya ca śriyam ||

Oh King, the Great Goddess of True Wealth gave the Spirit of All-Pervading Knowledge to the Creative Capacity as a wife, and to the Reliever of Suffering She gave She Who is Rays of Light, and to the Lord of True Wealth She gave the Ultimate Prosperity.

\- 27 -

स्वरया सह संभूय विरिञ्चोऽण्डमजीजनत् ।
बिभेद भगवान् रुद्रस्तद् गौर्या सह वीर्यवान् ॥

svarayā saha saṃbhūya viriñco-ṇḍamajījanat |
bibheda bhagavān rudrastad gauryā saha vīryavān ||

Thus the Creative Capacity with his wife, the Spirit of All-Pervading Knowledge, gave birth to the Cosmic Egg; and the Reliever of Suffering, along with his wife, She Who is Rays of Light, pierced the egg, causing it to crack.

- 28 -

अण्डमध्ये प्रधानादि कार्यजातमभून्नृप ।

महाभूतात्मकं सर्वं जगत्स्थावरजङ्गमम् ॥

aṇḍamadhye pradhānādi kāryajātama bhūnnṛpa |
mahābhūtātmakaṃ sarvaṃ
jagat sthāvarajaṅgamam ||

Oh King, within the egg were all the primary products, the capacity of the five elements to unite, and all this existence of movable and immovable forms came to be.

- 29 -

पुपोष पालयामास तल्लक्ष्म्या सह केशवः ।

संजहार जगत्सर्वं सह गौर्या महेश्वरः ॥

puposa pālayāmāsa tallakṣmyā saha keśavaḥ |
saṃjahāra jagat sarvaṃ saha gauryā maheśvaraḥ ||

Then the Goddess of True Wealth, along with the Consciousness That Pervades All, began to protect and to nourish creation, and at the appointed time, the Great Lord with His wife, She Who is Rays of Light, will cause its dissolution.

- 30 -

महालक्ष्मीर्महाराज सर्वसत्त्वमयीश्वरी ।

निराकारा च साकारा सैव नानाभिधानभृत् ॥

mahā lakṣmīr mahārāja sarva sattva mayīśvarī |
nirākārā ca sākārā saiva nānābhidhānabhṛt ||

Oh Great King, the Great Goddess of True Wealth is the Ruler of All Truth and of the quality of Light. She is the inconceivable formless, and again She is with form and is known by many names.

- 31 -

नामान्तरैर्निरूप्यैषा नाम्ना नान्येन केनचित् ॥

nāmāntarair nirūpyaiṣā nāmnā nānyena kenacit ||

Only Her attributes can be named, and yet She cannot be explained by only one name.

ॐ

oṃ

अथ वैकृतिकं रहस्यम्

atha vaikṛtikaṃ rahasyam

The Modified Secret

Devi: 28

ऋषिरुवाच

ṛṣi ruvāca

The Ṛṣi said:

\- 1 -

ॐ त्रिगुणा तामसी देवी सात्त्विकी या त्रिधोदिता ।

सा शर्वा चण्डिका दुर्गा भद्रा भगवतीर्यते ॥

oṃ triguṇā tāmasī devī sāttvikī yā tridhoditā |

sā śarvā caṇḍikā durgā bhadrā bhagavatīryate ||

The Goddess who is composed of the three qualities, who is predominant in Light, yet differentiated as Darkness, etc., is spoken of as the Energy That Slays with Arrows, the Energy That Tears Apart Thought, the Reliever of Difficulties, the Excellent One, the Possessor of Wealth.

\- 2 -

योगनिद्रा हरेरुक्ता महाकाली तमोगुणा ।

मधुकैटभनाशार्थं यां तुष्टावाम्बुजासनः ॥

yoganidrā hareruktā mahākālī tamoguṇā |

madhu kaiṭabhanāśārthaṃ yāṃ tuṣṭāvāmbujāsanaḥ ||

She who is of the quality of Darkness, who held the Consciousness That Pervades All in the mystic Sleep of Divine Union, who was praised by the Creative Capacity for the purpose of slaying Too Much and Too Little, She is called the Great Remover of Darkness.

\- 3 -

दशवक्त्रा दशभुजा दशपादाञ्जनप्रभा ।

विशालया राजमाना त्रिंशल्लोचनमालया ॥

daśavaktrā daśabhujā daśapādāñjana prabhā |

viśālayā rājamānā triṃśallocana mālayā ||

She has ten faces, ten arms, and ten feet. Her immense body is dark and shining brilliantly like collyrium. Her thirty eyes are all large and of equal proportion.

- 4 -

स्फुरद्दशनदंष्ट्रा सा भीमरूपापि भूमिप ।

रूपसौभाग्य कान्तीनां सा प्रतिष्ठा महाश्रियः ॥

sphuraddaśanadaṃṣṭrā sā bhīma rūpāpi bhūmipa |
rūpasaubhāgya kāntīnāṃ sā pratiṣṭhā mahāśriyaḥ ||

Oh Protector of the Earth, Her teeth and fangs are shining, making Her form frightful, and yet that form is as beautiful as lustrous beauty enhanced by love, for She establishes the Great Prosperity.

- 5 -

खड्गबाणगदाशूलचक्रशङ्खभुशुण्डिभृत् ।

परिघं कार्मुकं शीर्षं निश्च्योतद्रुधिरं दधौ ॥

khaḍgabāṇa gadā śūla cakra śaṅkha bhuśuṇḍibhṛt |
parighaṃ kārmukaṃ śīrṣaṃ
niścyotadrudhiraṃ dadhau ||

In Her hands She holds the sword, the arrow, the club, the spear, the discus, the conch, the sling, the iron bar, the bow, and a severed head dripping blood.

- 6 -

एषा सा वैष्णवी माया महाकाली दुरत्यया ।

आराधिता वशीकुर्यात् पूजाकर्तुश्चराचरम् ॥

eṣā sā vaiṣṇavī māyā mahākālī duratyayā |
ārādhitā vaśīkuryāt pūjākartuścarācaram ||

This is the Energy of the Consciousness That Pervades All, the Measurement of the All-Pervading Consciousness, the incomparably Great Remover of Darkness. Pleased by worship and meditation, She awards to the aspirant domination over all that moves and moves not.

- 7 -

सर्वदेवशरीरेभ्यो याऽऽविर्भूतामितप्रभा ।

त्रिगुणा सा महालक्ष्मीः साक्षान्महिषमर्दिनी ॥

sarva deva śarīrebhyo yā--virbhūtāmita prabhā |
triguṇā sā mahālakṣmīḥ sākṣān mahiṣamardinī ||
The Great Goddess of True Wealth came forth shining from the bodies of all the Gods, bearing the three qualities of nature. She is the actual slayer of the Great Ego.

\- 8 -

श्वेतानना नीलभुजा सुश्वेतस्तनमण्डला ।
रक्तमध्या रक्तपादा नीलजङ्घोरुरुन्मदा ॥
śvetānanā nīlabhujā suśveta stana maṇḍalā |
rakta madhyā rakta pādā nīla jaṅghorurunmadā ||
Her face is light, Her arms blue, and Her breast area is extremely white. The middle part of Her body is red, the feet are red, and Her shanks and thighs are blue.

\- 9 -

सुचित्रजघना चित्रमाल्याम्बरविभूषणा ।
चित्रानुलेपना कान्तिरूपसौभाग्यशालिनी ॥
sucitra jaghanā citra mālyām bara vibhūṣaṇā |
citrā nulepanā kānti rūpa saubhāgya śālinī ||
Her hips are beautiful and attractive, and of varied hues are Her garlands, cloth, and ornaments. Unguents are smeared upon Her body. She is the form of beauty enhanced by love and reflects all auspiciousness.

\- 10 -

अष्टादशभुजा पूज्या सा सहस्रभुजा सती ।
आयुधान्यत्र वक्ष्यन्ते दक्षिणाधःकरक्रमात् ॥
aṣṭā daśa bhujā pūjyā sā sahasra bhujā satī |
āyudhānyatra vakṣyante dakṣiṇādhaḥ kara kramāt ||
Even though She has a thousand arms, yet She should be worshipped with eighteen hands. The weapons She holds are enumerated in order beginning from the lower right:

\- 11 -

अक्षमाला च कमलं बाणोऽसिः कुलिशं गदा ।
चक्रं त्रिशूलं परशुः शङ्खो घण्टा च पाशकः ॥

akṣmālā ca kamalaṃ bāṇo-siḥ kuliśaṃ gadā |
cakraṃ triśūlaṃ paraśuḥ śaṅkho ghaṇṭā ca pāśakaḥ ||

- 12 -

शक्तिर्दण्डश्चर्म चापं पानपात्रं कमण्डलुः ।
अलंकृतभुजामेभिरायुधैः कमलासनाम् ॥

śaktirdaṇḍaścarma cāpaṃ pānapātraṃ kamaṇḍaluḥ |
alaṃkṛta bhujāmebhirāyudhaiḥ kamalāsanām ||

11-12. the rosary of alphabets, a lotus, an arrow, a sword, lightning, a club, discus, trident, battle axe, a conch, bell, net, energy, staff, shield, bow, drinking vessel, and the bowl of renunciation. She is seated on a lotus seat.

- 13 -

सर्वदेवमयीमीशां महालक्ष्मीमिमां नृप ।
पूजयेत्सर्वलोकानां स देवानां प्रभुर्भवेत् ॥

sarva deva mayī mīśāṃ mahā lakṣmīmimāṃ nṛpa |
pūjayet sarva lokānāṃ sa devānāṃ prabhur bhavet ||

Oh King, composed of all the Gods, She is the Ruler of the Gods. Who worships this Great Goddess of True Wealth becomes master of all the worlds and of the Gods.

- 14 -

गौरीदेहात्समुद्भूता या सत्त्वैकगुणाश्रया ।
साक्षात्सरस्वती प्रोक्ता शुम्भासुर निबर्हिणी ॥

gaurī dehāt samudbhūtā yā sattvaika guṇāśrayā |
sākṣāt sarasvatī proktā śumbhāsura nibarhiṇī ||

The actual Spirit of All-Pervading Knowledge has manifested from the body of She Who is Rays of Light. She is the repository of the quality of Truth. It is She who slew the manifestation of ego known as Self-Conceit.

- 15 -

दधौ चाष्टभुजा बाणमुसले शूलचक्रभृत् ।
शङ्खं घण्टां लाङ्गलं च कार्मुकं वसुधाधिप ॥

dadhau cāṣṭabhujā bāṇa musale śūla cakrabhṛt |
śaṅkhaṃ ghaṇṭāṃ lāṅgalaṃ ca
kārmukaṃ vasudhādhipa ||

Oh King of the Earth, in Her eight hands She displays the arrow, pestle, pike, discus, conch, bell, plow, and bow.

\- 16 -

एषा सम्पूजिता भक्त्या सर्वज्ञत्वं प्रयच्छति ।
निशुम्भमथिनी देवी शुम्भासुरनिबर्हिणी ॥

eṣā sampūjitā bhaktyā sarva jñatvaṃ prayacchati |
niśumbha mathinī devī śumbhāsura nibarhiṇī ||

This is the Goddess who slew Self-Conceit and Self-Deprecation. Whoever will worship Her with devotion will attain all wisdom.

\- 17 -

इत्युक्तानि स्वरूपाणि मूर्तीनां तव पार्थिव ।
उपासनं जगन्मातुः पृथगासां निशामय ॥

ityuktāni svarūpāṇi mūrtīnāṃ tava pārthiva |
upāsanaṃ jagan mātuḥ pṛthagāsāṃ niśāmaya ||

Oh King, the intrinsic nature of these embodiments has been described. Now understand how to continually meditate upon the Mother of the Universe in these forms.

\- 18 -

महालक्ष्मीर्यदा पूज्या महाकाली सरस्वती ।
दक्षिणोत्तरयोः पूज्ये पृष्ठतो मिथुनत्रयम् ॥

mahā lakṣmīr yadā pūjyā mahā kālī sarasvatī |
dakṣiṇot tarayoḥ pūjye pṛṣṭhato mithunatrayam ||

When the Great Goddess of True Wealth is to be worshipped, She should be established in the center with the Great Remover of Darkness to Her right and the Great Spirit of All-Pervading Knowledge to Her left. Directly behind them the three pairs should be worshipped as follows:

\- 19 -

विरञ्चिः स्वरया मध्ये रुद्रो गौर्या च दक्षिणे ।
वामे लक्ष्म्या हृषीकेशः पुरतो देवतात्रयम् ॥

virañciḥ svarayā madhye rudro gauryā ca dakṣiṇe |
vāme lakṣmyā hṛṣīkeśaḥ purato devatā trayam ||

Shining One (Brahmā) and Melody (Sarasvatī) in the middle, the Reliever of Suffering and She Who is Rays of Light on Her right, and on Her left, Prosperity and the Ruler of the Senses. In front, the Goddesses should be worshipped.

- 20 -

अष्टादशभुजा मध्ये वामे चास्या दशानना ।
दक्षिणेऽष्टभुजा लक्ष्मीर्महतीति समर्चयेत् ॥

aṣṭā daśa bhujā madhye vāme cāsyā daśānanā |
dakṣiṇe-ṣṭabhujā lakṣmīr mahatīti samarcayet ||

In the center, the eighteen-handed one; on Her right, the one with ten faces; and on Her left, the eight-handed one. Thus the greatness of the Goddess of True Wealth is to be worshipped.

- 21 -

अष्टादशभुजा चैषा यदा पूज्या नराधिप ।
दशानना चाष्टभुजा दक्षिणोत्तरयोस्तदा ॥

aṣṭā daśa bhujā caiṣā yadā pūjyā narādhipa |
daśānanā cāṣṭa bhujā dakṣiṇottarayos tadā ||

Oh King of Men, when only the eighteen-handed Goddess is worshipped, or only the ten-faced or the eight-handed,

- 22 -

कालमृत्यू च सम्पूज्यौ सर्वारिष्टप्रशान्तये ।
यदा चाष्टभुजा पूज्या शुम्भासुरनिबर्हिणी ॥

kāla mṛtyū ca sampūjyau sarvāriṣṭa praśāntaye |
yadā cāṣṭa bhujā pūjyā śumbhāsura nibarhiṇī ||

then, for the removal of all obstacles, on the right side Time should be worshipped, and on the left side, Death. When the eight-handed Slayer of Self-Conceit is worshipped,

- 23 -

नवास्याः शक्तयः पूज्यास्तदा रुद्रविनायकौ ।
नमो देव्या इति स्तोत्रैर्महालक्ष्मीं समर्चयेत् ॥

navāsyāḥ śaktayaḥ pūjyās tadā rudravināyakau |
namo devyā iti stotrair mahālakṣmīṃ samarcayet ||
then Her nine energies (Brahmī, Māheśvarī, Kaumarī, Vaiṣṇavī, Vārāhī, Nārasiṃhī, Aindrī, Śivadūtī, and Cāmuṇḍā) are to be worshipped, along with Rudra and Gaṇeśa. The hymn of praise that says, "I bow to the Goddess," should be sung for the Great Goddess of True Wealth.

- 24 -

अवतारत्रयार्चायां स्तोत्रमन्त्रास्तदाश्रयाः ।
अष्टादशभुजा चैषा पूज्या महिषमर्दिनी ॥
avatāra trayārcāyāṃ stotramantrās tadā śrayāḥ |
aṣṭādaśa bhujā caiṣā pūjyā mahiṣamardinī ||
The mantras and songs of praise from the three episodes should be sung for their respective deities. The pūjā for the Great Goddess of True Wealth, the Slayer of the Great Ego, must be conducted specially,

- 25 -

महालक्ष्मीर्महाकाली सैव प्रोक्ता सरस्वती ।
ईश्वरी पुण्यपापानां सर्वलोकमहेश्वरी ॥
mahālakṣmīr mahākālī saiva proktā sarasvatī |
īśvarī puṇya pāpānāṃ sarva loka maheśvarī ||
because She is the Great Goddess of True Wealth, the Great Remover of Darkness, the Spirit of All-Pervading Knowledge, the Controller of all virtues and sins, the Great Lord of all the Worlds.

- 26 -

महिषान्तकरी येन पूजिता स जगत्प्रभुः ।
पूजयेज्जगतां धात्रीं चण्डिकां भक्तवत्सलाम् ॥
mahiṣāntakarī yena pūjitā sa jagat prabhuḥ |
pūjayejjagatāṃ dhātrīṃ caṇḍikāṃ bhaktavatsalām ||
Who worships with devotion the Great Goddess of True Wealth, the Destroyer of the Great Ego, will become the Master of the Universe. Therefore, worship the Supporter of the Universe, She Who Tears Apart Thought, Bestower of Grace to devotees.

- 27 -

अर्घ्यादिभिरलंकारैर्गन्धपुष्पैस्तथाक्षतैः ।

धूपैर्दीपैश्च नैवेद्यैर्नानाभक्ष्यसमन्वितैः ॥

arghyādibhir alaṃkārair
gandha puṣpais tathākṣataiḥ |
dhūpair dīpaiśca naivedyair
nānābhakṣya samanvitaiḥ ||

With the offering of various objects that demonstrate respect, ornaments, scented flowers, whole grains, incense, lights, and various dishes of food,

- 28 -

रुधिराक्तेन बलिना मांसेन सुरया नृप ।

(बलिमांसादि पूजेयं विप्रवर्ज्या मयेरिता ॥

rudhirāktena balinā māṃsena surayā nṛpa |
(bali māṃsādi pūjeyaṃ vipravarjyā mayeritā ||

तेषां किल सुरामांसैर्नोक्ता पूजा नृप क्वचित् ।)

प्रणामाचमनीयेन चन्दनेन सुगन्धिना ॥

teṣāṃ kila surāmāṃsair noktā pūjā nṛpa kvacit |)
praṇāmācamanīyena candanena sugandhinā ||

with passionately devoted sacrifices, meat, spirituous liquors. Oh King, (the sacrificial offering of meat and alcohol or offerings drenched in blood is forbidden to the twice-born knowers of Wisdom.) They will worship with bowing down devotedly, and offering water for rinsing the hands and mouth, fragrant sandal paste,

- 29 -

सकर्पूरैश्च ताम्बूलैर्भक्तिभावसमन्वितैः ।

वामभागेऽग्रतो देव्याश्छिन्नशीर्षं महासुरम् ॥

sakarpūraiśca tāmbūlair bhakti bhāva samanvitaiḥ |
vāma bhāge-grato devyāś
chinna śīrṣaṃ mahāsuram ||

betel leaves with camphor, and mouth-refreshing mints and nuts. With a greatly devoted attitude, one should offer all these to the Goddess. In front of the Goddess, on the left side, one should offer worship to the severed head

- 30 -

पूजयेन्महिषं येन प्राप्तं सायुज्यमीशया ।
दक्षिणे पुरतः सिंहं समग्रं धर्ममीश्वरम् ॥

pūjayen mahiṣaṃ yena prāptaṃ sāyujyamīśayā |
dakṣiṇe purataḥ siṃhaṃ
samagraṃ dharmamīśvaram ||

of the Great Ego who attained complete union with the Goddess. And similarly, in the front right, the lion should be worshipped, the Lord of Dharma, the Way of Truth to Wisdom,

- 31 -

वाहनं पूजयेद्देव्या धृतं येन चराचरम् ।
कुर्याच्च स्तवनं धीमांस्तस्या एकाग्रमानसः ॥

vāhanaṃ pūjayed devyā dhṛtaṃ yena carācaram |
kuryācca stavanaṃ dhīmāṃstasyā ekāgramānasaḥ ||

the vehicle of the Goddess, Maintainer of all that moves and moves not. Wise beings will sing songs of praise to the Goddess with one-pointed attention.

- 32 -

ततः कृताञ्जलिर्भूत्वा स्तुवीत चरितैरिमैः ।
एकेन वा मध्यमेन नैकेनेतरयोरिह ॥

tataḥ kṛtāñjalir bhūtvā stuvīta caritairimaiḥ |
ekena vā madhyamena naikenetarayoriha ||

Then with folded hands one should recite the three episodes of the Chaṇḍī. If it is possible to recite only one episode, then recite only the middle one. One should not recite only the first or only the last of the episodes.

- 33 -

चरितार्धं तु न जपेज्जपञ्छिद्रमवाप्नुयात् ।
प्रदक्षिणानमस्कारान् कृत्वा मूर्ध्नि कृताञ्जलिः ॥

caritārdhaṃ tu na japej japañ chidrama vāpnuyāt |
pradakṣiṇā namaskārān kṛtvā mūrdhni kṛtāñjaliḥ ||

\- 34 -

क्षमापयेज्जगद्धात्रीं मुहुर्मुहुरतन्द्रितः ।
प्रतिश्लोकं च जुहुयात्पायसं तिलसर्पिषा ॥

kṣamāpayej jagaddhātrīṃ muhur muhuratandritaḥ |
prati ślokaṃ ca juhuyāt pāyasaṃ tilasarpiṣā ||

33-34. Also one should not recite only half an episode; that recitation does not bring fruit. After completing the recitation, the aspirant should circumambulate the image and bow down, and fold his hands on top of his head, and again and again pray for forgiveness for any mistakes committed. For every one of the Seven Hundred Verses, milk, sesame, and ghee should be mixed together and offered as oblations to the sacrificial fire.

\- 35 -

जुहुयात्स्तोत्रमन्त्रैर्वा चण्डिकायै शुभं हविः ।
भूयो नामपदैर्देवीं पूजयेत्सुसमाहितः ॥

juhuyātstotra mantrairvā caṇḍikāyai śubhaṃ haviḥ |
bhūyo nāma padair devīṃ pūjayet susamāhitaḥ ||

Whatever mantras or songs of praise that are offered to She Who Tears Apart Thought should be accompanied by pure oblations to the sacrificial fire. After performing the fire ceremony, again worship should be performed in the name of the Goddess with a concentrated mind.

\- 36 -

प्रयतः प्राञ्जलिः प्रह्वः प्रणम्यारोप्य चात्मनि ।
सुचिरं भावयेदीशां चण्डिकां तन्मयो भवेत् ॥

prayataḥ prāñjaliḥ prahvaḥ praṇamyāropya cātmani |
suciraṃ bhāvayedīśāṃ caṇḍikāṃ tanmayo bhavet ||

Then controlling the mind and the senses, with hands folded, he should bow to the Goddess, and seating the Ruler of All, She Who Tears Apart Thought, in his heart, he should meditate upon Her presence. Thus meditating, he will become full of Her.

- 37 -

एवं यः पूजयेद्भक्त्या प्रत्यहं परमेश्वरीम् ।

भुक्त्वा भोगान् यथाकामं देवीसायुज्यमाप्नुयात् ॥

evaṃ yaḥ pūjayed bhaktyā
pratyahaṃ parameśvarīm |
bhuktvā bhogān yathā kāmaṃ
devī sāyujyamāpnuyāt ||

Whoever will always worship the Supreme Sovereign in this way with full devotion will enjoy all the pleasures he contemplates, and ultimately attain to complete union with the Goddess.

- 38 -

यो न पूजयते नित्यं चण्डिकां भक्तवत्सलाम् ।

भस्मीकृत्यास्य पुण्यानि निर्दहेत्परमेश्वरी ॥

yo na pūjayate nityaṃ caṇḍikāṃ bhaktavatsalām |
bhasmī kṛtyāsya puṇyāni nirdahet parameśvarī ||

Whoever does not worship the Gracious She Who Tears Apart Thought regularly, the Supreme Sovereign burns to ashes all the merits that have been accrued.

- 39 -

तस्मात्पूजय भूपाल सर्वलोकमहेश्वरीम् ।

यथोक्तेन विधानेन चण्डिकां सुखमाप्स्यसि ॥

tasmāt pūjaya bhūpāla sarvaloka maheśvarīm |
yathoktena vidhānena caṇḍikāṃ sukhamāpsyasi ||

Therefore, Oh King, worship the Great Lord of All the Worlds according to the system of the scriptures. From this you will attain the highest happiness.

ॐ

oṃ

Devi 29

अथ मूर्तिरहस्यम्

atha mūrti rahasyam

And Now, The Secret of the Manifestations

ऋषिरुवाच

ṛṣi ruvāca

The Ṛṣi said:

- 1 -

ॐ नन्दा भगवती नाम या भविष्यति नन्दजा ।
स्तुता सा पूजिता भक्त्या वशीकुर्याज्जगत्त्रयम् ॥

oṃ nandā bhagavatī nāma yā bhaviṣyati nandajā |
stutā sā pūjitā bhaktyā vaśīkuryāj jagat trayam ||

Oṃ The Goddess who is Possessor of the Wealth of Bliss, who will take birth from Delight, to those who will praise Her with song and worship Her with devotion, She will give command over the three worlds.

- 2 -

कनकोत्तमकान्तिः सा सुकान्तिकनकाम्बरा ।
देवी कनकवर्णाभा कनकोत्तमभूषणा ॥

kanakottama kāntiḥ sā sukānti kananakāmbarā |
devī kanakavarṇābhā kanakottama bhūṣaṇā ||

Her body shines resplendently like excellent gold, golden is the color of Her beautiful garment, golden is Her lustrous aura, and golden are the ornaments that She wears.

- 3 -

कमलाङ्कुशपाशाब्जैरलंकृतचतुर्भुजा ।
इन्दिरा कमला लक्ष्मीः सा श्री रुक्माम्बुजासना ॥

kamalāṅkuśa pāśābjair alaṃkṛta catur bhujā |
indirā kamalā lakṣmīḥ sā śrī rukmām bujāsanā ||

In Her four hands She holds the lotus, curved sword, net, and conch. She is called the Energy That Rules, Lotus One, the Goddess of True Wealth, Ultimate Prosperity, and who sits on the golden lotus.

- 4 -

या रक्तदन्तिका नाम देवी प्रोक्ता मयानघ ।
तस्याः स्वरूपं वक्ष्यामि शृणु सर्वभयापहम् ॥

yā raktadantikā nāma devī proktā mayānagha |
tasyāḥ svarūpaṃ vakṣyāmi śṛṇu sarvabhayāpaham ||

I had introduced to you the Goddess named She with Red Teeth. Listen as I elucidate Her intrinsic nature, which alleviates all fear.

- 5 -

रक्ताम्बरा रक्तवर्णा रक्तसर्वाङ्गभूषणा ।
रक्तायुधा रक्तनेत्रा रक्तकेशातिभीषणा ॥

raktāmbarā rakta varṇā rakta sarvāṅga bhūṣaṇā |
raktāyudhā raktanetrā raktakeśāti bhīṣaṇā ||

Her wearing apparel is red, Her body is red, and all the ornaments She wears are red. Her weapons are red, Her eyes are red, her hair is red, and thus Her appearance is terrifying.

- 6 -

रक्ततीक्ष्णनखा रक्तदशना रक्तदन्तिका ।
पतिं नारीवानुरक्ता देवी भक्तं भजेज्जनम् ॥

rakta tīkṣṇa nakhā rakta daśanā rakta dantikā |
patiṃ nārīvānuraktā devī bhaktaṃ bhajejjanam ||

Her sharp nails are red, Her fangs are red, and red are Her teeth. Just as a devoted wife serves her husband, just so the Goddess adores Her devotees.

- 7 -

वसुधेव विशाला सा सुमेरुयुगलस्तनी ।
दीर्घौ लम्बावतिस्थूलौ तावतीव मनोहरौ ॥

vasudheva viśālā sā sumeru yugalastanī |
dīrghau lambāvati sthūlau tāvatīva manoharau ||

Her form is vast as the earth, and Her two breasts, like the mountain Sumeru. They are long and wide, very large, and extremely beautiful.

- 8 -

कर्कशावतिकान्तौ तौ सर्वानन्दपयोनिधी ।

भक्तान् सम्पाययेद्देवी सर्वकामदुघौ स्तनौ ॥

karkaśāvati kāntau tau sarvā nanda payonidhī |
bhaktān sampāyayed devī sarvakāmadughaustanau ||

They are hard and fully an ocean of perfect bliss. Those two breasts fully satisfy all the desires of the devotees who drink from them.

- 9 -

खड्गं पात्रं च मुसलं लाङ्गलं च बिभर्ति सा ।

आख्याता रक्तचामुण्डा देवी योगेश्वरीति च ॥

khaḍgaṃ pātraṃ ca musalaṃ
lāṅgalaṃ ca bibharti sā |
ākhyātā rakta cāmuṇḍā devī yogeśvarīti ca ||

In Her four hands She holds the sword, drinking vessel, pestle, and plow. She is also known as the Extremely Devoted Slayer of Passion and Anger, and as the Ruler of Union (female).

- 10 -

अनया व्याप्तमखिलं जगत्स्थावरजङ्गमम् ।

इमां यः पूजयेद्भक्त्या स व्याप्नोति चराचरम् ॥

anayā vyāptamakhilaṃ jagat sthāvara jaṅgamam |
imāṃ yaḥ pūjayedbhaktyā sa vyāpnoti carācaram ||

She pervades the entire universe of movable and non-movable objects. Who worships the Goddess with devotion, She with Red Teeth, becomes diffused in the universe of movable and immovable objects.

- 11 -

(भुक्त्वा भोगान् यथाकामं देवीसायुज्यमाप्नुयात् ।)

अधीते य इमं नित्यं रक्तदन्त्या वपुःस्तवम् ।

तं सा परिचरेद्देवी पतिं प्रियमिवाङ्गना ॥

(bhuktvā bhogān yathā kāmaṃ
devī sāyujya māpnuyāt |)
adhīte ya imaṃ nityaṃ raktadantyā vapuḥ stavam |
taṃ sā paricared devī patiṃ priya mivāṅganā ||

(He will enjoy pleasurable experience to the extent of his desires and ultimately attain union with the Goddess.) For he who constantly studies the songs of praise of the Goddess She with Red Teeth, the Goddess will serve and protect him as a loving wife serves her husband.

- 12 -

शाकम्भरी नीलवर्णा नीलोत्पलविलोचना ।
गम्भीरनाभिस्त्रिवलीविभूषिततनूदरी ॥

śākambharī nīla varṇā nīlot palavilocanā |
gambhīranābhistrivalī vibhūṣita tanūdarī ||

The Goddess She Who Nourishes with Vegetables is of a blue color, with eyes like blue lotuses. Her navel is very deep, and Her slender belly is beautiful because of three wrinkles on it.

- 13 -

सुकर्कशसमोत्तुङ्गवृत्तपीनघनस्तनी ।
मुष्टिं शिलीमुखापूर्णं कमलं कमलालया ॥

sukarkaśasa mottuṅga vṛtta pīna ghanastanī |
muṣṭiṃ śilīmukhāpūrṇaṃ kamalaṃ kamalālayā ||

Her two breasts are extremely hard, equally large, and round. She sits on a lotus, and in Her hands the Lotus One has a fist full of arrows, a lotus, a bow,

- 14 -

पुष्पपल्लवमूलादिफलाढ्यं शाकसञ्चयम् ।
काम्यानन्तरसैर्युक्तं क्षुत्तृणमृत्युभयापहम् ॥

puṣpa pallavamūlādi phalāḍhyaṃ śākasañcayam |
kāmyānantarasairyuktaṃ
kṣuttṛṇ mṛtyu bhayāpaham ||

flowers, sprouts, roots, and various fruits and vegetables filled with desirable tastes that will destroy hunger, thirst, and fear of death.

- 15 -

कार्मुकं च स्फुरत्कान्ति बिभ्रती परमेश्वरी ।

शाकम्भरी शताक्षी सा सैव दुर्गा प्रकीर्तिता ॥

kārmukaṃ ca sphurat kānti bibhratī parameśvarī |

śākambharī śatākṣī sā saiva durgā prakīrtitā ||

The Supreme Sovereign, who holds a bow of great beauty, is known as She Who Nourishes with Vegetables, also famous as She with a Hundred Eyes, and also as She Who Removes Difficulties.

- 16 -

विशोका दुष्टदमनी शमनी दुरितापदाम् ।

उमा गौरी सती चण्डी कालिका सा च पार्वती ॥

viśokā duṣṭa damanī śamanī duritāpadām |

umā gaurī satī caṇḍī kālikā sā ca pārvatī ||

She nullifies sorrow, suppresses evil, and destroys difficulties and confusion. She is the Mother who Nourishes, She is Rays of Light, the Remover of Darkness, and She Who Wears the Body of Nature.

- 17 -

शाकम्भरीं स्तुवन् ध्यायञ्जपन् सम्पूजयन्नमन् ।

अक्षय्यमश्नुते शीघ्रमन्नपानामृतं फलम् ॥

śākambharīṃ stuvan dhyāyañ

japan sampūjayannaman |

akṣayyamaśnute śīghram anna pānāmṛtaṃ phalam ||

One who sings praise, meditates, repeats mantras, worships, and adores She Who Nourishes with Vegetables quickly receives the everlasting presence of food and drink and freedom from death.

- 18 -

भीमापि नीलवर्णा सा दंष्ट्रादशनभासुरा ।

विशालल्लोचना नारी वृत्तपीनपयोधरा ॥

bhīmāpi nīlavarṇā sā daṃṣṭrā daśana bhāsurā |

viśāla locanā nārī vṛttapīna payodharā ||

The Goddess of Fearful Form is of a blue color. Her fangs and teeth glisten, and Her eyes are massive. This woman has breasts large and round.

- 19 -

चन्द्रहासं च डमरुं शिरः पात्रं च बिभ्रती ।

एकवीरा कालरात्रिः सैवोक्ता कामदा स्तुता ॥

candrahāsaṃ ca ḍamaruṃ śiraḥ pātraṃ ca bibhratī |
ekavīrā kālarātriḥ saivoktā kāmadā stutā ||

In Her hands She holds a scimitar, a small drum, a severed head, and a drinking vessel. She is called Solely Attentive to the Battle, the Dark Night, and the Grantor of Desires.

- 20 -

तेजोमण्डलदुर्धर्षा भ्रामरी चित्रकान्तिभृत् ।

चित्रानुलेपना देवी चित्राभरणभूषिता ॥

tejomaṇḍala durdharṣā bhrāmarī citra kānti bhṛt |
citrā nulepanā devī citrā bharaṇa bhūṣitā ||

She who has a bee-like nature is of various hues. Because of the brilliance of Her aura of light, She is safe from attack. Her body is also of various colors, as are Her ornaments.

- 21 -

चित्रभ्रमरपाणिः सा महामारीति गीयते ।

इत्येता मूर्तयो देव्या याः ख्याता वसुधाधिप ॥

citra bhramara pāṇiḥ sā mahā mārīti gīyate |
ityetā mūrtayo devyā yāḥ khyātā vasudhādhipa ||

Her hands manifest as a bee, and Her glory is sung as the Great Destroyer. Oh King of the Earth, thus the manifestations of the Goddess have been explained.

- 22 -

जगन्मातुश्चण्डिकायाः कीर्तिताः कामधेनवः ।

इदं रहस्यं परमं न वाच्यं कस्यचित्त्वया ॥

jaganmātuś caṇḍikāyāḥ kīrtitāḥ kāmadhenavaḥ |
idaṃ rahasyaṃ paramaṃ na vācyaṃ kasyacittvayā ||

The Mother of the Perceivable Universe, the Energy That Tears Apart Thought, She is famed as the Cow That Satiates all Desire. This is the Supreme Secret, not to be indiscriminately divulged.

- 23 -

व्याख्यानं दिव्यमूर्तीनामभीष्टफलदायकम् ।
तस्मात् सर्वप्रयत्नेन देवीं जप निरन्तरम् ॥

vyākhyānaṃ divya mūrtīnām
abhīṣṭa phala dāyakam ।
tasmāt sarva prayatnena devīṃ japa nirantaram ॥

The divine incarnations described are givers of the desired fruit, and therefore, with right effort, one should continually repeat the names of the Goddess in meditation.

- 24 -

सप्तजन्मार्जितैर्घोरैर्ब्रह्महत्यासमैरपि ।
पाठमात्रेण मन्त्राणां मुच्यते सर्वकिल्बिषैः ॥

saptajanmārjitair ghorair brahma hatyā samairapi ।
pāṭha mātreṇa mantrāṇāṃ mucyate sarvakilbiṣaiḥ ॥

By merely reading the Seven Hundred Mantras in Praise of She Who Removes All Difficulties (Chaṇḍī Pāṭhaḥ), all the impurities and terrible sins, such as killing a knower of divinity, are removed for up to seven births previous.

- 25 -

देव्या ध्यानं मया ख्यातं गुह्याद्गुह्यतरं महत् ।
तस्मात् सर्वप्रयत्नेन सर्वकामफलप्रदम् ॥

devyā dhyānaṃ mayā khyātaṃ
guhyādguhyataraṃ mahat ।
tasmāt sarvaprayatnena sarva kāmaphala pradam ॥

Thus the greatest of esoteric secrets, the meditation of the Goddess, has been described to you. Therefore, if a full and complete effort is made, all desires will be fulfilled.

(एतस्यास्त्वं प्रसादेन सर्वमान्यो भविष्यसि ।
सर्वरूपमयी देवी सर्वं देवीमयं जगत् ।
अतोऽहं विश्वरूपां तां नमामि परमेश्वरीम् ॥)

(etasyāstvaṃ prasādena sarva mānyo bhaviṣyasi |
sarva rūpa mayī devī sarvaṃ devī mayaṃ jagat |
ato-haṃ viśva rūpāṃ tāṃ namāmi parameśvarīm)

(With Her grace you will attain the highest respect. The Goddess pervades every form, and the entire universe is the form of the Goddess. Therefore I bow down to the Supreme Sovereign who is the form of the Universe.)

ॐ

oṃ

क्षमा-प्रार्थना

kṣamā prārthanā

Prayer for Forgiveness

\- 1 -

अपराधसहस्राणि क्रियन्तेऽहर्निशं मया ।
दासोऽयमिति मां मत्वा क्षमस्व परमेश्वरि ॥

**aparādha sahasrāṇi kriyante-harniśaṃ mayā |
dāso-yamiti māṃ matvā kṣamasva parameśvari ||**

Continually I commit thousands of mistakes, Oh Supreme Goddess, but understanding that I am only trying to serve you, please forgive them all.

\- 2 -

आवाहनं न जानामि न जानामि विसर्जनम् ।
पूजां चैव न जानामि क्षम्यतां परमेश्वरि ॥

**āvāhanaṃ na jānāmi na jānāmi visarjanam |
pūjāṃ caiva na jānāmi kṣamyatāṃ parameśvari ||**

I don't know how to welcome you, nor do I know to say good-bye. I don't know how to worship you, Oh Supreme Goddess, please forgive me.

\- 3 -

मन्त्रहीनं क्रियाहीनं भक्तिहीनं सुरेश्वरि ।
यत्पूजितं मया देवि परिपूर्णं तदस्तु मे ॥

**mantrahīnaṃ kriyāhīnaṃ bhaktihīnaṃ sureśvari |
yatpūjitaṃ mayā devi paripūrṇaṃ tadastu me ||**

Oh Empress of the Gods, I know nothing of mantras. I don't know the ways of righteous conduct. I am devoid of devotion. But Oh my Goddess, please be satisfied with my worship, and let it be complete.

\- 4 -

अपराधशतं कृत्वा जगदम्बेति चोच्चरेत् ।
यां गतिं समवाप्नोति न तां ब्रह्मादयः सुराः ॥

aparādhaśataṃ kṛtvā jagadambeti coccaret |
yāṃ gatiṃ samavāpnoti na tāṃ brahmādayaḥ surāḥ ||
One who commits a hundred faults, yet calls for the Mother of the Perceivable Universe, neither Brahmā nor the other Gods can rise to the upliftment that is received.

- 5 -

सापराधोऽस्मि शरणं प्राप्तस्त्वां जगदम्बिके ।
इदानीमनुकम्प्योऽहं यथेच्छसि तथा कुरु ॥

sāparādho-smi śaraṇaṃ prāptastvāṃ jagadambike |
idānīmanukampyo-haṃ yathecchasi tathā kuru ||
Oh Mother of the Universe, I am guilty of error, and I take refuge in you. I am worthy of compassion. Do as you will.

- 6 -

अज्ञानाद्विस्मृतेर्भ्रान्त्या यन्न्यूनमधिकं कृतम् ।
तत्सर्वं क्षम्यतां देवि प्रसीद परमेश्वरि ॥

ajñānādvismṛter bhrāntyā
yannyūnamadhikaṃ kṛtam |
tat sarvaṃ kṣamyatāṃ devi prasīda parameśvari ||
Oh Goddess, whatever performance that was committed through ignorance, forgetfulness, or confusion, all of that, Oh Supreme Goddess, please forgive, oh may you be so gracious!

- 7 -

कामेश्वरि जगन्मातः सच्चिदानन्दविग्रहे ।
गृहाणार्चामिमां प्रीत्या प्रसीद परमेश्वरि ॥

kāmeśvari jaganmātaḥ saccidānandavigrahe |
gṛhāṇārcāmimāṃ prītyā prasīda parameśvari ||
Oh Ruler of Desire, Mother of Existence, Embodiment of Truth-Consciousness-Bliss, please accept this offering with love. Oh Supreme Divinity, be pleased.

\- 8 -

गुह्यातिगुह्यगोप्त्री त्वं गृहाणास्मत्कृतं जपम् ।
सिद्धिर्भवतु मे देवि त्वत्प्रसादात्सुरेश्वरि ॥

guhyātiguhyagoptrī tvaṃ gṛhāṇāsmatkṛtaṃ japam |
siddhir bhavatu me devi tvat prasādāt sureśvari ||

Oh Goddess, you are the protector of the most secret of mystical secrets. Please accept the recitation that I have offered, and grant to me the attainment of perfection.

ॐ

oṃ

अथ दुर्गाद्वात्रिंशन्नाममाला
atha durgā dvātriṃśannāma mālā
The Rosary of Thirty-two Names of Durgā

दुर्गा दुर्गार्तिशमनी दुर्गापद्विनिवारिणी ।
दुर्गमच्छेदिनी दुर्गसाधिनी दुर्गनाशिनी ॥

durgā durgārti śamanī durgā padvinivāriṇī |
durgamacchedinī durga sādhinī durga nāśinī ||

1. The Reliever of Difficulties
2. Who Puts Difficulties at Peace
3. Dispeller of Difficult Adversities
4. Who Cuts Down Difficulties
5. The Performer of Discipline to Expel Difficulties
6. The Destroyer of Difficulties

दुर्गतोद्धारिणी दुर्गनिहन्त्री दुर्गमापहा ।
दुर्गमज्ञानदा दुर्गदैत्यलोकदवानला ॥

durgatod dhāriṇī durga nihantrī durgamāpahā |
durgamajñānadā durga daityaloka davānalā ||

7. Who Holds the Whip to Difficulties
8. Who Sends Difficulties to Ruin
9. Who Measures Difficulties
10. Who Makes Difficulties Unconscious
11. Who Destroys the World of Difficult Thoughts

दुर्गमा दुर्गमालोका दुर्गमात्मस्वरूपिणी ।
दुर्गमार्गप्रदा दुर्गमविद्या दुर्गमाश्रिता ॥

durgamā durgamālokā durgamātmasvarūpiṇī |
durgamārgapradā durgamavidyā durgamāśritā ||

12. The Mother of Difficulties
13. The Perception of Difficulties
14. The Intrinsic Nature of the Soul of Difficulties
15. Who Searches through Difficulties

16. The Knowledge of Difficulties
17. The Extrication from Difficulties

दुर्गमज्ञानसंस्थाना दुर्गमध्यानभासिनी ।
दुर्गमोहा दुर्गमगा दुर्गमार्थस्वरूपिणी ॥

durgamajñāna saṃsthānā durgamadhyāna bhāsinī |
durga mohā durgamagā durgamārtha svarūpiṇī ||

18. The Continued Existence of Difficulties
19. Whose Meditation Remains Brilliant When in Difficulties
20. Who Deludes Difficulties
21. Who Resolves Difficulties
22. Who is the Intrinsic Nature of the Object of Difficulties

दुर्गमासुरसंहन्त्री दुर्गमायुधधारिणी ।
दुर्गमाङ्गी दुर्गमता दुर्गम्या दुर्गमेश्वरी ॥

durgam āsura saṃhantrī durgam āyudha dhāriṇī |
durgamāṅgī durgamatā durgamyā durgameśvarī ||

23. The Annihilator of the Egotism of Difficulties
24. Bearer of the Weapon Against Difficulties
25. The Refinery of Difficulties
26. Who is Beyond Difficulties
27. Accessible with Difficulty
28. The Empress of Difficulties

दुर्गभीमा दुर्गभामा दुर्गभा दुर्गदारिणी ।
नामावलिमिमां यस्तु दुर्गाया मम मानवः ।

durgabhīmā durgabhāmā durgabhā durgadāriṇī |
nāmāvalimimāṃ yastu durgāyā mama mānavaḥ ||

29. Who is Terrible to Difficulties
30. The Lady of Difficulties
31. The Illuminator of Difficulties
32. Who Cuts Off Difficulties

Whoever will recite this garland of the names of Durgā,

पठेत् सर्वभयान्मुक्तो भविष्यति न संशयः ॥

paṭhet sarva bhayān mukto bhaviṣyati na saṃśayaḥ ||
the Reliever of Difficulties, will be freed from every type of fear without a doubt.

ॐ

oṃ

अथ देव्यपराधक्षमापनस्तोत्रम्
atha devyaparādha kṣamāpana stotram
And Now, A Song Seeking Forgiveness from
the Goddess for the Commission of Offences

- 1 -

न मन्त्रं नो यन्त्रं तदपि च न जाने स्तुतिमहो
न चाह्वानं ध्यानं तदपि च न जाने स्तुतिकथाः ।
न जाने मुद्रास्ते तदपि च न जाने विलपनं
परं जाने मातस्त्वदनुसरणं क्लेशहरणम् ॥

na mantraṃ no yantraṃ tadapi ca na jāne stutimaho
na cāhvānaṃ dhyānaṃ tadapi ca na jāne stutikathāḥ |
na jāne mudrāste tadapi ca na jāne vilapanaṃ
paraṃ jāne mātastvadanusaraṇaṃ kleśaharaṇam ||

Mother, I don't know mantras nor yantras, nor can I sing your praise. I don't know how to welcome you, nor how to meditate on your presence. Neither do I know how to sing your glories, nor how to show your mystical signs, nor even how to lament. But I shall keep on calling you, you who take away the difficulties of all.

- 2 -

विधेरज्ञानेन द्रविणविरहेणालसतया
विधेयाशक्यत्वात्तव चरणयोर्या च्युतिरभूत् ।
तदेतत् क्षन्तव्यं जननि सकलोद्धारिणि शिवे
कुपुत्रो जायेत क्वचिदपि कुमाता न भवति ॥

vidherajñānena draviṇavirahenālasatayā
vidheyāśakyatvāt tava caraṇayoryā cyutirabhūt |
tadetat kṣantavyaṃ janani sakaloddhāriṇi śive
kuputro jāyeta kvacidapi kumātā na bhavati ||

Oh Energy of Infinite Goodness, Mother of the Universe, I don't know the systems of worship. Neither have I sufficient wealth with which to serve you. My nature is lazy, and I don't know the correct performance of worship. For these reasons, whatever deficiencies exist in my service to your lotus feet, please pardon, Oh Mother, because a child can be bad, but a Mother can never be bad.

- 3 -

पृथिव्यां पुत्रास्ते जननि बहवः सन्ति सरलाः
परं तेषां मध्ये विरलतरलोऽहं तव सुतः ।
मदीयोऽयं त्यागः समुचितमिदं नो तव शिवे
कुपुत्रो जायेत क्वचिदपि कुमाता न भवति ॥

pṛthivyāṃ putrāste janani bahavaḥ santi saralāḥ
paraṃ teṣāṃ madhye viralataralo-haṃ tava sutaḥ |
madīyo-yaṃ tyāgaḥ samucitamidaṃ no tava śive
kuputro jāyeta kvacidapi kumātā na bhavati ||

Mother, on this earth you have so many honest and simple children, and among them I am your extremely fickle child. I alone am the most inconstant. Oh Goddess of Goodness, it is not fitting for you to discard me, because a child can be bad, but a Mother can never be bad.

- 4 -

जगन्मातर्मातस्तव चरणसेवा न रचिता
न वा दत्तं देवि द्रविणमपि भूयस्तव मया ।
तथापि त्वं स्नेहं मयि निरुपमं यत्प्रकुरुषे
कुपुत्रो जायेत क्वचिदपि कुमाता न भवति ॥

jagan mātar mātas tava caraṇasevā na racitā
na vā dattaṃ devi draviṇamapi bhūyastava mayā |
tathāpi tvaṃ snehaṃ mayi nirupamaṃ yatprakuruṣe
kuputro jāyeta kvacidapi kumātā na bhavati ||

Oh Mother of the Universe, Oh Goddess, I have yet to serve your respected lotus feet. I have not offered my wealth to you lavishly. Even still you show your most excellent love to this worthless being, because a child can be bad, but a Mother can never be bad.

\- 5 -

परित्यक्ता देवा विविधविधसेवाकुलतया
मया पञ्चाशीतेरधिकमपनीते तु वयसि ।
इदानीं चेन्मातस्तव यदि कृपा नापि भविता
निरालम्बो लम्बोदरजननि कं यामि शरणम् ॥

parityaktā devā vividhavidha sevākulatayā
mayā pañcā śīter adhikamapanīte tu vayasi I
idānīṃ cenmātastava yadi kṛpā nāpi bhavitā
nirālambo lambodara janani kaṃ yāmi śaraṇam II

Oh Mother of all Auspiciousness, I have abandoned the service of various Gods, being absorbed in multifarious activities for many years (at least fifty). Now I am fully dependant on you. If you don't show your grace to me, where else shall I go to take refuge?

\- 6 -

श्वपाको जल्पाको भवति मधुपाकोपमगिरा
निरातङ्को रङ्को विहरति चिरं कोटिकनकैः ।
तवापर्णे कर्णे विशति मनुवर्णे फलमिदं
जनः को जानीते जननि जननीयं जपविधौ ॥

śvapāko jalpāko bhavati madhupākopamagirā
nirātaṅko raṅko viharati ciraṃ koṭikanakaiḥ I
tavāparṇe karṇe viśati manu varṇe phalamidaṃ
janaḥ ko jānīte janani jananīyaṃ japavidhau II

Mother of Excellence, your mantra has such power that if even one letter should touch the ear, a fool becomes an eloquent speaker and his discourse becomes an excellent exposition. When hearing but one letter can produce such an effect, then who can speak for those souls who regularly perform your worship according to the injunctions of scripture, what excellent result will be attained by them?

- 7 -

चिताभस्मालेपो गरलमशनं दिक्पटधरो
जटाधारी कण्ठे भुजगपतिहारी पशुपतिः ।
कपाली भूतेशो भजति जगदीशैकपदवीं
भवानि त्वत्पाणिग्रहणपरिपाटीफलमिदम् ॥

citābhasmālepo garalamaśanaṃ dikpaṭadharo
jaṭādhārī kaṇṭhe bhujagapatihārī paśupatiḥ |
kapālī bhūteśo bhajati jagadīśaikapadavīṃ
bhavāni tvat pāṇi grahaṇa paripāṭī phalamidam ||

He who besmears his body with ashes from the funeral pyre, who consumes the poison, who remains naked, who has long matted locks of hair, and wears the king of snakes around his neck as a garland, who has in his hand a cup made of bone, that Lord of Spirits, Lord of Animals, who is known as the Lord of the Universe, how did He acquire His Greatness? He simply accepted your hand in marriage, Oh Empress of Being, that is the method of His attainment.

- 8 -

न मोक्षस्याकांक्षा भवविभववाञ्छापि च न मे
न विज्ञानापेक्षा शशिमुखि सुखेच्छापि न पुनः ।
अतस्त्वां संयाचे जननि जननं यातु मम वै
मृडानी रुद्राणी शिव शिव भवानीति जपतः ॥

na mokṣasyākāṃkṣā bhavavibhavavāñchāpi ca na me
na vijñānāpekṣā śaśimukhi sukhecchāpi napunaḥ |
atastvāṃ saṃyāce janani jananaṃ yātu mama vai
mṛḍānī rudrāṇī śiva śiva bhavānīti japataḥ ||

Oh Mother from whose face shines forth the luster of the moon, I have no desire for liberation nor expectation of status in the eyes of others. Neither do I search for worldly knowledge or comfort. From you I have only one earnest entreaty, that I pass my life in contemplation of the names the Compassionate One, Reliever of Sufferings, Infinite Goodness, Infinite Goodness, the Female Ruler of Being.

- 9 -

नाराधितासि विधिना विविधोपचारैः
किं रुक्षचिन्तनपरैर्न कृतं वचोभिः ।
श्यामे त्वमेव यदि किञ्चन मय्यनाथे
धत्से कृपामुचितमम्ब परं तवैव ॥

nārādhitāsi vidhinā vividhopacāraiḥ
kiṃ rukṣacintana parairna kṛtaṃ vacobhiḥ |
śyāme tvameva yadi kiñcana mayyanāthe
dhatse kṛpā mucitamamba paraṃ tavaiva ||

Oh Unknowable One, I have no such capacity to please you with worship according to the scriptures with the offering of various articles. Always thinking of my own deficient circumstances, what mistakes has my speech not revealed? Still, Oh Mother, you make the effort to place your gracious look upon me, this helpless one. That verifies your worthiness. You are such a compassionate mother as to be able to give even a bad child like me a refuge and mercy.

- 10 -

आपत्सु मग्नः स्मरणं त्वदीयं
करोमि दुर्गे करुणार्णवेशि ।
नैतच्छठत्वं मम भावयेथाः
क्षुधातृषार्ता जननीं स्मरन्ति ॥

āpatsu magnaḥ smaraṇaṃ tvadīyaṃ
karomi durge karuṇārṇaveśi |
naitacchaṭhatvaṃ mama bhāvayethāḥ
kṣudhātṛṣārtā jananīṃ smaranti ||

Oh Mother, Reliever of Difficulties, Ocean of Mercy, I am remembering you today, having fallen into difficulties. I request you to disregard my wickedness. We call you as children perplexed by hunger and thirst would remember their mother, being away from her breast.

- 11 -

जगदम्ब विचित्रमत्र किं
परिपूर्णा करुणास्ति चेन्मयि ।
अपराधपरम्परापरं
न हि माता समुपेक्षते सुतम् ॥

jagadamba vicitra matra kiṃ
paripūrṇā karuṇāsti cenmayi |
aparādhaparam parā paraṃ
na hi mātā samupekṣate sutam ||

Mother of the Universe, it is no surprise that you bestow your abundant mercy and grace on me, your child, who commits error after error continually. You are Mother, hence you cannot disregard or ignore me, your child.

- 12 -

मत्समः पातकी नास्ति पापघ्नी त्वत्समा न हि ।
एवं ज्ञात्वा महादेवि यथायोग्यं तथा कुरु ॥

matsamaḥ pātakī nāsti pāpaghnī tvatsamā na hi |
evaṃ jñātvā mahādevi yathā yogyaṃ tathā kuru ||

Oh Great Goddess, there is no greater evil doer than I, and there is no other who takes away sin as you. With such understanding, do what is proper.

ॐ

oṃ

सिद्धकुञ्जिकास्तोत्रम्
siddha kuñjikā stotram
The Song That Gives the Key to Perfection

शिव उवाच

śiva uvāca

Śiva said:

\- 1 -

श्रृणु देवि प्रवक्ष्यामि कुञ्जिकास्तोत्रमुत्तमम् ।
येन मन्त्रप्रभावेण चण्डीजापः शुभो भवेत् ॥

śṛṇu devi pravakṣyāmi kuñjikā stotram uttamam |
yena mantraprabhāveṇa caṇḍījāpaḥ śubho bhavet ||

Listen, Oh Goddess, while I elucidate the excellent Song That Gives the Key to Perfection. By means of the brilliance of these mantras, the meditation of the Goddess Chaṇḍī becomes easy.

\- 2 -

न कवचं नार्गलास्तोत्रं कीलकं न रहस्यकम् ।
न सूक्तं नापि ध्यानं च न न्यासो न च वार्चनम् ॥

na kavacaṃ nārgalā stotraṃ
kīlakam na rahasyakaṃ |
na sūktaṃ nāpi dhyānaṃ ca
na nyāso na ca vārcanam ||

Not the Armor, nor the Praise That Unlocks the Bolt, nor the Praise That Removes the Pin, nor the Secrets; neither the hymns, nor even the meditations, nor the establishment of the mantras into the body, nor the offering of worship and adoration;

\- 3 -

कुञ्जिकापाठमात्रेण दुर्गापाठफलं लभेत् ।
अति गुह्यतरं देवि देवानामपि दुर्लभम् ॥

kuñjikā pāṭha mātreṇa durgā pāṭha phalaṃ labhet |
ati guhyataraṃ devi devānāmapi durlabham ||

the recitation of the mantras that Give the Key to Perfection will grant the fruits of the recitation of the Glory of the Goddess. Oh Goddess, this is extremely secretive and difficult even for the Gods to attain.

- 4 -

गोपनीयं प्रयत्नेन स्वयोनिरिव पार्वति ।
मारणं मोहनं वश्यं स्तम्भनोच्चाटनादिकम् ।
पाठमात्रेण संसिद्ध्येत् कुञ्जिकास्तोत्रमुत्तमम् ॥

gopanīyaṃ prayatnena svayoniriva pārvati |
māraṇaṃ mohanaṃ vaśyaṃ
stambhanoccāṭa nādikam |
pāṭha mātreṇa saṃsiddhyet
kuñjikā stotram uttamam ||

Oh self-born Goddess, Pārvati, with right effort Māraṇa (the capacity to slay anger, passion, and the Ego), Mohaṇa (to become stupefied knowing none other than the Goddess, Vaśīkāraṇa (to make the mind sit still), Stambhana (to restrain the senses from wandering), Ucchātana (to become solely absorbed in the attainment of enlightenment), and all other attainments all come to perfection by means of the recitation of the excellent mantras of the Song That Gives the Key to Perfection. Hence this is to be kept secret by all means.[1]

ॐ ऐं ह्रीं क्लीं चामुण्डायै विच्चे ॥
ॐ ग्लौं हुं क्लीं जूं सः ज्वालय ज्वालय ज्वल ज्वल प्रज्वल प्रज्वल ऐं ह्रीं क्लीं चामुण्डायै विच्चे ज्वल हं सं लं क्षं फट् स्वाहा ॥

oṃ aiṃ hrīṃ klīṃ cāmuṇḍāyai vicce ||
oṃ glauṃ huṃ klīṃ jūṃ saḥ jvālaya jvālaya jvala jvala prajvala prajvala aiṃ hrīṃ klīṃ cāmuṇḍāyai vicce jvala haṃ saṃ laṃ kṣaṃ phaṭ svāhā ||

And Now, the Mantra

Oṃ The Infinite Beyond Conception
Aiṃ Creation, Rajo Guṇa, Energy of Desire, Mahāsarasvatī
Hrīṃ Preservation, Sattva Guṇa, Energy of Action, Mahālakṣmī
Klīṃ Destruction, Tamo Guṇa, Energy of Wisdom, Mahākālī
Cāmuṇḍā The Slayer of Passion and Anger, Moves in the Head
Yai The Grantor of Boons
Vic In the Body of Knowledge; in the Perception
Ce of Consciousness
Oṃ The Infinite Beyond Conception
Glauṃ Mahāgaṇeśa, the Great Lord of Wisdom
Huṃ Cutting the Ego
Klīṃ Dissolving Bondage to Physical Attachment
Jūṃ Saḥ Pure Consciousness
Jvālaya Jvālaya Flame, Bright Light of Illumination
Jvala Jvala Burning, Blazing, Shining
Prajvala Prajvala To Begin to Blaze or Flash

that the three guṇas, energies, and Goddesses - Creation, Preservation, and Destruction - are in constant movement, transformation in the perception of Consciousness

Jvala (and this) Illumination
Haṃ (is the) Divine I
Saṃ in all
Laṃ manifested beings
Kṣaṃ (to) the end of existence
Phaṭ without a doubt
Svāhā I am One with God!

That is the mantra.

- 1 -

नमस्ते रुद्ररूपिण्यै नमस्ते मधुमर्दिनि ।

नमः कैटभहारिण्यै नमस्ते महिषार्दिनि ॥

namaste rudra rūpiṇyai namaste madhu mardini |
namaḥ kaiṭabha hāriṇyai namaste mahiṣārdini ||

We bow to She Who has the Capacity to Express the form of Rudra, the Reliever from Sufferings. We bow to the Slayer of Too Much. We bow to She Who Takes Away Too Little. We bow to the Annihilator of the Great Ego.

- 2 -

नमस्ते शुम्भहन्त्र्यै च निशुम्भासुरघातिनि ॥

namaste śumbha hantryai ca niśumbhāsuraghātini ||

We bow to the destroyer of Self-Conceit and to the Destroyer of Self-Deprecation as well.

- 3 -

जाग्रतं हि महादेवि जपं सिद्धं कुरुश्व मे ।

ऐंकारी सृष्टिरूपायै ह्रींकारी प्रतिपालिका ॥

jāgratam hi mahā devi japam siddham kuruśva me |
aiṃkārī sṛṣṭi rūpāyai hrīṃkārī prati pālikā ||

Arise to wakefulness, Oh Great Goddess! Grant me the perfection of meditation. The sound Aiṃ is the sound of creation. The syllable Hrīṃ is the entire existence preserved.

- 4 -

क्लींकारी कामरूपिण्यै बीजरूपे नमोऽस्तु ते ।

चामुण्डा चण्डघाती च यैकारी वरदायिनी ॥

klīṃkārī kāma rūpiṇyai bīja rūpe namo-stu te |
cāmuṇḍā caṇḍa ghātī ca yai kārī varadāyinī ||

The syllable Klīṃ is the intrinsic form of all desire. We bow to you, the ultimate objective, in the form of Seed Mantras. As the Slayer of Passion and Anger, you slay Passion, and as the syllable Yai, you are the Grantor of Boons.

- 5 -

विच्चे चाभयदा नित्यं नमस्ते मन्त्ररूपिणि ॥

vicce cābhayadā nityaṃ namaste mantra rūpiṇi ||

Vicce gives eternal freedom from fear. We bow to you in the form of mantras.

\- 6 -

धां धीं धूं धूर्जटिः पत्नी वां वीं वूं वागधीश्वरी ।

क्रां क्रीं क्रूं कालिका देवि शां शीं शूं मे शुभं कुरु ॥

dhāṃ dhīṃ dhūṃ dhūrjaṭeḥ patnī
vāṃ vīṃ vūṃ vāgadhīśvarī |
krāṃ krīṃ krūṃ kālikā devi
śāṃ śīṃ śūṃ me śubhaṃ kuru ||

Dhāṃ dhīṃ dhūṃ the wife of Śiva (literally the one with matted hair), Vāṃ vīṃ vūṃ Vāgadīśvarī (the Ruler of all Vibrations). Krāṃ krīṃ krūṃ kālikā devi (the Goddess Who Takes Away the Darkness), Śāṃ śīṃ śūṃ (She who is Peace in the gross body, Peace in the suble body, Peace in the causal body) be easily attained by me.

\- 7 -

हुं हुं हुंकाररूपिण्यै जं जं जं जम्भनादिनी ।

भ्रां भ्रीं भ्रूं भैरवी भद्रे भवान्यै ते नमो नमः ॥

huṃ huṃ huṃkāra rūpiṇyai
jaṃ jaṃ jaṃ jambhanādinī |
bhrāṃ bhrīṃ bhrūṃ bhairavī bhadre
bhavānyai te namo namaḥ ||

In the form of the syllables Huṃ huṃ huṃ, Jaṃ jaṃ jaṃ as the restrained sound of constant vibration emanating as a yawn from the junction of the eyes, ears, nose and throat. Brāṃ brīṃ brūṃ to the Excellent Energy that is Extremely Fierce, to Bhavāṇī, the female Lord of Being, we bow, we bow to you.

\- 8 -

अं कं चं टं तं पं यं शं वीं दुं ऐं वीं हं क्षं ।

धिजाग्रं धिजाग्रं त्रोटय त्रोटय दीप्तं कुरु कुरु स्वाहा ॥

aṃ kaṃ caṃ ṭaṃ taṃ paṃ yaṃ śaṃ vīṃ duṃ aiṃ vīṃ haṃ kṣaṃ |
dhijāgraṃ dhijāgraṃ troṭaya
troṭaya dīptaṃ kuru kuru svāhā ||

Aṃ kaṃ caṃ ṭaṃ taṃ paṃ yaṃ śaṃ vīṃ duṃ aiṃ vīṃ haṃ kṣaṃ[2]

Rise up! Break asunder! Illuminate the brilliant light!
I am One with God![3]
Vīṃ to eagerly approach
Duṃ the Reliever of Difficulties
Aiṃ the Body of Universal Knowledge
Vīṃ to eagerly approach
Aspirates: Haṃ, the Supreme I; Kṣaṃ, the end of duality

पां पीं पूं पार्वती पूर्णा खां खीं खूं खेचरी तथा ॥

pāṃ pīṃ pūṃ pārvatī pūrṇā
khāṃ khīṃ khūṃ khecarī tathā ॥

Pāṃ pīṃ pūṃ Pārvatī, the wife of Śiva; the Potentiality of Nature is full and complete. Khāṃ khīṃ khūṃ (the three stages of khecarī where one levitates) as a heavenly being we fly up into the atmosphere.

- 9 -

सां सीं सूं सप्तशती देव्या मन्त्रसिद्धिं कुरुष्व मे ॥

sāṃ sīṃ sūṃ saptaśatī devyā
mantra siddhiṃ kuruṣva me ॥

Sāṃ sīṃ sūṃ as other divine beings born of these Seven Hundred Verses, give to me the perfect attainment of the mantras.

इदं तु कुञ्जिकास्तोत्रं मन्त्रजागर्तिहेतवे ।
अभक्ते नैव दातव्यं गोपितं रक्ष पार्वति ॥

idaṃ tu kuñjikā stotram mantra jāgarti hetave ।
abhakte naiva dātavyaṃ gopitaṃ rakṣa pārvati ॥

This is the Song That Gives the Key to Perfection, the primary cause of awakening these mantras. This must be kept hidden from non-devotees. Oh Pārvati, the secret must be protected.

यस्तु कुञ्जिकया देवि हीनां सप्तशतीं पठेत् ।
न तस्य जायते सिद्धिररण्ये रोदनं यथा ॥

yastu kuñjikayā devi hīnāṃ saptaśatīṃ paṭhet |
na tasya jāyate siddhir araṇye rodanaṃ yathā ||
Oh Goddess, whoever will recite the Seven Hundred Verses without the key will not attain success, and his recitation will produce an effect similar to crying in the forest.

ॐ ऐं ह्रीं क्लीं चामुण्डायै विच्चे ॥ ॐ ग्लौं हुं क्लीं जूं सः ज्वालय ज्वालय ज्वल ज्वल प्रज्वल प्रज्वल ऐं ह्रीं क्लीं चामुण्डायै विच्चे ज्वल हं सं लं क्षं फट् स्वाहा ॥

oṃ aiṃ hrīṃ klīṃ cāmuṇḍāyai vicce ||
oṃ glauṃ huṃ klīṃ jūṃ saḥ jvālaya jvālaya jvala jvala prajvala prajvala aiṃ hrīṃ klīṃ cāmuṇḍāyai vicce jvala haṃ saṃ laṃ kṣaṃ phaṭ svāhā ||

Oṃ	The Infinite Beyond Conception
Aiṃ	Creation, Rajo Guṇa, Energy of Desire, Mahāsarasvatī
Hrīṃ	Preservation, Sattva Guṇa, Energy of Action, Mahālakṣmī
Klīṃ	Destruction, Tamo Guṇa, Energy of Wisdom, Mahākālī
Cāmuṇḍā	The Slayer of Passion and Anger, Moves in the Head
Yai	The Grantor of Boons
Vic	In the Body of Knowledge; in the Perception
Ce	of Consciousness
Oṃ	The Infinite Beyond Conception
Glauṃ	Mahāgaṇeśa, the Great Lord of Wisdom
Huṃ	Cutting the Ego
Klīṃ	Dissolving Bondage to Physical Attachment
Jūṃ Saḥ	Pure Consciousness
Jvālaya Jvālaya	Flame, Bright Light of Illumination
Jvala Jvala	Burning, Blazing, Shining
Prajvala Prajvala	To Begin to Blaze or Flash

that the three guṇas, energies, and Goddesses - Creation, Preservation, and Destruction - are in constant movement, transformation in the perception of Consciousness

Jvala	(and this) Illumination
Haṃ	(is the) Divine I
Saṃ	in all
Laṃ	manifested beings
Kṣaṃ	(to) the end of existence
Phaṭ	without a doubt
Svāhā	I am One with God!

1 There are three types of aspirants who may have occasion to utter these mantras, and they are distinguished by the diverse forms of nature: Sāttvika, Rājasika, and Tāmasika. The Rājasika quality is active in the perfection of the individual's status, power, and authority. Tāmas seeks to cause injury to another. The Sāttvika perception seeks the ultimate knowledge of unity in self-surrender.

2 The Saṃskṛta alphabet includes all of the possible sounds for all of the possible names of all of the possible objects of creation. The letters themselves symbolize the entire range of evolution of all possibilities, the full and complete transformation of the saṃsāra, the totality of all objects and relationships. Creation begins with A, the first vowel and letter of the alphabet. Thereafter, the alphabet proceeds through the sixteen vowels to the first consonant Ka. From thence it is arranged in groups called Vargas:

Gutturals:	ka kha ga gha ña
Palatals:	ca cha ja jha ṅa
Cerebrals:	ṭa ṭha ḍa ḍha ṇa
Dentals:	ta tha da dha na
Labials:	pa pha ba bha ma
Semi Vowels:	ya ra la va
Sibilants:	śa ṣa sa
Aspirates:	haṃ kṣaṃ

3 According to Pannini, in the individual this journey begins in the Viśuddha Cakra, and working its way down to the Mūlādhāra, it calls to the Kuṇḍaliṇī, "Rise up! Break asunder! Illuminate the brilliant light! I am One with God!" And it takes that luminous energy back up to the Ājña Cakra, having pierced the cakras with its rising force, cutting asunder all attachments to duality.

चण्डी माँ की आरती
caṇḍī mām̐ kī āratī
Be Victorious!

जय चण्डी जय जय (माँ) जय चण्डी जय जय
भयहारिणि भवतारिणि भवभामिनि जय जय
ॐ जय चण्डी जय जय

jaya caṇḍī jaya jaya (mām̐) jaya caṇḍī jaya jaya
bhaya hāriṇi bhava tāriṇi (2)
bhava bhāmini jaya jaya
oṃ jaya caṇḍī jaya jaya

Be Victorious! Oh Goddess Who Tears Apart Thought! Be Victorious! You take away all fear and illuminate the intensity of reality. Be Victorious!

\- 1 -

तू ही सत-चित-सुखमय शुद्ध ब्रह्मरूपा (माँ)
सत्य सनातन सुन्दर पर-शिव सूर-भूपा
ॐ जय चण्डी जय जय

tū hī sata cita sukhamaya śuddha brahmarūpā (mām̐)
satya sanātana sundara (2) para śiva sūra bhūpā
oṃ jaya caṇḍī jaya jaya

You are the essence of Truth, Consciousness, Happiness, the form of Pure Conscious Being. You are the beauty of Eternal Truth. Beyond infinite goodness, you rule over all the Gods. Be Victorious!

\- 2 -

आदि अनादि अनामय अविचल अविनाशी (माँ)
अमल अनन्त अगोचर अज आनन्दराशी
ॐ जय चण्डी जय जय

ādi anādi anāmaya avicala avināśī (mām̐)
amala ananta agocara (2) aja ānandarāśī
oṃ jaya caṇḍī jaya jaya

The beginning, without beginning, unseverable; motionless and indestructible; Bright, infinite, imperceptible, unborn, the great collection of Bliss. Be Victorious!

- 3 -

अविकारी अघहारी अकल कलाधारी (माँ)
कर्त्ता विधि भर्त्ता हरि हर सँहारकारी
ॐ जय चण्डी जय जय

avikārī aghahārī akala kalādhārī (mām̐)
karttā vidhi bharttā hari (2) hara sam̐hārakārī
oṃ jaya caṇḍī jaya jaya

Changeless, holy One, sinless, bearer of individual phenomena; created by Brahmā, sustained by Viṣṇu, and Śiva who dissolves this creation. Be Victorious!

- 4 -

तू विधि वधू रमा तू उमा महामाया (माँ)
मूलप्रकृति विद्या तू तू जननी जाया
ॐ जय चण्डी जय जय

tū vidhi vadhū ramā tū umā mahā māyā (mām̐)
mūlaprakṛti vidyā tū (2) tū jananī jāyā
oṃ jaya caṇḍī jaya jaya

You are the wife of Brahmā, the wife of Viṣṇu (Ramā), the wife of Śiva (Umā), the Great Measurement of Consciousness. You are the knowledge of primordial existence, the Mother who gives birth to all. Be Victorious!

- 5 -

राम कृष्ण तू सीता ब्रजरानी राधा (माँ)
तू वाञ्छाकल्पद्रुम हारिणि सब बाधा
ॐ जय चण्डी जय जय

rāma kṛṣṇa tū sītā brajarānī rādhā (mām̐)
tū vāñchā kalpadruma (2) hāriṇi saba bādhā
oṃ jaya caṇḍī jaya jaya

You are the consciousness of the subtle light of wisdom that merges with the ultimate. You are the Doer of All. You are Sītā, the pure white one, the Queen of the multitude; Rādhā, the Ruler of all success. You are the desire of the wish-fulfilling tree, taking away all obstructions. Be Victorious!

- 6 -

दश विद्या नव दुर्गा नानाशस्त्रकरा (माँ)
अष्टमातृका योगिनि नव नव रूप धरा
ॐ जय चण्डी जय जय

daśa vidyā nava durgā nānāśastra karā (māṁ)
aṣṭa mātṛkā yogini (2) nava nava rūpa dharā
oṃ jaya caṇḍī jaya jaya

You are the ten branches of knowledge (Mahā Vidyās) and the nine Relievers of Difficulties (nine Durgās). All of the scriptures present you. The eight Mothers of union. Various are the forms that you assume. Be Victorious!

- 7 -

तू परधामनिवासिनि महाविलासिनि तू (माँ)
तु ही श्मशानविहारिणि ताण्डवलासिनि तू
ॐ जय चण्डी जय जय

tū paradhāma nivāsini mahā vilāsini tū (māṁ)
tū hī śmaśāna vihāriṇi (2) tāṇḍavalāsini tū
oṃ jaya caṇḍī jaya jaya

You are the inhabitant of the highest residence. Yours is the greatest beauty. You wander about the cremation grounds dancing to the rhythmic music. Be Victorious!

- 8 -

सुर मुनि मोहिनि सौम्या तू शोभाऽऽधारा (माँ)
विवसनविकट-सरूपा प्रलयमयी धारा
ॐ जय चण्डी जय जय

sura muni mohini saumyā tū śobhā--dhārā (māṁ)
vivasana vikaṭ sarūpā (2) pralaya mayī dhārā
oṃ jaya caṇḍī jaya jaya

You mesmerize the Gods and munis when you present your radiant beauty. All are helpless seeing your dreadful appearance at the time when you assume the form of total dissolution. Be Victorious!

- 9 -

तू ही स्नेह-सुधामयि तू अति गरलमना (माँ)
रत्नविभूषित तू ही तू ही अस्थि तना
ॐ जय चण्डी जय जय

tū hī sneha sudhāmayi tū ati garalamanā (māṁ)
ratna vibhūṣita tū hī (2) tū hī asthi tanā
oṃ jaya caṇḍī jaya jaya

You pervade Love and ease. You are extremely eminent. You are the Brilliance of the jewel. You are the invisible existence. Be Victorious!

- 10 -

मूलाधारनिवासिनि इह पर सिद्धि प्रदे (माँ)
कालातीता काली कमल तू वरदे
ॐ जय चण्डी जय जय

mūlādhāra nivāsini iha para siddhi prade (māṁ)
kālātītā kālī (2) kamala tū varade
oṃ jaya caṇḍī jaya jaya

You reside in the Mūlādhāra Chakra. You grant the highest attainment in this world. At the appointed time you are Kālī, the Remover of Darkness, and as the Lotus One you grant blessings. Be Victorious!

- 11 -

शक्ति शक्तिधर तू ही नित्य अभेदमयी (माँ)
भेदप्रदर्शिनि वाणी विमले वेदत्रयी
ॐ जय चण्डी जय जय

śakti śakti dhara tū hī nitya abheda mayī (māṁ)
bheda pradarśini vāṇī (2) vimale vedatrayī
oṃ jaya caṇḍī jaya jaya

You are every form of energy, the eternal undistinguishable essence, the vibration that exposes change and distinction, and the spotlessly pure three Vedas. Be Victorious!

- 12 -

हम अति दीन दुखी माँ विपत-जाल घेरे (माँ)

हैं कपूत अति कपटी पर बालक तेरे

ॐ जय चण्डी जय जय

ham ati dīna dukhī māṁ vipat jāla ghere (māṁ)
haiṃ kapūt ati kapaṭī (2) para bālaka tere
oṃ jaya caṇḍī jaya jaya

For so many days we have been in pain, Maa. We are bound by adversities and suffering. We are negligent and insincere, but still we are your children. Be Victorious!

- 13 -

निज स्वभाववश जननी दया दृष्टि कीजै (माँ)

करुणा कर करुणामयि चरण-शरण दीजै

ॐ जय चण्डी जय जय

nija svabhāva vaśa jananī dayā dṛṣṭi kījai (māṁ)
karuṇā kara karuṇā mayi (2) caraṇa śaraṇa dījai
oṃ jaya caṇḍī jaya jaya

Endow us with your very own nature, Mother. Give us your mercy, Oh Merciful Mother! Give us the refuge of your lotus feet. Be Victorious!

जय चण्डी जय जय (माँ) जय चण्डी जय जय

भयहारिणि भवतारिणि भवभामिनि जय जय

ॐ जय चण्डी जय जय

jaya caṇḍī jaya jaya (māṁ) jaya caṇḍī jaya jaya
bhaya hāriṇi bhava tāriṇi (2)
bhava bhāmini jaya jaya
oṃ jaya caṇḍī jaya jaya

Be Victorious! Oh Goddess Who Tears Apart Thought! Be Victorious! You take away all fear and illuminate the intensity of reality. Be Victorious!

देवीमयी

devīmayī

Manifestation of the Goddess

तव च का किल न स्तुतिरम्बिके
सकलशब्दमयी किल ते तनुः ।
निखिलमूर्तिषु मे भवदन्वयो
मनसिजासु बहिःप्रसरासु च ॥

tava ca kā kila na stutirambike
sakalaśabdamayī kila te tanuḥ ।
nikhilamūrtiṣu me bhavadanvayo
mansijāsu bahiḥprasarāsu ca ॥

Oh Mother! Is there any vibration that is not your song? Your body is the form of all sound. In cognizing your imminent form of divinity, my mind has moved beyond thoughts and reflections.

इति विचिन्त्य शिवे शमिताशिवे
जगति जातमयत्नवशादिदम् ।
स्तुतिजपार्चनचिन्तनवर्जिता
न खलु काचन कालकलास्ति मे ॥

iti vicintya śive śamitāśive
jagati jātamayatnavaśādidam ।
stutijapārcanacintanavarjitā
na khalu kācana kālakalāsti me ॥

Oh Destroyer of all Obstructions, Grantor of Welfare! Recognizing you as such, as She who gives birth to all that moves and moves not, even these brief moments of my appearance in life should be spent without other thoughts in singing your praises, chanting your names, and offering of my devotion.

भगवतीस्तुतिः

bhagavatīstutiḥ

A Song of Praise to the Supreme Goddess

प्रातः स्मरामि शरदिन्दुकरोज्ज्वलाभां
सद्रत्नवन्मकरकुण्डलहारभूषाम् ।
दिव्यायुधोजितसुनीलसहस्रहस्तां
रक्तोत्पलाभचरणां भवतीं परेशाम् ॥

prātaḥ smarāmi śaradindukarojjvalābhāṃ
sadratnavanmakarakuṇḍalahārabhūṣām |
divyāyudhojitasunīlasahasrahastāṃ
raktotpalābhacaraṇāṃ bhavatīṃ pareśām ||

In the morning I remember the Foremost, She who shines like the autumn moon, wearing a shining necklace and earrings studded with fine jewels. She holds divine weapons in Her thousand arms of excellent blue, She gives divine life. The soles of her feet are red like a lotus. She is the Highest Divinity.

प्रातर्नमामि महिषासुरचण्डमुण्ड-
शुम्भासुरप्रमुखदैत्यविनाशदक्षाम् ।
ब्रह्मेन्द्ररुद्रमुनिमोहनशीललीलां
चण्डीं समस्तसुरमूर्तिमनेकरूपाम् ॥

prātarnamāmi mahiṣāsuracaṇḍamuṇḍa-
śumbhāsurapramukhadaityavināśadakṣām |
brahmendrarudramunimohanaśīlalīlāṃ
caṇḍīṃ samastasuramūrtimanekarūpām ||

In the morning I bow down to the Foremost, to the Slayer of the Great Ego, Anger and Passion, and the Destroyer of other negativities of duality led by Self-Conceit. Her graceful activities delude even Brahmā, the Creative Consciousness, Indra, the Rule of the Pure, Ṛudra, the Reliever of Sufferings, and other wise beings. She is Chaṇḍī, She Who Tears Apart Thought, the image of divinity to all the Gods in so many forms.

प्रातर्भजामि भजतामभिलाषदात्रीं
धात्रीं समस्तजगतां दुरितापहन्त्रीम् ।
संसारबन्धनविमोचनहेतुभूतां
मायां परां समधिगम्य परस्य विष्णोः ॥

prātarbhajāmi bhajatāmabhilāṣadātrīṃ
dhātrīṃ samastajagatāṃ duritāpahantrīm |
saṃsārabandhanavimocanahetubhūtāṃ
māyāṃ parāṃ samadhigamya parasya viṣṇoḥ ||

In the morning I laud the Foremost, the Fulfiller of all Desires for those who worship, the Creator of all the worlds and Remover of all difficulties. Take away all the bondage from the world of objects and relationships, and bring us to the pure intuitive vision of the Supreme Consciousness that resides beyond Māyā.

प्रणामः

Praṇāmaḥ

Bowing Down with Devotion

ॐ दुर्गां शिवां शान्तिकरीं ब्रह्माणीं ब्रह्मणः प्रियाम् ।
सर्वलोक प्रणेत्रीञ्च प्रणमामि सदा शिवाम् ॥

oṃ durgāṃ śivāṃ śānti karīṃ
brahmāṇīṃ brahmaṇaḥ priyāṃ ।
sarva loka praṇetrīñca praṇamāmi sadā śivām ॥

The Reliever of Difficulties, Exposer of Goodness, Cause of Peace, Infinite Consciousness, Beloved by Knowers of Consciousness, She who Motivates and Guides the three worlds, always I bow to Her, and I am bowing to Goodness Herself.

मङ्गलां शोभनां शुद्धां निष्कलां परमां कलाम् ।
विश्वेश्वरीं विश्वमातां चण्डिकां प्रणमाम्यहम् ॥

maṅgalāṃ śobhanāṃ śuddhāṃ
niṣkalāṃ paramāṃ kalām ।
viśveśvarīṃ viśva mātāṃ
caṇḍikāṃ praṇamāmyaham ॥

Welfare, Radiant Beauty, Completely Pure, without limitations, the Ultimate Limitation, the Lord of the Universe, the Mother of the Universe, to you Chaṇḍī, to the Energy That Tears Apart Thought, I bow in submission.

सर्वदेवमयीं देवीं सर्वरोगभयापहाम् ।
ब्रह्मेशविष्णुनमितां प्रणमामि सदा शिवाम् ॥

sarva deva mayīṃ devīṃ sarva roga bhayāpahām ।
brahmeśa viṣṇu namitāṃ praṇamāmi sadā śivām ॥

She is composed of all the Gods, removes all sickness and fear, Brahmā, Maheśvara, and Viṣṇu bow down to Her, and I always bow down to the Energy of Infinite Goodness.

विन्ध्यस्थां विन्ध्यनिलयां दिव्यस्थाननिवासिनीम् ।
योगिनीं योगजननीं चण्डिकां प्रणमाम्यहम् ॥

vindhyasthāṃ vindhya nilayāṃ
divyasthāna nivāsinīm ।
yoginīṃ yoga jananīṃ caṇḍikāṃ praṇamāmyaham ॥

The dwelling place of Knowledge, residing in Knowledge, Resident in the place of Divine Illumination, the Cause of Union, the Knower of Union, to the Energy That Tears Apart Thought, we constantly bow.

ईशानमातरं देवीमीश्वरीमीश्वरप्रियाम् ।
प्रणतोऽस्मि सदा दुर्गां संसारार्णवतारिणीम् ॥

īśānamātaraṃ devīm īśvarīm īśvarapriyām ।
praṇato-smi sadā durgāṃ saṃsārārṇava tāriṇīm ॥

The Mother of the Supreme Consciousness, the Goddess Who is the Supreme Consciousness, beloved by the Supreme Consciousness, we always bow to Durgā, the Reliever of Difficulties, who takes aspirants across the difficult sea of objects and their relationships.

The Pronunciation of Sanskrit Transliteration

a	org*a*n, s*u*m
ā	f*a*ther
ai	*ai* sle
au	s*au*erkr*au*t
b	*b*ut
bh	a*bh*or
c	*ch*ur*ch*
ḍ	*d*ough
d	*d*ough slightly toward the *th* sound of *th*ough
ḍh	a*dh* ere
dh	a*dh*ere slightly toward the *theh* sound of brea*the-h*ere
e	pr*ey*
g	*g*o
gh	do*gh*ouse
ḥ	slight aspiration of preceding vowel
h	*h*ot
i	*i*t
ī	pol*i*ce
j	*j*ump
jh	lo*dgeh*ouse
k	*k*id
kh	wor*kh*orse
l	*l*ug
ṃ	resonant nasalization of preceding vowel
m	*m*ud
ṅ	si*ng*
ṇ	u*n*der
ñ	pi*ñ*ata
n	*n*o
o	n*o*
p	*p*ub
ph	u*ph*ill
ṛ	no English equivalent; a simple vowel *r*, such as appears in many Slavic languages
r	*r*oom
ś	*sh*awl pronounced with a slight whistle; German *s*prechen
ṣ	*sh*un
s	*s*un
ṭ	*t* omato
t	wa*t*er

ṭh	*Th*ailand
u	p*u*sh
ū	r*u*de
v	*v*odka midway between *w* and *v*
y	*y*es

More Books by Shree Maa and Swami Satyananda Saraswati

Annapūrṇa Thousand Names
Before Becoming This
Bhagavad Gītā
Chaṇḍi Pāṭh
Cosmic Pūjā
Cosmic Pūjā Bengali
Devī Gītā
Devī Mandir Songbook
Durgā Pūjā Beginner
Ganeśa Pūjā
Gems From the Chaṇḍi
Guru Gītā
Hanumān Pūjā
Kālī Dhyānam
Kālī Pūjā
Lakṣmī Sahasra Nāma
Lalitā Triśati
Rudrāṣṭādhyāyī
Sahib Sadhu
Saraswati Pūjā for Children
Shree Maa's Favorite Recipes
Shree Maa - The Guru & the Goddess
Shree Maa, The Life of a Saint
Śiva Pūjā Beginner
Śiva Pūjā and Advanced Fire Ceremony
Sundara Kāṇḍa
Swāmī Purāṇa
Thousand Names of Ganeśa
Thousand Names of Gayatri
Thousand Names of Viṣṇu and
Satya Nārāyaṇa Vrata Kathā

CDs and Cassettes

Chaṇḍi Pāṭh
Durgā Pūjā Beginner
Lalitā Triśati
Mantras of the Nine Planets
Navarṇa Mantra
Oh Dark Night Mother
Oṃ Mantra
Sādhu Stories from the Himalayas
Shree Maa at the Devi Mandir
Shree Maa in the Temple of the Heart
Shiva is in My Heart
Shree Maa on Tour, 1998
Śiva Pūjā Beginner
Śiva Pūjā and Advanced Fire Ceremony
The Goddess is Everywhere
The Songs of Ramprasad
The Thousand Names of Kālī
Tryambakaṃ Mantra

Videos

Across the States with Shree Maa & Swamiji
Meaning and Method of Worship
Shree Maa: Meeting a Modern Saint
Visiting India with Shree Maa and Swamiji

Please visit us at www.shreemaa.org
Our email is info@shreemaa.org